No

For Ron Rosbottom,

With much appreciation
for your support of my
work, and for your
supportive and encouraging
presence here overall.

[signature]

In the Mirror of Memory

SUNY Series in Buddhist Studies
Matthew Kapstein, editor

In the Mirror of Memory

Reflections on Mindfulness and Remembrance in Indian and Tibetan Buddhism

EDITED BY
JANET GYATSO

State University of New York Press

Published by
State University of New York Press, Albany

Printed in the United States of America

For information, address State University of New York
Press, State University Plaza, Albany, N.Y., 12246

Production by Diane Ganeles
Marketing by Dana E. Yanulavich

Library of Congress Cataloging-in-Publication Data

In the mirror of memory : reflections on mindfulness and remembrance
in Indian and Tibetan Buddhism / edited by Janet
Gyatso.
p. cm. — (SUNY series in Buddhist studies)
Includes index.
ISBN 0-7914-1077-3. — ISBN 0-7914-1078-1 (pbk.)
1. Buddhism—Psychology. 2. Memory—Religious aspects—Buddhism.
I. Gyatso, Janet. II. Series.
BQ4570.P76I5 1992
153.1'2'0882943—dc20 91-25555
CIP

10 9 8 7 6 5 4 3 2 1

Contents

Acknowledgments vii

Introduction
JANET GYATSO 1

Memories of the Buddha
DONALD S. LOPEZ, JR. 21

Smṛti in the Abhidharma Literature and the Development of Buddhist Accounts of Memory of the Past
PADMANABH S. JAINI 47

The Omission of Memory in the Theravādin List of Dhammas: On the Nature of *Saññā*
NYANAPONIKA THERA 61

Mindfulness and Memory: The Scope of *Smṛti* from Early Buddhism to the Sarvāstivādin Abhidharma
COLLETT COX 67

Memory in Classical Indian Yogācāra
PAUL J. GRIFFITHS 109

Buddhist Terms for Recollection and Other Types of Memory
ALEX WAYMAN 133

The *Mātikās:* Memorization, Mindfulness, and the List
RUPERT GETHIN 149

Letter Magic: A Peircean Perspective on the Semiotics of Rdo Grub-chen's Dhāraṇī Memory
JANET GYATSO 173

Commemoration and Identification in *Buddhānusmṛti*
PAUL HARRISON 215

The Amnesic Monarch and the Five Mnemic Men: "Memory" in Great Perfection (Rdzogs–chen) Thought
MATTHEW KAPSTEIN 239

Remembering Resumed: Pursuing Buddhism and Phenomenology in Practice
EDWARD S. CASEY 269

Glossary 299

Contributors 305

Acknowledgments

I am grateful to Amherst College for two faculty research grants that aided in the completion of this volume.

Special thanks to contributors Ed Casey, Matthew Kapstein, Donald Lopez, and Paul Griffiths, as well as to Jay Garfield, Steven Collins, manuscript readers Roger Jackson and two anonymous others, and finally to Fur Friend, all of whom offered valuable suggestions concerning the volume as a whole at various stages in the project. John Pettit assisted in the editing of the volume, and Nicole Freed, Jon Gold, and Evan Specter helped in typing it. Bill Eastman, Diane Ganeles, and the SUNY Press staff expertly facilitated a smooth publication process.

Introduction

Buddhist discussions of memory range from epistemological analyses of the nature of recognition or the mind's ability to store data, to spectacular claims concerning memory of innumerable past lives, memorization of vast volumes, and the reduction of those volumes into highly condensed mnemonic devices. In addition, meditative concentration, which requires that an object be held in mind, has been associated with types of memory by several Buddhist theorists. The special strings of syllables in the Buddhist dhāraṇīs, which are used as reminders of philosophical principles, also are associated with kinds of memory. The practices of devotion to, and visualization of, the Buddha involve a variety of memory akin to commemoration. Even the awareness that is enlightenment itself is considered by some traditions to consist in a "mnemic engagement" with reality, or ultimate truth.[1]

Yet, despite this impressive array of phenomena and practices that involve distinctively Buddhist species of memory, many labeled by Sanskrit terms derived from the same verbal root *smṛ* or other roots displaying a similar semantic scope, very little has been written by Buddhologists on memory, with the exception of several articles on the recollection of past lives.[2] This silence may be attributed to a certain tendency to consider as memory only that which consists expressly in the recollection of previous experience. And because discussion of this sort of memory, at least in theoretical discourse, apparently occurs in but few passages in Buddhist literature, Buddhologists seem to have concluded that Buddhism does not have much to say about memory at all.

But if memory is reduced to recollection, a wide range of mnemic phenomena that have a central role both in Buddhist practice and thought will be overlooked. Some of these phenomena involve forms of memory that work in concert with recollection; others can be shown to entail types of memory that are not primarily recollective. As several of the studies in the present volume demonstrate, important but hitherto unstudied passages in Buddhist doctrinal literature address explicitly the question of how recollection of past experience is related to some of the other faculties and practices that are also denoted by *smṛti* or other terms. To fail to examine those mnemic phenomena in the Buddhist tradition that lie at the limits, or on the margins, of what is normally thought to be memory is to miss an opportunity to expand and to deepen our understanding of memory as a whole.

In fact, to restrict memory to recollection would be to reflect a bias that may be associated more with Western strains of thought than with Buddhist ones themselves. And yet, in several Western academic disciplines and areas of research, including philosophy, psychoanalytic theory, cognitive psychology, and anthropology, increasing attention is being paid to types of memory that do not consist mainly in the recollection of past events, particularly that aspect of recollection associated with the mental representation of an object or episode in the rememberer's personal past. An outstanding example of a type of memory that is not at all recollective is "primary memory," recognized first by William James and Edmund Husserl and since observed in laboratory settings; such memory consists in the initial retention of experience that takes place in a brief stretch of time as the experience retreats from momentary awareness. Also receiving notice is the spectrum of types of memory that are habitual in nature, studied by Henri Bergson and others. Closely related to habit memory is what Edward Casey has called "body memory." The "abstract, timeless knowledge of the world that [a person] shares with others," termed "semantic memory" by Endel Tulving is another form of nonrecollective memory. Well known, of course, are Freud's and his successors' investigations of the vicissitudes of repressed memory traces in psychopathological symptoms; here again, the mnemic mode is not primarily recollective. Deserving of mention as well are recent anthropological analyses of the embodiment of social memory in cultural processes, material media, and places, in which the emphasis is put upon the performative function of memory in the present, rather than on the mental storage or representation of past events.[3]

The present volume is in some respects continuous with the growing fascination with the range and manifold nature of memory, of both the recollective and nonrecollective sorts, although the Buddhist traditions treated here are often concerned with mnemic modes distinct from those that have received the most attention in the West. But even such Buddhist traditions that speak of the commemoration of buddhahood, or that would characterize enlightenment as a memory of ultimate truth, have long had counterparts in Western discussions of memory, from St. Augustine's reflections on human memory of God to Heidegger's discussion of memory as "the gathering of the constant intention of everything that the heart holds in present being."[4] On another note, a certain mistrust of memory can also be observed to be shared by Western theorists—from Descartes to Nietzsche to Freud—and by Buddhist ones, particularly the Buddhist logicians discussed in Alex Wayman's article in this volume, who consider some types of memory to be unreliable and deceptive.[5] In the Buddhist case, the devaluation of certain kinds of memory, particularly mundane recollection and the recognition of objects of the past, is to be attributed ultimately to the conviction that these are obstacles to progress on the Buddhist path. Yet once again, when recollection's privileged position as the researcher's paradigm of memory is revoked, it becomes possible to identify other varieties of memory, varieties suggested in a significant number of areas in Buddhist thought and practice, which are considered beneficial for soteriological development and are deliberately cultivated for that purpose.

The following essays have as their focus the many kinds of memory—be they deemed detrimental, beneficial, or neutral—that have been identified in the Buddhist tradition. The sources utilized in these essays include Abhidharmic analysis, sutraic discourse and exegesis, meditation instruction, myth, allegory, and prayer.[6] One of the striking themes emerging from these essays is the alliance that some Buddhist thinkers forged between types of memory, and the manner in which a present object is noted, identified, and registered during the perceptual process. Such a link is asserted both in theoretical descriptions of ordinary states of mind and in discussions of religious practice in which special sorts of memory are made to inform the act of perception so as to transform it into a salvific experience. Of considerable interest too is the variety of Buddhist traditions in which types of reminders, both linguistic and imagistic, are cultivated in order to engender religiously valued realizations. Commemorative ritual is shown to have a central role in Buddhist practice as well. The issue of how the Buddhists account, or fail to account, for the ability to remember the past also occupies several of the volume's contributors. It is the investigation of these diverse modes and uses of memory in various Buddhist contexts that is the primary aim of this book.

An essay by Edward Casey, author of a recent book entitled *Remembering* that studies memory from a phenomenological perspective, has also been included in the collection.[7] In *Remembering* Casey contends that memory, once investigated in its philosophical, literary, psychological, and social manifestations, turns out to be far from univocal; hence his treatment in separate chapters of the phenomena of recollection, reminiscing, recognition, reminders, body memory, commemoration, and what he calls "place memory." Casey's response to the papers in the current volume was invited not only because his treatment of the varieties of memory in the West complements the exploration of the multiplicity of the phenomenon in Buddhist terms. It was also thought to be valuable to have a Western philosopher, one who has worked on the subject of memory at length, respond to the distinctive meanings that notions like *smṛti* have in the Buddhist context, notions that might point to some fundamental peculiarities about Buddhist philosophy and religion. Comparative reflections are needed all the more insofar as Buddhologists are still very much engaged in the project of arriving at satisfactory translations and interpretations of primary texts, where the problem of which Western word should render a Buddhist technical term is frequently a vexing one: the translation of many of the most foundational concepts is still not standardized. Sustained investigation of divergences between basic assumptions in Buddhism and other traditions is critical if one is to assess the appropriateness of a given translation. Such investigation is also important if scholars of Buddhism are to engage in the larger and even more challenging project of entering into genuine conversation with other traditions on philosophical, religious, psychological, or social issues. It is with these various concerns in mind that, in addition to Casey, several of the Buddhologists writing in this volume have considered non-Buddhist Indian and Western traditions in a comparative mode.

Two Meanings of *Smṛti?*

The primary discrepancy obtaining between Buddhist concepts denoted by *smṛ-* derivatives and Western senses of memory revolves around the significance of the two basic meanings that *smṛ-* derivatives can have: recollective memory (or more generally, memory of the past), and what is most often rendered as "mindfulness." The nature of this distinction, and particularly the question as to whether mindfulness should be considered a type of memory at all, are attended to in several of the chapters here. A variety of positions on these issues is represented, with a corresponding range of ways of handling the technical Sanskrit terminology and its translation into English. Several authors have chosen to leave *smṛti* and cognate terms untranslated to avoid adjudicating between the alternate meanings. Both Padmanabh Jaini and Alex Wayman distinguish carefully between the contexts in which *smṛ-* derivatives (and other terms) mean mindfulness and those contexts in which they mean recollective memory of past objects and experiences. Paul Harrison opines that *anusmṛti*, like *smṛti*, has a range of meanings, finding that its primary sense in the traditions he studies implicate a species of "commemoration" that exceeds personal recollection. Matthew Kapstein has adopted English terms based on the Greek root *mnā*, which, like the Sanskrit *smṛ* (Tib. *dran*), can mean recollection as well as mindfulness. In this Kapstein is asserting that the two senses of *smṛti* (actually Kapstein identifies three distinct senses) are continuous and that the use of the same word for such various meanings in Great Perfection texts is deliberate. He is joined in asserting a close linkage between the varying uses of *smṛti* by Collett Cox, who translates all instances of *smṛti* as "mindfulness," and who attempts to demonstrate that recollection of the past as such is in fact understood in some schools of Buddhism to be a subtype of mindfulness. Interestingly, Paul Griffiths also finds that the various Buddhist uses of *smṛti*, which he often leaves untranslated, represent what is by and large a single semantic set, although he is in accord with Jaini and Wayman in maintaining a critical distinction between memory of past experiences and mindfulness. For Griffiths, *smṛti* mainly denotes active attention in Buddhism, whereas advertance to the past as this is understood in the West is a quite different matter. Although remembering the past is sometimes discussed in terms of *smṛti,* Griffiths maintains that it is not essential to the meaning of the word as it manifestly is to *memory* in the West. Finally, Gyatso, discussing not *smṛ-* related words but *dhāraṇī,* tends also to employ a single word, *memory* itself, to refer to the variety of types of content of the literal formula, as well as to the types of ways those contents are held in store.

It will be noted that the decision to use the word *memory* (along with the adjective *mnemic*) in a broad way for the purpose of discussion in this Introduction, so as to accommodate recollection, reminding, mindfulness, holding in mind, memorization, recognition, and commemoration, reflects the position that these various phenomena have features that qualify them for a single general label. However, it is undebatable that important distinctions are to be drawn between types of mnemic practices and faculties, as is recognized even by the authors who attempt to establish a link between them. Cox, for example, differentiates religious praxis from mundane psychological functions; Kapstein draws distinctions between various types of "mnemic engagement" in cosmogonic and soteriological terms; and Gyatso distinguishes several kinds of contents of dhāraṇī memory.

Meditative Mindfulness and Mnemic Engagement with Enlightenment

The classic instance of what is usually translated as "mindfulness" in Buddhism would be the practice of the four applications of mindfulness (*smṛtyupasthāna*). The history and operating principles of this practice are traced out in some detail as the starting point for Cox's study. In this instance *smṛti* is what is normally thought of as meditation: the mind is focused, concentrated, fastened on a mark. In this mindful observing of the objects of meditation, the practitioner observes their impermanence, lack of self, and so forth. Because mindfulness comes to be associated closely with insight (*prajñā*), which for Buddhism performs the critical function of destroying the defilements, and because that destruction is synonymous with enlightenment, mindfulness is in these cases affiliated with the realization of enlightenment itself.

According to Kapstein's analysis of the Great Perfection tradition, soteriologically beneficial mindfulness may be divided into that required for study and meditation and that which forms the noetic content of enlightened awareness. The latter thus constitutes a special type of mnemic engagement, consisting in the reflexivity of primordial awareness as such. According to the Great Perfection exegetes, this awareness is at the ground of our existence as well as at the apex of the Buddhist path. Because it has been forgotten by deluded sentient beings, its recovery through meditative practice is a sort of memory, despite its nonintentional character. But it is also the very self-referentiality of this awareness that makes it mnemic in nature, and the Great Perfection's thematization of such reflexivity constitutes a distinctive contribution to Buddhist discussions of the nature of memory.

As is evident in a number of studies in this volume, including those by Harrison, Gethin, Kapstein, Cox, and Gyatso, the realizations engendered through various Buddhist practices of mindfulness and retention of teachings are preceded by the learning of doctrinal principles, memorization of linguistic formulations and images, and cultivation of meditative skills. However, it is not on the ground of such a temporal sequence alone that the resulting realizations are sometimes characterized in terms of memory. The Buddhist practitioner is not thought merely to be recollecting his prior religious training when he "holds in mind" or "remembers" the Dharma, or emptiness, or awareness, or when he commemorates buddhahood. Rather, the sorts of memory operative in such cases are akin to what have been called "semantic memory" and "habit memory" in the West, where previously learned categories and skills inform present experience without being recollected as such.[8] But in the Buddhist varieties, even more pertinent than the role of previous training is the sense of "recognizing" the ultimate truth of what is realized, and of gaining personal mastery and an internalized, thorough-going identification with it.[9] Additionally, in those Buddhist traditions that call upon some notion of "buddha nature" (best represented in this volume in Kapstein's study of the Great Perfection), the practitioner may be said to be remembering buddhahood, or emptiness, or self-reflexive awareness, because he is felt in some sense to have been already imbued with such realization anyway, independent of all training. In such a view, learning and memorization of techniques are but aids in recovering what has been lost track of or obscured due to adventitious defilement.

Connections Between Mindfulness, Perception of Present Objects, and Recollection of the Past

Cox is interested in a link that was explicitly established between meditative mindfulness and mundane recollection in the Sarvāstivāda tradition. Although mindfulness in the early Abhidharma was classified exclusively as a virtuous factor, implying that it occurs only in those states of mind that are religiously valued such as meditation, mindfulness came to be reclassified by the Northern Abhidharma school of the Vaibhāṣikas/Sarvāstivādins as present in all states of mind, be they good, bad, or neutral. This reclassification reflects the view that every mental event consists in a conglomoration of simultaneous factors, instead of the serial view of mental functioning, whereby only one factor operates at a time. *Smṛti*'s inclusion in the group of ubiquitous factors proves for Cox first of all that it is now being understood not exclusively as an occasional meditative state, but rather as one of the basic elements of all mental functioning. This is the basis of an assertion by the Sarvāstivādin exegete Saṅghabhadra that it is mindfulness's fixing, directed at a present object, that makes that object's later recollection in memory possible at all. Further, he claims that this same fixing is what functions to retain the object over time so that it can be recollected later. Here then is forged a connection between mindful fixing upon present objects, and recollection, which also functions by virtue of such fixing.

A related point is made by Nyanaponika Thera on the basis of the Theravāda tradition. Nyanaponika's contribution is the only one in the volume reprinted from a previous publication; it was originally written as part of the author's subcommentary to the *Dhammsaṅgaṇi,* and was meant to be in conformity with the Theravāda tradition.[10] The essay suggests a critical dimension of the early Buddhist understanding of memory of past objects. Nyanaponika's discussion focuses not on the Vaibhāṣika notion of dharmas present in all states of mind, but on a category from one of Buddhism's oldest doctrinal strata, namely, the skandhas, or aggregates. He argues that memory was not listed as one of the dharmas because it was already included in the aggregate of *saṃjñā* (Pāli *saññā*). It should be noted that Nyanaponika, influenced by a Buddhological convention no longer current because it is not sufficiently precise, renders *saññā* as "perception," in the broad sense of this term that connotes the perception of an object in light of a conception or notion (indeed, the other contributors to this volume translate *saṃjñā* as "conception," or occasionally, "recognition.") Nyanaponika's discussion shows that *saṃjñā* is what might be termed *perception-as;* it consists in assigning an object a label, classifying it in a category, seeing it *as* something and so forth, and it is to be distinguished from the Buddhist logicians' understanding of *pratyakṣa* ("direct perception") discussed below that lacks conceptuality altogether. Nyanaponika identifies two types of *saññā* that are suggested in Theravāda sources, and both involve kinds of memory. One consists in the explicitly memorial act of recognizing an object that has already been noticed previously; such recognition occurs on the basis of the object's distinguishing mark. The other is the "making" or identifying of such a mark itself; this occurs in every act of "fully perceiving" or conceptualizing an object, according to Theravāda doctrine, even a new object never noted before. But as Nyanaponika points out, this fixing upon and registering of an object's marks already involves a rudimentary type of memory: the object must be maintained in mind, or "remembered," over several [sub-] moments in order for the identifying and registering of the mark to take place; further, the label or category by virtue of which such a mark is identified is itself remembered from previous acts of conception. And finally, this mark will be what is grasped later when the object is recognized again. Thus Nyanaponika finds that it is the process of fully perceiving/conceiving a present object that memorializes it and is central to the occurrence of memory, even though the Buddhist sources he cites do not call this *smṛti*.

Another link that Cox locates between mindfulness and recollection emerges in a dispute about the relationship between meditative insight and mindfulness, concerning whether they occur simultaneously or whether one precedes the other. Vasubandhu, in his influential *Abhidharmakośabhāṣya*, asserts that mindfulness follows insight, functioning to retain and fix what was first penetrated by insight. Cox understands this assertion to imply that even in the flow of meditation itself, a retention akin to that in mundane recollection of the past is already occurring, this retention being the same principle that allows an object to be held for years.

The idea that holding on to the thread (to use one of Nyanaponika's metaphors) is critical in many mental acts is also evident in other Buddhist doctrines. For example, Jaini, whose article introduces the problem of memory of the past in the Abhidharma literature as a whole, suggests that the "having the same object" moment of the Theravāda "mental series" could also perform the function of registering and consigning the object of perception to memory. However, it is only in Northern Abhidharmic analyses that the object of *smṛti* is stated explicitly to be of the past. Griffiths supplies several critical Yogācāra passages from Sthiramati and other sources on this issue. Here the reader will note an interesting suggestion of ambiguity in Sthiramati's position, whereby Griffiths and Jaini are able to read the same statement in a different way than Cox. Whereas for Cox the holding and nonloss (*asampramoṣa*) of a past object mentioned by Sthiramati is an element of mundane psychological states, Griffiths and Jaini understand this nonloss to be primarily a matter of meditation; that is, as referring to a lack of distractions from the appointed object of concentration. Another difference in interpretation concerns the implications of the Vaibhāṣika classification of *smṛti* among the mental factors that occur in all mental states; although Cox sees this development as evidence of the increasingly psychological orientation of Abhidharma analyses, Jaini maintains that since memory of the past does not always occur, the *smṛti* that is a ubiquitous mental factor cannot be identified as memory of this sort.

Cox, Jaini, and Griffiths are in agreement that meditative categories provide the overarching framework for Buddhist psychological analysis. Indeed, not only did the Buddhist virtuosi recommend meditative concentration as the optimal condition for reaching buddhahood, they also investigated the nature of mundane mental states while *in* meditation. Thus it is perhaps to be expected that meditational terminology would have influenced their description of all mental states, even the mundane mental states of those who are far from ever having attempted meditation themselves.

A final point concerning the relationship between the various sorts of memory in Buddhism emerges in many of the studies here; namely, that they affect each other. As already suggested, Harrison's study of the commemoration of the Buddha would indicate that memorization of attributes of the Buddha must precede the salutary effects that the act of commemoration itself is thought to engender, especially the personal identification with those attributes. Similarly, the use of the *mātikās* discussed by Rupert Gethin requires an initial memorization of mnemonic lists in order to achieve the more profound memory needed to preach the Dharma. The realization of dhāraṇī memory also involves an initial learning of conventions. Sometimes the direction of influence goes from the meditative to the more mundane: as both Donald Lopez and Alex Wayman demonstrate, the feat of remembering large sections of one's personal past require meditative mindfulness as a necessary condition; in Cox's article it is shown that doctrines associated with meditative concentration historically led to doctrines describing ordinary psychological states; the Gyatso reports the Tibetan exegete Rdo Grub-chen's claim that remembering emptiness clears the head so as to allow for memory of specific texts. Griffiths shows how meditative mindfulness serves as an antidote to the deleterious self-absorption that memory of one's personal past is thought to entail. We can also see the flip side of this point in Kapstein's findings concerning the Great Perfection, where the loss of primordial awareness of the ground constitutes the first of all mnemic phenomena, a loss that leads to the sort of discursive memory that in turn can obstruct salvific mnemic engagement.

Interestingly, the Buddhist tendency to subordinate recollection of the past to profound mnemic awareness may be contrasted to Lopez's analysis of the Buddha's night of enlightenment: here an act of diachronic memory par excellence, that is, a recollection of infinite past lives (albeit of a special, valued sort and itself already conditioned by meditative mindfulness) in fact sets the stage for buddhahood itself. Thus it would appear that some personal memories of the past have substantial soteriological benefits. Lopez meditates on this issue at length in the opening essay of this volume, noting that here "it is not a case of memory but of the mythology of memory." As Paul Demiéville and Gregory Schopen have already demonstrated, the Buddhist tradition itself has not assigned sacred status to the memory of past lives as such, but Lopez maintains that as part of Buddhism's founding myth its significance needs to be explored. Lopez critically reviews several theories concerning this significance, especially that of Mircea Eliade. More suggestive for Lopez is Freud's notion of "screen memories," which can account for the flat and formulaic quality of the Buddha-to-be's recollection noticed also by

Griffiths. In accord with this notion, Lopez memorably suggests, perhaps the Buddha "needed to remember in order to forget."

Remembering the Past: The Paucity of Buddhist Analyses

The first Buddhist analysis of the mechanism of memory of the past as such seems to occur in the *Mahāvibhāṣā*, an early North Indian collection of Abhidharma texts. The analysis was developed by Vasubandhu in the *Abhidharmakośabhāṣya;* it is summarized here by Jaini and also considered by Griffiths. But recollection as well as other types of memory already had long been implicated in several domains of Buddhist practice, if not discussed or described theoretically. A variety of types of Buddhist recollection is surveyed in Wayman's chapter, including the already-mentioned recollection of past lives.

Griffiths finds the descriptions of memory of past lives disappointing. Indeed, one might expect such passages to explore self-consciousness and subjectivity, but they do not, at least not in Indic literature. Griffiths is correct in noting that a systematic phenomenology of remembering as a whole is almost completely absent in Buddhism, despite Sthiramati's use of a suggestive phenomenological category, *ākāra*. Even those passages that may be discovered in Buddhist literature that discuss recollection in most cases are terse, dwarfed by other concerns in Buddhist epistemology and psychology.

Griffiths suggests a number of reasons why recollective memory in particular never received the interest that so many other phenomena did in the Abhidharma. One such reason is related to his intriguing theory that the purported memory of past lives in Buddhism should be described more properly as consisting in active contemplative attention; the fact that the events attended to in this contemplation occurred in the past is not a central component of the active attention involved. According to Griffiths, buddhas don't engage in remembering their personal past as this is understood in all of its phenomenological richness in the West. (And further, as he has argued elsewhere, they can't).[11] And since Buddhists are interested only in emulating buddhas, they are not interested in studying recollective memory. There is merit in this point, and yet it does not fully explain the absence of sustained discussion of the topic, because, for example, buddhas also do not have defilements, yet there is a considerable amount of investigation in Buddhist literature into the nature of defilements.

A different reason for the paucity of Buddhist accounts of memory of the past is also considered in this volume, concerning which Jaini, Griffiths, and Cox each make valuable contributions. This has to do with the widely held conviction that memory of what is past can be possible only if there is some sort of enduring subjective substratum; the fact that memory occurs at all would, according to this theory, prove that such a substratum exists. This constitutes a serious challenge to the Buddhist doctrine that a substratum or enduring self is an illusion, and it is explicitly raised by several non-Buddhist Indian schools and by some Buddhist sects as well. Jaini shows that it is just this challenge that is the principal occasion for the Buddhist account of memory of the past in the first place. But the Buddhists did not give such an account often, and the suggestion is clear: perhaps they shied away from considering the issue of how the past can be remembered because its discussion would give their critics an opening to attack the central Buddhist theory of no-self.

The Buddhists, however, do not concede that the occurrence of memory of the past proves that there must be an enduring self. Vasubandhu's *Abhidharmakośa* account describes a memory in which both the remembered content and the rememberer are causally connected and part of the same stream as their past identities, yet are not identical with those past identities. Griffiths points out that Vasubandhu's theory does not supply an explanation of how, and where, the traces of objects that are as yet unremembered persist; such traces would have to be available so as to provide the basis for the resemblance or relation to the original object that Vasubandhu claims is noted when the remembering occurs. Recourse to the metaphors of the "store consciousness," "seeds," and "perfuming tendencies," which reach full development in the Yogācāra texts, would provide such an explanation, both of the place, and the mode of persistence, of latent memories. But as Griffiths indicates, the store consciousness would seem to amount to an enduring substance with attributes, and hence a surrender of the Buddhist theory of no-self; indeed, Yogācāra theory has been critiqued at some length by the Madhyamaka Buddhist philosopher Candrakīrti. According to Cox, the problems entailed by the Yogācāra's store consciousness and unrealized potentialities are circumvented in the Sarvāstivāda account of memory of the past. The Sarvāstivādins claim that actualized, instead of latent, mindfulness of the past object continues to be repeated in successive moments, as part of the entire mental "bundle." This mindfulness then provides the basis for a particular act such as recollection, which, as in Vasubandhu's theory, occurs only when the right combination of conditions obtain, some of which are external to the rememberer. At issue here would be the hallmark Sarvāstivāda doctrine that everything always exists; since the Sarvāstivādins also are laying claim to the Buddhist doctrine of momentariness, they are invoking a pair of doctrines that are difficult to reconcile. Still another possible place for a theory of remembering the past in Buddhism is ingeniously devised by Jaini, based on the Theravāda "mental series" doctrine—albeit with the addition of a few modifications that contradict that doctrine's central presuppositions!

Ultimately, the issues at stake for a Buddhist account of memory are not limited to memory, but pertain to any aspect of personal identity, since Buddhism's no-self doctrine does not allow for an essential, enduring element of any sort. Yet, given the problems that a theory of an enduring substratum entails (for example, how could a substance that is subject to change with respect to its parts or properties be said to endure?), its proponents also encounter difficulties in accounting for the occurrence of memory of the past, difficulties a Buddhist such as Vasubandhu does not hesitate to exploit.

Finally, a further proposal as to why memory of the past as such receives little attention in Buddhist epistemology deserves consideration. According to Nyanaponika, if the primary distinguishing feature of memory is that its object is of the past, it would not be of particular interest to the authors of the *Dhammasaṅgaṇi*, who did not classify states of mind according to the temporality of those states' objects. If the issue of time is not of central importance, it follows that memory would be considered in terms of its mode of operation, which for many Buddhists is closely aligned with mindfulness, rather than in terms of its occasional manifestation as recollection of particular past objects.

Critiques of Memory

Even if not sufficient to explain why Buddhists rarely discuss memory of the past as such, there are reasons, emerging in this volume, as to why Buddhists do not value mundane recollection. One such reason is articulated in Rdo Grub-chen's dhāraṇī theory: recollection, which in this case refers to the memory of specific verbal statements that one has heard, is not only limited, but also superficial, failing to come to grips with the "profound situation" that is the content of the most enlightened type of memory. The basic premise of Rdo Grub-chen's argument is more fully formulated in terms of Kapstein's Great Perfection study (and this is no accident, as Rdo Grub-chen was deeply influenced by the Great Perfection tradition): the most authentic mnemic engagement is that which engages the ground of primordial awareness; any other sort of mnemic activity/cogitation is a distraction. But even if such a primordial ground is not admitted, as it is not in the so-called first and second "turnings of the wheel" in Buddhism, memories of particular things are widely perceived to be distractions from soteriologically beneficial praxis; this is seen as early as the scriptural references to "remembrance and intention rooted in ordinary life" that need be abandoned in order to practice mindfulness.[12]

That certain sorts of memory are classified pejoratively as types of discursive thought (*vikalpa*) is evident in many Buddhist texts. Wayman's essay in this volume draws attention to several important passages that explain why some sorts of memory are excluded by the Buddhist logicians from the category of "authoritative source of knowledge." One variety of memory so excluded is mundane recognition, which involves the identification of something perceived in the present with something perceived in the past. Since the Buddhists believe that everything is in flux, and therefore different from moment to moment, such an identification must, strictly speaking, be false. In fact, it is precisely the act of ignoring this flux that makes possible the superimposition of an essential, enduring identity such as "I" onto a "stream," this in turn leading to misguided emotions such as the "conceit that I am." This is the principal error pinpointed by Griffiths as the danger, from the Buddhist perspective, attendant upon recollection; yet for Lopez the perception of this error would give memory of past lives educational value.

To the degree that language is viewed as inaccurate and misleading in Buddhism, the fact that some types of memory are connected with verbal articulation becomes another reason for the denigration of mnemic phenomena. Mundane recognition, for example, often entails the articulation of the semantic or conceptual identity it imputes. Even mindfulness comes, in some readings, to be associated with verbal noting or chatter, one of the senses of *abhilapana* that Cox documents as contributing to the secularization of mindfulness. In a set of verses from the *Pramāṇavārttika* presented here by Wayman, recollection is contrasted with "direct perception" (*pratyakṣa*), which for the Buddhist logicians does not involve language or discursive thought, but attends instead to unarticulable and unique characteristics. Direct perception, unlike recollection, is considered in this tradition to be an authoritative source of knowledge. Wayman also discusses a difference between recollective memory and sense perception that is indicated both by Dharmakīrti and by Śāntarakṣita: the senses perceive things that are real and possess efficacy, whereas recollective memory concerns an object that is gone, or is merely a sign, both of which are deprived of efficacy. Because of memory's engagement with signs, language, and general categories, its mode of operation is more like that of inference, the second type of authoritative source of knowledge for the Buddhist logicians, than like direct perception, although memory is not admitted as a valid type of inference either. The Buddhist logicians compare several types of memory with direct perception, from which category they adamantly exclude memory, reserving direct perception as a source of knowledge completely devoid of discursive thought and language.[13]

The Conjoining of Memory and Perception in Buddhist Practice: Mindful and Self-Reflexive Looking; Commemorative Visualization; Reminders

Whereas the Buddhist logicians are at pains to distinguish mundane recognition and memory-as-discursive-thought from what they consider to be authentic perception, certain discussions of Buddhist practice recommend a drawing together of mnemic engagement and perception in the larger sense of this term, so as to make possible a mode of perception that is indeed informed by memory, albeit a sort of memory that is not villified but valorized. Perception is the mode in which the applications of mindfulness operate; the meditator is instructed to observe (*anu-paś*) the four objects of that practice while maintaining mindfulness and awareness. Great Perfection instructions also use the verb *to look/regard/perceive* (*lta*) for what is optimally a non-intentional perception that takes on a reflexive character: here perception and mnemic engagement with the percept's primordial nature are simultaneous, each reflecting the other as in a mirror, a common metaphor in this tradition albeit not mentioned in the texts Kapstein discusses here.

Types of perception seem to be especially critical in practices where a special image or sign is formulated as a mediating device. This is the case in *buddhānusmṛti* practice, which, as documented by Harrison, began as a calling to mind of the abstract virtues of the Buddha, but increasingly came to involve the visualization of an image of the Buddha's body. In his reflections on the nature of this cultivated and constructed sort of perception, Harrison invokes anthropologist Lawrence Babb's study of the Hindu practice of "glancing" (*darśana*), which consists in a kind of interchange whereby the viewer comes to take on the qualities that he perceives. Harrison shows that this interchange occurs both for the *buddhānusmṛti* practitioner who imagines himself receiving teachings in a buddha-field and for the tantric sādhana adept who identifies subjectively with a visualized buddha. It leads Harrison to conclude that *buddhānusmṛti* practice is a form of commemoration, which he compares with the types of commemoration identified by Casey in *Remembering* as largely communal in their enactment. *Buddhānusmṛti* also is sometimes practiced communally, but even when it is not, it involves a process of "psychical incorporation" of another person or identity, and it is mediated by text and ritual, all of which Casey has shown to be central elements of commemorative remembering. The ultimate goal of *buddhānusmṛti* practice is the transformation of the viewer, who comes to identify himself with the sublime buddha image that he views.

In the "forebearance dhāraṇī" practice examined in my essay, perception is directed upon letters or other linguistic signs, which are perceived as reminders of Buddhist philosophical principles. This "perception-as" ultimately has similar effects to those of *buddhānusmṛti* practice, in that it engenders an identification of the perceiver with the sublime content exemplified and embodied by the perceived letter. This ultimate identification is preceded by the establishment of the letter as a sign, which can then function in a variety of ways to remind the practitioner of that sublime content. I am particularly interested in the semiotics of this reminding, and find that the role of the sign in Rdo Grub-chen's and other Buddhist analyses of dhāraṇī practice can be usefully analyzed in terms of the semiological theory of the influential American philosopher Charles Sanders Peirce. Semiotic features of memory in Buddhism are also clearly evident in the "making of marks" mentioned in Nyanaponika's Theravāda passages on conception and recognition, and in Dharmakīrti's and Śāntarakṣita's characterizations of the object of memory as a sign, as discussed by Wayman. In the case of dhāraṇī practice, it emerges that the iconic sign, which resembles that of which it reminds, is the most efficacious type of reminder when the content to be remembered is emptiness. It will be observed that *buddhānusmṛti* commemorative visualization also employs icons, albeit by virtue of other sorts of features than those of the dhāraṇī letters.

The early Buddhist *mātikās* also serve as reminders, yet in a different way from dhāraṇīs. In his essay in this volume, Gethin corrects certain misconceptions concerning the *mātikās'* relationship with the first formulation of the Abhidharma Piṭaka. His analysis of the function of the *mātikās* shows that they evoke a type of memory more akin to the realization of basic Buddhist principles seen in dhāraṇī practice than to a memory of particular items, even if memorization of lists forms the basis of their mode of operation. Gethin finds that the list is not merely to be learned by rote; it also teaches the practitioner about the Dharma's inner structure. It is a creative source, a pregnant word, as it were, according well with the maternal metaphor that *mātikā* itself suggests. Not only does the *mātikā* "give birth to various dhammas," Gethin cites Kassapa of Coḷa as claiming, it also "looks after them and brings them up so that they do not perish."[14]

Further Directions

This brings me to several areas that might have been studied in this volume, but, for reasons of space, were not. The essays here draw primarily on Sanskrit, Pāli, and some Tibetan sources, with very limited use of East or Southeast Asian materials. This in itself suggests the array of still other Buddhist traditions that could be explored to carry the work of this volume further. Additional topics and themes that might be considered include, for instance, the role that memory plays in the formulation of the Buddhist scriptures. It was Ānanda's purported recitation by heart of the words of the Buddha at the so-called First Council that served to legitimize those scriptures as canonical; and his emblematic testimony to recollection—"thus have I heard at one time"—continues to be repeated as the introduction to later canonical materials and/or apocryphal texts.[15] We might contrast here *smṛti's* usage in

Vedic traditions, where it is distinguished from revelation that is "heard" (*śrūti*) and denotes instead received tradition that is not revelation.

A type of Buddhist memory that only has been touched on in this volume is associated with the practice of tantric sādhanas. Harrison establishes here an important connection between sūtraic *buddhānusmṛti* and tantric visualization; we can add that the act of visualization is sometimes itself called *smṛti* (Tib. *dran-pa*) in Tibetan sources. In this regard there is the Tibetan technical term *dag-dran* ("memory of purity"), referring to the practitioner's appreciation of and identification with the elements of the "pure realm" of visualized deities and maṇḍalas, which has been noted briefly in my essay on dhāraṇī.

Contemplative "non-memory," or oblivion to worldly distractions marked by freedom from discursive thought (i.e., Kapstein's E *dran-med,* to which he pays minimal attention, as the term barely occurs in the material he covers here), is an important notion in Mahāmudrā and related traditions, and deserves study. For example, toasts to such non-memory are preserved among the various collections of songs of the Zhi-byed "fifty-four male and female siddhas," allegedly translated from an Indic language by the eleventh century Indian master known in Tibet as Pha Dam-pa Sangs-rgyas.[16]

I would also submit that we need to consider the practices related to relics in Buddhism in terms of the sort of memory they make possible. Anthropologist Stanley Tambiah has already thematized the function of relics as reminders.[17] But once we remember anthropological data we can think of a host of ways in which memory plays an important role in Buddhist rituals and practices, only adumbrated in the present volume and deserving of detailed study.

Finally, I would draw the reader's attention to the copious hagiographical and especially auto/biographical literature produced by Buddhists. The fact that these genres became popular in Buddhism—from the life stories of the Buddha and the *Jātakas* to the many accounts of masters in Tibet and East Asia—attests to the value attached to remembering the lives of exemplars, be these accounts fact or fiction. Autobiographies in particular have been produced in exceptional quantity by Tibetan Buddhists, some of which present not idealized didactic stories, but critical and self-aware explorations of the nature of their authors' personal identity.[18] These autobiographers engage in, even if they do not analyze, a type of reminiscent and nostalgic recollective memory missing in the writings of Indian Buddhist scholastics. The continuing popularity of autobiography and biography, along with the several other modes of Buddhist memory uncovered in this collection, suggest that even if the Buddha needed to remember in order to forget, many Buddhists want to remember in order to remember.

Notes

1. A general terminological note for the purpose of this introduction is in order here, the rationale of which will emerge in the following paragraphs. *Memory* is used in a broad way to encompass a variety of phenomena discussed in this volume. Because no sufficiently general adjective exists (*memorial*'s principal connotation concerns the commemeration of the dead), I have adopted the adjective *mnemic*, following the lead of Matthew Kapstein who uses *mnemic engagement* and other phrases based on the Greek root *mnā* for certain Tibetan terms formed on *dran* (= Skt. *smṛ*) in his chapter in this volume. (*Mnemic* was coined first perhaps by Richard Semon to refer to an even broader set of psychological phenomena; see *The Mneme*, translated from the German by Louis Simon, London: George Allen & Unwin, 1921; and *Mnemic Psychology*, translated by Bella Duffy, London: George Allen & Unwin, 1923.) *Recollection* refers to the mental representation of particular objects, events, and experiences of one's personal past, to be distinguished from the special meaning the term has when it translates the Platonic *anamnesis*, as well as from the sense in which it is sometimes used in English for memory as a whole.

2. Most notably Paul Demiéville, "Sur la mémoire des existences antérieures," *Bulletin de l'École Française d'Extrême Orient* 27 (1927), and Gregory Schopen, "The Generalization of an Old Yogic Attainment in Medieval Mahāyāna Sūtra Literature: Some Notes on *Jātismara*," *Journal of the International Association of Buddhist Studies* 6, no. 1 (1983): 109–147; both are summarized in Donald Lopez's chapter, along with other treatments of this subject. A recent discussion of the memorization of texts and its role in the preservation of Buddhist teachings is to be found in R. Gombrich, "How the Mahāyāna Began," in *The Buddhist Forum, Volume I: Seminar Papers 1987–1988* (London: School of Oriental and African Studies, 1990), pp. 21–30.

3. On primary memory, see William James, *Principles of Psychology* (New York: Holt, 1890), I.646 et seq.; Edmund Husserl, *The Phenomenology of Internal Time-Consciousness*, trans. J. Macquarrie and E. Robinson (New York: Harper and Row, 1962), sections 11–29 and 34–45; Robert G. Crowder, *Principles of Learning and Memory* (Hillsdale, N.J.: Lawrence Erlbaum Associates, 1976), Chapter 6 and throughout; see also Casey's article *infra*. On habit memory, see Henri Bergson, *Matter and Memory*, trans. Nancy Margaret Paul and W. Scott Palmer (New York: Zone Books, 1988), p. 80 et seq.; note that Bergson does not consider habit memory to be "true memory" (p. 151). For body memory, see Edward S. Casey, *Remembering: A Phenomenological Study* (Bloomington: University of Indiana Press, 1987), Chapter 8. Regarding semantic memory, see Endel Tulving, *Elements of Episodic Memory*, Oxford Psychology Series No. 2 (Oxford: Oxford University Press, 1983), brief definition on p.v; see Chapter 2 and especially p. 35 for a summary of the principal differences between semantic memory and what he calls "episodic memory," which is the recollection of concrete, dateable experiences. Freud's principal thinking on the fate of repressed memories may be seen in "The Unconscious" and "Repression,"

The Standard Edition of the Complete Psychological Works of Sigmund Freud, trans. James Strachey (London: The Hogarth Press, 1953–74), vol. 14; and Josef Breuer and Sigmund Freud, *Studies in Hysteria, Standard Edition,* vol. 2. An influential work in anthropological circles, which focuses on bodily performative memory as distinct from personal and cognitive memory, is Paul Connerton, *How societies remember* (Cambridge: Cambridge University Press, 1989). Examples of anthropological studies that take into account the embodiment of memory include Nancy D. Munn, "Constructing Regional Worlds in Experience: Kula Exchange, Witchcraft and Gawan Local Events," *Man* (N.S.) 25, no. 1 (1990): 1–17; and Debbora Battaglia, "The Body in the Gift: Memory and Forgetting In Sabarl Mortuary Exchange," *American Ethnologist,* in press.

4. For Saint Augustine's thoughts on memory of God, see *The Trinity,* trans. Stephen McKenna (Washington, D.C.: The Catholic University of America Press, 1963), Book 14, Chapter 12, and Book 15, Chapters 21–23. Some of Martin Heidegger's reflections on memory may be found in *What Is Called Thinking,* trans. J. Glenn Gray (New York: Harper & Row, 1968); see p. 141, and discussion pp. 138–153.

5. On Descartes and memory, see Dalia Judovitz, *Subjectivity and Representation in Descartes* (Cambridge: Cambridge University Press, 1988), p. 58 seq. One example of Nietzsche's views on memory may be had from Matthew Kapstein's chapter herein, p. 259. An example of Freud's skepticism concerning memory of childhood is expressed in "Screen Memories," *Standard Edition,* vol. 3, p. 332; see Casey, *Remembering,* p. 8.

6. An earlier version of some of the chapters in this volume were read at a panel on memory in Buddhism that I, with the enthusiastic encouragement of Donald Lopez, organized for the American Academy of Religion meeting held in Boston in December 1987. Volume contributors Padmanabh Jaini, Lopez, and myself, in addition to John Keenan whose paper is not published here, and Edward Casey as respondent, participated in that panel.

7. Casey's book *Remembering* is cited in note 2.

8. Some of the relevant sources for semantic, habit, and related types of memory are cited in note 2.

9. Identification is particularly thematized in Harrison's study; see p. 230 for a suggestive quote from anthropologist Lawrence Babb, who notes that certain practices, in this case in the Hindu tradition, create "possibilities for self-transformation that are, whatever their origins in social experience, already internalized as part of his personality structure." My use of the term *recognizing* in this sentence should be distinguished from the mundane recognition of persons and things that is critiqued by the Buddhist logicians, as discussed below. In the mundane variety of recognition, a specific object perceived now is identified with a specific object perceived previously. In contrast, recognition of the "ultimate truth" of something, in Buddhist terms, would entail the perception of that thing in light of a principle such as no-self or emptiness, which the Buddhist practitioner endeavors to see in all things. See Wayman's chapter

for Buddhist usage of the term *pratyabhijñāna* to mean recognition of the mundane sort. *Pratyabhijñāna* also occurs in the *Ratnagotravibhāgavyākhyā;* but here it refers to the recognition of reality in the special sense that such a notion would have in the Buddhist *tathāgatagarbha* and related traditions, where the idea is that the reality being recognized is innate to all sentient beings, an idea that may be connected to certain Brahmanical traditions: see David Ruegg, *Le traité du tathāgatagarbha de Bu ston Rin chen grub* (Paris: École Française D'Extrême-Orient, 1973), p. 78, n. 1; and *Buddha-nature, Mind and the Problem of Gradualism in a Comparative Perspective: On the Transmission and Reception of Buddhism in India and Tibet* (London: School of Oriental and African Studies, 1989), p. 139.

10. *Abhidhamma Studies: Researches in Buddhist Psychology,* 2d. ed. (Kandy, Ceylon: Buddhist Publication Society, 1965), pp. 68–72. See also his Introduction.

11. Paul J. Griffiths, "Why Buddhas Can't Remember Their Previous Lives," *Philosophy East and West* 39, no. 4 (October 1989): 449–52.

12. See Cox, p. 91, n. 9.

13. According to Masaaki Hattori, *Dignāga, On Perception,* Harvard Oriental Series, vol. 47 (Cambridge, Mass.: Harvard University Press, 1968), p. 81, n. 17, the object of recognition is viewed by Buddhist logicians as a particular, not a universal. This suggests some ambivalence concerning the classification of at least one type of memory, i.e., recognition, which on the grounds of the nature of its object would have a significant affinity with perception. Hattori remarks, "Dignāga's theory of a sharp distinction between the objects of *pratyakṣa* [direct perception] and *anumāna* [inference] is hardly applicable to the case of re-cognition."

14. See Gethin's chapter, p. 161.

15. I argue that memory becomes synonymous with revelation of scripture in the Tibetan Gter-ma tradition in my "Signs, Memory and History: A Tantric Buddhist Theory of Scriptural Revelation," *Journal of the International Association of Buddhist Studies* 9, no. 2 (1986): 7–35.

16. *The Tradition of Pha Dam-pa Saṅs-rgyas,* ed. Barbara Aziz. Reproduced from a Unique Collection of Manuscripts Preserved with 'Khrul-źig Rin-po-che of Roṅ-phu Monastery at Diṅ-ri Glaṅ-skor (Thimphu: Druk Sherik Parkhang, 1979), 5 vols. See, for example, vol. 1, pp. 351–58, for a collection of songs sung "over a full container of wine" by thirty-five ḍākinīs after a *gaṇacakra* ceremony at Śītavana, especially the songs of Ral-pa'i Thor-lcog-can, Ye-shes Rdo-rje, Pad-ma'i Zhabs, and Gzi-brjid-kyi Rgyal-mo.

17. Stanley Tambiah, *The Buddhist saints of the forest and the cult of the amulets* (Cambridge: Cambridge University Press, 1984), pp. 200 et seq.

18. An initial study of these matters can be found in my "Autobiography in Tibetan Religious Literature: Reflections on Its Modes of Self-Presentation," to be published in the proceedings of the Fifth Seminar of the International Association of Tibetan Studies (Narita, Japan: Naritasan Shoji, 1992).

Memories of the Buddha

DONALD S. LOPEZ, JR.

Memory's images, once they are fixed in words, are erased.

——— *Italo Calvino*

Extraordinary feats of memory continue to captivate the imagination. Pliny the Elder calls memory "the boon most important for life," and tells of King Cyrus of Persia, who knew the names of all of the soldiers in his army, and of King Mithridates, who could render judgments in the twenty-two languages of his realm.[1] The sixteenth-century Jesuit missionary Matteo Ricci, in an effort to convince his Chinese hosts of the glories of Christianity, employed his now famous memory palace to recite forward and backward a long and random list of Chinese characters after a single reading.[2] And in 1952, a Russian journalist known to us simply as "S", a patient of the Soviet neurologist A. R. Luria, employed his synaesthetic memory to recite in Italian (a language he did not know) the first four lines of the *Divine Comedy,* fifteen years after the first and only time he heard them.[3]

But who among these mnemonists can surpass the feat of the Gautamid prince, seated beneath the tree on that full moon night? He recounts that prior to his achievement of buddhahood at dawn:

> I directed my mind to the knowledge and recollection of former abodes. I remembered a variety of former abodes: one birth, two births, three births, four births, five births, ten births, twenty births, thirty births, forty births, fifty births, a hundred births, a thousand births, a hundred thousand births, and many aeons of creation, many aeons of destruction, and many aeons of creation and destruction. There I was so named, of such a clan, of such a caste, such food, such experience of pleasure and pain, such a life span. Passing away there, I appeared elsewhere, and there too I was so named, of such a clan, of such a caste, such food, such experience of pleasure and pain, such a life span. Passing away there, I appeared here. Thus I remembered various former abodes in all their modes and details.[4]

Contexts of Memory

Many issues could be explored in connection with the memory of former abodes (*pūrva-nivāsa-ānusmṛti-jñānam*) that the bodhisattva Siddhārtha is said to have experienced on the night he became the Buddha. How, for example, is this knowledge gained? Is this extraordinary memory a natural byproduct of a particular stage on the Buddhist path, or must one engage in specific practices in order to acquire it? The fifth century Theravādin scholar Buddhaghosa seems to hold the latter view, outlining in the *Visuddhimagga* a regimen in which the meditator recalls his or her life in reverse order.[5] She begins with the most recent act of sitting down to meditate and then proceeds to trace the events of this life back to the moment of conception, back to the moment of death in the previous existence, and so on through the eons; non-Buddhists can recollect as far back as forty eons, ordinary disciples (*śrāvakas*) 1,000 eons, the eighty great disciples 100,000 eons, Śāriputra and Maudgalyāyana could recollect an incalculable age and 100,000 eons of their past lives, pratyekabuddhas two incalculable eons and 100,000 eons, and buddhas can recall limitless past lives.

As in any theory of memory, there are philosophical questions to be asked concerning the memory of past lives. What is it that distinguishes memory from thought; that is, what is the quality of memory that causes the subject to recognize the content as something experienced rather than something dreamed or imagined? What is the relationship between the memory image that is the present object of consciousness and the past object that is the referent of that memory?[6] And if, as Buddhist philosophers so often declare, the past is nonexistent, what is the object that the bodhisattva perceived as he meditated under the tree? What precisely did he remember?[7]

The clinical psychologist might compare the Buddha's recollection of his former abodes with documented cases of extraordinary reminiscence. This occurs in incidents of incontinent nostalgia brought about by anamnestic seizure in the temporal lobe, when scenes or sounds from the long forgotten past are replayed in vivid hallucination, or in forced reminiscence induced by the drug L-dopa, in which the most trivial details of the past are brought into present awareness.[8] Such cases have suggested to some researchers that every human being constantly carries in the brain "fossilized memory sequences" of all past experiences. These dormant memories remain indefinitely and can be reactivated under special conditions, such as those brought about by brain injury, the electrical stimulation of epileptogenic points in the cerebral cortex, or states of extreme excitement.[9] Those interested in the physiognomy of altered states of consciousness might wonder whether these memories can also be activated by the Buddhist meditative practice of dhyāna, a question that immediately evokes the fascination of twenty years ago (today) with the apparent parity of yogic and psychedelic experience.[10]

But the Buddha remembers not only the events of this life but of an infinite number of past lives. Further, as we will see, his reminiscences differ significantly in tone from those just described. The memories experienced through the stimulation of the temporal lobe are described in the language of presence and possession, with events recounted as if they are being fully relived in the moment. The memory of the mnemonist S was of a synaesthetic character in which all the senses were stimulated by a sound or visual object.[11] The great fictional mnemonist, Borges' Funes the Memorious, whose prodigious memory (as in many clinical cases) resulted from an injury, was cursed to perceive everything in vivid detail and then to remember it all, rendering him incapable of abstraction: "It was not only difficult for him to understand that the generic term *dog* embraced so many unlike specimens of differing sizes and different forms; he was disturbed by the fact that a dog at three-fourteen (seen in profile) should have the same name as the dog at three-fifteen seen from the front."[12] Funes, lying on his bed in the darkness so as to protect himself from the sensory onslaught, is in some ways a morbid parody of yogic direct perception (*yogipratyakṣa*) as described in certain Tibetan expositions of the Buddhist Sautrāntika position, where direct perception is exalted over the abstraction of thought. The authors of these expositions perhaps fail to grasp what it would mean for someone to live only in direct perception, without abstraction and forgetfulness.[13] Nietzsche argued that, "there could be no happiness, no cheerfulness, no hope, no pride, no *present* without forgetfulness. The man in whom this apparatus of repression is damaged and ceases to function properly may be compared (and more than merely compared) with a dyspeptic—he cannot 'have done' with anything."[14] This was the case with Funes. We will have occasion below to consider whether the Buddha needed to remember in order to forget, whether the vision of his former lives served to digest the past so that he could eliminate it and be freed from its effects.

The comparison of the Buddha to modern mnemonists can be taken to its parodic extreme with the case of the twins described in Oliver Sacks' *The Man Who Mistook His Wife for a Hat.* Variously diagnosed as severely retarded, psychotic, or autistic, their memory seems closest to that of the Buddha. The twins could tell you instantly and correctly the day of the week of any date over a period of 80,000 years. But their skill was not merely one of computation, for they could also recount the weather, the news, and their experiences of any day of their life when specified by date.[15] Unlike S or Funes, their memory lacked excessive richness, but rather was documentary and disinterested. They could move immediately to see any moment of the past, much as buddhas, in order to recall a specific moment of the past, "descend with the lion's descent wherever they want, even skipping over many millions of aeons as though there were an elision in the text."[16]

In the end, however, the Buddha differs from all these cases. His recounting of his prodigious past is entirely flat and formulaic. In particular, unlike these others, he seems to have made no great sacrifice for his preternatural memory. Those who experienced incontinent nostalgia or forced reminiscence suffered from neurological disorders resulting from injury or disease: Funes lay crippled on his bed as result of the equestrian accident that triggered his memory, the Russian mnemonist's synaesthetic memory of things barred him forever from the world of ideas, and the twins remained seated in the corner of a psychiatric ward communicating with each other in twenty-digit prime numbers.

The Buddha's recollection of his former lives is topographically flat, without affect, with none of the imagery of eidetic memory, with none of the wistfulness of reminiscence, with none of the spontaneity of *mémoire involontaire*, with none of the forgetfulness of selective memory whereby the past is woven each day and unraveled each night.[17] The memory of the Buddha is comprehensive, disinterested, continuous, closed, dissolving singular events into a formula.

The case of the Buddha does not bear fruitful comparison with these others because the recollection of past abodes that the Buddha experienced in the first watch of the night is not a case of memory but of the mythology of memory. Hence our task is not to account for its fact but for its fiction and its function. Why is it that among the scores of powers attributed to the Buddha, the recollection of past abodes figures so prominently in the seminal legend of Buddhism, the account of the Buddha's enlightenment? The remainder of this essay will attempt to provide some reflections on why memory, specifically the memory of past lives, is recounted as part of the enlightenment of the Buddha. To consider this question, we must first survey briefly the occurrences of the memory of former abodes in the early Buddhist scriptures as they pertain to the experience of enlightenment.

Memory of Former Abodes in the Pāli Canon

Memory of former lives, literally "of former abodes," the places of past rebirth (*nivāsa* has the sense of habitation, a dwelling place, a place to pass the night), appears most commonly as a component of one or another list. It often occurs in the lists of the superknowledges (*abhijñā*, Pāli: *abhiññā*), the gnoses (*vidyā*, Pāli: *vijjā*), or the powers (*bala*). Although lists of five, six, and seven superknowledges appear in Buddhist literature,[18] the most common listing is of six:

1. Knowledge of thaumaturgy (*ṛddhi-vidhi-jñānam*), which includes the ability to produce manifold forms, to appear and disappear, to walk through walls and mountains, to walk on water, to fly in the cross-legged posture, to touch and stroke the sun and moon with one's hands, and to physically travel as far as the world of Brahmā;[19]
2. The divine ear (*divyaṃ-śrotram*) or clairaudience;

3. The knowledge of others' minds (*parasya cetaḥ-paryāya jñānam*) or telepathy;

4. The knowledge of former abodes (*pūrva-nivāsa-anusmṛti-jñānam*), which is the memory of one's own former lives;

5. The divine eye (*divyaṃ cakṣuḥ*), whereby one can see the present karmic fate of beings throughout the various universes and realms of rebirth, faring well or ill according to their deeds;[20]

6. The knowledge of the destruction of the defilements (*āsrava-kṣaya-jñānam*), the salvific knowledge of the four truths that puts an end to future rebirth.[21]

In other texts, the memory of former abodes is called the first of the three gnoses, the other two being the divine eye and the knowledge of the destruction of the defilements. In another list, the memory of former abodes occurs as the eighth of the ten powers of the tathāgata.[22]

In situating the memory of former abodes as a component of the path to enlightenment, the Nikāyas present two general descriptions of the process involved. In one, the Buddha describes the path of an average monk; and in the other, the Buddha relates his own experience. There are at least four varieties of the first type, the longest and most detailed of which occurs in the *Sāmaññaphalasutta* of the *Dīghanikāya,* repeated throughout its first section. Here, the Buddha describes the benefits of the homeless life to King Ajātasatta and provides a chronological catalogue of the attainments of one who follows the path, from the occasion of first hearing the Dhamma to the final attainment of arahantship and nirvāṇa. Among those attainments are the six superknowledges (although they are not identified as such in the sutta) in the order given above, culminating with the knowledge of the destruction of the defilements.[23] In another, abbreviated model of the arahant's path, the monk attains each of the four concentrations (*jhāna*), and then comes to understand that a living being (*jīvam*) is not the same as or different from the body; in this version there is no mention of any of the superknowledges.[24] Yet another variety of the arahant's path is described in great detail in the *Cūḷahatthipadopamasutta* of the *Majjhimanikāya.* As in the longer account in the *Dīgha,* the Buddha here describes the proper behavior and practice of a monk on the path from the first hearing of the Dhamma through enlightenment. But this account differs from that in the *Dīgha* with respect to the superknowledges in that here, having attained the fourth concentration, the monk achieves only the last three of the superknowledges: the knowledge of former abodes, the divine eye, and the knowledge of the destruction of the defilements.[25] Elsewhere, these three are referred to as the three gnoses (*tevijjā*).[26] Finally, there is the so-called dry insight (*sukkha-vipassanā*) whereby monks become arahants without recourse to either deep concentration or superknowledge.[27]

Second, there are the "autobiographical" narratives of the Buddha's enlightenment. These appear in two forms in the Nikāyas. In the *Ariyapariyesanasutta* of the *Majjhimanikāya* the Buddha recalls his days as a disciple of Āḷārakālāma and Uddakarāmaputta and his attainment of the concentrations and superknowledges under their tutelage, but does not specify what the superknowledges are. The description of his attainment of nirvāṇa is surprisingly brief; the concentrations and superknowledges are not mentioned as constituents of the enlightenment experience.[28] But this account was less popular than the second variety, a longer version of Gautama's achievement of buddhahood that occurs in full form in the *Bhayabheravasutta* of the *Majjhimanikāya* and that seems to have served as the source for the accounts in the *Buddhacarita* and the *Lalitavistara*. Here, the bodhisatta becomes the Buddha by gaining the three gnoses: in the first watch of the night, the knowledge of former abodes; in the second watch, the divine eye; and in the third watch of the night, the knowledge of the destruction of the defilements.[29] It is this version of enlightenment that concerns us here, a version in which the memory of past lives holds such a prominent place. The various mundane superknowledges are reduced to only two: the memory of past lives and the divine eye. These two extraordinary visions are then placed in apparent propaedeutic proximity to the final liberating knowledge, the supramundane superknowledge (*lokuttara-abhiññā*) that the causes of all future birth have been destroyed.

Before considering the specific place of the memory of former abodes in the Buddha's enlightenment, we can survey briefly the scholarship on the general topic of the memory of past lives in Buddhism. Paul Demiéville catalogued the references to this memory in the Pāli Nikāyas, the Chinese Āgamas, and the Abhidharma literature in his 1927 article, "Sur la mémoire des existences antérieures."[30] It is clear from Demiéville's study that the memory of former abodes is regarded with a pronounced ambivalence by the Abhidharma scholastics: on the one hand, they are obliged to afford it at least a modicum of importance because it occurs as a constituent of the enlightenment of both the arahant and the Buddha; but, on the other hand, memory of past abodes is a common byproduct of deep levels of concentration that are accessible even to non-Buddhists. Hence, in the Abhidharma literature the memory of former abodes is legitimized through being invested with some point of Buddhist doctrine, with which it may be related only tangentially. For example, it is said of the three gnoses (of which memory of former abodes is the first), "In the first, one overcomes ignorance about the past; in the second, ignorance about the future; in the third, ignorance about nirvāṇa. . . . In the first, one overcomes misunderstanding of the skandhas [aggregates]; in the second, misunderstanding of sentient beings; in the third, misunderstanding of dharmas.''[31] This leads Demiéville to conclude: ''Given the importance of the doctrine of transmigration in the Buddhist system, one would expect to find an original and well-established Buddhist theory concerning the memory of former lives. This does not seem to have been brought out by our brief inquiry. . . . It has no saintly character in and of itself; it only takes on religious value by the reflections it inspires.''[32]

The ambiguity of the tradition toward the memory of former births is further confirmed in the work of Gregory Schopen, who has surveyed medieval Mahāyāna sūtras to discover that there the memory of former births (*jātismara*) is not the result of deep states of concentration but is a benefit achieved through certain meritorious deeds. Further, this memory brings about not a profound realization of impermanence that inspires the quest for liberation, but instead a modification in behavior less grand in purpose: having seen the sufferings one experienced in the past, one resolves to eschew evil and live a virtuous life so that one will never again be reborn in hell.[33]

The studies of Demiéville and Schopen demonstrate a wide range of Buddhist interpretations of the significance of the memory of past lives. None of these pertain specifically, however, to the question of how such memory functions in the enlightenment of the Buddha. Richard Robinson has turned to comparative religion for such an interpretation, noting that the memory of former lives is a feature of certain shamanic ecstasies. Thus, Robinson sees the enlightenment that occurred over the three watches of the night as ''two-thirds shamanism ethically transformed and one-third philosophy.''[34] But the experience of native American shamans seems to be quite different from Robinson's characterization, involving memories of prenatal existence rather than memories of numerous former incarnations.[35] That the shamanic can be civilized into the philosophical or ethical has been made evident by the work of Karl Meuli and others on the origins of Plato's theory of anamnesis.[36] That the same is true in the case of the Buddha's enlightenment, as Robinson suggests, should not be automatically conceded.[37] But Robinson's evocation of shamanism directs us toward perhaps the most sustained attempt to discover some significance in the Buddha's memory of his former lives.

Eliade on the Buddha's Memory

In *Cosmos and History: The Myth of the Eternal Return,* Mircea Eliade distinguishes between what he calls the primitive (or archaic, traditional, anthropological, or archetypal) and the historical (or existentialist) visions of time. The former first negates, and then renews both time and the world via the periodic return to the atemporal moment before the beginning of time.

The primary vehicles for this return are myth and ritual, both of which rely strongly on memory to conjure the primordial. Eliade finds universal evidence for the primitive quest to gain control over time and its ravages, discerning it in India in various hymns and sacrifices of the Saṃhitās and Brāhmanas. The view of time in the Yoga and Buddhist schools represents for Eliade a different vision, the historical position, in which "the reactualization of auroral time" is no longer considered an effective means of dealing with suffering. Rather, these systems imagine time itself as suffering; instead of using the law of karma to justify the human condition and account for history, they seek to destroy karma, "the very symbol of man's 'slavery'."[38]

Without pausing to evaluate his manipulation of the doctrine of karma, we can note that Eliade's placement of Buddhism in the primitive/historical dichotomy shifts in his later writings. With his reading of the Buddha's memory of former lives, Eliade returns Buddhism to the realm of the archaic. In this context, he enumerates the initiation rites of primitive societies that entail a symbolic *regressus ad uterum* of the initiate as a means of healing the individual or even repeating the cosmogony, "by reimmersing him in the primordial fullness."[39] Eliade perceives a structural analogy in the Buddhist practice of remembering former lives, which he sees as a means of destroying karmic residue and gaining deliverance from time. He writes:

> To re-live one's past lives would also be to understand them and, to a certain degree, "burn up" one's "sins"; that is, the sum of the deeds done in the state of ignorance and capitalised from one life to the next by the law of *karma*. But there is something of ever greater importance: one attains to the beginning of Time and enters the Timeless—the eternal present which preceded the temporal experience inaugurated by the "fall" into human existence. In other words, it is possible, starting from a moment of temporal duration, to exhaust that duration by retracing its course to the source and so come out into the Timeless, into eternity. But that is to regain the non-conditioned state, which preceded the fall into Time and the wheel of existences.[40]

For Eliade the two orders of time, the primordial and the historical, seem to be collapsed in the Buddha's vision of his former lives, because this vision at once destroys karma (which for Eliade stands for the historical) and returns the Buddha to the primordial moment.

But if we examine Eliade's reading of the Buddha's experience in light of early Buddhist soteriological theory, it is clear that he goes too far, demonstrating a tendency evident elsewhere in his works to ubiquitize, almost nostalgically, the archaic motif of the return to the origin. To find this motif in Buddhism, he must misrepresent the Buddhist delineation of both the problem and the solution. The problem, for the Buddha, is not, as Eliade claims, that man lives in Time.[41] In the Abhidharma, time is the most tenuous of abstractions; like the person (*pudgala*), it is a construct associated with neither form nor consciousness (*viprayukta-saṃskāra*). In seeking the Buddhist correlate of time, that which for Eliade is to be overcome by the return to the primordial, he sees only the law of karma. But although karma functions in time, it is not itself time. Eliade does not look beyond karma to the deeper causes of suffering that motivate karma: the various defilements of attachment, hatred, and delusion. Although one could, indeed, extrapolate from the classical Buddhist categories of causation, impermanence, and construction (*saṃskāra*) a Buddhist critique of time, Eliade makes no move in this direction, seeing only history as the negatum of Buddhist insight. Consequently, Eliade comes to imagine that the Buddha's purpose in recollecting his former abodes is the return to a primordial moment whereby he will escape the confines of time; "This mystical ability made it possible to reach the 'beginning of time' which . . . implied 'emerging from time.' "[42] Although he notes correctly that the Buddha was not concerned with first causes, he easily succumbs to the lure of the archaic: "His aim is to sever the succession of transmigrations; and one of the methods is this retracing of the course of one's previous lives, through the memory of them, back to the moment when the Cosmos came into existence."[43] But there is no such moment in Buddhist cosmogony.[44]

Indeed, we find in Indian Buddhist thought a pronounced aversion to origins and endtimes. Despite the fact that creation myths continued to be written into the Hindu tradition, from the *Ṛg Veda* to the Brāhmaṇas, Upaniṣads, Dharmaśāstras, and Purāṇas, we discover in Buddhism a conspicuous absence of such retrospective speculation. This is due, at least in part, to the fact that Indian Buddhist philosophy above all is a theory of causation, showing that all things are constructed in the process of cause and effect, and that behind this tenuous and transient construction there is no essence, no identity. For there to be a first cause, an origin, there must be that which is unconstructed. But for the Buddhists the unconstructed occurs not at the beginning but at the end, at nirvāṇa, at the destruction of all causes. If the Buddhists were to speak of an origin they would be obliged to posit a pristine identity prior to the forging of the chains of causation, before the beginning of movement, where all movement would be movement toward loss and all liberation would imply retrieval. The origin is "a metaphysical extension that arises from the belief that things are most precious and essential at the moment of birth."[45] In the Nikāyas, the Buddha seems to be arguing very strongly against such an extension and hence against original purity. To say that saṃsāra has no beginning is to declare that there is no primordial essence of things, behind and before the world.

The Buddha does engage in retrogressive reflection to discover an origin, however, and, according to some accounts, this reflection constitutes his enlightenment. It is the tracing of aging and death back through its preceding causes that substitutes for cosmogony in Buddhism. The ''origin'' he discovers, however, is ignorance at the beginning of a twelvefold process of dependent origination. This ignorance is not a primal origin, but one produced from an earlier causal chain, a specific cause that is itself an effect, rather than some first cause. The components of the twelvefold sequence are discussed not as a line but as a wheel, with ignorance as the hub, aging and death as the rim, and the other ten components as the spokes.[46]

Eliade apparently misses this, insisting that the Buddha returned to the moment before the beginning. Yet, nowhere is it stated that the Buddha returned to any particular moment in his past, but that he remembered it all. Nowhere is it said that karma is destroyed by the memory of past lives, that liberation is gained, in Eliade's words, by ''retracing of the course of one's previous lives, through the memory of them, back to the moment when the Cosmos came into existence.''[47] Otherwise, Siddhārtha would have been enlightened in the first watch of the night, rather than the third. Instead, such memory is seen by both Buddhist and non-Buddhist schools as a byproduct of deep concentration (as in *Yogasūtra* III.18). The memory itself carries with it no salvific power. Indeed, in the *Brahmajālasutta,* the Buddha explains that certain ascetics, who gain the ability to remember their past lives, conclude on the basis of that experience that the self and the world are eternal.[48]

In fact, the function of the memory of past lives in the enlightenment of the Buddha is a question on which the tradition itself is significantly silent. It is our purpose here to explore both that function and that silence. We must resist, however, the reductionist interpretation of Eliade who, influenced by the fact that recollection is to be found in the myths of primitive cultures, in Platonic philosophy, and in Freud, came to conclude:

> Whatever the differences between these images and formulae, in the final reckoning they all mean the same thing: that *the essential human condition preceded the actual human condition,* that the decisive deed took place before us, and even before our parents: that decisive deed having been done by the mythic Ancestor. . . . Better still, man is obliged to return to the actions of this Ancestor, either to confront or else repeat them; in short, never to forget them, whatever way he may choose to perform this *regressus ad originem.*[49]

Eliade's position is different from what we might loosely characterize as the Freudian view. For Freud, one returns through memory to a past ''event'' and thereby is freed from the deleterious effects of that specific event. For

Eliade, the return to the primordial origin provides freedom from the effects of all intervening history. A Freudian reading of the Buddha's recollection of his former abodes is indeed a tempting one. In Freud's prepsychoanalytic theory of abreaction, an emotional discharge liberates one from the affect associated with the memory of a traumatic event in such a way that the affect no longer is pathogenic.[50] Freud and Breuer hold that a massive abreaction, in the form of an emotional catharsis, is the only way for the subject to become free from the deleterious effects of a repressed memory. Yet the Buddha's account of his recollection of former abodes has nothing of the character of catharsis, but is emotionally flat and formulaic. Nonetheless, there are apparent parallels between Freud's theory of repetition and recollection on the one hand, and Buddhist karmic theory and insight on the other. For Freud (as paraphrased by Laplanche and Pontalis), "the compulsion to repeat is an ungovernable process originating in the unconscious. As a result of its action, the subject deliberately places himself in distressing situations, thereby repeating an old experience, but he does not recall this prototype; on the contrary, he has the strong impression that the situation is fully determined by the circumstances of the moment."[51] Thus, in 1909, and in language reminiscent of the Buddhist terms saṃsāra, *avidyā* ("ignorance"), and *vidyā* ("gnosis"), Freud wrote, "a thing which has not been understood inevitably reappears; like an unlaid ghost, it cannot rest until the mystery has been solved and the spell broken;"[52] saṃsāra as the return of the repressed, if you will. But we cannot reduce the recollection of past lives to these terms; we have already dismissed as inappropriate to the Buddhist model Eliade's view that simply to see the past is to be freed from it, or, more precisely, to return to the primordial past is to be freed from the historical past. For Eliade, "the important thing is to recollect even the most insignificant details of one's life (present or past), for it is only by virtue of this recollection that one can 'burn up' one's past, master it, keep it from affecting the present."[53] Rather, we must seek a further link between the recollection of former abodes and the Buddha's liberating knowledge of the destruction of the defilements.

Further Speculations on the Buddha's Memory

It would seem that a number of purposes are served in ascribing to the Buddha the ability to recall limitless past lives. One reflects the tendency to ascribe to the Buddha all possible powers to the highest degree, surpassing the accomplishments, or *siddhis*, of all other yogins. This superordination of virtues, of course, is a common motif of the hagiographic.

The Buddha's remarkable memory also provides a scriptural justification for the appropriation of a diverse body of folklore into the canon. The

Jātakas (*Birth Stories*), of which there are 547 by Fausböll's count, are transformed from an Indian version of Aesop's *Fables* into the word of the Buddha. This is evident in the appended conclusion to each story, in which the Buddha represents the tale as the recollection of one of his former lives and inevitably identifies himself as the protagonist ("In that existence the otter was Ānanda, the jackal was Moggallāna, the monkey was Sāriputta, and I was the wise hare."). As the Greek goddess Mnemosyne, the deification of memory, serves as the poet's muse, so the Buddha's prodigious memory provides a seemingly limitless fount of narrative by which simple fables come to illustrate the Dharma.[54]

Turning to questions of doctrine that are more central to the scholastic tradition, we may venture to link the Buddha's memory to his discovery of the four noble truths. Because the bodhisattva vows to achieve enlightenment at a time when no buddhas are present in the world, he must come to an understanding of those truths—that is, suffering, its origin, its cessation, and the path to that cessation—without a teacher. This factor of the presence or absence of a teacher appears to be the primary distinction between the Buddha and an arahant in the early tradition. The recollection of former abodes is not reported as integral to the realizations of the arahant (nor the stream-enterer, once-returner, or never-returner). In the *Vangīsasutta* of the *Saṃyuttanikāya*, the Buddha notes that of the 500 arahants in his audience, 320 were liberated by insight alone, without recourse to the recollection of former abodes, construed as either one of the three gnoses or one of the six superknowledges.[55] Thus, it would seem that the recollection of former lives is a necessary prerequisite only for the enlightenment of the Buddha (at least for those sūtra authors who include it in their renditions of the enlightenment event.) It is with this recollection, and with the divine eye of the second watch, that the bodhisattva sees, rather than infers, the fact of suffering in his own past and its immediate origin in the functioning of the karma of all beings in the universe. That the bodhisattva is not simply regressing through time in memory, as Buddhaghosa instructs the neophyte in the practice, but rather is seeing the causal relationship between one lifetime and the next, is evident from the progressive character of the narration: "Then, passing away there, I was born here." And, indeed, Aśvaghoṣa (second century CE), in the fourteenth chapter of the *Buddhacarita,* uses the occasion of the first two watches to describe the sufferings of saṃsāra in vivid detail.[56] Hence, the memory of former abodes seems to serve as a substitute for a teacher, instructing the bodhisattva on the first truth, the truth of suffering.

Only in the third watch, however, as the bodhisattva enters into liberating insight (*vipassanā*), does he see the deep cause of suffering and bring about its cessation. If the recollection of former abodes is necessary for the attainment of nirvāṇa, then, it is not in itself sufficient for it. According to the commentary on the *Nidānakathā,* the recollection of former abodes and the divine eye are merely two of the many powers already commanded by the bodhisattva Sumedha, four innumerable eons and one hundred eons before his last birth as Prince Siddhārtha. For the Buddha, again, it is not the case, as Eliade claims, that "he who remembers his former lives succeeds in freeing himself from karmic conditionings."[57]

On closer examination, however, even this constructive reading suggesting the autodidactic role of memory in the enlightenment sequence becomes problematic. Despite the fact that Aśvaghoṣa connects the truth of suffering to the vision of the first watch of the night, the texts do not suggest that the bodhisattva did so. As André Bareau has noted:

> In effect, the notion of suffering is entirely absent in the knowledge of the memory of past lives, which serves to prove only the doctrine of transmigration. Nothing in the description expresses the lassitude, anguish, and fright at the prospect of the endless series of rebirth. In the description of the second knowledge this notion of suffering is evident, but it is also countered by the contrary notion of happiness. The lesson that can be extracted is twofold, corresponding poorly to the foundation of Buddhist doctrine, in that it encourages people to act properly and to think wholesomely, not in order to escape possible existences but to avoid being reborn in hell and to be reborn in heaven in a happy journey.[58]

For Bareau, the knowledge gained in the first two watches of the night suggests not the first two truths of suffering and origin, but simply the laws of transmigration and karma: virtuous action leads to a happy rebirth, nonvirtuous action leads to future sorrow. And although these are fundamental Buddhist doctrines, they are not the first two truths: that all conditioned existence is somehow suffering and the cause of that suffering is craving and ignorance. Indeed, for Bareau, the view that heaven can be gained by wholesome deeds "est étrangère à l'essence profonde du Bouddhisme" and constitutes a lower teaching addressed to a laity who cannot hope to attain deliverance from rebirth soon, who can only strive, for the present, for a favorable rebirth.[59] Without pausing to consider whether Buddhism has a profound essence and, if so, what it might possibly be, we can observe only that the visions of the first two watches of the night seem for Bareau to imply exactly the simple ethical message of karmic conscientiousness that Gregory Schopen discerned in the Mahāyāna sūtras concerning memory of past lives. This concordance provides support for the argument that bodhi, or full enlightenment, stood as a remote if not mythical goal for much of Indian Buddhism.

If, then, we are unable to integrate neatly the knowledges gained in the first watch of the night with the salvific knowledge of the destruction of the defilements gained in the third, how can we interpret the memory of former abodes in the enlightenment narrations? If we attempt, though vainly, to divine the intention of the authors of the sūtras, we can ponder the historical circumstances that contributed to the inclusion of the memory of former abodes in so many versions of the enlightenment. As Bareau notes, the doctrines implied by the first two watches, of rebirth and karma, preceded the rise of Buddhism and, indeed, may have represented a world-view widely accepted in northern India at the time of the Buddha.[60] If these beliefs were universally held, there would be no need to include them in the account of the Buddha's enlightenment.[61] On the other hand, if the doctrines of karma and rebirth were new and controversial, the knowledge of former abodes would have been represented as a more prominent and integral part of a unitary (rather than tripartite) experience of enlightenment, and it would have received a fuller treatment in subsequent commentary than it actually does. That the knowledges of the first two watches of the night occur on the night of the enlightenment but prior to and separate from the final and most important knowledge suggests that the authors of the sūtras regarded these first two knowledges with a certain ambivalence, reflected also in the distinction between mundane and supramundane superknowledges: non-Buddhists can achieve the knowledges of the first two watches but only Buddhists can achieve the third. This would lead us to conclude, obviously, that it was the knowledge of destruction of the defilements that was exalted by the authors as the unique discovery of the Buddha. But it was also a discovery that they apparently felt compelled to embed in the familiar context of the doctrines of rebirth and karma. Bareau proposes three possible motives for the inclusion of the memory of former abodes and the divine eye in the enlightenment accounts. He argues that the authors wanted either (1) to sanction the already long-established idea of transmigration, (2) to introduce a new idea into Buddhist doctrine, or (3) to clarify a poorly defined point.[62]

Bareau does not speculate further on these three motives and warns against making imprudent hypotheses. Ignoring his counsel, we can observe that the first of the three appears the most plausible, unless, following the second, we revive the nineteenth-century claim that the doctrine of rebirth was absent in "original Buddhism," its introduction representing a concession to vulgar concerns. Yet in following the first we can see not simply the tradition's need to stamp a Buddhist seal onto the doctrine of transmigration, but also to connect, albeit ambivalently, the commonly held doctrines of karma and rebirth represented by the knowledge gained in the first watches with the revolutionary view of *anattā* represented by the third. Such a connection demonstrates both the Buddha's continuity with and supersession of the contemporary brahmanical tradition, appropriating its presuppositions in order to transcend them.[63]

But these reflections remain tentative and unsatisfying, and we are led inevitably to seek a further function of the memory of former lives in the accounts of the enlightenment. As we have already discussed, that the Buddha is able to recollect an infinite number of past lives does not seem to entail some return to the primordial before the commencement of the world, pure and uncorrupted by time. The Buddha's recollection of his former abodes at this primal moment must, however, carry some implications for the Buddhist notions of personal identity, and its relation to enlightenment.

Memory and the Rememberer

That memory is the fundamental component of personal identity is suggested by Proust, in the Overture to *Remembrance of Things Past,* when he describes waking at midnight:

> I was more destitute of human qualities than a cave-dweller; but then the memory, not yet of the place in which I was, but of various other places where I had lived, and might now very possibly be, would come like a rope let down from heaven to draw me up out of the abyss of not-being, from which I could never have escaped by myself; in a flash I would traverse and surmount centuries of civilisation, and out of a half-visualized succession of oil lamps, followed by shirts with turned-down collars, would put together by degrees the component parts of my ego.[64]

Here memory becomes the history that writes the individual, the narrative that creates the continuity called the person. If memory constitutes the person, then to remember what was is to be aware of who is, and to remember everything would be to see the person in its manifest fullness. Thus, for the bodhisattva to see all of his past lives was to see who he was, both in its plenitude and its paucity. The persistence of the person is multiplied through its continuity over time, through eons of evolution and dissolution as, grasping the rope of memory, he rises to the karmic present.

And what he remembers is also significant. Contained in the formula of the memory of former abodes are all of the constituents of Indian social identity: place, name, caste, food. But it is this very identity that the Indian renunciates, whether Hindu or Buddhist, abandon when going forth in search of an identity that is not defined in terms of social hierarchy.[65] They go forth from the house and the responsibilities of the householder, giving up a permanent dwelling place, renouncing their former abode. In the case of the Buddha then, one could surmise that the vision of past lives amounts to an insight into his personal identity as it had been constructed in saṃsāra. He sees, in their entirety, those constituents from which the presence of the person had been deduced.

This diachronic vision, encompassing the entire past, enhances by contrast the potency of the vision of the third watch in which the bodhisattva sees in the instantaneous present that this person is a mere projection, that before and behind the chain of dependent origination there is no agent, no person, no self, and that the liberating identity beyond saṃsāra is without self (*anattā*). The personal continuity recollected in the vision of his past abodes is proved a fiction by the actualization of cessation (*nirodha*), where there is no self to be seen.[66] Thus, the bodhisattva sees the past and present order of the world in the first two watches of the night. But when he sees that that ordered world has no essence, he is awakened. That the tension between personal identity and identitylessness, between saṃsāra and nirvāṇa, between continuity and cessation, between the historical and ahistorical, which is played out throughout Buddhist philosophy, also occurs in the paradigmatic event of the tradition should, upon reflection, come as no surprise.

However, we must pause one last time to examine the content of the memory that occurs in the bodhisattva's first watch. We might recall that what the sūtras describe about the night of the enlightenment is not the past but a memory of the past; it is a representation of the past, in effect, its substitute. In a similar vein, recent scientific research has questioned the assumption of nineteenth-century neurobiology that memories are permanent and accurate records, localized in different brain centers, of all past experience. Memory is now described not as a fossil of the past but rather as a system of categorization in which the past is re-created in ways appropriate for the present.[67]

Freud was among the first to discern the fragmentary and selective nature of memory. In his letter to Fliess of December 6, 1896, he wrote, "I am working on the assumption that . . . the material present in the shape of memory-traces is from time to time subjected to a rearrangement in accordance with fresh circumstances—is, as it were, transcribed."[68] He observed that the same processes of displacement and condensation found in dreams also occur in reminiscences during waking hours. It had generally been believed that, for an event to be remembered, it must arouse a powerful emotion in the subject at the time or prove to be of a significance that is recognized shortly after its occurrence. But Freud noted that this did not explain why we recall events that seem insignificant, often in our earliest childhood memories. He called such recollections "screen memories," which are characterized by unusual clarity and persistence as well as banality of content. They are compromise-formations resulting from the conflict of repressed childhood experiences and unconscious fantasies, on the one hand, and the wish to remember significant events of the past, on the other.

> The result of the conflict is therefore that, instead of the memory which would have been justified by the original event, another memory is produced which has been to some degree associatively *displaced* from the former one. And since the elements of the experience which aroused objection were precisely the important ones, the substituted memory will necessarily lack those important elements and will in consequence most probably strike us as trivial.[69]

Screen memories can be recollected as having occurred before or after the objectionable event and may be contrary to the actual content of the suppressed experience. In addition to their apparent ordinariness and their clarity, screen memories are also marked by detached observation; the subject sees himself or herself objectified as part of the scene that is remembered, whereas in the actual experience one must have been a participant rather than a bystander. This indicates that the original impression has been "worked over," that a memory has been "translated into a plastic and visual state at a later date—the date of the memory's 'revival'."[70] Thus, memories of childhood do not simply emerge in adulthood; rather, they are selected and formed during adulthood, and for a wide range of motives.

The Buddha's memory of his earlier existences carries many of the marks of screen memories in its clarity, insignificance, and objectification of the subject. His memory shows a leveling of experience into an affectless formula. Without hoping to discover what specific fantasies the bodhisattva was seeking to repress through the revival of this memory, we can at least discern a motive. We have in his description of his past a devaluation of the world into a sphere of tedium and repetition, where each lifetime serves only as a duplication, without specificity, of a pattern characterized as "such a caste, such food, such experience of pleasure and pain." Hidden just below the surface of this portrayal of memory is the ideology of saṃsāra, the pervasive suffering of conditioning (*saṃskāra-duḥkhatā*). And in accordance with this ideology, the conception of the person is desubjectivized as another constituent of the scene, as another element in the process of cause and effect. Thus, the content of the Buddha's memory of former abodes, like all memory, is a construction of the past, a remolding of the past for the purposes of the present. In this sense, the Buddha's formulaic memory of his earlier existence destroys the past as a source of identity and attachment and replaces it with the memory of an existence that is happily abandoned.

The authors of the account of the enlightenment thus construct a model against which all memory is to be measured, a model of an original memory that reaches back without beginning. All worldly experience can be subsumed under the formula of the Buddha's memory, revelatory of the tedium of saṃsāra. The past is manipulated, decomposed, and reconstituted from a suprahistorical perspective according to the demands of the Dharma.[71] As an experience of the Buddha, indeed as a constituent of enlightenment itself, this memory is invested with the power and authority of the origin, demonstrating that the Buddhist view of the world has always been the case. The Buddha's understanding of the human condition, though yet to occur in the third watch of the night, already is dramatized by the memory and projected retroactively into the measureless past as the setting against which all experience is to be observed. We have in the Buddha's memory of his former abodes a case of deferred revision, in which unassimilated experience from the past is reworked so that it may be incorporated into a meaningful context, namely, that of the four noble truths.

But we must also recall that the narrative of the night of the enlightenment, more than an historical document providing the scholar with insights into the early development of the Buddhist religion or a source for the implication of nascent philosophical doctrines, is a story. It is to that structure that we must at last turn. The introduction to the *Jātakas* recounts that after Prince Siddhārtha resolved to go forth from Kapilavastu in search of a state beyond birth and death, he crept into his wife's chamber to look upon his infant son. He resisted the urge to hold him, knowing that to do so would awaken Yaśodharā and prevent his departure from the world. It is this last look, looking at but not touching what he was to leave behind, that forms one of the most poignant moments in the narrative. It is this backward glance that recurs six years hence under the tree, as the prince looks back one last time at what he had been and thus at who he is, looking at but not being touched by that person made of memory. It is then that he declares, "Birth is finished."

In *Totem and Taboo* Freud wrote: "There is an intellectual function in us which demands unity, connection and intelligibility from any material, whether of perception or thought, that comes within its grasp; and if, as a result of special circumstances, it is unable to establish a true connection, it does not hesitate to fabricate a false one."[72] We see this compulsion to unity at work in our attempts to integrate the memory of former lives into the enlightenment of the Buddha. It is a task at which the commentator has long struggled. Hence, the Ābhidhārmikas upgrade this extraordinary memory from a superknowledge to a gnosis but then demoted it to a mundane knowledge. Aśvaghoṣa has the vision of former lives make the bodhisattva feel compassion for sentient beings who must abandon their families as they cycle in saṃsāra.[73] Sir Edwin Arnold, in his nineteenth-century bestseller *The Light of Asia*, makes the vision of former lives into a retrospective *Pilgrim's Progress:*

thus Buddha did behold
Life's upward steps long-linked, from levels low
Where breath is base, to higher slopes and higher
Whereon the ten great Virtues wait to lead
The climber skyward.[74]

Herman Hesse takes the knowledge of former abodes and the knowledge of the divine eye and conflates them into Siddhārtha's crypto-Vedāntin vision of the river, in which the voices of all beings merge into Oṃ.[75] André Bareau discerns the scriptural authors' intention to connect the new Buddhist doctrines to the contemporary philosophical ethos of India. Mircea Eliade sees still further evidence of the archaic *regressus ad uterum*. And I see, among other things, screen memories. Without suggesting that it is impossible to judge some of these readings to be more cogent than others, it can be observed nonetheless that the process of interpretation, in its attempt to impose a coherent narrative on the discontinuity that has gone before, imitates the movements of memory.

Notes

All Pāli texts cited refer to the Pali Text Society editions.

1. Pliny, *Natural History*, vol. 2, trans. H. Rackham (Cambridge, Mass.: Harvard University Press, 1942), pp. 562–65.

2. See Jonathan D. Spence, *The Memory Palace of Matteo Ricci* (New York: Viking Press, 1984), pp. 136–37.

3. See A. R. Luria, *The Mind of a Mnemonist* (Cambridge, Mass.: Harvard University Press, 1986), pp. 45–48.

4. *Majjhimanikāya*, I.22.

5. *Visuddhimagga*, XIII,13 et seq.

6. For a modern discussion of this problem, see Chapter 5 of C. D. Broad, *Mind and Its Place in Nature* (London: K. Paul, Trench, Trubner & Co., 1925). Classic discussions of memory include those of Locke in *Essay Concerning Human Understanding* (Book 2, Chapter 10) and William James, *Principles of Psychology*, vol. 1 (New York: Henry Holt and Company, 1904), pp. 643–89. For recent surveys and analyses of Western philosophical treatments of memory, see Mary Warnock, *Memory* (London: Faber and Faber, 1987) and Edward S. Casey, *Remembering: A Phenomenological Study* (Bloomington: University of Indiana Press, 1987).

7. Because the object of his consciousness must exist in the present, one might speculate that the bodhisattva actually had an acute insight into his own karmic seeds,

but many of those seeds had long since fructified. Furthermore, where is it said that karmic seeds contain visible representations of their origins? The mental factor (*caitta*) called mindfulness or memory (*smṛti*) cannot provide present simulacra of all past states because, according to the Pāli Abhidhamma it accompanies only virtuous moments of consciousness. (See Nyanaponika's essay in this volume.) This leaves discrimination (*saṃjñā*), the ubiquitous mental factor (*sarvatragacaitta*) that perceives the characteristics of objects, as the best choice of that present mental state which carries the memories of past lives. But there appears to be no such explanation of the technical function of memory of past lives in the major Abhidharma works. See also Paul J. Griffiths, "Why Buddhas Can't Remember Their Previous Lives," *Philosophy East and West* 39, no. 4 (October 1989): 449–52.

8. Such cases are discussed by Oliver Sacks in *The Man Who Mistook His Wife for a Hat* (New York: Harper and Row, 1987), pp. 132–52.

9. See ibid., p. 152.

10. See Jay Stevens, *Storming Heaven: LSD and the American Dream* (New York: Atlantic Monthly Press, 1987).

11. For example, he recalls, "I heard the bell ringing. A small round object rolled right before my eyes . . . my fingers sensed something rough like a rope. . . . Then I experienced a taste of salt water . . . and something white." Luria, *The Mind of a Mnemonist*, p. 81.

12. Jorge Luis Borges, *A Personal Anthology* (New York: Grove Press, 1967), p. 42.

13. For a Dge-lugs-pa presentation of the categories of direct perception (*mngon sum*) and thought (*rtog pa*) and their respective objects, see Bstan-dar-lha-ram-pa, *Rang mtshan spyi mtshan gyi rnam gzhag* in *Collected gSung 'bum of Bstan-dar Lha-ram of A-lag-sha*, vol. 1 (New Delhi: Guru Deva, 1971). See also Anne Klein, *Knowledge and Liberation* (Ithaca, N.Y.: Snow Lion Publications, 1986), pp. 89–140.

14. Friedrich Nietzsche, *On the Genealogy of Morals*, trans. Walter Kaufmann and R. J. Hollingdale (New York: Random House, 1969), p. 58.

15. See Sacks, *The Man Who Mistook His Wife for a Hat*, p. 198.

16. *Visuddhimagga*, XIII.18.

17. The image of Penelope is drawn by Walter Benjamin in his essay on Proust in *Illuminations* (New York: Schocken Books, 1968), p. 202.

18. For descriptions and discussions of the *abhijñā*, see Har Dayal, *The Bodhisattva Doctrine in Buddhist Sanskrit Literature* (Delhi: Motilal Banarsidass, 1975), pp. 106–34; *Encyclopedia of Buddhism*, s.v. "Abhiññā" by H. G. A. van Zeyst; *Visuddhimagga*, XII–XIII (English trans. Bhadantācariya Buddhaghosa, *The Path of Purification* (*Visuddhimagga*), trans. by Bhikku Ñyanamoli [sic], 2d ed., (Colombo, Ceylon: A. Semage, 1964), pp. 409–78); É. Lamotte, *Le traité de la grande vertu de la sagesse*, vol. 4 (Louvain: Université de Louvain, Institut Orientaliste, 1976), pp.

1809–16; Louis de la Vallée Poussin, "Le bouddha et les abhijñās," *Le Museon* 44 (1931): 334–42. Vasubandhu considers the *abhijñā* in *Abhidharmakośa*, ed. Swami Dwarikadas Shastri (Varanasi: Buddha Bharati, 1970–73), VII.42–46. For a Tibetan exposition, see 'Jam-dbyangs-bzhad-pa, *sKabs dang po'i mtha' dpyod blo gsal yid gsos 'jam dbyangs bzhad pa'i rdo rjes bgyis pa legs bshad dga' ston yid bzhin nor bu* (Varanasi: Mongolian Lama Guru Deva, 1963), pp. 341–52.

19. This standard list occurs in full at *Dīghanikāya* I.78. For other magical powers, see Dayal, ibid., pp. 112–16, and the *Encyclopedia of Buddhism,* s.v. "Abhiññā," pp. 99–100.

20. The divine eye is often misrepresented to be the knowledge of past lives of others, as if it were a universalized form of the preceding superknowledge. It is clear from Buddhaghosa (in *Visuddhimagga,* XIII.124), however, that the divine eye has only the present as its object; it is synchronic whereas the knowledge of former abodes is diachronic. For corrections of this misconception, see the *Encyclopedia of Buddhism,* s.v. "Abhiññā," p. 101, and Paul Demiéville, "Sur la mémorie des existences antérieures," *Bulletin de l'École Française d'Extrême Orient* 27, (1927): 291, n. 2.

21. For a long discussion of how the difficult term *āsrava* has been variously translated and how *āsrava-kṣaya-jñānam* has been variously interpreted, see Dayal, *Bodhisattva Doctrine,* pp. 116–34.

22. For the ten powers of the tathāgata, see *Majjhimanikāya* I.69–71. In his *Madhyamakāvatāra* (XI.22–31), Candrakīrti describes the ten powers and provides a long explanation of each. For a Tibetan edition of the root text and autocommentary, see Louis de la Vallée Poussin, ed., *Madhyamakāvatāra par Candrakīrti,* Bibliotheca Buddhica IX (Osnabruck: Biblio Verlag, 1970), pp. 369–95. Candrakīrti deviates from the Pāli tradition in defining the knowledge of former abodes as the Buddha's memory of the past lives of others as well as himself; see XI.29 (pp. 388–90). On the ten powers, also see Étienne Lamotte, *Le traité,* vol. 3, pp. 1505–66.

23. The six *abhiññā* are described in *Dīghanikāya* I.77–85.

24. This version of the path occurs in the sixth and seventh suttas of the *Dīghanikāya,* the *Mahālisutta* and the *Jāliyasutta* (Dīghanikāya I.150–60). It is unclear from the sutta whether this knowledge that the living being (*jīvam*) is neither the same nor different from the body constitutes the culmination of the path or whether some further insight is required before the monk can declare, "There is nothing further here." In the *Kevaddhasutta* (*Dīghanikāya* I.211–23), the long version of the path presented in the *Sāmaññaphalasutta* occurs but with the omission of those verses dealing with the first five *abhiññā*. In this sutta the Buddha denounces the performance of miracles (specifically magic [*iddhi-pāṭihāriya*] and prophecy [*ādesanā-pāṭihāriya*]) as a means of gaining converts to the Dhamma and favors instead the miracle of teaching (*anusāsani-pāṭihāriya*). It would seem only circumspect in this context that he not mention the five *abhiññā* as components of the path. Thus, it is not justifiable to consider this particular description of the path as a separate variety of the arahant's path.

25. The description of the path occurs in *Majjhimanikāya* I.179–84. The three *abhiññā* are described in *Majjhimanikāya* I.182–83.

26. See *Dīghanikāya* III.220. Here, the second knowledge is referred to as "the knowledge of the death and birth of sentient beings" (*sattānaṁ cutupapāte ñānaṁ vijjā*) rather than as the divine eye. This is just one of the many glosses of the term *tevijjā* (coined presumably to counter brahmanical claims to superiority based on their three Vedas) that occurs in the Nikāyas and commentaries. For others, see T. W. Rhys Davids and William Stede, eds., *Pāli-English Dictionary* (London: Pali Text Society, 1972), pp. 617–18, sv. *vijjā*.

27. The Buddha refers to such arahants at *Saṃyuttanikāya* I.191. Buddhaghosa uses the term in *Visuddhimagga* XXI.112 and XXIII.18.

28. The account occurs in *Majjhimanikāya* I.163–67.

29. *Majjhimanikāya* I.22–23. In addition to these two versions of the enlightenment in the Nikāyas, of course, there are many others in Sanskrit literature. For an exegesis of the extant Hīnayāna accounts and a discussion of their relative chronology, see André Bareau, *Recherches sur la biographie du Buddha dans les Sūtrapiṭaka et les Vinayapiṭaka anciens: de la quête de l'éveil a la conversion de Śāriputra et de Maudgalyāyana*, Publications de l'École Française d'Extrême Orient 51 (Paris: Ecole Française d'Extrême Orient, 1963), pp. 75–91.

30. For a full reference, see note 20.

31. Demiéville, "Sur la mémoire," p. 293. My translation.

32. Ibid., p. 298. My translation.

33. Gregory Schopen, "The Generalization of an Old Yogic Attainment in Medieval Mahāyāna Sūtra Literature: Some Notes on *Jātismara*," *Journal of the International Association of Buddhist Studies* 6, no. 1 (1983): 109–47.

34. See Richard H. Robinson and Willard L. Johnson, *The Buddhist Religion: A Historical Introduction*, 3d ed. (Belmont, Calif.: Wadsworth Publishing Company, 1982), pp. 13–14. See also Mircea Eliade, *Myths, Dreams, and Mysteries* (New York: Harper and Row, 1975), pp. 162ff.

35. See Ake Hultkrantz, *Conceptions of the Soul Among North American Indians* (Stockholm: 1953), pp. 418–26.

36. See Karl Meuli, "Scythica," *Hermes* 70 (1935): 121–76.

37. It can be noted, however, that the tradition makes its own "two-thirds, one-third" division: the recollection of former abodes and the divine eye are mundane superknowledges (*laukikābhijñā*, Pāli: *lokiyābhiññā*) whereas the knowledge of the destruction of the defilements is supramundane, implying that it, unlike the others, is not within the gnoseological purview of non-Buddhists. Bareau notes that Mahīśāsakas and the Dharmaguptakas hold that the six *abhijñā* and the three *vidyā*

can be attained only by Buddhists. See Bareau, *Recherches sur la biographie du Buddha*, p. 82.

38. Mircea Eliade, *Cosmos and History: The Myth of the Eternal Return*, trans. Willard R. Trask (New York: Harper and Row, 1959), p. 117. A different, and more sophisticated, view of what constitutes the primitive mentality with regard to suffering is presented by Paul Ricoeur in *The Symbolism of Evil* (Boston: Beacon Press, 1967), pp. 25–46.

39. Mircea Eliade, *Myth and Reality*, trans. Willard R. Trask (New York: Harper and Row, 1975), p. 85.

40. Mircea Eliade, *Myths, Dreams and Mysteries: The Encounter between Contemporary Faiths and Archaic Realities*, trans. Philip Mairet (New York: Harper and Row, 1975), p. 50. The same passage is quoted verbatim in *Myth and Reality*, p. 86.

41. Eliade, *Myths, Dreams and Mysteries*, p. 49.

42. Mircea Eliade, *Yoga: Immortality and Freedom*, trans. Willard R. Trask, Bollingen Series 51 (Princeton, N.J.: Princeton University Press, 1973), p. 183.

43. Eliade, *Myth, Dreams and Mysteries*, p. 51.

44. Richard Gombrich notes Eliade's error on this point (as well as many others) in "Eliade on Buddhism," *Religious Studies* 10 (1974): 225–31. This particular point is discussed on p. 229.

45. Friedrich Nietzsche, *The Wanderer and his Shadow*, 3. Cited by Michel Foucault in *Language, Counter-Memory, Practice*, trans. Donald F. Bouchard (Ithaca, N.Y.: Cornell University Press, 1977), p. 143.

46. See *Visuddhimagga* VII.7–8. See also Steven Collins, *Selfless Persons* (Cambridge: Cambridge University Press, 1982), pp. 103–10.

47. Eliade, *Myths, Dreams and Mysteries*, p. 51.

48. *Dīghanikāya* I.13–16. Ironically, Eliade cites this passage in *Yoga: Immortality and Freedom*, p. 181.

49. Eliade, *Myths, Dreams and Mysteries*, pp. 54–55. Ananda Coomaraswamy makes a similar error in trying to find Plato's doctrine of recollection in Buddhism in his article, "Recollection, Indian and Platonic." He does this by translating *sati* in *Dīghanikāya* I.19–20 as "memory" rather than "mindfulness" thereby causing the gods to fall from heaven because they fail to remember. He offers no justification for this reading. He derives further support for his position by translating *aggaññam . . . pajānāmi* in *Dīghanikāya* III.28 as "I have prior knowledge of the ultimate beginning" rather than simply "I know the beginnings," thus portraying the Buddha as having knowledge of some Eliadean ur-moment. He seems to have overlooked the *Aggaññasutta* (*Dīghanikāya* III.80–97) in which the notion of ultimate origins is debunked. See Roger Lipsey, ed. *Coomaraswamy: 2: Selected Papers, Metaphysics*,

Bollingen Series 89 (Princeton, N.J.: Princeton University Press, 1977), pp. 49–65. The passage just discussed occurs on p. 54, n. 16.

50. For Freud's earliest paper dealing with abreaction (written in collaboration with Breuer), see "On the Physical Mechanism of Hysterical Phenomena," in Sigmund Freud, *Collected Papers*, vol. 1 (London: Hogarth Press, 1950), pp. 24–41.

51. Jacques Laplanche and J. B. Pontalis, *The Language of Psychoanalysis* (New York: Norton, 1973), p. 78.

52. Sigmund Freud, *The Standard Edition of the Complete Psychological Works of Sigmund Freud*, vol. 10 (London: Hogarth Press, 1953–74), p. 122.

53. Eliade, *Myth and Reality*, p. 89.

54. In the *Bodhisattvabhūmi*, Asaṅga mentions that the bodhisattva uses his memory of past lives to tell stories. See Dayal, *Bodhisattva Doctrine*, p. 111. This evokes Walter Benjamin's comparison of the sage and the storyteller, of whom he writes: "For it is granted to him to reach back to a whole lifetime (a life, incidentally, that comprises not only his own experience but no little of the experience of others; what the storyteller knows from hearsay is added to his own). His gift is the ability to relate his life: his distinction, to be able to tell his entire life. The storyteller: he is the man who could let the wick of his life be consumed completely by the gentle flame of his story." Walter Benjamin, *Illuminations* (New York: Schocken, 1968), pp. 108–9.

55. *Saṃyuttanikāya*, I.191.

56. For a Sanskrit edition and English translation of the *Buddhacarita*, see E. H. Johnston, *The Buddhacarita or Acts of the Buddha* (Delhi: Motilal Banarsidass, 1978).

57. Mircea Eliade, *Myth and Reality* (New York: Harper and Row, 1975), p. 90.

58. Bareau, *Recherches sur la biographie du Buddha*, p. 90.

59. Ibid., p. 90.

60. Ibid., p. 90. For an excellent study of the intellectual climate at the time of the Buddha regarding the issues of karma and rebirth, see Steven Collins, *Selfless Persons* (Cambridge: Cambridge University Press, 1982), pp. 28–64.

61. As, indeed, the Sarvāstivādin version does not. See Bareau, ibid., p. 76.

62. Ibid., p. 89.

63. At this point, Bareau's third option, that the memory of former abodes was tied to the enlightenment to clarify a poorly defined point is increasingly attractive, although we would concede that that point remains poorly defined.

64. Marcel Proust, *Remembrance of Things Past*, vol. 1, trans. C. K. Scott Moncrieff (New York: Random House, 1934), p. 5.

65. For this reason Louis Dumont claims that it is the renunciate who is the true "individual" in the Western sense of the term. He makes this point repeatedly in his writings. See, for example, the article "World Renunciation in Indian Religions" which appears as Appendix B in his *Homo Hierarchicus* (Chicago: University of Chicago Press, 1980).

66. There is a question as to whether the Buddha has any direct realization of selflessness at the moment of enlightenment, technically, at the achievement of *kṣayajñāna*, the knowledge of the destruction of the afflictions. According to Vasubandhu's *Abhidharmakośa* VII.12, the knowledge of destruction possesses understanding of all sixteen aspects of the four truths, with the exception of emptiness and selflessness. However, according to *Abhidharmakośa* II.44 and VI.24, the bodhisattva achieves enlightenment by traversing the portion of path from the path of preparation (*prayogamārga*) through the achievement of enlightenment in a single sitting of thirty-four moments. The fourth of these moments is the knowledge of selflessness, the last of the four aspects of the truth of suffering. Thus, although there seems to be no explicit realization of selflessness in the actualization of cessation, such a realization occurs earlier in the same meditative session beneath the bodhi tree.

67. For a study of past and current neurological theories of memory, see Israel Rosenfield, *The Invention of Memory* (New York: Basic Books, 1988).

68. Sigmund Freud, *The Origins of Psychoanalysis* (New York: Basic Books, 1954), p. 173.

69. Freud, "Screen Memories" in *Collected Papers*, vol. 5, p. 52.

70. Ibid., p. 68.

71. The suprahistorical perspective is, according to Foucault, "a history whose function is to compose the finally reduced diversity of time into a totality fully closed upon itself; a history that always encourages subjective recognitions and attributes a form of reconciliation to all the displacements of the past; a history whose perspective on all that precedes it implies the end of time, a completed development." See Michel Foucault, *Language, Counter-Memory, Practice*, p. 152.

72. Sigmund Freud, "Totem and Taboo," in *The Standard Edition*, vol. 13 p. 95. Freud is writing here about secondary revision, a theory he developed years earlier in *The Interpretation of Dreams*.

73. Aśvaghoṣa, *Buddhacarita*, XIV.4–5.

74. Edwin Arnold, *The Light of Asia* (Boston: Roberts Brothers, 1880), p. 167.

75. Herman Hesse, *Siddhartha*, trans. Hilda Rosner (New York: New Directions, 1951), pp. 110–11.

Smṛti in the Abhidharma Literature and the Development of Buddhist Accounts of Memory of the Past

PADMANABH S. JAINI

Despite the extraordinary preoccupation of the ancient Buddhists in explaining the process of cognition, memory is conspicuous by its absence in the long list of mental events and concomitant mental factors (*citta-caitta-dharmas*). In the Theravādin Abhidhamma the word *sati* (*smṛti*) appears as a conditioning factor (*saṃskāra*) that occurs only in good (*kuśala*) consciousness and hence is invariably called "right-mindfulness" (*sammā-sati*).[1] The author of the *Dhammasaṅgaṇi* admits that even a person holding a wrong view can have a sort of "awareness," but seeks to reserve the term *sati* only for right-mindfulness.[2] The Vaibhāṣikas appear to have noticed some error here, for in their Abhidharma literature, *smṛti* is no longer restricted to good mental events, but is enumerated in the list of the factors invariably found in every mental event (*mahābhūmika-dharmas*), together with feeling (*vedanā*), thinking (*cetanā*), and conceptual identification (*saṃjñā*).[3] Vasubandhu (fourth or fifth century CE), in his *Abhidharmakośabhāṣya,* defines *smṛti* as the "retention of" or "not letting drop the object" (*ālambana-asampramoṣa*).[4] He however does not specify if the term *object* in this definition is past or present and thus leaves open the possibility that the term could be taken to mean either memory of the past or mindfulness of the present. Yaśomitra (eighth century) in his *Sphuṭārthābhidharmakośavyākhyā* is more specific and says: "*Smṛti* is that factor on account of which the mind does not forget the object; it is as if it repeats it."[5] The fact that *smṛti* is found in every mental event can only lead one to conclude that here too the term *smṛti* is understood to mean mindfulness and not memory of the past, for the latter is not a phenomenon that occurs at all times. Vasubandhu must have perceived some anomaly here, for in his *Pañcaskandhaprakaraṇa, smṛti* is not included in the group of mental factors that occur invariably, but in the next group of five factors that are found only in certain mental events (*viniyata-dharmas*). Other such occasional factors are zest (*chanda*), confidence (*adhimokṣa*), meditational concentration (*samādhi*), and insight (*prajñā*). There *smṛti* is defined as "the non-forgetting of a range of events towards which there is acquaintance and is a certain kind of discourse of consciousness (*citta*)."[6] This definition is almost identical with the one given by Sthiramati (c. 470–550) in his *bhāṣya* on Vasubandhu's *Triṃśikā* (verse 10), where *smṛti* is also classified with the factors that occur only in certain moments. According to Sthiramati *smṛti* is the nondropping (*asampramoṣa*) of a familiar entity; it is a mental repetition.[7] Sthiramati goes on to gloss the expression "familiar entity" as "a previously experienced object" (*vastu pūrvānubhūtam*), but even here the recollection of this past object is described in terms traditionally associated with meditative mindfulness. For example, he also glosses *smṛti* as "that which brings about non-distraction" (*avikṣepa-karmikā*). Why the Buddhists with their otherwise thorough analysis of the mental factors should have paid so scant attention to the phenomenon of memory of the past as such has remained a riddle and needs to be examined.

The term *asampramoṣa* in the above definitions of *smṛti* is derived from the root *muṣ* (of the ninth *gaṇa*) having the meaning "to release," or "to let go." *Asampramoṣa* therefore would be this root's opposite; namely, "retention" or "holding on to an object." In early Buddhist sources this referred primarily to a special kind of *smṛti* as one finds in the Buddhist term "applications of mindfulness" (*smṛtyupasthāna;* Pāli *satipaṭṭhāna*) that maintains awareness of one of the four objects; namely, the body (*kāya*), the feelings (*vedanā*), the mind (*citta*), and the remaining factors (*dharmas*), the foundation of all Buddhist meditation.[8]

This is not the meaning, however, in which other Indian philosophical schools understand the word *smṛti*. In the *Pātañjalayogasūtra,* for example, *smṛti* is defined as "not letting drop an object that has been experienced" (*anubhūta-viṣaya-asampramoṣa*),[9] almost identical with Sthiramati's gloss: "not letting drop . . . a previously experienced object." The most ancient commentator Vyāsa (c. fifth century CE) was silent on the meaning of the term *asampramoṣa*. Vācaspati Miśra (ninth century), the foremost expositor of the Yoga system, however, in his *Tattvavaiśāradī* commentary interprets the word *asampramoṣa* in quite a different way. He derives the word from the same root *muṣ* as the Buddhists do, but having the meaning "to steal." *Asampramoṣa* thus comes to mean "not adding surreptitiously [to a once experienced object]." He explains this aspect further by saying that whereas other "fluctuations" (*vṛttis,* e.g., perception or inference) give access to a hitherto inaccessible object, memory does not go beyond the limits of previous experience. It corresponds with the previous experience or with less than that, but it does not correspond to any experience *in addition* to that. This is called *asampramoṣa,* (i.e., "not adding surreptitiously").[10] Vācaspati Miśra's derivation seems a trifle too artificial and suggests the possibility that in totally ignoring the alternative meaning of the root *muṣ,* he was showing his disagreement with the Buddhist explanation of the term *smṛti*.

Probably the first Theravādin to notice this omission of *smṛti* as memory in the Abhidharmma Piṭaka is Nyanaponika Thera whose discussion of this topic has been reprinted in the present volume. Nyanaponika's transference of the function of *smṛti* to the aggregate of conceptual identification (*saṃjñā-skandha*), however, does not fully solve the problem of memory. We still need to account for the specific kind of cognition of the previous object alone that could be properly designated as memory of the past. Nevertheless, Nyanaponika's suggestion is worth noting because he asks us not to look for *smṛti* in that catch-all of dharmas called the *aggregate of conditioning factors* (*saṃskāra-skandha*), but in the act of cognition itself.

Nyanaponika's survey is limited to the Pāli Abhidharma texts and commentaries and does not cover the Sanskrit Abhidharma material, especially the *Abhidharmakośabhāṣya* of Vasubandhu. We already have referred to Vasubandhu's brief definition of *smṛti* and how it was understood as mindfulness by the Vaibhāṣikas. However, in his appendix to the *Abhidharmakośabhāṣya*, called the *Pudgalaviniścaya*,[11] Vasubandhu provides us with detailed material on *smṛti*, not as he defined it earlier as mindfulness, but as memory of the past. The context for his account of memory is provided by the Pudgalavādin Vātsīputrīya, the Buddhist heretic, who apparently uses the phenomenon of *smṛti* as a valid ground for his doctrine of a durable entity called *pudgala* (translated variously as "person," "self," or "soul"). Their debate on this particular point is highly informative in revealing Vasubandhu's understanding of the process involved in the event of memory (*smṛti*) and therefore may be briefly summarized here:

> Pudgalavādin: If the self does not absolutely exist how can the momentary mental events (*cittas*) be capable of the remembrance or recognition of an object experienced (*anubhūta*) a long time ago?[12]
>
> Vasubandhu: A special type of mental event connected (*anvaya*) with the conceptual identification (*saṃjñā*) of the object already perceived—which is hence called "object of memory"—produces memory and recognition.[13]
>
> Pudgalavādin: What is this special condition of the mental event which is immediately followed by memory (*smṛti*)?[14]
>
> Vasubandhu: The following conditions are required:[15]
>
> 1. *tadābhoga:* There should be "bending" (*ābhoga*) of the mental event, i.e. a turning of attention towards that object.
>
> 2. *sadṛśa-saṃjñā:* That mental event should have a conceptual identification which resembles the [conceptual identification of the past] object,

should such a resemblance exist [e.g., a memory of a fire seen in the past aroused by its resemblance to the conceptual identification of a fire in the present.]

3. *sambandha-saṃjñā:* Or, that mental event should have a conceptual identification suggesting a relation (*sambandha*) to the past object [e.g., a memory of a past fire aroused by the conceptual identification of smoke seen in the present].[16]

4. *praṇidhāna:* The mental event should have a certain resolution (*praṇidhāna*), for example, "I shall remember this at a certain time."[17]

5. *anupahata-prabhāva:* There should be no impairment of the mental event on account of bodily pain, grief or distraction, etc.

These conditions are necessary but not adequate to produce a memory. If these conditions are fulfilled but the mental event is not connected with a previous concept of the object to be remembered then also there can be no memory. On the other hand, if the mental event *is* so connected but the above conditions are absent, it likewise is not able to produce the memory. Both factors, namely, connection to the previous conceptual identification and a suitable state of mind, are necessary for the emergence of a memory. A mental event which is not like this is incapable of evoking memory.[18]

Vasubandhu's stipulation that *smṛti* is a special type of mental event (*citta-viśeṣa*), a representative cognition of the past object, removes the necessity to postulate a separate dharma called *smṛti*. By being a type of mental event, *smṛti* thus already is included in the consciousness aggregate (*vijñāna-skandha*), and hence there is no need to postulate a new dharma by that name.

Vasubandhu's use of the term *connection* (*anvaya*) is extremely important here. In ordinary cognition, the object is a present one, and both the conceptual identification aggregate (*saṃjñā-skandha*) and the consciousness aggregate have the same object: the present object. But in the case of memory, the present consciousness with a present conceptual identification has to connect itself with a past concept, either on the basis of a resemblance (*sādṛśya*) or a relationship (*sambandha*) between the two concepts. If the Buddhist doctrine that all conditioned factors are momentary is to be valid, then the past concepts must be considered to have perished and thus be inaccessible to the present mental event. The Buddhist, therefore, must address the question of how the present can be linked with the past. This is the next stage in the debate.

Pudgalavādin: [If there were absolutely nothing permanent, it would mean that] one mental event has perceived the object and another remembers it. How could this possibly be? Surely it is not correct to say that Yajñadatta remembers an object perceived by Devadatta?[19]

> Vasubandhu: There is no analogy here. Devadatta and Yajñadatta are not connected, whereas the two mental events are bound by the relation of cause and effect. Indeed, we do not say that one mental event sees an object and that [an altogether] different mental event remembers this object; for [although the two occur at different times] both mental events belong to the same series (*santāna*). What we do maintain is that one mental event of the past, which perceives a certain object and hence can be designated as a "seeing mental event" (*darśana-citta*) brings about the existence of another, namely the present mental event, which can be called "remembering mental event" (*smṛti-citta*) as it is capable of remembering this object. The two are causally related in the same manner of seed and its fruit, because both belong to the same series (*santati*).[20]

At this point we will not examine the validity of the doctrine of series or its alleged ability to explain the phenomenon of memory. It should be noted, however, that the use of the memory issue in defense of a theory of a person (*pudgala*) is not attested in the Pāli Nikāyas nor in the earlier Abhidharma works, including the *mātṛkā* texts, nor in the *Kathāvatthu*, which opens with the person theory as the main point of debate. The problem of memory of the past is a relatively new one, with perhaps its earliest appearance in the *Mahāvibhāṣā*.[21] That it was raised primarily in non-Buddhist circles is suggested even in the passage concerning the Pudgalavādins just mentioned. In that passage, the examination of *smṛti* begins at the end of the first section where Vasubandhu condemns the two heresies, namely the *pudgalagrāha* (the "dogma of a person" of the Vāstsīputrīya) and the *sarvanāstitāgrāha* (the "nihilism" of the Mādhyamika, according to Yaśomitra). Then Vasubandhu introduces the heterodox teachers, the Tīrthakaras (identified by Stcherbatsky with the Sāṅkhya and the Vaiśeṣika schools),[22] who maintain a doctrine of the self (*ātman*) as an independent substance.[23] But the arguments that are put in the mouth of the Buddhist Pudgalavādin in the following section employ the non-Buddhist word *self* (*ātman*), and not *person* (*pudgala*) as we might expect.[24] Thus Vasubandhu seems to be anticipating here not a Buddhist critique, but rather that of the Naiyāyika Vātsyāyana's (c. 400 CE) *Nyāyasūtrabhāṣya*, where the latter seeks to prove the existence of an eternal self (*ātman*) by pointing to the phenomenon of memory: "Memory is properly explained if it is [accepted] as a quality (*guṇa*) of the [abiding] self (*ātman*), for one does not remember [an object] seen [earlier] by some other person."[25] Vasubandhu's defense of the Buddhist theory of *smṛti* in his *Pudgalaviniścaya*, therefore, is a relatively novel one, unknown to the earlier Buddhist traditions prior to the Vaibhāṣika Abhidharma.

The only other Buddhist work of this period to address the problem of memory of the past in any detail is the *Abhidharmadīpavibhāṣāprabhāvṛtti*. This text is distinguished for its strident opposition to the Sautrāntika bias exhibited by Vasubandhu in his *Abhidharmakośabhāṣya*. The (anonymous) author of this work does not relegate the topic of *smṛti* to an appendix as does Vasubandhu, but introduces it in the first chapter of the *Abhidharmadīpa*, while expounding on the nature of the aggregate of consciousness (*vijñāna-skandha*). Having dealt with the varieties of the representative consciousness (*mano-vijñāna*) as listed in the *mātṛkā*, he embarks on a new topic in the following manner:[26]

> Now this must be discussed: How, in the absence of an eternal self (*ātman*) and in the absence of its quality (*guṇa*) called *smṛti*, can the consciousness (*vijñāna*) which cease momentarily and [hence] cannot establish a connection between each other, produce memory (*smṛti*) of an object experienced in the past?
>
> Answer: This doctrine [of the eternal self] has already been refuted;[27] even so we address this question as it is relevant to the topic at hand:
>
> Memory (*smṛti*) of an object experienced by a past consciousness is produced in the [present] consciousness on account of attention (*prayoga*), proximity of the causes (*aṅga-sānnidhya*), and the continuity of the same series (*sabhāga-santati*). [I, verse 27].
>
> When resolution, experience, expertise, repetition and other such efficient causes are present, memory arises of form and other objects, which have been experienced by a past consciousness belonging to the same series.
>
> Objection: Memory is produced on account of the impressions (*saṃskāra*) when there is a contact (*saṃyoga*) of the mind (*manas*) with the self (*ātman*).
>
> Answer: That is not so. The contact between the impressions, the mind and the soul is not proven because an eternal entity called self is like the horn of a hare and cannot be established . . . [28]
>
> [And] when those conditions [of attention, proximity, etc.] are not obtained, and when one is overcome by indolence, passion and sickness, then non-remembrance (*vismṛti*) is produced pertaining to those objects which were known previously. [I, verse 28].

The *Abhidharmadīpa*'s exposition of memory of the past is merely a restatement of Vasubandhu's description. But the terms appearing in the statement of the opponent, viz., *ātman, guṇa, saṃskāra, anubhava,* and so forth, reflect his familiarity with the Nyāya-Vaiśeṣika position, and their criticism of the Buddhist theory of memory perpetuated by a series of consciousness.

In this connection, Vātsyāyana's *Nyāyasūtrabhāṣya*, III.i.14, dealing with *smṛti* may be compared with the arguments appearing in both Vasubandhu's *Abhidharmakośabhāṣya* and the *Abhidharmadīpavṛtti:*

> Now if the being (*sattva*) [who is the agent in all these several cognitions and re-cognitions] were a mere "series of impressions" (*saṃskāra-santati-mātre*) [as the Buddhist opponent holds], then inasmuch as every impression would [by its nature] disappear as soon as it has come into existence, there could not be a single impression which could do the apprehending (*anubhava*) of the cognition (*jñāna*) and the remembrance (*smṛti*), an apprehending that has been shown to pertain to all three points of time; and without such comprehending [by a single agent] there could be no recognition (*pratisandhāna*) [or recollecting] of cognition or of remembrance; and there would be no such conception of "I" or "my"; just in the same way as we have no such conception [as "I" and "mine"] with regard to the bodies of other persons.[29]

This single paragraph from Vātsyāyana's *bhāṣya* probably sums up the entire range of objections repeatedly raised by the Advaita Vedāntin[30] and the Jaina[31] teachers against the Buddhist doctrines of karma, its fruition (*vipāka*), the holy path, and the attainment of nirvāṇa. The problem of the evocation of memory is analogous to the problem of connecting the past agent of an action with the present experience of its result. The Buddhist must explain the mechanism whereby the past impressions (*saṃskāra*) of objects or the traces of the past actions are stored and await their fruition if everything in the series of consciousness is momentary.

In the case of actions, the Buddhists have maintained that the karmic potency (*phaladāna-śakti*) is carried unimpeded through the continuous chain of consciousness (*vijñāna-santati*).[32] The same principle seems to apply to the function of memory. Although there are no statements in the Abhidharma literature to the effect that the impressions of past objects are preserved in any concrete manner, a stray occurrence of the term *seed of memory* (*smṛti-bīja*) appearing in connection with the discussion of the latent passions (*anuśayas*) in the *Abhidharmakośabhāṣya* may be of interest here. Vasubandhu employs this term there in discussing his theory of the "seed" (*bīja*). The passions (*kleśas*) in their dormant stage are said to endure in the form of seeds in consciousness, just as the capacity to produce rice that belongs to the rice plant is engendered by the rice seed (*śāli-bīja*) and carried through various stages in between. Vasubandhu argues there that if the passions in their dormant state were to have any other substratum than the series of consciousness (e.g., a *citta-viprayukta-saṃskāra,* a factor which is distinguished from both mind and matter), then the opponent (the Vātsīputrīya) may also have to admit a similar substratum dharma, one totally dissociated from the mind, to account for the seeds of memory.[33] Vasubandhu does not develop this theory of seeds of memory beyond this laconic remark and his commentator Yaśomitra chose to ignore it altogether; but we may be certain that the Ābhidharmikas at some stage must have debated this problem of explaining the retention of past impressions through a series of momentary consciousnesses.

The Theravādin Abhidharma texts are totally silent on this matter, although their notion of the *bhavaṅga* (lit., "constituent of becoming") consciousness could have been exploited to serve this purpose.[34] As is well known, the Theravādins propose a theory of perception whereby a series (*vīthi*) of several mental events (*citta*) with the same object is maintained, after which the basic consciousness resumes until the next series begins. The series (of mental events) can be maintained for as many as seventeen moments when material objects are cognized (*pañca-viññāṇa*), or even longer for a mental cognition (*mano-viññāṇa*). Under certain circumstances there arises a mental event called "having the same object" (*tadārammaṇa*)[35] before the series is terminated. This regrasps the object for a moment before the object is lost, the series is terminated, and the *bhavaṅga* instantaneously reemerges. It is conceivable that this having-the-same-object mental event could perform, in addition to reregistering the object, the function of passing on the mark (*nimitta*) of the vanishing object to the *bhavaṅga* consciousness where it could be stored. Of course, the Theravādins do not make any such claim, nor could they, given their rule that a consciousness or mental event (*citta*) can have only a single object at one time. Because the *bhavaṅga* consciousness already was provided with its object at the time of its first occurrence, that is, at the rebirth of a person, and that object remains the same for the entire duration of its successive appearances during one lifetime, it would not be correct to make the *bhavaṅga* a carrier of the countless impressions made by the other consciousnesses that repeatedly interrupted the *bhavaṅga*'s stream.[36] But, in any case, the concept of *bhavaṅga* clearly anticipates the emergence of the Yogācāra theory of the store consciousness (*ālaya-vijñāna*), and multilayered storehouse of all seeds (*sarva-bījaka*),[37] a convenient structure that traditionally is considered to explain adequately the operations of both action (*karma*) and memory (*smṛti*).

Notes

1. *saranti etāya, sayaṃ vā sarati, saraṇamattam eva vā esā ti sati . . . sati kusaladhamme apilāpeti—ime cattāro satipaṭṭhānā . . . ,ime lokuttarā dhammā ti . . . aparo pana nayo-apilāpanalakkhaṇā sati, . . . ārammaṇe daḷhaṃ patiṭṭhitattā pana esikā viya.* Bapat and Vadekar, 1942, pp. 99–100.

2. *asaddhiyacitte pana sati n'atthī ti na gahitā. kiṃ diṭṭhigatikā attanā katakammaṃ na sarantī ti? saranti. sā pana sati nāma na hoti. kevalaṃ tenākārena akusalacittappavatti. tasmā sati na gahitā. atha kasmā micchāsatī ti suttante vuttā? sā pana akusalakkhandhānaṃ sativirahitattā satipaṭipakkhattā ca micchāmaggamic-*

chattānaṃ pūraṇatthaṃ tattha pariyāyena desanā katā. nippariyāyena pan' esā n'atthi. Ibid., p. 202.

3. *vedanā cetanā saṃjñā cchandaḥ sparśo matiḥ smṛtiḥ,*
manaskāro 'dhimokṣaś ca samādhiḥ sarvacetasi.
Abhidharmakośa, II, 24. (Shastri, 1970, I, p. 186).

4. . . . *saṃjñā saṃjñānaṃ viṣayanimittodgrahaḥ . . . smṛtirālambanāsampramoṣaḥ . . . samādhiś cittasyaikāgratā. Abhidharmakośabhāṣya*, II, 24.5 (ibid., I, p. 187).

5. *viśeṣanimittagrāha iti. viṣayaviśeṣarūpagrāha ity arthaḥ . . . smṛtir ālambanāsampramoṣa iti. yadyogād ālambanaṃ mano na vismarati, tac cābhilapatīva, sā smṛtiḥ. Sphuṭārthā-Abhidharmakośavyākhyā*, II, 24 (ibid., p. 1870).

6. *Pañcaskandha-prakaraṇa*, Anacker, 1984, p. 67.

7. *smṛtiḥ saṃstute vastuny asampramoṣaś cetaso 'bhilapanatā. saṃstutaṃ vastu pūrvānubhūtam. ālambanagrahaṇāvipraṇāśakāraṇatvād asampramoṣaḥ. pūrvagṛhītasya vastunaḥ punaḥ punar ālambanākārasmaraṇam abhilapanatā. abhilapanam evābhilapantā. sā punar avikṣepakarmikā. ālambanābhilapane sati cittasyālambanāntare ākārāntare vā vikṣepābhāvād avikṣepakarmikā.* Lévi, 1925, pp. 25–26.

8. *tesu tesu ārammaṇesu okkhanditvā pakkhanditvā upaṭṭhānato upaṭṭhānaṃ. sati yeva upaṭṭhānaṃ satipaṭṭhānaṃ. kāyavedanācittadhammesu pan'assā . . . pavattito catudhā bhedo hoti; tasmā cattāro satipaṭṭhānā ti vuccanti. Visuddhimagga*, xxii, 34 (Warren, 1950, p. 583). For a detailed discussion of *smṛtyupasthāna*, see Cox's chapter in this book.

9. *pramāṇavikalpanidrāsmṛtayaḥ.* I, 6. . . . *anubhūtaviṣayāsampramoṣaḥ smṛtiḥ.* I, 11. Bhattacarya, 1963, pp. 10 and 15.

10. *sampramoṣaḥ steyam. kasmāt? sādṛśyāt muṣa steye ity asmāt pramoṣapadavyutpatteḥ. etad uktaṃ bhavati—sarve pramāṇādayo 'nadhigatārthaṃ sāmānyataḥ prakārato vā 'dhigamayanti. smṛtiḥ punar na pūrvānubhavamaryādām atikrāmati. tadviṣayā vā tadūnaviṣayā vā na tu tadadhikaviṣayā. so 'yaṃ vṛttyantarād viśeṣaḥ smṛter iti.* Ibid., p. 15. See translation by Woods, 1914, p. 33.

11. Translated as *The Soul Theory of the Buddhists* by Stcherbatsky, 1920.

12. Shastri, 1973, p. 1215.

13. *smṛtiviṣayasaṃjñānvayāc cittaviśeṣāt.* Ibid., p. 1215.

14. *kīdṛśāc cittaviśeṣāt yato 'nantaraṃ smṛtir bhavati?* Ibid.

15. *tadābhogasadṛśasambandhisaṃjñādimato 'nuphataprabhāvād āśrayaviśeṣaśokavyākṣepādibhiḥ.* Ibid., p. 1216.

16. Added from the *Sphuṭārthāvyākhyā: sadṛśasaṃjñādimataḥ, yatra sādṛśyāt smṛtir bhavati. sambandhisaṃjñādimataḥ, yatrāntareṇāpi sādṛśyaṃ dhūmādidarśanāt smṛtir bhavati.* Ibid.

17. The term *praṇidhāna* is found in Yasomitra's gloss on the word *ādi* ("and so forth") appearing in Vasubandhu's *bhāṣya*. See n. 15.

18. *tādṛśo 'pi hy atadanvayaś cittaviśeṣo na samarthas tāṃ smṛtiṃ bhāvayitum, tadanvayo 'pi cānyādṛśo na samarthas tāṃ smṛtiṃ bhāvayitum. ubhayathā tu samartha ity evaṃ smṛtir bhavati; anyasya sāmarthyādarśanāt.* Ibid.

19. *katham idānīm anyena cetasā dṛṣṭam anyat smarati, evaṃ hi Devadattacetasā dṛṣṭaṃ Yajñadattaḥ smaret?* Ibid.

20. *na, asambandhāt. na hi tayoḥ sambandho 'sti; akāryakāraṇabhāvād yathaikasantānikayoḥ. na ca brūmaḥ—anyena cetasā dṛṣṭam anyat smaratīti, api tu darśanacittāt smṛticittam anyad evotpadyate, santatipariṇatyā yathoktam iti ka evaṃ iti ka evaṃ sati doṣaḥ?* Ibid., pp. 1216–17.

21. See Cox's chapter in this book, pp. 85–86.

22. Stcherbatsky, 1920 (reprint, 1970), p. 65.

23. *ye 'pi ca dravyāntaram evātmānaṃ manyante tīrthakarāḥ* . . . Shastri, 1973, p. 1215.

24. *yadi tarhi sarvathā 'pi nāsty ātmā, kathaṃ kṣaṇikeṣu citteṣu cirānubhūtasya smaraṇaṃ bhavati? . . . katham idānīm anyena cetasā dṛṣṭam anyat smarati . . . asaty ātmani ka eṣa smarati? . . .* Ibid., p. 1215.

25. *yadi smṛtir ātmaguṇaḥ, evaṃ sati smṛtir upapadyate, nānyadṛṣṭam anyaḥ smaratīti . . . ekas tu cetano 'nekārthadarśī bhinnanimittaḥ pūrvadṛṣṭam arthaṃ smaratīty ekasyānekārthadarśino darśanapratisandhānāt smṛter ātmaguṇatve sati sadbhāvaḥ, viparyaye cānutpattiḥ . . . saṃskārāsantatimātre tu sattve utpadyotpadya saṃskārās tirobhavanti. sa nāsty eko 'pi saṃskāro yas trikālaviśiṣṭaṃ jñānaṃ smṛtiṃ cānubhavet. na cānubhavam antareṇa jñānasya smṛteś ca pratisandhānam ahaṃ mameti cotpadyate, dehāntaravat. Nyāyasūtra-Bhāṣya,* III, 1, 14. See Shastri, 1969, pp. 185–87.

26. Jaini, 1959a, p. 22.

27. *yady api dattotara eṣa vādaḥ* . . . Ibid. It is not clear whether the author of the *Vibhāṣāprabhāvṛtti* refers here to a refutation of his own (which is not extant) or to the *Pudgalaviniścaya* of Vasubandhu discussed earlier.

28. *ātmamanaḥsaṃyogāt saṃskārāpekṣā tadutpattir iti cet, na. ātmamanaḥsaṃyogaḥ saṃskārāṇāṃ śaśaviṣāṇavad asiddhatvān nityasyātmanaḥ saṃskārāṇām anutpatteḥ.* Ibid., p. 22.

29. Quoted from Jha, 1939, p. 272.

30. *anusmṛteś ce. . . . anubhavam upalabdhim anūtpadyamānaṃ smaraṇam evānusmṛtiḥ, sā copalabhdhyekakartṛkā satī sambhavati, puruṣāntaropalabdhiviṣaye puruṣāntarasya smṛtyadarśanāt . . . Brahmasūtra-Śāṅkara-Bhāṣya,* II, 25. See Dhundhiraj Shastri, 1929, pp. 535–58.

31. *kṛtapraṇāśākṛtakarmabhoga-bhavapramokṣa-smṛtibhaṅgadoṣān, upekṣya sākṣāt kṣaṇabhaṅgam icchan aho mahāsāhasikaḥ paras te. Anyayogavyavaccheda-dvātriṃśikā* of Hemacandra (1089–1172), xviii. See Dhruva, 1933, pp. 122–30; translation by Thomas, 1960, pp. 119–25.

32. For a detailed exposition, see Vasubandhu's *Pudgalaviniścaya* in Shastri, 1973, pp. 1229–32.

33. *ko 'yaṃ bījabhāvo nāma? ātmabhāvasya kleśajā kleśotpādanaśaktiḥ, yathānubhavajñānajā smṛtyutpādanaśaktiḥ, yathā cāṅkurādīnāṃ śāliphalajā śāliphalotpādanaśaktir iti. yas tu [Sphuṭārthā—yas tv iti Vātsīputrīyaḥ] kleśānāṃ bījārtham arthāntaraṃ viprayuktam anuśayaṃ kalpayati, tena smṛtibījam apy arthāntaraṃ kalpayitavyaṃ bhavati.* See Shastri, 1972, pp. 763–64. This discussion takes place in the context of a debate at *Abhidharmakośa,* v.1 over the nature of the dharmas called the (six) *anuśayas*—beginning with sexual desire (*kāmarāga*) and ending with skepticism (*vicikitsā*)—that are eliminated through the supermundane (*lokottara*) path. The Sautrāntika believes that *anuśayas* are latent forces, which remain dormant (like seeds [*bījas*] of a plant) awaiting an opportunity for their outburst (*paryavasthāna*) when they are recognized as passions (*kleśa*). According to this view the *anyśayas* are always "present" in the stream of consciousness. Whether a dormant dharma can be called "present" in a given stream of thought forms the crux of the debate. The Vaibhāṣika rejects the theory of latency altogether on the grounds that the "presence" of these evil dharmas will preclude all possibility of having a wholesome (*kuśala*) mental event (*citta*) at any time, since the two are incompatible. The Vaibhāṣika therefore maintains that the *anyśayas* are identical with their so-called outbursts, the passions (*kleśa*). Another school (identified by Yaśomitra as the Vātsīputrīya) seeks to overcome this difficulty (of the incompatibility of the latent passion and the active purity in a single moment of mental event) by postulating that the *anuśayas* are dharmas of the category known as the *viprayukta-saṃskāras,* "forces disassociated both from mind and matter." In this theory the *anuśayas* will be morally neither wholesome nor unwholesome, but neutral and thus can abide side by side with any kind of mental event. (For details on this debate, see Jaini, 1959b, and 1959c.) Drawing on the similarity that exists between the latent forces (*anuśaya*) and the past impressions (i.e., the objects of memory), the Sautrāntika (Vasubandhu) retorts by asking if the Vātsīputrīya would also favor a theory of the "disassociated forces" to explain the operation of memory. Because the opponent remains silent, it can be presumed that the Vātsīputrīya does not pursue the matter further. This inconclusive debate shows the difficulty the various schools of Abhidharma encounter when, in the absence of an appropriate theory to account for past impressions, they try to explain the operation of passions or memories that spring from them.

34. For the canonical references to the *bhavaṅga-citta,* see Wijesekera, 1976, pp. 348–52.

35. . . . *javanānubandhāni ca dve tadārammaṇapākāni yathārahaṃ pavattanti, tato paraṃ bhavaṅgapāto. Abhidhammatthasaṅgaho,* IV, 8. *javanānubandhānī ti paṭisotagāminiṃ nāvamiva udakaṃ, imāni tadārammaṇāni kiñci kālaṃ javanam*

anubandhanti. yasmā imāni bhavaṅgassa ārammaṇaṃ muñcitvā javanārammaṇe pavattanti, tasmā tadārammaṇānī ti vuccanti. Navanītaṭīkā, IV, 8. See Kosambi, 1941, p. 69.

36. The object (*ālambana*) of the *bhavaṅga* will depend on the kind of consciousness at the time of one's rebirth. For example, if a being is to be born in the realm of desire (*kāmadhātu*), its *bhavaṅga* will be appropriate to the destinies within that realm (e.g., animal, human) and it will have any object available to the mind-consciousness (*mano-vijñāna*) at the time of conception. Similarly, if the rebirth took place in the realm of form (*rūpadhātu*), the *bhavaṅga* will be of a *rūpāvacara* variety and its object will have to be the meditational object appropriate to the particular *rūpa* heaven. Since the *bhavaṅga* does not change its quality for the duration of a particular life, its object (*ālambana*), with which it came into existence at the time of rebirth (*pratisandhi*), also remains the same. This precludes any possibility of endowing the current *bhavaṅga-citta* with a new object in midstream as it were, for that can only mean the beginning of a new life, a new *bavaṅga* with its own object.

37. *tatrālayākhyaṃ vijñānaṃ vipākaḥ sarvabījakam. Triṃśikā, 2cd.* See Lévi, 1925, p. 18.

Bibliography

Anacker, Stefan. 1984. *Seven Works of Vasubandhu* (trans. of the *Pañcaskandhaprakaraṇa*, pp. 49–82). Delhi: Motilal Banarsidass.

Bapat, P. V., and Vadekar, R. D., 1942. *Aṭṭhasālinī*. Poona: Bhandarkar Oriental Series, No. 3.

Bhattacarya, R. S. 1963. *Pātañjala-Yogadarśanam, Tattvavaiśāradī-saṃvalita-VyāsaBhāṣyasametam*. Banares: Bharatiya Vidya Prakashan.

Dhruva, A. B. 1933. *Malliṣeṇa's Syādvādamañjarī with Anyayoga-vyavavaccheda-dvātriṃśikā of Hemacandra*. Bombay Skt & Pkt. Series, No. 83.

Dhundhiraj, Shastri. 1929. *Brahmasūtra-śāṅkarabhāṣyam* (Pt. I). Kashi Sanskrit Series No. 71.

Jaini, P. S. 1959a, *Abhidharmadīpa with Vibhāṣāprabhā-Vṛtti*, Tibetan Sanskrit Works Series, No. 4. Patna: K. P. Jayaswal Research Institute (reprinted, 1977).

———. 1959b, "The Sautrāntika theory of *bīja*." *Bulletin of the School of Oriental and African Studies* [University of London] 22, no. 2:236–49.

———. 1959c, "The origin and development of the *viprayukta-saṃskāras*." *Bulletin of the School of Oriental and African Studies* [University of London] 22, no. 3:532–47.

Jha, Ganganath. 1939. *Gautama's Nyāyasūtras with Vātsyāyana's Bhāṣya* (trans.). Poona: Poona Oriental Series No. 59.

Kosambi, D. 1941. *Abhidhammatthasaṅgaho of Anuruddhācariya with Navanītaṭīkā.* Sarnath, Banares: Mahabodhi Society.

Lévi, Sylvain. 1925. *Vijñaptimātratāsiddhi: Deux Traites de Vasubandhu Viṃśatikā et Triṃśikā.* Paris: Librairie Ancienne Honoré Champion.

Nyanaponika Thera. 1965. *Abhidhamma Studies,* 2d ed. Kandy, Sri Lanka: Buddhist Publication Society.

Shastri, Dvarikadas. 1969. *VātsyāyanaBhāṣyasaṃvalitaṃ Gautamīyaṃ Nyāyadarśanam.* Banares: Bharatiya Vidya Prakshan.

———. 1970–73. *ĀcāryaVasubandhuviracitaṃ Svopajñabhāṣyasahitam Abhidharmakośa Yaśomitrakṛta Spuṭhārthāvyākhyopetam,* Pts. 1–4. (*Pudgala-Viniścayaḥ,* Pt. 4, pp. 1189–1234).

Stcherbatsky, T., 1920 (reprinted, 1970). *The Soul Theory of the Buddhists,* ed. Jaidev Singh. Banares: Bharaitya Vidya Prakashan.

Thomas, F. W. 1960. *The Flower-Spray of the Quodammodo Doctrine* (trans. of the *Syādvādamañjarī* of Malliṣeṇa). Berlin: Akademie-Verlag.

Warren, H. C. 1950. *Visuddhimagga of Buddhaghosācariya.* Cambridge, Mass.: Harvard Oriental Series, Vol. 41.

Wijesekera, O. H. De A. 1976. "Canonical References to Bhavaṅga." In *Malalasekera Commemoration Volume,* ed. O. H. De A Wijesekera. Colombo.

Woods, J. H. 1914. *The Yoga System of Patañjali.* Cambridge, Mass.: Harvard Oriental Series, Vol. 17.

The Omission of Memory in the Theravādin List of Dhammas: On the Nature of *Saññā*[1]

NYANAPONIKA THERA

With the first occurrence of mindfulness (*sati;* Skt. *smṛti*) in the *Dhammasaṅgaṇi's* list of dhammas, we would draw attention to a problem.[2] *Sati* occurs only in good consciousness (*sobhaṇa citta*). This implies that mindfulness means here first of all "right mindfulness" (*sammā-sati*), referring to the four applications of mindfulness (*satipaṭṭhāna*). The original meaning of *sati* as memory is, however, not quite excluded, since it has its place in the definition given in the *Dhammasaṅgaṇi* as "controlling heedlessness," but it stands rather in the background and refers always to good consciousness. The question now suggests itself: why has such an important and frequent mental function as that of memory not been expressly included in the *Dhammasaṅgaṇi*'s list of dhammas in its quality as an ethically neutral factor? We cannot suppose that it has simply been forgotten. Against any such explanation stands the fact that this list of dhammas is too obviously the product of a mind working with the greatest accuracy. The list is undoubtedly the result of careful investigation supported by introspective intuition. Certainly no essential aspects of the subject matter have been overlooked here; though, of course, the list does admit of condensation as well as extensions.

This question of memory as an ethically neutral function was actually raised in *Atthasālinī*. Here is the passage in full:

> In a mind devoid of [right] faith (*asaddhiya-citte*) there is no mindfulness (*sati*). How then, do not adherents of wrong views remember actions performed by them? They do. But that is not mindfulness (*sati*). It is merely an unwholesome thought process occurring in that aspect.[3] That is why mindfulness is not included [in unwholesome consciousness]. But why, then, is wrong mindfulness (*micchā-sati*) mentioned in the Suttantas? For the following reasons: because unwholesome aggregates are devoid of mindfulness, and in order to complete the group of factors of the wrong path (*micchā-magga*). For these reasons wrong mindfulness is mentioned in an exposition of relative validity (*pariyāyena*). But in an exposition of absolute validity (*nippariyāyena*) it has no place.[4]

We cannot say that these explanations are very satisfactory. They still leave unanswered the question why memory has not been included in the list under some other name, such as *paṭissati,* to distinguish it from right mindfulness (*sammā-sati*).

In the sub-commentary (*Mūlaṭīkā*) to the passage just quoted from the *Atthasālinī,* we find, however, a hint for a plausible theory about the omission of memory. There it is said: "[According to that passage in the *Atthasālinī,*] wrong mindfulness is explained as the unwholesome aggregates which are void of mindfulness and contrary to it. This again should be understood as follows: when reflecting on previous actions, for example, in the case of inimical feelings, those unwholesome aggregates are associated with keen perception."[5]

Taking up this suggestion we can assume that ancient Buddhist psychology ascribed the main share in the process of recollecting to perception (*saññā*), regarding it merely as a department of the latter. It should be recalled that perception belongs to the "pentad of sense impression" and to the factors common to all consciousness (*sabbacittasādhāraṇa*), so that the requirement of universal occurrence as a neutral and general factor is fulfilled. We are supported in our theory by the definition of perception found in *Atthasālinī.*[6] There two sets of explanations are supplied, given in the customary categories used for definitions (*lakkhaṇa, rasa,* etc.). According to the first explanation the characteristic (*lakkhaṇa*) of perception, applicable to all cases, is "perceiving" (*sañjānana,* lit. "cognizing well"). The essential property or function (*rasa*) of perception is "re-cognizing" (*paccabhiññāṇa*), said to be applicable only to certain cases, namely, when perception proceeds with the help of a distinctive mark of the object, either fixed to it intentionally (as by woodcutters to trees), or a characteristic of the object itself (e.g., a mole on the face of a man). The second explanation is said to apply to all cases of perception. The characteristic is again that of perception. The essential property given here is: "making marks as a condition for a repeated perception (i.e., for recognizing or remembering)."[7] So we may sum up: perception (*saññā*) is the taking up, the making, and the remembering of the object's distinctive marks.[8] In this connection it is noteworthy that "mark" or "signal" is also one of the different meanings of the word *saññā* itself.

Not only the taking up, but also the making and the remembering of marks may be relevant to all cases of perception if it is understood as follows: what really happens in the simple act of perception is that some features of the object (sometimes only a single striking one) are selected. The mental note made of that perception is closely associated with those selected features. We attach, as it were, a tag to the object, or make a mark on it as woodcutters do on trees. So every perception is a making of marks (*nimitta-karaṇa*). In order to understand how remembering or recognizing too is implied in every act of perception, we should mention that according to the deeply penetrative analysis of the Abhidamma the apparently simple act of seeing a rose, for example, is in reality a very complex process composed of different phases.[9] Each phase consists in numerous smaller combinations of conscious processes (*citta-vīthi*) which again are made up of several single moments of consciousness (*citta-kkhaṇa*) following each other in a definite sequence of diverse functions. Among these phases there is one that connects the present perception of a rose with a previous one, and there is another that attaches to the present perception the name "rose" remembered from previous experience. Not only in relation to similar experiences in a relatively distant past, but also between those infinitesimally brief single phases and successive processes must the connecting function of rudimentary "memory" be assumed to operate, because each phase and each lesser successive state has to remember the previous one—a process called by the later Ābhidhammikas "grasping the past" (*atīta-gghahana*). Finally, the individual contributions of all those different perceptual processes have to be remembered and coordinated in order to form the final and complete perception of a rose.

Not only in such microscopic analysis of sense-perception, but also in every consecutive thought process, for example, in reasoning can the phase of grasping the past be observed, as when the parts of an argument are connected, that is, when conclusions are built on premises. If that grasp of the past is too weak to be effective, one says that one has "lost the thread." The way in which one remembers the earlier phases of one's thought-process is likewise through selected marks (*nimitta-karaṇa*) because it is neither possible nor necessary to consider all the minor aspects of a thought. But if the selection is too incomplete and overlooks essential features or consequences of the past thought, then a faulty argument built on wrong premises follows.

In these two ways we can understand how remembering, i.e., connecting with the past, is a function of perception in general. We can now formulate the following definition: *saññā* is cognition as well as recognition, both occurring by way of selected marks.

We can summarize our findings as follows:

1. Memory as we usually understand it is not mentioned in the Pāli Abhidhamma as a separate component of a moment of consciousness because it is not a single mental factor but a complex process.

2. The mental factor which is most important for the arising of memory is perception (*saññā* = *sañjānana*), being that kind of elementary cognition (*jānana*) which proceeds by way of taking up, making and remembering (i.e., identifying) marks.

3. Apart from that which, in common usage, is called "remembering," the reminiscent function of perception in general operates also (a) in the imperceptibly brief phases of a complete perceptual process, the sequence of which is based on the connecting function of grasping the past phases; and

(b) in any consecutive train of thoughts where this grasping of the past is so habitual, and refers to an event so close to the present, that in normal parlance it is not called "memory," though it is not essentially different from it.

Another reason for the omission of memory in the Pāli Abhidhamma lists from either the components or the classes of consciousness is this. Remembrance means merely the fact that a state of consciousness has objects of the past (*atītārammaṇa*). But in the *Dhammasaṅgaṇi* the object side of the perceptual process is used for the classification of consciousness only in a single instance and refers only to the division into visual objects, etc. The time relation of objects, in particular, does not enter into the classification or analysis of consciousness at all, being irrelevant to them. Still less could a time relation, for example, that of memory, be counted as a separate component of consciousness. In the *Dhammasaṅgaṇi* the time relation of objects is treated separately in the triad of things with past, etc., objects (*atītārammaṇa-tikā*). But the fact that a moment of consciousness has objects of the past does not warrant the listing of a separate factor called "memory."

As a point of comparison between the Pāli Abhidhamma of the Theravādins and the Abhidhamma of later Buddhist schools, it deserves mentioning that in the lists of dhammas composed by the Sarvāstivādins and by the Mahāyānist Vijñānavādins, *sati* (= *smṛti*) is given as a neutral factor. It is included there in a group called *mahābhūmikā*, which is composed of factors common to all consciousness, and corresponds to the category of *sabbacittasādhāraṇa* in Theravāda. The fact that *smṛti* is really intended there as an ethically neutral and not a wholesome factor, is also proved by the definition of *smṛti* given, in this same connection, in the commentary to the *Abhidharmakośa:* "the non-forgetting of that which has been experienced."[10] This divergence from the list given in the *Dhammasaṅgaṇi* shows that these old thinkers too had noticed the absence of memory in that list, assuming perhaps that it had been forgotten. But for the reasons given above we think that this omission was not only deliberate but fully justified. In other cases of divergence, too, we have found that on close examination the Theravādin's list of dhammas is far preferable, being based on a much more mature judgment of psychological facts. But here we are not concerned with any such comparative study of Abhidhamma systems.

Notes

[Editor's note] This chapter was originally published as "The Omission of Memory in the List—On the Nature of *Saññā*," in Nyanaponika Thera, *Abhidhamma Studies: Researches in Buddhist Psychology*, Island Hermitage Publications, vol. 2 (Colombo: Frewin & Co., 1949; 2d ed: Kandy, Ceylon: Buddhist Publication Society,

1965, pp. 68–72.) It is reprinted by permission of the author and the Buddhist Publication Society.

1. [Editor's note] N.B. The author translates *saññā* as "perception," but more recently the tendency in Buddhist Studies has been to render *saññā* as "conception," "recognition," or "notion."

2. [Editor's note] *Sati* first appears in the *Dhammasaṅgaṇi*'s list of dhammas among the faculties (*indriya*). It is also present as one of the path factors (*magg'anga*); powers (*bala*); and helpers (*upakāraka*).

3. *ten'ākārena akusalacittappavatti.*

4. P. 249.

5. *patu-saññā-sampayutta.*

6. P. 110.

7. *puna-sañjānana-paccaya-nimitta-karaṇa.*

8. According to the commentary to the *Patisambhidāmagga*: "Perception means taking up the appearance of a thing (*ākāragāhika saññā*)." Note that the Latin word *per-cipere* from which the English *perceive* is derived, means literally "to seize or take up thoroughly"; the prefix *per* corresponding to the Pāli *sam* in *sañ-jānana* = *saññā*.

9. Cf. *Compendium of Philosophy* (*Abhidhammatthasangaha*) trans. by S. Z. Aung (London, 1929) p. 32 seq. The perceptual "phases" treated there and briefly mentioned above, are elaborations by later Abhidhamma scholars and not found in older works.

10. *Anubhūtasya asampramoṣa.*

Mindfulness and Memory: The Scope of *Smṛti* from Early Buddhism to the Sarvāstivādin Abhidharma

COLLETT COX

Introduction

For virtually any Indian tradition, an examination of the cognitive process designated in the West as memory must begin with an investigation of the term *smṛti*. This Sanskrit designation, however, is used in a variety of contexts and has a range of meanings or connotations not indicated by *smṛti*'s standard English translation as memory. These various contexts would seem to suggest two distinct functions of *smṛti:* first, as a technique central to religious praxis; and second, as an aspect of ordinary psychological processes. As employed and refined in religious praxis, *smṛti* is a mode of attentiveness operative in several Buddhist models for practice. The second function of *smṛti* appears to coincide with some of the psychological operations normally associated in the West with memory: specifically, retention and recollection. Such a twofold distinction, though appealing in its descriptive simplicity, obscures a complex historical evolution during which the traditional meanings of the single term *smṛti* were preserved and accommodated to newly emerging meanings and shifts of emphasis. This twofold distinction also conceals the determinative historical and doctrinal constraints specific to a Buddhist context that frame any discussion of doctrinal issues, which in turn affect the further shaping of those very constraints. Finally, limiting one's examination of *smṛti* to a dichotomous framework also precludes an understanding of the connotative scope of *smṛti,* a scope that illumines both the interconnections among the various contexts in which *smṛti* is used and the connections with other similarly functioning terms.

In this chapter, I adopt another interpretative model, whereby the apparent twofold distinction in the functioning of *smṛti* does not represent a semantic bifurcation, but rather an interrelated semantic complex. Specifically, *smṛti*'s functions as a central component of religious praxis and as a psychological factor are mutually determining; underlying these two contexts of use is a common aspect of the functioning of *smṛti* that is otherwise obscured in a dichotomous model.

Thus, this chapter proceeds with the assumption that the variant meanings of the term *smṛti* suggested by the dichotomous framework reflect an underlying unity and interaction between models of memory and religious praxis and not a secondary and thereby negligible semantic overlap. For this reason, the inclusive and initially ambiguous term *mindfulness* has been chosen to translate *smṛti* in all of its contexts. Mindfulness is chosen here not, as in many cases, to avoid confusion with the psychological function of *smṛti* as memory, but precisely for the opposite reason; that is, to indicate at the outset what this chapter will illustrate: that the contexts for the operation of *smṛti* suggested by the term *mindfulness* actually encompass the psychological functions of memory as they were understood within Indian Buddhism.

To demonstrate this alternative interpretative model for *smṛti,* I will explore the range of technical uses of mindfulness. I will attempt to demarcate the boundaries of the psychological functioning of mindfulness and clarify its specific operations in religious praxis and in memory. First, I examine the various formulaic descriptions of mindfulness in early Buddhist scripture to uncover the role of mindfulness in religious praxis and, in particular, its most frequent occurrence in the practice of the applications of mindfulness (*smṛtyupasthāna*). Next, I explore the further specification and refinement of these descriptions undertaken in the taxonomies of the early scholastic Abhidharma texts. This will reveal the reorganization of the traditional descriptions of practices involving *smṛti* and their incorporation into the complex path structure that forms the centerpiece of Abhidharma doctrinal synthesizing. Finally, the ordinary psychological functions of mindfulness that are carefully analyzed in later Abhidharma treatises will be examined in the context of *smṛti*'s continuing functions in praxis. Throughout, attention will be directed to the differences that occur in descriptive formulas. Even in the early period, the descriptions of mindfulness had attained a formulaic regularity, reflecting the didactic and mnemonic requirements of scriptural transmission and the predilection of the growing tradition to utilize repeatedly stereotypical characterizations. Consequently, deviations in the standard formulas, even within the earliest sources, are instructive either as a remnant of an earlier stratum, or as a sign of further intentional development.

Mindfulness in Early Buddhist Scriptures

In the early Buddhist scriptural collections, *mindfulness* refers almost exclusively to techniques of religious praxis. Its importance is amply indicated by its inclusion in many of the lists of exercises or qualities that the early scriptural collections recommend as aids in abandoning all defilements and attaining enlightenment. Mindfulness occurs, for example, within the five or seven forces (*bala*), the five controlling factors (*indriya*), the seven limbs of enlightenment (*bodhyaṅga*), and the eightfold noble path.[1] Mindfulness is often paired with awareness (*samprajanya*). It also appears in the mindfulness of respiration (*ānāpānasmṛti*), an independent practice, which serves as the prerequisite for advanced stages of trance (*dhyāna*) or equipoise (*samāpatti*) in the later Abhidharma.[2] The closely related term *anusmṛti*, or "reflection," occurs in discussions of distinctly religious exercises, and is said to be of six, eight, or ten varieties. *Anusmṛti* is also applied to previous rebirth states (*pūrvanivāsānusmṛti*).[3]

The most frequent context in which mindfulness occurs within the early materials is the four applications of mindfulness (*smṛtyupasthāna*): mindfulness of the body (*kāya*), mindfulness of feelings (*vedanā*), mindfulness of mind events (*citta*), and mindfulness of factors (*dharma*). Like the mindfulness of respiration (*ānāpānasmṛti*), the set of four applications of mindfulness becomes the topic of individual dialogues in the early scriptures. This is an indication of their importance within the as yet relatively unstructured array of alternative techniques for praxis, an array characteristic of this early period in the development of Buddhism.[4] Further, mindfulness in its other praxis-related functions as a force, controlling factor, limb of enlightenment, or member of the eightfold noble path is also customarily defined in terms of these four applications of mindfulness.[5]

The Four Applications of Mindfulness as a Path to Enlightenment

The development of the four applications of mindfulness in the early scriptural collections has been examined in depth by both Lin Li-kouang and Lambert Schmithausen.[6] Lin Li-kouang suggests that the standard set of four applications found from the early scriptural period onward represents an expansion of an original single application of mindfulness with regard to the body.[7] Schmithausen admits the probable antiquity of the body-focused practice, but suggests that Lin's assertion that the canonical account of the four applications is an amplification of an original mindfulness of the body does not withstand a text-historical analysis of the relevant early scriptural materials.[8]

Whatever the origin of the four applications, their significance among the range of early Buddhist practices is underscored by the formulaic passages that proclaim the objectives and results of the practice of mindfulness. The separate dialogue on the mindfulness of the body declares that through that practice, "one abandons remembrance and intention rooted in ordinary life and becomes inwardly stilled, concentrated," and so on.[9] As a result, one is able to enter the four trance states, from which one gains ten beneficial results culminating in the destruction of the fluxes, which is the last of the three clear intuitions (*vidyā*) that together constitute the experience of enlightenment.[10] Moreover, the general formula that introduces the dialogues on the four applications unequivocally declares that the four constitute the single path of practice, leading ultimately to the final goal of all praxis, the realization of nibbāna.[11] Elsewhere, the four applications are said to constitute the basis from which Buddhas of the past, present, and future cultivate the seven limbs of enlightenment and finally attain the incomparable right complete enlightenment.[12] According to other formulas, the four applications lead to the abandonment of inclinations (*chanda*) that arise from the objects of each of the four applications or to the state of having completely understood (*pariññāta*) and, thereby, having removed the defilements dependent upon these four objects. This understanding and removal results ultimately in the realization of the deathless (*amata*).[13]

Such descriptive formulas suggest that the practice of mindfulness is tantamount to the central praxis of Buddhism: namely, as the single path leading to the ultimate soteriological goal of enlightenment and nirvāṇa. However, mindfulness also plays a prominent role in stylized scriptural enumerations of various practices that function together as a comprehensive path. According to one account, praxis begins with the purification of discipline (*sīlaṃ suvisuddham*) and straight views (*diṭṭhi ujukā*), which constitute the foundation of virtuous factors (*kusaladhamma*). It then proceeds through the cultivation of the four applications of mindfulness and culminates in the growth of virtuous factors and the recognition that constitutes the verification of one's enlightenment and one's status as an arhat: namely, that "birth is exhausted, the religious life (*brahmacariya*) is lived, what is to be done is done, and there is nothing further after this life."[14] In the Buddha's directive that his disciples should abide taking themselves and the Dharma as their lamp and refuge, mindfulness is identified as the proper mode of abiding.[15] Conversely, the failure to cultivate the four applications is cited as the primary reason for the decline of the teaching.[16]

Scriptural Descriptions of the Operation of Mindfulness and its Relation to Other Mental Functions

Although the early formulaic descriptions of the four applications of mindfulness do not provide a comprehensive picture of the operation of mindfulness per se, some passages do offer clues as to those states and activities with which mindfulness is associated. The standard formula states: "a monk abides observing the body in the body, zealous, possessed of awareness and mindfulness, having restrained covetousness and dejection in the world; [a monk] abides observing the feelings in the feelings" and so on, for each of the four applications.[17] According to a slightly different pattern, "you should abide observing the body in the body, zealous, possessed of awareness, focussed, having a clear mind, composed, having one-pointedness of mind, for the sake of knowledge of the body as it truly is,'' and so on, for each of the four applications.[18] The former formula emphasizes the moral preconditions for the practice of mindfulness, whereas the latter pattern, the concomitant meditative concentration.[19] The cultivation of each of the four applications includes several stages, each of which concludes with three formulas: first, one observes an object inwardly, outwardly, and both inwardly and outwardly; next, one observes the facts of arising (*samudaya*) and passing away (*vaya*) as regards the object; and third, mindfulness, while observing the object, is established to the point of possessing knowledge (*ñāna*) and recollection (*patissati*), and one abides being not dependent (*anissita*) and not grasping anything in the world.[20] One who practices thus attains one of two fruits: either final knowledge in this life, that is, the ultimate state of arhatship; or, if accompanied by some remainder of substratum (*upādi*), the penultimate state of the nonreturner.[21]

In some dialogues, this standard formulaic description of the four applications is expanded to include meditative techniques attendant to the practice of mindfulness.[22] Mindfulness can be cultivated either by fastening (*paṇidhāya*) or not fastening the mind. In the first case, as one ''abides observing the body in the body,'' for example, the mind may become outwardly distracted due to physical pain or mental sluggishness, and so on. To counteract this distraction, the mind should then be fastened on some worthy (*pasādanīya*) mark, which results in delight (*pāmojja*), joy (*prīti*), quieting of the body (*passaddhakāya*), ease (*sukha*), and concentrated mind. Having been fastened thus on a worthy mark, the mind is withdrawn and no initial inquiry (*vitakka*) or investigation (*vicāra*) remains; one becomes aware simply, ''I am without initial inquiry or investigation, I am inwardly mindful and at ease.''[23] Mindfulness may also be cultivated without fastening the mind: that is, one becomes aware that the mind is outwardly unfastened and that it is unfastened (*appaṇihita*), uncollected (*asaṇkhitta*), and liberated (*vimutta*) with regard to what comes after or before (*pacchāpure*). One then engages in the traditional practice of the four applications: that is, ''one abides observing the body in the body,'' and so on.[24] Another dialogue sets out the requisites for the proper cultivation of mindfulness using the example of unskillful and skillful cooks.[25] An unskillful cook does not grasp the marks characterizing the tastes of the employer and, therefore, receives no reward. So also, an unskillful monk, though practicing the four applications in accordance with the formulaic description, does not grasp (*na uggaṇhāti*) the marks of the mind and, therefore, does not experience concentration of the mind and the abandonment of defilements.[26] The skillful monk, in contrast, grasps the marks of the mind, experiences concentration of the mind and, thus, abandons defilements.

Although these two dialogues do not present a uniform picture of the activity of mindfulness, they do touch on certain factors important in its operation. The first dialogue suggests that mindfulness, as cultivated in the practice of the four applications, does not require that the mind be either fastened or unfastened on an object. The mind, if distracted, can be prepared for mindfulness through fastening on a mark. However, this initial fastening of the mind is followed by withdrawal from the mark and the disappearance of both initial inquiry and investigation.[27] Mindfulness also can be cultivated without the aid of a mark on which to fasten the mind, in which case one is aware of one's undirected state of mind and is openly mindful from the outset. By contrast, the second dialogue suggests a different view: the successful practice of mindfulness that leads to concentration of the mind and the abandonment of defilements, in fact, is contingent on the process of grasping marks, presumably the marks of the mind involved in the practice of mindfulness.

Further clues to the operation of mindfulness are found in the close connection between mindfulness (*smṛti*) and awareness (*samprajanya*). References to awareness appear in virtually all formulaic definitions of the four applications of mindfulness, as well as in descriptions of other praxis-related varieties of mindfulness and reflection (*anusmṛti*).[28] In other contexts, mindfulness and awareness characterize a state of concentration[29] or function as stages in hierarchies of practice culminating, for example, in one-pointedness of mind or in liberation and nirvāṇa.[30] This frequent linkage of mindfulness and awareness indicates that, in many contexts, the cultivation of mindfulness alone functions not as a self-sufficient practice, but rather as a necessary stage of simple observation that is merely preparatory to a subsequent stage of cognitive awareness. It is then possible that in those cases in which mindfulness does appear as a self-sufficient practice, for example, in the four applications, simple observation and cognitive awareness are conflated and subsumed within the category of mindfulness, here understood in a wider sense. However, when mindfulness and awareness do appear as a pair, mindfulness is defined using the standard formula of the four applications, whereas awareness is defined using the formula that appears particularly in the concrete description of mindfulness of the body. In these contexts, awareness functions as a conscious attentiveness in action: for example, one acts with awareness in going out and returning, or looking forward and backward, and so on.[31] Or awareness may be defined as the fact that feelings (*vedanā*), initial inquiry (*vitakkā*), and conceptions (*saññā*) are known as arising, remaining, and disappearing.[32] Thus, when paired with awareness, mindfulness is but a stage of calm and settled preparedness, which can be directed toward an object, as in the case of the four applications of mindfulness, but which, in itself, does not require such direction. However, as in the example of the skillful cook cited earlier, mindfulness may also be described as involving the grasping of marks; in those cases, the sphere of mindfulness includes cognitive operations that in other contexts are associated with awareness.

Mindfulness as a Technique of Religious Praxis in Abhidharma

The northern Indian Abhidharma texts continue the tradition of mindfulness as a technique of religious praxis, but not without significant changes in its character and operation.[33] The four applications of mindfulness are no longer recommended as a completely independent and self-sufficient technique of praxis, but rather are included as the first four members in the standardized list of thirty-seven aids to enlightenment (*bodhipakṣya*).[34] The thirty-seven aids are further incorporated within a new path structure detailed in northern Indian Sarvāstivādin Abhidharma texts. This new gradualist path of theoretically successive stages begins with the stage of initial action (*ādikarmika*), in which one has not yet begun the cultivation expounded exclusively within the Buddha's teaching. This nonexclusive stage is followed by the distinctively Buddhist paths of preparation (*prayogamārga*), vision (*darśanamārga*), and cultivation (*bhāvanāmārga*), each of which contains substages. The four applications of mindfulness, as the first group among the thirty-seven aids, are identified as the predominant form of practice within the first nonexclusive stage of initial action. The second group among the thirty-seven aids, the four right efforts (*samyakpradhāna*), is predominant in the first stage of the subsequent path of preparation: namely, the stage of heat. The third group, the four bases of magic powers (*ṛddhipāda*), is predominant in the second stage of the path of preparation, the stage of the summit, and so on, through the seven groups of thirty-seven aids.[35] Thus, the four applications of mindfulness are incorporated into the Sarvāstivādin path structure at its very basis in the stage of initial action, prior to the distinctively Buddhist practices of the three paths of preparation, vision, and cultivation. Therefore, they can, theoretically, be practiced by non-Buddhists as well.

Though particularly associated with and predominant in this initial stage of praxis, the four applications, like all of the subsequent aids, nonetheless are said to characterize the entire path from their stage of predominance onward. Therefore, they continue to be practiced throughout the entire path up to the final stage of arhatship, in which one attains the ultimate knowledge of the future nonarising of all defilements. We can hypothesize that the practice of mindfulness was incorporated at the initial stage of the path because of its strong traditional association with simple observation or calm preparedness, which would serve as a propaedeutic to subsequent practice. But, despite its relegation to a merely preparatory and nonexclusive role, mindfulness was not omitted from the rest of the path because of an inherited precedent: namely, the widespread scriptural tradition establishing the importance of the practice of mindfulness.

When discussing the four applications of mindfulness, Abhidharma texts focus on three issues: the nature of their respective objects; the distinctive character of their mode of operation; and their relation to other techniques of religious praxis.

The Objects of the Applications of Mindfulness

In Abhidharma texts, the objects of the four applications—the body, feelings, mind events, and factors—taken together, are extended to encompass all possible factors.[36] This extension is especially evident in the ever more inclusive explanations offered for the object of the fourth application, the factors (*dharma*). In the early scriptures, the objects of the application of factors include the five hindrances, the five aggregates, the fetters that depend on the six sense bases, the seven limbs of enlightenment, and, in certain versions, the knowledge of the four noble truths.[37] In the Abhidharma, both traditional and new categories define the objects of the four applications so that they form four mutually exclusive sets, which together exhaustively encompass the range of potential experience. Some Abhidharma texts define the object of the fourth application as containing all factors not included in the other three.[38] Others employ the taxonomy of the five aggregates, identifying the conception (*saṃjñāskandha*) and motivations aggregates (*saṃskāraskandha*) as the contents of the factors application.[39] Still others employ both the aggregate and sense sphere taxonomies and identify the object of the fourth application with that portion of the nonmaterial dharma sense sphere (*dharmāyatana*) not included within the feelings aggregate (*vedanāskandha*).[40] Finally, the *Mahāvibhāṣā* completes the expansion by also subsuming unconditioned factors (*asaṃskṛtadharma*) within the fourth application. This expansion of the contents of the fourth application reflects the general purpose underlying the Abhidharma enterprise as a whole: namely, to provide a soteriologically coherent enumeration of all experienced phenomena.

Another innovation in the Abhidharma interpretation of the objects of the four applications is that the objects themselves are understood to encourage soteriologically significant recognitions. One early Abhidharma text states that the objects of each of the four applications of mindfulness promote the recognition of the impurity, impermanence, suffering, voidness, and nonself of the four objects of the body, feelings, mind events, and factors.[41] In later Abhidharma texts, each of the four applications is considered to be, respectively, a counteragent to one of the four mistaken views (*viparyāsa*) of purity, ease, permanence, and self.[42] Post- *Vibhāṣā* Abhidharma compendia link this function of the four applications as counteragents to a description of their true intrinsic characteristics. To observe the objects of the four applications correctly is to observe their true characteristics, which are identified, in one case, as impurity, impermanence, suffering, and nonself.[43] In another case, these true characteristics are said to comprise both the particular (*svalakṣaṇa*) and generic characteristics (*sāmānyalakṣaṇa*) of the four objects: the particular characteristic refers to their distinctive intrinsic nature (*svabhāva*) or to their nature as belonging to a particular sense sphere (*āyatana*) and the generic characteristic is their general fourfold nature as impermanence, and so on.[44]

Relationships between Mindfulness and Insight: The Bridge to the Psychological Understanding of Mindfulness

The functioning and character of mindfulness itself also receives increased attention in later Abhidharma texts. The *Mahāvibhāṣā* offers a threefold interpretation of the scriptural term *applications of mindfulness.*[45] First, some scriptural passages are said to refer to the applications of mindfulness in their intrinsic nature (*svabhāvasmṛtyupasthāna*), here identified as insight (*prajñā*).[46] As an example, the *Mahāvibhāṣā* cites the scriptural passage that equates the applications with the single path.[47] Second, some passages refer to applications of mindfulness through connection (*saṃsargasmṛtyupasthāna*). In other words, the term *mindfulness* can refer either to the mental forces or to the dissociated forces (*cittaviprayuktasaṃskāra*) that occur in the same moment as a particular application of mindfulness and have the same effect as that application. Therefore, these factors are called *applications of mindfulness* in connection with the principal application: for example, the passage that identifies the four applications as a heap of virtue.[48] Third, still other scriptural passages use the term *applications of mindfulness* to refer to the object-support (*ālambana*) of mindfulness: for example, the passage that identifies the four applications as all factors.[49] In short, *applications of mindfulness* denotes not only that insight with which mindfulness is intrinsically identified, but also those factors occurring simultaneously with the operation of this insight, as well as the objects to which this insight is applied.[50]

The *Mahāvibhāṣā* and all later northern Indian Abhidharma texts devote particular attention to the first sense of the applications of mindfulness in their intrinsic nature, which is identified as insight (*prajñā*).[51] The four applications, originally classified within the mindfulness component among the controlling factors, forces, limbs of enlightenment, and members of the eightfold noble path, are reclassified in later Abhidharma texts among the corresponding insight components.[52] As the *Mahāvibhāṣā* notes, if the intrinsic nature of the applications of mindfulness were not insight but mindfulness (*smṛti*), then the scriptural formula that identifies the operation of the applications of mindfulness as observation (*anupaśyanā*) would be contradicted, because observation is itself a form of insight.[53] Furthermore, the particular and generic characteristics said to be discerned through the applications of mindfulness actually can be cognized only through insight.[54] The later Kāśmīra Sarvāstivāda-Vaibhāṣika master Saṅghabhadra (fifth century AD) adds a second reason for identifying the intrinsic nature of the applications of mindfulness as insight: the four applications are identified with the single path by which nirvāṇa is ultimately attained, and that single path is the eradication of defilements. Because insight is always required for eradicating defilements, the applications must be of the nature of insight.[55]

This shift from mindfulness to insight in the Abhidharma characterization of the applications of mindfulness, however, raises new problems significant to this study. Specifically, if the applications of mindfulness are identified with insight, then what connection do they retain to mindfulness? The *Mahāvibhāṣā* offers eight possible solutions, five of which suggest differing relationships between mindfulness and insight.[56] In four of these five relationships, mindfulness performs a preparatory function that provides the requisite conditions for the subsequent proper functioning of insight: namely, stability, attentiveness, and retention with regard to the object-support. The remaining relationship suggests a reciprocity between insight and mindfulness: either the practitioner first applies mindfulness to the object-support and afterward investigates it, presumably through insight; or the practitioner penetrates the object-support first, again presumably through insight, and then afterward applies mindfulness. In the latter case, mindfulness protects that initial insight like a gatekeeper. Elsewhere, the *Mahāvibhāṣā* summarily characterizes this reciprocal relationship between mindfulness and insight in a similar manner: either insight is applied to an object-support through the initial power of mindfulness, or the initial power of insight enables the subsequent application of mindfulness to the object-support.[57]

The *Abhidharmakośabhāṣya* by Vasubandhu (fourth or fifth century AD), in the context of analyzing the compound *smṛtyupasthāna* (mindfulness applications), also presents these two alternative relationships between insight and mindfulness: namely, either insight is applied through mindfulness (*tad evaṃ smṛtyo 'patiṣṭhate*), or mindfulness is applied through insight (*smṛtir anayo 'patiṣṭhate*).[58] Though both alternatives are attested in the *Mahāvibhāṣā*, as indicated above, Vasubandhu attributes the first, whereby mindfulness is the cause of insight, to the Sarvāstivāda-Vaibhāṣikas, while he endorses the second, whereby mindfulness is the consequence of insight. As

Vasubandhu explains, in the operation of these applications, one fixes or notes (*abhilapana*) the object through mindfulness as it had already been seen through insight.[59]

Saṅghabhadra also explores various relationships between mindfulness and insight, correlating them to the *Mahāvibhāṣā*'s three senses of the scriptural term *applications of mindfulness* as discussed above.[60] In the case of the first sense, that is, the applications as intrinsic nature, Saṅghabhadra, apparently reflecting the view attributed to the Sarvāstivāda-Vaibhāṣikas by Vasubandhu, asserts that insight is established and retained through the initial power of mindfulness; insight can be applied to the object only if assisted by the power of mindfulness. In the case of the second sense, that is, the applications through connection, mindfulness and insight are simultaneous and function reciprocally; insight is able to cognize the object clearly only if it is retained by the power of mindfulness, and mindfulness is able to fix the object only if retained by the power of insight. Finally, in the case of the third sense, that is, the applications as object-supports, initial insight applies mindfulness to a given object-support.

In the later Abhidharma literature, therefore, the set of applications of mindfulness lose their earlier scriptural status as a set of independent and self-sufficient practices and, instead, are incorporated within a comprehensive path structure. As a part of this larger set of practices, the applications of mindfulness become reinterpreted as modes of insight. In all probability, this reinterpretation results from a recognition that insight is indispensable for the eradication of defilements—the primary objective of the Abhidharma path. Further, the integration of the applications of mindfulness with insight is consistent with the earlier scriptural link between mindfulness and awareness (*samprajanya*) and indicates the partial assimilation of the operation of awareness by mindfulness. One moment of this reinterpretation, represented by the Sarvāstivāda-Vaibhāṣikas, stresses the traditional observational and preparatory aspect of mindfulness; hence, they would traditionally be associated with the view that mindfulness precedes insight. This emphasis on the preparatory aspect of mindfulness parallels meditational interpretations in other traditions.[61] The other moment, represented by Vasubandhu, who places insight before mindfulness, stresses, by implication, the psychologically retentive, and possibly recollective, aspects of mindfulness.

The Development of a Psychological Description of Mindfulness in Abhidharma

Parallel to the reinterpretation of the applications of mindfulness as varieties of insight, there emerges a new analysis of the function of mindfulness as an ordinary psychological operation or, in Abhidharma terminology, as a mental factor concomitant with the mind (*caittadharma*). Evidence of this new psychological function of mindfulness is found not only in overtly psychological descriptions of mental processes, but also in Abhidharma formulas that define traditional mindfulness praxes. Such passages no longer simply equate the mindfulness force, controlling factor, limb of enlightenment, and member of the eightfold noble path with the soteriologically oriented four applications of mindfulness. Rather, the definition of these praxes is extended to include particular psychological operations, which are directed toward objects of contemplation.

In fact, some scriptural definitions of mindfulness techniques allude to this extended, more prosaic sense of mindfulness. For example, one recurrent scriptural formula describes the practice of mindfulness as involving the "retention or reflection upon what has been done or said in the past by one possessed of utmost mindfulness and prudence."[62] Another scriptural passage distinguishes two varieties of correct mindfulness (*samyaksmṛti*): that which tends toward the fluxes; and that which does not tend toward the fluxes, but which instead is directed toward the notion of the four noble truths. Both varieties operate through retention (**smaraṇa*) and recollection (**pratismaraṇa, *saṃsmaraṇa*).[63]

Psychological description becomes the norm in Abhidharma definitions of the praxis-related modes of mindfulness and largely displaces the previously cited definitions of mindfulness in terms of the four applications. Among the Pāli Abhidhamma texts, the *Dhammasaṅgaṇi* and the *Vibhaṅga* use the same formula in defining virtually all modes of mindfulness: "that mindfulness, which is reflection, recollection; mindfulness which is retentiveness, the state of supporting, the state of nondrifting (or fixing), the state of nonlosing; mindfulness, which is the mindfulness controlling factor, the mindfulness force, correct mindfulness."[64] Northern Indian Abhidharma texts employ a similar definition of the psychological functioning of mindfulness: "mindfulness is reflection, remembering, recollection, the nonremoving, the nonlosing, the nonleaving, the nonflowing away, the state of the nonlosing of factors, the state of the nondrifting (or fixing or noting) of the mind."[65]

Whereas the *Dharmaskandha* combines the psychological description with the more traditional definition in terms of the four applications,[66] the psychological definition of the new function of *smṛti* as a discrete mental factor concomitant with the mind also appears alone in Abhidharma passages, with no reference to the four applications or to any other soteriologically oriented praxes. These psychological definitions tend to be similar, though they lack the formulaic regularity of the praxis-related definitions. This freer pattern of definition suggests a growing interest in psychological events per se, and results in an innovative analytic categorization and investigation of individual psychological phenomena. Whereas the *Dhātukāya* offers a relatively lengthy definition very similar to that presented above,[67] the *Prakaraṇapāda*, *Śāriputrābhidharmaśāstra*, and **Abhidharmahṛdayaśāstra*, as well as later Abhidharma texts offer more abbreviated definitions that emphasize the retentive function of mindfulness with regard to a particular object: for example, mindfulness is the nonloss (or nondrifting) of mind events;[68] or mindfulness is retention (**smaraṇa*) and recollection (**pratismaraṇa*, **saṃsmaraṇa*).[69] In these abbreviated definitions, the early Abhidharma formulas that combine religious and psychological functions are reduced: the psychologically significant aspect is extracted, and the inherited meditational context along with its soteriological orientation is omitted. The occurrence of these reduced formulas confirms that the middle-period Abhidharma texts are no longer interested only in conditions necessary for religious praxis, but are now interested also in the general psychological components of all mental functioning.

Excursus: The Development of the Psychological Function of Mindfulness

The development of the psychological characterization of mindfulness can be illumined by tracing the history and reinterpretation of key terms that provide transitional links between the early Abhidharma formulas and the succinct definitions of the mature Abhidharma compendia. The most problematic of these transitional terms are, in Pāli, *apilāpana*, and the apparently analogous Sanskrit term *abhilapana*, which becomes so important in the later Abhidharma psychological definitions of mindfulness. The complicated and often obscure history of these terms, in fact, encapsulates the transformation of mindfulness and its emergence as an ordinary psychological component.

In Pāli Abhidhamma texts, the term *apilāpana* appears consistently in definitions of mindfulness as "the state of *apilāpana*" (*apilāpanatā*) and "the state of nonlosing" (*asammusanatā*). Later Pāli postcanonical texts set the two defining characteristics of mindfulness as *apilāpana* and *upagaṇhana*, or "sustaining" (as of an object).[70] Although the exact sense of *apilāpana* in these formulas is unclear, its usage in the postcanonical texts and the later commentarial explanations would suggest two possible interpretations. First, the *Milindapañha*, in explaining this *apilāpana* function of mindfulness, employs the simile of a storekeeper, who reminds (*sarāpeti*) the king of the contents of his stores. Mindfulness, likewise, notes (*api-lāpeti*) or causes one to be attentive to factors, in particular to those virtuous factors such as the thirty-seven aids to enlightenment, calming, discerning, intuition, and liberation. Through this process of duly noting, mindfulness thereby enables one to cultivate those factors that are to be cultivated, and not to cultivate those that are not to be cultivated, and so on.[71] As a second interpretation, later commentaries explain *apilāpana* as "plunging," in the sense of entering into the object-support; it is the state of "not drifting" (*a-pilāpana-tā*), unlike gourd vessels, and so on, that float (*plavanti*) and do not enter the water.[72]

Both later Abhidharma and non-Abhidharma Sanskrit treatises use what would appear to be an analogous term, that is, *abhilapana,* in discussions of the psychological operation of mindfulness. Defining mindfulness as a separate mental factor, several Sanskrit sources use the term *abhilapana,* which involves some type of operation directed toward the object of consciousness. For example, the *Yogācārabhūmiśāstra* defines mindfulness as "having *abhilapana* that conforms to any given familiar object."[73] The *Abhidharmāvatāraśāstra* and the later *Abhidharmadīpavibhāṣāprabhāvṛtti* explain mindfulness as "*abhilapana* with regard to the object-referent of the mind, which is precisely the nonloss of past, present, or future action."[74] Vasubandhu's *Abhidharmakośabhāṣya* specifies mindfulness simply as "the nonloss (*asampramoṣa*) of the object-support;" Yaśomitra (c. eighth century AD) glosses this nonloss with the verb *abhilapati:* mindfulness is "that by connection with which the mind does not forget the object-support, and, as it were, *abhilapati* that [object-support]."[75] Sthiramati (sixth century AD) also, in commenting on the definition of mindfulness in Yogācāra treatises, includes the term *abhilapana.*[76] In his commentary on the *Triṃśikā,* Sthiramati identifies mindfulness as both the "nonloss of a familiar object and the state of *abhilapana* of the mind," thereby underscoring a close connection between nonloss (*asampramoṣa*) and *abhilapana* in the operation of *smṛti.*[77]

The precise meaning of *abhilapana* in these passages, however, is far from clear. One might expect that the sense of this term and its relationship to the Pāli *apilāpana* would be clarified by an examination of the early northern Indian Abhidharma materials. However, a precise terminological investigation using the extant Chinese versions of these texts, unfortunately, is virtually impossible. This is due in part to the absence of any detailed exegesis of the terms *abhilapana* or *apilāpana* in the early Abhidharma texts. Equally as important, however, is the obfuscating effect of the Chinese translations of the term, particularly those of Hsüan-tsang (seventh century AD), who translated the majority of the Abhidharma treatises.[78] Hsüan-tsang's translations would appear to betray a systematic homogenizing that has retrospectively standardized the variation of the original Abhidharma materials according to norms derived from his earlier translations.[79] It is possible that Hsüan-tsang was influenced in his understanding of mindfulness by Sthiramati, specifically Sthiramati's glosses on mindfulness in his commentary on the *Abhidharmasamuccaya,* which Hsüan-tsang translated prior to any early Abhidharma texts.[80]

What then is the meaning of the term *abhilapana* in the later Sanskrit treatises, and how is it related historically either to the Pāli term *apilāpana* or to the analogous term as used in the early Abhidharma materials? The difficulty posed by these questions would be mitigated if the literature itself offered a univocal derivation of these terms. However, as was clear from the variant interpretations of *apilāpana* within the Pāli postcanonical and commentarial literature, no univocal derivation is recognized. As mentioned previously, later Pāli postcanonical texts connect *apilāpana* and *upagaṇhana,* or "sustaining," in the definition of mindfulness. Reminiscent of this connection are Yaśomitra's comments on Vasubandhu's use of the term *abhilapana* to explain the function of mindfulness in the applications of mindfulness.[81] Here Yaśomitra characterizes the activity of *abhilapana* toward the object of mindfulness as that of "taking up," or "sustaining," or perhaps more appropriately "noting" or "fixing." Such a sense would be consistent with the traditional connection between mindfulness and attentiveness. As noted previously, however, there are at least two possible derivations for the terms *apilāpana* and *abhilapana,* each of which would lend a different sense to the operation of mindfulness: one derived from the root *plu,* "to float," with a privative prefix (*a-pilāpana*); and the other apparently derived from the root *lap* possibly in the sense "to repeat" or, especially in the causative, "to note" with a prefix *api,* or possibly *abhi.*[82] The derivation from the root *plu* with a privative would support the sense of "not drifting," "entering," or "fixing." The derivation from the root *lap* could have the sense of "to repeat" or, especially in the causative, "to note," or possibly the sense of "to chatter" or "to express." Indeed some of the later Sanskrit commentators, especially Sthiramati, appear to have understood *abhilapana* as derived from the root *lap* with the sense, "to chatter" or "to express," by analogy with other related technical derivations such as *abhilāpa.*[83]

Given the vicissitudes of textual transmission and translation, it is impossible to determine which derivation, if either exclusively, is assumed by the early northern Indian Abhidharma treatises. It is possible that *apilāpana* and *abhilapana* were seen to have different derivations in some contexts, but were held to be equivalent in the context of *smṛti.* But it is also possible that a bifurcation in a once single term occurred through a later divergent derivation assumed by either the Pāli or Sanskrit commentators. Although the relationship between these terms cannot be unraveled, we should not assume that in the early northern Indian Abhidharma literature *abhilapana* necessarily has the technical sense of "mental chatter" that was later assigned to *abhilāpa* by commentators such as Sthiramati.[84] Indeed, *apilāpana, abhilapana,* and mindfulness itself in its early development as a mental factor may have no connection with verbal expression and its attendant negative connotations. Instead, these terms, whether derived from *plu* or *lap,* may be intended simply to suggest an attentive noting or fixing. This function of noting or fixing is critical both to mindfulness in religious praxis and, as will be shown, to mindfulness in the ordinary psychological sense.

Irrespective of their original sense or etymological derivation, the terms *apilāpana* or *abhilapana* become prominent in Abhidharma analyses of the psychological functions of mindfulness. However, the use of the term *abhilapana* in the mature Abhidharma literature should not be interpreted in terms of the technical sense of mental chatter, a sense that probably represents a special, divergent interpretation associated with mindfulness by the later commentators. Rather, *apilāpana* and *abhilapana* should be seen as part of a progressive reinterpretation and reappropriation of a single, inherited tradition concerning mindfulness that traces back to the earliest sources.

The Psychological Operation of Mindfulness in Abhidharma

Though the early Abhidharma formulaic definitions of the psychological function of mindfulness as a discrete mental factor are not sufficient to provide a clear picture of its operation, later Abhidharma treatises furnish more information. This is provided in descriptions of the relation of mindfulness to other mental factors, in arguments concerning its existential status, and finally, in examinations of the events of retention and recollection, in which mindfulness plays a central role. In these passages, the operation of mindfulness and, in particular, its role in the act of recollection must be understood in terms of the general Buddhist model of psychological functioning.

The basic model of psychological functioning proposed in virtually all Abhidharma materials analyzes each mental event into its constituent factors; however, the number, identity, and modes of interaction among these mental factors become major points of disagreement among Buddhist Abhidharma schools. The Kāśmīra Sarvāstivādin school holds that each moment is defined by one mind event (*citta*). This mind event performs only the most general function of cognition; it serves primarily to define one moment of the mind, and to demarcate it from the next in the psychic stream. However, every mind event is accompanied by a number of concomitant mental factors (*caittadharma*), each of which fulfills a specific function occurring in that single moment. But certain Abhidharma masters, for example, the Dārṣṭāntikas, deny the discrete psychological functions and separate existence of the majority of these mental factors; therefore, they reject the model of the simultaneous occurrence of a mind event with other concomitant mental factors.[85] Instead, they propose a serial model of psychological functioning, in which a mind event and its concomitant mental factors operate in succession. They also drastically reduce the number of mental factors, and conflate their activities to only a few recognized factors. Thus, there are two divergent interpretative models: that supported by the Kāśmīra Sarvāstivādins of a single mind event associated with concomitant factors; and that advanced by the Dārṣṭāntikas of a mind event followed by mental factors in a series. These two models of psychological functioning entail a radically different understanding of the operation of mindfulness and the event of recollection.

Among the over forty-six possible concomitant mental factors enumerated by the Kāśmīra Sarvāstivādin school, ten, including mindfulness, are associated with and function in each and every mind event (*caittā mahābhūmikāḥ*).[86] These ten factors, whether by grasping the given object or discerning a particular quality of it, carry out some function integral to the constantly repeated process of perception that constitutes each moment.[87] As noted previously, mindfulness functions to cause the nonloss (*asampramoṣa*) of the object, and the fixing or noting (*abhilapana*) by the mind of the object. Such a definition is ambiguous—it could refer either to functions critical to the maintenance of meditative concentration, or to the more prosaic act of retention. However, there is some evidence to indicate that such a definition of mindfulness refers explicitly to the ordinary psychological event of recollection. In the course of a discussion on the relation between mindfulness and insight, the *Mahāvibhāṣā* presents several distinctive functions of mindfulness that relate to the event of recollection: for example, through the power of mindfulness, the object is not lost, enabling one to give rise to both specific and general activities with regard to it; or through the power of mindfulness, the practitioner thoroughly fixes or notes the object-support, and even if the object-support is forgotten, it can be recollected once again; or, mindfulness stabilizes or sustains the object-support, enabling insight to investigate it, or supports insight itself.[88] Here mindfulness performs the functions of retention, noting or fixing, and stabilizing that are requisite for recollection.

This connection between the operation of mindfulness and recollection is made explicit in an argument about the existential status of mindfulness. The argument occurs between the Kāśmīra Sarvāstivāda-Vaibhāṣika master Saṅghabhadra, and his major opponent, Sthavira, identified as the Dārṣṭāntika master, Śrīlāta (fourth–fifth century AD).[89] Saṅghabhadra identifies the activity of mindfulness as that of fixing or noting (*ming-chi*, **abhilapana*), which must occur when the mind cognizes any object.[90] But Śrīlāta, who denies the separate existence of all but three mental concomitants—feelings, conception, and volition[91]—claims that mindfulness is not a separate mental factor operating on present objects in each momentary mind event. Instead, mindfulness, which for Śrīlāta means specifically memory of the past, is used merely as a provisional designation to refer to mental operations directed toward past objects.[92] The activity of fixing or noting attributed to mindfulness by Saṅghabhadra, for Śrīlāta, is simply a feature of the operation of knowledge in general (*jñānākāra*) and does not necessitate the existence of mindfulness as a separate factor.

Saṅghabhadra's response indicates that it is precisely fixing or noting, which is the distinctive activity of mindfulness, that links mindfulness to ordinary memory:

> [Śrilāta's statement that mindfulness] is used as a provisional designation with regard to past objects establishes unequivocally that it functions with regard to present object-supports, [for] if there is no fixing (or noting) (*ming-chi*, **abhilapana*) with regard to a present object, no recollection (**pratismaraṇa*, **saṃsmaraṇa*) of the past object will be produced afterward.[93]

In other words, memory of a past object occurs through the functioning of mindfulness, specifically in its operation of fixing or noting that occurs in each moment. Further, Saṅghabhadra contends that the features of knowledge (investigation and repeated examination of an object) are to be distinguished from those of mindfulness (fixing or noting and causing nonloss). For that reason, Saṅghabhadra claims, tradition asserts that mindfulness is that "fixing (or noting) which causes the mind not to lose the experienced object."[94]

Thus, for Saṅghabhadra, mindfulness is not simply the recollection of past objects, but rather the activities of fixing or noting and retention as they occur with regard to every present object. Indeed, in the absence of this activity of mindfulness, which fixes or notes the present object in each and every moment, subsequent recollection would be impossible.[95] This interpretation of the activity of mindfulness undoubtedly shows the influence of the Sarvāstivādin model of psychological functioning that views all psychological events as separate factors, some of which, including mindfulness, occur in each moment. It is also, however, completely consistent with the traditional praxis-related function of mindfulness, which stabilizes and attentively observes a present object without distraction.

These different views of mindfulness as functioning with regard to past or present objects reflect different views of its role in the events of retention and recollection. For those who claim that mindfulness pertains only to past objects, *smṛti* provisionally refers to the conventional experience of memory: it is the recollection of a previously experienced object. Śrīlāta, Sthiramati, and Hsüan-tsang would all accept this view.[96] Memory is then not a distinct function attributed to a discrete and actually existing mental factor. Instead, as Vasubandhu explains, memory refers to a process whereby recollection arises as a result of a complex set of conditions.[97]

For the Sarvāstivāda-Vaibhāṣikas, however, *smṛti* is a separately existing factor that operates on present objects in each and every moment; it is this present functioning of fixing or noting that enables the subsequent event of recollection. Therefore, though the Sarvāstivāda-Vaibhāṣikas would accept that the process of recollection generally occurs as Vasubandhu describes, they would not limit *smṛti* to the event of recollection.

The Problem of Accounting for Continuity: Sarvāstivādin Solutions

The source for the general model of recollection accepted by both Vasubandhu and the later Sarvāstivāda-Vaibhāṣikas can be found in the *Mahāvibhāṣā*, in a passage containing a lengthy refutation of eight Buddhist and non-Buddhist theories concerning ordinary memory.[98] All the refuted theories attempt to explain memory by postulating a continuing objective or subjective substratum that underlies, and thereby unites, prior experiences and subsequent recollections. For example, some non-Buddhists propose a theory of impregnation, whereby essences of events exist latent in one another, providing the impetus for their mutual recollection. Some suggest a theory of transformation, whereby the events of one moment transform to become the events of the next moment. Others adopt a theory of transference, whereby the events of one moment are transferred to, or continue to exist within, the events of the next moment. Still others shift the unchanging substratum from an objective sphere to a subjective one. This position asserts that cognition is singular in essence, uniting the activities of both performance and recollection; the prior momentary mental event conveys its experiences to a subsequent moment of mind that is capable of recollection. Among the refuted Buddhist theorists, some propose a personality (*pudgala*) that unites prior and subsequent events within the same being. Others propose an additional mind element (**manodhātu*) that underlies all specific and transitory moments of perceptual consciousness and is able to remember their contents. Still others maintain that two aggregates constitute each being—a transitory active aggregate and a permanent fundamental aggregate that recollects events performed previously by the active aggregate. Other Buddhists propose a subtle transmission of mind, from a prior moment that performs action, to a subsequent moment that cognizes or recognizes that action.

All such theories, the *Mahāvibhāṣā* recommends, are to be rejected by true Buddhists in favor of a model that assumes no unchanging substratum or essential transference but, nonetheless, accounts for recollection. The model endorsed by the *Mahāvibhāṣā* anticipates later equations of *smṛti* with recollection: "through the power of familiarity, sentient beings obtain knowledge homogeneous with a certain factor, which enables them to cognize [that factor] in the same way in which it was previously experienced."[99] Later in the same passage, a slightly different model is offered: a receptive moment of mind becomes the primary cause of mindfulness of an object-support, which is then not lost.[100] In this definition, *mind* refers to a previously produced mental "bundle" (*kalāpa*), which was receptive in the sense that it assumed either the features (*ākāra*) of a particular object-support or the object-support (*ālambana*) itself.[101] *Mindfulness* then refers to the subsequently produced mental bundle; its nonloss is further said to be contingent on the mind being not distracted and not oppressed by suffering.

In this definition from the *Mahāvibhāṣā*, mindfulness is one operational moment in the event of recollection. It requires the successful coordination of three conditions: (1) securely grasped characteristics of the object previously experienced; (2) the present occurrence of a series homogeneous with that previous experience; and (3) the nonloss of mindfulness.[102] Using Buddhist terminology, an object, once forgotten, can be recollected when knowledge that accords with that object arises within the homogeneous stream of a particular sentient being. Therefore, recollection requires a single causally connected, that is, homogeneous, stream of experiences and some experience that is similar to that prior object. For example, recollection can be stimulated by repetition, by a similar object, or by circumstances conducive to recollection.[103] Contrariwise, an object, once recollected, can be forgotten once again. Forgetfulness, or lapse of mindfulness, ensues from distraction of the mind, which can be attributed to a number of causes: oppression by suffering at birth or death; the present occurrence of other deliberations; dulled sense organs occupied with other cognitive activity; oppression by the suffering of an undesirable rebirth state; the distraction, wavering, and carelessness of the five sense organs with regard to an object; the present occurrence of heavy obscurations due to defilements; or mental distraction due to the absence of the cultivation of concentration.[104]

Saṅghabhadra clarifies the process of recollection described in the *Mahāvibhāṣā* and renders explicit the function of mindfulness as a discrete mental factor in this process. He rejects the position of Śrīlāta, who argues that recollection of an object from the distant past arises not from the past object itself, but rather through the mediation of a series of successively dependent causes, originating from the prior perceptual consciousness of that object.[105] For Saṅghabhadra, who accepts the Sarvāstivādin view that factors of all three time periods exist, even a past object actually exists and can itself serve as the direct object of and, therefore, direct cause for a later recollection.

Saṅghabhadra also rejects Śrīlāta's theory that a residue of past experience, or a subsidiary element (*sui-chieh, *anudhātu*) produced as a result of the original perception, is preserved and awakened in subsequent recollection.[106] Similarly, Saṅghabhadra rejects other theories that assign mindfulness a provisional existential status as a seed (*smṛtibīja*) or a potency, which, once generated from a prior experience of knowledge, remains dormant until, with the proper conditions, it produces a subsequent experience of memory.[107] For Saṅghabhadra, mindfulness cannot be a "mindfulness seed" that exists merely as a provisional designation for a complex process. Rather, in accordance with Sarvāstivādin psychological analysis, mindfulness is a discrete and actually existing mental factor that arises together with each mind event. That mindfulness, which arises simultaneously with the knowledge of a prior experience, has the capability to initiate a series of mindfulness factors, one of which will arise simultaneously with the subsequent recollecting knowledge. Thus, Saṅghabhadra, like Vasubandhu, Śrīlāta, and others, does assert that a successive cause and effect relation underlies the event of recollection. But, unlike them, he denies that this serial cause-and-effect relation is one simply between two moments of knowledge: one moment that grasps the original object and a subsequent one that is provisionally described as its recollection. Instead, according to Saṅghabhadra, the causal series consists of successive moments of *smṛti*, each of which is an actually existing concomitant mental factor, which appears simultaneous with mind events and performs a function essential to the process of recollection.[108]

Conclusion

If the Abhidharma analysis of mindfulness ends as a psychological theory of recollection, it begins in the praxis-oriented cultivation of calm preparedness. Thus, an interpretation of mindfulness merely as an operational aspect of cognition and a corresponding translation as memory ignore not only its initial significance, but also the transformational history of its development, from the early scriptures through the various phases of Abhidharma literature. This transformation occurs through both a selective emphasis of components of the traditional formulaic definitions, and a progressive incorporation of new elements that reflect dogmatic and philosophical innovation. The development of the term *mindfulness* results not simply from an internal dynamic of independent inquiry, but reflects the broader evolution of Buddhist thought. Central to this evolution is a shift of emphasis from praxis-concerned formulations to analytical investigations and taxonomies. In the Abhidharma, this entails the expansion of the analytical categories to include exhaustively all aspects of experience and an increasingly detailed study of both individual phenomena and their dynamic interrelations. In the case of mindfulness this shift of emphasis is evident in the expansion of the traditional objects of the praxis-related applications of mindfulness to include all phenomena, in the integration of the formerly independent praxis-related variety of mindfulness into the larger path structure, in the reinterpretation of the four applications of mindfulness as a mode of insight, and in the emergence of mindfulness as an independent event in the developing structural analysis of cognitive and psychological functioning.

The mature description of the function of mindfulness in recollection cannot be understood except as an outcome of continual molding and adaptation of the primary senses of mindfulness as an attentiveness operative in praxis. Even the later debates between the different Abhidharma schools still echo this original primary sense within the confines of their respective doctrinal concerns. For the Sarvāstivāda-Vaibhāṣikas, mindfulness is a mental event that occurs with regard to each object in every moment of psychic life. It enables the simultaneous insight or cognition of that object to occur and provides a necessary condition for later recollection. This specific doctrinal position, like many others, is both a motive for and a consequence of the general Sarvāstivādin philosophical model: that factors exist as real entities in the past, present, and future, but are radically momentary in terms of their activity; and that each moment of psychological functioning consists of a demarcating mind event, which is accompanied by discrete simultaneous mental factors. Therefore, mindfulness, as one such mental factor, can occur together with other mental activities, and even when past, can itself serve as the real cause for present recollection. In fixing or noting every present object, mindfulness performs an action essential for subsequent recollection. Other Abhidharma schools accept a serial view of psychological functioning, whereby each moment consists in only one mental activity; therefore, the cognition of an object cannot be simultaneous with any other mental activity, including mindfulness. Rejecting the reality of anything other than present factors, they relegate mindfulness to the status of a provisional designation referring to subsequent recollection.

Both these theories, the Sarvāstivādin and the serial view, must be understood within the context of the general Buddhist cognitive model. As its central feature, that model rejects the existence of a stable perduring self (*ātman*) capable of serving as the basis for the transmission of memories and as the locus for the occurrence of recollection. But certain Abhidharma schools, for example, those that adhere to the theory of seeds, invoke a commonsense model of memory by implying a virtual substratum, even though they claim not to have incurred the consequences of positing a continuous self. Their system of storage and retrieval via the preservation of dormant seeds and their awakening at recollection becomes the basis for later Yogācāra models.

The Sarvāstivāda-Vaibhāṣika model exhibits the strictest adherence to the Buddhist doctrine of nonself and momentariness, and the praxis-related function of *smṛti* as mindfulness. The problem of providing a coherent account of experience, including memory, in the face of this strict adherence entailed the ontological position for which they are famous: that factors of all three time periods exist and can function as causes. In this Sarvāstivādin Buddhist model, the contradiction posed to Buddhist premises by a continuous substratum implicit within a strictly linear classical model of memory is avoided. However, there emerges the different problematic of, first, discriminating among the particular factors within the universe of equally real and available past, present, and future events that now constitute the experience of any individual and, second, distinguishing the experience of one individual from that of another. The Sarvāstivādins find the solution to these practical problems in a panoply of causes, mindfulness among them, whose purpose is to demarcate specific events for specific activities. Recollection then becomes a function of whether or not the mindfulness that is forever associated with a particular experienced object is activated by the requisite conditions in any given subsequent moment.

From the Buddhist perspective, the ingenuity of the Sarvāstivādins lies in their devising an ontological model that mediates experience in a way consistent with the Buddhist premises. Their model for mindfulness and recollection preserves the praxis emphasized in the early texts within a self-denying and moment-directed analysis, while still countering the obvious philosophical challenge of other models that assume the continuity of moral and psychic experience based on a self. From the Western perspective, which views memory primarily in terms of the simple recollection of past events, however, the Sarvāstivādin emphasis on the initial moment of a simultaneous attentive observation, cognitive fixing or noting, and retention, not only presents an alternative account for memory, but also suggests a radical reconsideration of Western models of psychological functioning.

Notes

See list of abbreviations below.

1. For a brief survey of uses of and references to *smṛti* throughout Indian Buddhist literature, see Kōgen Mizuno, *Pāri Bukkyō o chūshin to shite Bukkyō no shinshikiron* (1964; reprint, Tokyo: Pitaka, 1978), pp. 603ff. See also Étienne Lamotte, trans., *Le traité de la grande vertu de sagesse,* 5 vols., Publications de l'Institut Orientaliste de Louvain 2 (Louvain: Institut Orientaliste Université de Louvain, 1979), vol. 3, pp. 1121–23; and Ryūjō Yamada, *Daijō Bukkyō seiritsuron josetsu* (Tokyo: Heirakuji shoten, 1959), pp. 49–51ff.

2. See SN 54 *Ānāpānasaṃyutta* 5: 311ff, SA 29 #803–814 T.2 206a–209b; MN #118 *Ānāpānasatisutta* 3: 78ff; cf. *Fo shuo ch'ih-i ching* T.1 (96) 918a–b. For mindfulness of respiration as a component of mindfulness with regard to the body, see MN #10 *Satipaṭṭhānasutta* 1: 56; MA 24 #98 T.1 582c12ff.

3. For the list of ten reflections, characteristic of the *Aṅguttaranikāya* and the *Ekottarāgama*, see AN 1.16 *Ekadhamma* 1: 30, EA 1 T.2 550b17–19, 1 T.2 552c–553c; and EA 2 T.2 554a–557a. Cf. also AN 1.20 *Aparaaccharāsaṅghātavaggo* 1: 42; EA 42 T.2 779c26ff, 42 T.2 780c4ff, 43 T.2 781a2ff. For six reflections, excluding the last four in this group of ten, that appear in the *Dīrghāgama* and *Saṃyuktāgama*, see DA 2 #2 T.1 12a13–15, 9 #11 T.1 58a20–21; SA 30 #858 T.2 218b27–28; cf. AN 11.2 *Anussativaggo* 5: 329ff, passim; SA 20 #550 T.2 143b18ff, 33 #932–33 T.2 238b24–27, 33 T.2 238c22–23; cf. AN 6.3.25–26 *Anussatiṭṭhanasutta* and *Mahākaccānasutta* 3: 312ff. Only the six reflections appear in northern Indian Abhidharma texts: see SP 16 T.26 433a2ff, Valentina Stache-Rosen, *Das Saṅgītisūtra und sein Kommentar Saṅgītiparyāya 1, Dogmatische Begriffsreihen im älteren Buddhismus 2*, Sanskrittexte aus den Turfanfunden 9 (Berlin: Akademie-Verlag, 1968), 172; DS 8 T.26 492c6ff; ŚAŚ 16 T.28 637a20ff; MVB 15 T.27 74c22, 97 T.27 503c17–18, 106 T.27 547c19. For eight reflections, see **Mahāprajñāpāramitāsūtropadeśa* 21 T.25 218c21ff. For reflection on previous rebirth states as one of the supernormal powers, see, for example, MN #6 *Ākaṅkheyyasutta* 1: 35; SA 29 #815 T.2 209c27, passim.

4. Major dialogues on the four applications of mindfulness occur in the *Majjhimanikāya* and *Madhyamāgama* (MN #10 *Satipaṭṭhānasutta* 1: 55ff; MA 24 #98 T.1 582b9ff), and *Dīghanikāya* (DN #22 *Mahāsatipaṭṭhānasutta* 2: 290–315). Cf. also MA 18 #74 T.1 543c1ff; EA 5 T.2 568a1ff. The *Aṅguttaranikāya* (AN 9.7 *Satipaṭṭhānavaggo* 4: 457ff), the *Saṃyuttanikāya* (SN 47 *Satipaṭṭhānasaṃyutta* 5: 141ff), and the *Saṃyuktāgama* (SA 24 #605–39 T.2 170c–77c) each contains a section of dialogues on the topic of the four applications. Chih-i's sixth century *Ssu nien-ch'u* T.46. (1918) testifies to the continuing importance of the four applications.

5. See SN 48.11 *Paṭilābhasutta* 5: 200; AN 5.2.15 *Daṭṭhabbasutta* 3: 12; SA 26 #655 T.2 183b29, 26 #658 T.2 184a4, 26 #675 T.2 185c12, 26 #691 T.2 188a27.

6. Lin Li-kouang, *L'aide-mémoire de la vraie loi* (*Saddharma-smṛtyupasthāna-sūtra*), *Recherches sur un Sūtra Développé du Petit Véhicule*, Publications du Musée Guimet Bibliothèque d'Études 54 (Paris: Adrien-Maisonneuve, 1949), pp. 118–27; Lambert Schmithausen, "Die vier Konzentrationen der Aufmerksamkeit: Zur geschichtlichen Entwicklung einer spirituellen Praxis des Buddhismus," *Zeitschrift für Missionswissenschaft und Religionswissenschaft* 4 (1976): 241–66. Cf. Leon Hurvitz, "Fa-sheng's Observations on the Four Stations of Mindfulness," in *Mahāyāna Buddhist Meditation, Theory and Practice*, ed. Minoru Kiyota, (Honolulu: University Press of Hawaii, 1978), pp. 207–48.

7. See Lin, *L'aide-mémoire*, pp. 122ff. See also the later Abhidharma text, the *Śāriputrābhidharmaśāstra* (ŚAŚ 15 T.28 625a10–11, 625a26ff), where mindfulness with regard to the body alone is identified as the path consisting of one member and is listed apart from the set of four applications, which is then identified as one instance of the path of four members.

8. Schmithausen, "Die vier Konzentrationen," pp. 253ff. The textual priority of the mindfulness of the body is based, he argues, on the unfounded assumption that

the breath and corpse observation are original elements of the account. Through a detailed comparative examination of the specific stages of practice in each of the four applications, as presented in the Pāli and Chinese scriptural sources of these dialogues, Schmithausen attempts to prove that the breath and corpse observation are secondary in both form and content. Instead, he contends that the stereotyped formulaic accounts of mindfulness of feelings and of mind events represent, in these textual accounts, the prior stratum common to all four applications, which was later supplemented with concretizing examples that are not original, but instead represent a formulaic reworking of independent material.

9. MN #119 *Kāyagatāsatisutta* 3: 89: *tassa evaṃ appamattassa ātāpino pahitattassa viharato ye gehasitā sarasaṅkappā te pahīyanti. tesaṃ pahānā ajjhattam eva cittaṃ santiṭṭhati sannisīdati ekodi hoti samādhiyati. evaṃ bhikkhave bhikkhu kāyagatāsatiṃ bhāveti.* Cf. MA 20 #81 T.1 555a14–17, passim. See also MN #125 *Dantabhūmisutta* 3: 136: . . . *ime cattāro satipaṭṭhānā cetaso upanibandhanā honti . . . gehasitānaṃ ceva sarasaṅkappānaṃ abhinimmadanāya.* Cf. MA 52 #198 T.1 758b5ff, where the Chinese translation reads "household" for *geha*, presuming a reading equivalent to the Sanskrit, *gṛha*, in contrast to both Vasubandhu and Yaśomitra, who cite *gardha*. Cf. AKB 6.70 p. 384.26ff: . . . *smṛtyupasthānāni cetasa upanibaddhāni bhavanti yāvad eva gardhāśritānāṃ smarasaṃkalpānāṃ prativinodanāya;* SAKV p. 604.1ff: *gardhāśritānāṃ tṛṣṇāśritānām ity arthaḥ. smarasaṃkalpānām ity anubhūtaviṣayasmṛtisaṃkalpānām ity arthaḥ. kāmasaṃkalpānām iti vā.* For another interpretation of *sarasaṅkappa*, see I. B. Horner, ed., *Papañcasūdanī Majjhimanikāyaṭṭhakathā of Buddhaghosācariya*, 5 parts, Indexes (London: The Pali Text Society, 1977), parts 4–5: p. 144.

10. Cf. MA 20 #81 T.1 557b7ff, for a listing of eighteen beneficial results.

11. See MN #10 *Satipaṭṭhānasutta* 1: 56; DN #22 *Mahāsatipaṭṭhānasutta* 2: 290; SN 47.1 *Ambapālisutta* 5: 141: *ekāyano ayaṃ bhikkhave maggo sattānaṃ visuddhiyā sokaparidevānaṃ samatikkamāya dukkhadomanassānaṃ atthaṅgamāya ñāyassa adhigāmāya nibbānassa sacchikiriyāya yad idaṃ cattāro satipaṭṭhānā.* Cf. SN 47.18 *Brahmasutta* 5: 167; SA 24 #607 T.2 171a9ff; MA 24 #98 T.1 582b9ff; and EA 5 T.2 568a2ff, which also offers a commentary on this formula. See also ŚAŚ 13 T.28 612b28ff, for an exegesis of this introductory formula, and MVB 188 T.27 943a19ff, for an extensive examination of its implications for the other members of the thirty-seven aids to enlightenment.

12. See MA 24 #98 T.1 582b11ff. Cf. SA 18 #498 T.2 131a11ff, SN 47.12 *Nālandāsutta* 5: 160ff.

13. SN 47.37–38 *Chandasutta* and *Pariññātasutta* 5: 181–82 (cf. SA 24 #634 T.2 176a7ff); AN 1.21 *Kāyagatāsativaggo* 1: 43ff. See SN 47.11 *Mahāpurisasutta* 5: 158, SA 24 #614 T.2 172a13ff; SN 47.50 *Āsavasutta* 5: 190. Cf. also SN 47.33 *Viraddhasutta* 5: 180; SN 47.31 *Ananussutasutta* 5: 179, where the four applications are identified with the noble path, through which one attains the knowledge (*ñāṇa*), insight (*paññā*), and intuition (*vijjā*) that characterize the enlightenment experience; or SN 47.32 *Virāgasutta* 5: 179, where the practice of the four applications results in

unalloyed aversion (*ekantanibbida*), dispassion (*virāga*), cessation (*nirodha*), calm (*upasama*), special knowledge (*abhiññā*), complete enlightenment (*sambodha*), and nibbāna.

14. SN 47.3 *Bhikkhusutta* 5: 142ff; SA 24 #636 T.2 176a19ff; SA #635 176a10ff; SN 47.15 *Bāhiyasutta* 5: 165ff: *khīṇā jāti vusitaṃ brahmacariyaṃ kataṃ karaṇīyaṃ nāparaṃ itthattāyā;* SA 24 #627 T.2 175a17ff. Cf. SN 47.46 *Pāṭimokkhasaṃvarasutta* 5: 187–88.

15. SN 47.13 *Cundasutta* 5: 161ff, SA 24 #638 T.2 177a7ff; SN 47.14 *Ukkacelasutta* 5: 164–65; SA 24 #639 T.2 177b2ff; DN #16 *Mahāparinibbānasutta* 2: 100, DN #26 *Cakkavattisutta* 3: 58, DA 6 #6 T.1 39a26ff. Cf. Hakuju Ui, "Agon ni arawaretaru bonten," in *Indo tetsugaku kenkyū* (Tokyo: Iwanami shoten, 1965), vol. 3, pp. 69ff; Shōkan Andō, "Shibu Shiagon ni okeru shinenjo ni tsuite," *Indogaku Bukkyōgaku kenkyū* 30, no. 2 (1982): 138–39.

16. SN 47.22 *Ciraṭṭhitisutta* 5: 172ff, passim.

17. MN #10 *Satipaṭṭhānasutta* 1: 56: . . . *bhikkhu kāye kāyānupassī viharati ātāpī sampajāno satimā vineyya loke abhijjhādomanassaṃ vedanāsu vedanānupassī viharati* . . . ; DN #22 *Mahāsatipaṭṭhānasutta* 2: 290 (quoted in SAKV p. 531.18ff). Cf. SN 47.1 *Ambapālisutta* 5: 141; SA 24 #623 T.2 174c8ff; DN #16 *Mahāparinibbānasutta* 2: 95; DA 2 #2 T.1 13c26ff. For various interpretations of the phrase, "*kāye kāyānupassī viharati,*" see Kusum Mittal, *Fragmente des Daśottarasūtra aus zentralasiatischen Sanskrit-Handschriften, Dogmatische Begriffsreihen im älteren Buddhismus 1*, Sanskrittexte aus den Turfanfunden 4 (Berlin: Akademie-Verlag, 1957), pp. 61–62, n. 6.

18. SN 47.4 *Sālasutta* 5: 144: . . . *tumhe* . . . *kāye kāyānupassino viharatha ātāpīno sampajānā ekodibhūtā vippasannacittā samāhitā ekaggacittā kāyassa yathābhūtaṃ ñāṇāya*. Cf. SA 24 #621 T.2 173c17ff. The majority of dialogues on the topic of mindfulness in the *Saṃyuktāgama* add to this introductory formula the threefold qualification of inwardly, outwardly, and both inwardly and outwardly: "A monk abides observing inwardly the body in the body, zealous," and so on. See SA 24 #610 T.2 171b17ff, 174a16ff, passim. Cf. EA 5 T.2 568a10ff; DS 5 T.26 475c27ff. The *Saṃyuktāgama* also contains several dialogues that simply list the four applications with no formulaic description: SA 24 #629 T.2 175b29ff, passim.

19. This formulaic definition is followed by detailed accounts of the specific stages through which one cultivates each of the four applications. Schmithausen ("Die vier Konzentrationen," 246ff) examines these concretized descriptions in great detail, in particular noting the similarity between the accounts of mindfulness of feelings and of the mind and their difference from the greatly expanded accounts of mindfulness of the body and of factors.

20. See Schmithausen, "Die vier Konzentrationen," 256. Cf. MN #10 *Satipaṭṭhānasutta* 1: 56ff, passim. These formulas, which conclude the description of mindfulness, vary. The *Madhyamāgama* (MA 24 #98 T.1 582b22–24, passim) omits the second formula concerning arising and passing away: "Observing the internal [i.e., one's own] body in [or as] the body, observing the external [i.e., another's] body

in [or as] the body, one establishes mindfulness in the body, and has knowledge, views, intuition, and penetration." The *Ekottarāgama* (EA 5 T.2 568c13ff, 569a11ff) includes all three formulas only in the description of the applications of feelings and of the mind, but with the first formula following the second and third. In the description of the application of factors, only the second and third formulas appear, and in the application of the body, none of the three is used. However, as with the majority of the versions in Chinese translation, the introductory formula listing all four applications includes a reference to internal and external observation (EA 5 T.2 568a10ff). The *Śāriputrābhidharmaśāstra* (ŚAŚ 13 T.28 613c20ff) recounts at length the observation internally, externally, and both, as the major portion of its presentation of each application, and concludes each discussion with the second and third concluding formulas (ŚAŚ 13 T.28 614ff, passim). For a description of the four applications in terms of internal and external observation alone, see SN 47.3 *Bhikkhusutta* 5: 143; for the observation of arising and passing away alone, see SN 47.40 *Vibhaṅgasutta* 5: 183.

21. MN #10 *Satipaṭṭhānasutta* 1: 62–63; MA 24 #98 T.1 584b22ff. Cf. SN 47.36 *Aññāsutta* 5: 181. The *Ekottarāgama* (EA 5 T.2 569b9ff) omits this concluding reference to two fruits. Cf. SA 24 #618 173a29ff, which claims that the four applications will lead to the four noble fruits of the stream-enterer, the once-returner, the nonreturner, and the arhat.

22. SN 47.10 *Bhikkhunupassayasutta* 5: 154ff; SA 24 #615 T.2 172a26ff.

23. SN 47.10 *Bhikkhunupassayasutta* 5: 156ff: *avitakko' mhi avicāro ajjhattaṃ satimā sukham asmī' ti pajānāti*. Cf. AN 1.21 *Kāyagatāsativaggo* 1: 44, which states that, if mindfulness with regard to the body is cultivated, then "the body is quieted, the mind is quieted, initial inquiry and investigation are calmed," and so on: . . . *kāyo pi passambhati cittaṃ pi passambhati vitakkavicārā pi vūpasammanti*.

24. SN 47.10 *Bhikkhunupassayasutta* 5: 157.

25. SN 47.8 *Sūdasutta* 5: 149ff; SA 24 #616 T.2 172b23ff.

26. SN 47.8 *Sūdasutta* 5: 150: . . . *cittaṃ na samādhiyati upakkilesā na pahīyanti so tam nimittaṃ na uggaṇhāti*. See SA 24 #616 T.2 172c4ff.

27. Cf. the descriptions of the four trance states (*dhyāna*), where initial inquiry and investigation and mindfulness do not occur together, but characterize respectively the first and third trance states: MA 36 #146 T.1 657c21ff; MN #27 *Cūḷahatthipadopamasutta* 1: 181–82; MVB 80 T.27 412a21ff; AKB 8.7–8a–b pp. 437.15ff.

28. For references to mindfulness and awareness in the practice of reflection (*anusmṛti*), see SA 20 #550 T.2 143b29ff.

29. See AN 4.20.195 *Vappasutta* 2: 198ff: . . . *neva sumano hoti na dummano upekkhako viharati sato sampanjāno*. Cf. MA 3 #12 T.1 434c19ff.

30. See MA 17 #72 T.1 536c24ff; MA 10 #44–46 T.1 485c22ff. Cf. AN 8.9.81 *Satisampajaññasutta* 4: 336–37; MA 18 #74 T.1 541c10ff, 542a26; MA 27 #109 T.1 598b25ff; AN 10.6.51 *Sacittasutta* 5: 93; MA 52 #196 T.1 753c22ff. See also AN

10.7.61–62 *Avijjāsutta* and *Taṇhāsutta* 5: 113ff, MA 10 #51 #52 #53 T.1 487b14ff, where both the mindfulness-awareness pair and the four applications of mindfulness appear separately in a list of practices.

31. See SN 47.2 *Satisutta* 5: 142; DN #16 *Mahāparinibbānasutta* 2: 94–95; SN 36.7 *Paṭhamagelaññasutta* 4: 211, where mindfulness and awareness function as the preparatory stage for observing impermanence of feelings in the body and the abandonment of the three defilements (*anusaya*). See MN #107 *Gaṇakamoggallānasutta* 3: 3; cf. MA 35 #144 T.1 652a25ff, where the mindfulness-awareness pair appears as one stage in a series of practices beginning with discipline and proceeding through guarding the doors of the senses; moderation in eating, wakefulness, mindfulness, and awareness; abandoning the five hindrances; and finally the four trance states. The *Dantabhūmisutta* (MN #125 3: 135ff; cf. MA 52 #198 T.1 758a8ff) contains the same definition of mindfulness and awareness, and a similar series, but after the abandonment of the five hindrances inserts the four applications of mindfulness, and to the end adds the three varieties of intuition that constitute enlightenment.

32. SN 47.35 *Satisutta* 5: 180–81.

33. Though, for the most part, one can proceed with the prima facie assumption that the corpus of Abhidharma literature follows, presumes, and builds on the scriptural corpus, in individual cases, the possibility cannot be excluded that the scriptural collections as currently extant have been influenced and modified by doctrinal and sectarian concerns usually considered characteristic of Abhidharma. The arrangement by numerical enumeration in the *Ekottarāgama* and *Aṅguttaranikāya,* and the topical arrangement of the *Saṃyuktāgama* and *Saṃyuttanikāya* serve as probable examples of this influence.

34. The later standardized list of thirty-seven members includes the four applications of mindfulness, the four exertions, the four bases of magical powers, the five controlling factors, the five forces, the seven limbs of enlightenment, and the eightfold noble path. For this list of thirty-seven, see, for example, SA 26 #684 T.2 186c8–10, 26 #694 T.2 188b26–27; MA 52 #196 T.1 753c6–7; MN #104 *Sāmagāmasutta* 2: 245; SA 24 #638 T.2 176c14–17, which includes the term *bodhipakṣyadharma;* DN #16 *Mahāparinibbānasutta* 2: 120; *Ta pan-nieh-p'an ching* T.1 (7) 193a2ff, which includes the term *bodhipakṣyadharma,* and the number thirty-seven; DN #28 *Sampasādanīyasutta* 3: 102; DN #29 *Pāsādikasutta* 3: 127–28. Cf. DA 3 #2 T.1 16c10ff, 12 #17 74a14ff, 12 #18 76c28ff, which add the four trance states to the list of thirty-seven. For further canonical references to this list of thirty-seven factors and the term *bodhipakṣya,* see Lamotte, *Le traité,* vol. 3, pp. 1119–21. The history of the development and transmission of the taxonomy of the thirty-seven aids still remains to be written. The evidence presents several interesting questions. In the Chinese translations of the northern Indian canonical collections, references to the term *aids to enlightenment* together with the number, thirty-seven, occur almost exclusively in the *Ekottarāgama.* See EA 1 T.2 551a4, passim, where the thirty-seven aids are declared to be the topic of the *Ekottarāgama* and the source of all factors (*dharma*). This suggests that the school with which the *Ekottarāgama* is associated was possibly influential in the development of the thirty-seven aids. See also *Ta-lou-t'an ching* T.1 (23)

309b26, *Ch'i-shih ching* T.1 (24) 364c15, and *Ch'i-shih yin-pen ching* T.1 (25) 419c16, which refer to the thirty-seven aids, whereas DA 22 #30 T.1 149c6 refers to the seven limbs of enlightenment. Though the thirty-seven aids are listed in several of the seven early Sarvāstivādin Abhidharma texts, the term *thirty-seven aids to enlightenment* is virtually absent: see DS 12 T.26 511b12ff; cf. Siglinde Dietz, ed., *Fragmente des Dharmaskandha: Ein Abhidharma-Text in Sanskrit aus Gilgit*, Abhandlungen der Akademie der Wissenschaften in Göttingen, Philologisch-historische Klasse 3, 142 (Göttingen: Vandenhoeck & Ruprecht, 1984), pp. 52–53; SP 6 T.26 389a23–24; VK 3 T.26 544a13ff. The term *thirty-seven aids to enlightenment* is mentioned in the **Āryavasumitrabodhisattvasaṅgītiśāstra* (8 T.28 788b18ff) and the **Abhidharmahṛdaya* (AHŚ-D 4 T.28 828a29ff, AHŚ-U 5 T.28 862b26ff). The *Śāriputrābhidharmaśāstra* concludes with a list of aids that far exceeds the standardized list of thirty-seven (ŚAŚ 30 T.28 719a15ff). The *Mahāvibhāṣā* (MVB 96 T.27 495c27ff), in introducing a detailed discussion of the thirty-seven aids, claims that though the term *aids to enlightenment* is mentioned in the presumably Sarvāstivādin scriptural canon, these aids are identified as the seven limbs and not as the standardized list of thirty-seven. Several reasons are given for this omission, including the possibility that the scriptures containing references to the thirty-seven have been lost. Cf. AVB 48 T.28 364b11ff; *A-p'i-t'an wu fa hsing ching* T.28 (1557) 998b14; AARŚ T.28 977a23ff. For Pāli references to the thirty-seven aids, see V. Trenckner, ed., *The Milindapañho* (London: Pali Text Society, 1962), pp. 237; C. A. F. Rhys Davids, ed., *The Vibhaṅga* (London: Pali Text Society, 1904), pp. 372. See also MPPS 19 T.25 197b19ff; Lamotte, *Le traité*, vol. 3, pp. 1138ff.

35. MVB 96 T.27 496c22ff, 188 T.27 943c22–24; AKB 6.70 p. 384.15ff; SAKV pp. 602.32ff; NAS 71 T.29.727c9ff; ADV #450c–d pp. 362.12ff. For a general description of the *ādikarmika*, see MVB 6 T.27 26c9ff. For the *ādikarmika* as one of three varieties of practitioners who cultivate the meditation on the repulsive (*aśubhā*), including also those who practice thoroughly (*kṛtaparijaya*) and those who have surpassing attention (*atikrāntamanaskāra*), see MVB 40 T.27 205b11ff; AKB 6.10 pp. 338.3ff; SAKV pp. 526.15ff; NAS 59 T.29. 671a14ff. These three varieties of practitioners are correlated with the applications of mindfulness, (see MVB 187 T.27. 937a29ff) and, more generally, with progressive stages in practice (see SAHŚ 5 T.28. 907c25ff; and Hurvitz, "Fa-sheng's Observations," p. 209). According to the *Abhidharmakośabhāṣya* (AKB 6.9ff p. 337.7ff), the practitioner first cultivates the repulsive and develops mindfulness of respiration, thereby attaining concentration or calming, which prepares one to cultivate the four applications of mindfulness (cf. MVB 26 T.27 134b17ff). Through the applications of mindfulness, one perfects discerning, and from their cultivation, one produces, in succession, the first stage of heat within the path of preparation, the second stage of the summit, and so on. Cf. MVB 17 T.27 83b21–22, passim; AHŚ-D 2 T.28 818a15ff, AHŚ-U 3 T.28 848c1ff; SAHŚ 5 T.28 908a20ff.

36. See MVB 187 T.27 936c22ff, where this identification of the four applications with all factors is attributed to scripture. See AKB 6.14 p. 341.14; SAKV pp. 529.30–31. Cf. SA 24 #633 T.2 175c27ff.

37. For a comparison of scriptural treatments of the contents of the object of this fourth application, see Schmithausen, "Die vier Konzentrationen," pp. 247–50. Cf. Ui, *Indo tetsugaku kenkyū*, vol. 3, pp. 69ff.

38. ŚAŚ 13 T.28 615b29ff.

39. DS 6 T.26 478b25ff.

40. SP 6 T.26 391b27ff; PP 12 T.26 (1542) 740c4ff; cf. AHŚ-U 5 T.28 862b15–17.

41. ŚAŚ 13 T.28 613a20ff, passim. For an examination of the Abhidharma treatment of the four applications of mindfulness and specifically of this innovation in the interpretation of their objects, see Kyōshō Tanaka, "Shoki Abidaruma ronsho ni okeru shinenjoron," in *Bukkyō kyōri no kenkyū, Tamura Yoshirō hakushi kanreki kinen ronshū* (Tokyo: Shunjūsha, 1982), pp. 195–215.

42. AARŚ T.28 977a29ff; MPPS 19 T.25 198c10ff; SAHŚ 5 T.28 908c9ff; AARŚ T.28 977a29; AKB 6.15b pp. 342.24ff; SAKV pp. 531.28ff; NAS 60 T.29 677a27ff; ADV pp. 316.4ff. The *Mahāvibhāṣā* (MVB 187 T.27 938a13ff) cites this correlation as one of six reasons why the applications were set at four. Cf. ADV pp. 316.8–9.

43. AHŚ-D 2 T.28 818a19ff.

44. AHŚ-U 3 T.28 848c14ff; SAHŚ 5 T.28 908b24ff; AKB 6.14b–c pp. 341.10ff; SAKV pp. 529.7ff. Cf. MVB 7 T.27 34b29, which identifies the generic characteristic as the sixteen aspects through which the four noble truths are to be observed, the first four of which are impermanence, suffering, voidness, and nonself. The fourfold generic characteristic is also identified as the fourfold aspect through which one observes combined objects (*sambhinna*) while stationed in the final application of mindfulness with regard to factors. See AHŚ-D 2 T.28 818a24ff, 3 T.28 848c27ff; MVB 187 T.27 937c15ff; SAHŚ 5 T.28 909b6ff; AKB 6.16 pp. 343.2ff; SAKV pp. 532.2ff; NAS 61 T.29 677c8ff; ADV #384–385a–b pp. 316.10ff. These passages suggest that the first three applications of mindfulness have only uncombined (*asambhinna*) objects or specific objects that are distinct from those of the other applications. Only the fourth application with regard to factors has both uncombined and combined objects: that is, two or more of the objects of any of the four applications. For various interpretations of particular and generic characteristics, see MVB 13 T.27 65a13ff, 127 T.27 665b1ff; AKB 1.10d pp. 7.18ff; SAKV pp. 28.10ff; NAS 60 T.29 675b3ff.

45. See MVB 187 T.27 936c8ff. The *Mahāvibhāṣā* (MVB 187 T.27 937a10ff) also notes that earlier Abhidharma texts refer implicitly to these three varieties and cites, for example, the *Saṅgītiparyāya:* SP 6 T.26 391b23ff. Cf. SAHŚ 5 T.28 909a8ff; MPPS 19 T.25 200c29ff; NAS 60 T.29 675c6ff; AKB 6.15 pp. 341.16ff.

46. This Abhidharma redefinition of the applications of mindfulness as insight extends also to other modes of mindfulness, such as the mindfulness of respiration (*ānāpānasmṛti*) and the reflection upon previous rebirth states (*pūrvanivāsānusmṛti*).

See MVB 26 T.27 134b3ff, 100 T.27 517b22; AKB 6.12 pp. 339.5ff; NAS 60 T.29 673b7ff.

47. See note 11.

48. See SA 24 #611 T.2 171b26ff; SN 47.45 *Kusalarāsisutta* 5: 186–87.

49. See SA 24 #633 T.2 175c27ff.

50. See NAS 60 T.29 676b12ff.

51. MVB 187 T.27 938b5ff; MPPS 19 T.25 201a12; AKB 6.15b p. 342.5ff; NAS 60 T. 29 676a2ff; ASPŚ 30 T.29 920a8ff. Not all Abhidharma schools accept this view that the intrinsic nature of mindfulness is insight. Saṅghabhadra (NAS 60 T.29 676b2ff) cites the view of the Vibhajyavādins, who claim that the intrinsic nature of the applications of mindfulness is, in accordance with their name, mindfulness and not insight. Saṅghabhadra responds that their intrinsic activity is indeed insight because they function through the two operations of observation (*anupaśyanā*) and awareness (*samprajanya*), which are both varieties of insight. However, these applications of mindfulness are not called *applications of insight* because this would exclude the second and third varieties of the applications of mindfulness through connection and with regard to the object-support, neither of which is identified with insight.

52. For this scriptural association of *smṛtīndriya* and the *smṛtyupasthāna*, see SA 26 #647 T.2 182b20, passim; SN 48.8 *Daṭṭhabbasutta* 5: 196, passim; AN 5.2.15 *Daṭṭhabbasutta* 3: 12; SA 26 #655 T.2 183b29, 26 #658 T.2 184a4, 26 #675 T.2 185c12, 26 #691 T.2 188a27. For the Abhidharma reclassification, see MVB 183 T.27 917c4ff; 187 T.27 937c22ff. The *Mahāvibhāṣā* (MVB 187 T.27 938b28ff) explains that this association in the scriptures of the applications with the controlling factor of mindfulness indicates the predominance of the activity of the controlling factor of mindfulness in their operation, which further (MVB 101 T.27 522c22ff) accounts for their name as applications of mindfulness and not insight.

53. See note 17. Cf. MVB 187 T.27 936c27–28, 187 T.27 938b5–8; AKB 6.15b pp. 342.6ff; SAKV p. 529.32ff; NAS 60 T.29 675c13ff.

54. See MVB 39 T.27 200b24ff; especially, 42 T.27 217a8ff.

55. NAS 60 T.29 675c7–13ff. For references illustrating the role of insight in the eradication of defilements, see C. Cox, "Attainment Through Abandonment: The Sarvāstivādin Path of Removing Defilements," in *Paths to Liberation: The Mārga and its Transformations in Buddhist Thought*, ed. Robert Buswell and Robert Gimello (Honolulu: Kuroda Institute, University of Hawaii Press, forthcoming). For a discussion of which of the three varieties of the applications of mindfulness is capable of eradicating defilements, see MVB 187 T.27 937b12ff; ADV #384c–d pp. 317.9ff. For a discussion of the definition of the four applications as the single path, see MVB 188 T.27 943a18ff; especially 188 T.27 943c15ff.

56. MVB 187 T.27 938b12ff. Cf. Kaidō 14 T.64 320c17ff.

57. MVB 141 T.27 724a19ff.

58. See AKB 6.15b pp. 342.9ff; SAKV pp. 530.12ff. Cf. P'u-kuang 23 T.41 343c5ff; Fa-pao 23 T.41 734a10ff; Kaidō 23 T.64 321a9ff.

59. AKB 6.15b p. 342.11: *yathādṛṣṭasyā 'bhilapanāt.* Cf. SAKV pp. 530.23–24: *yasmād yathādṛṣṭo 'rthaḥ prajñayā tathai 'vā 'bhilapyate. smṛtyo 'dgṛhyata ity arthaḥ.* Cf. the *Nibandhana* commentary on the *Arthaviniścayasūtra,* N. H. Samtani, *The Arthaviniścaya-sūtra and its Commentary (Nibandhana),* Tibetan Sanskrit Works Series (Patna: Kashi Prasad Jayaswal Research Institute, 1971), pp. 211.

60. NAS 60 T.29 676a4ff.

61. For a discussion of the analogous functioning of *smṛti* in the *Yogasūtra,* see Gerhard Oberhammer, *Strukturen Yogischer Meditation,* Österreichische Akademie der Wissenschaften, Philosophisch-historische Klasse 322, 13, (Vienna: Österreichische Akademie der Wissenschaften, 1977), pp. 143ff.

62. For this formula in the definition of *satindriya,* see SN 48.9 *Paṭhamavibhaṅgasutta* 5: 197: *satimā hoti paramena satinepakkena samannāgato cirakataṃ pi cirabhāsitaṃ pi saritā anussaritā.* For the same formula, see MN #53 *Sekhasutta* 1: 356. Buddhaghosa's commentary distinguishes *saritā* from *anussaritā* on the basis of remembering once or many times. See Horner, *Papañcasūdanī Majjhimanikāyaṭṭhakathā,*3: 30: . . . *tāya satiyā esa sakiṃ saraṇena saritā punappuna saraṇena anussaritā ti veditabbo.* Other passages refer to both the four applications and to retention or recollection: SN 48.10 *Dutiyavibhaṅgasutta* 5: 198. For this formula in the definition of *satisambojjhaṅga,* see C. A. F. Rhys Davids, *Vibhaṅga,* p. 227; and in the definition of *satibala,* see AN 5.2.14 *Vitthatasutta* 3: 11. Cf. SA 26 #675 T.2 185c12, 26 #691 T.2 188a27, which mention only the four applications. For this formula in the definition of *sammāsati,* see MA 7 #31 T.1 469b19ff; *Fo-shuo ssu ti ching* T.1 (32) 816c7ff; cf. MN #141 *Saccavibhaṅgasutta* 3: 252, which mentions only the four applications of mindfulness.

63. SA 28 #785 T.2 203c25ff.

64. For this formula in the definition of *satindriya,* see E. Müller, ed., *The Dhammasaṅgaṇi* (London: Pali Text Society, 1885), p. 11: . . . *yā tasmiṃ samaye sati anussati paṭissati sati saraṇatā dhāraṇatā apilāpanatā asammusanatā sati satindriyaṃ satibalaṃ sammāsati* . . . , and 12, 13, 16, 19, 21, 22; Rhys Davids, *Vibhaṅga,* pp. 124, 250; J. Kashyap, ed., *Cullaniddesa,* Nālandā-Devanāgarī-Pāli-Series (Bihar: Pali Publication Board, 1959), pp. 32, 34, 167. Cf. Müller, *Dhammasaṅgaṇi,* pp. 62, 64, 65, 67; and Rhys Davids, *Vibhaṅga,* pp. 107, 229, 237, for the same formula, to which is added "a limb of enlightenment, a limb of the path, contained within the path": . . . *satisambojjhaṅgo maggaṅgaṃ maggapariyāpannaṃ.* The *Mahāniddesa* adds, "a limb of enlightenment, the single path": *satisambojjhaṅgo ekāyanamaggo.* See Louis de La Vallée Poussin and Edward J. Thomas, eds., *The Mahā-Niddesa* (London: Pali Text Society, 1916–17), p. 347

65. See DS 2 T.26 460b10ff, 2 T.26 462a15ff, 2 T.26 463a20ff, 6 T.26 482a6ff, 10 T.26 499c3ff; SP 2 T.26 372a18ff, 7 T.26 395a19ff, 16 T.26 433a7ff, 16 T.26 435a21, 17 T.26 437a13ff; PP 5 T.26 (1541) 652b25ff, 7 T.26 (1542) 720b25ff; PP 5

T.26 (1541) 654a12ff, 8 T.26 (1542) 723b14ff; cf. ŚAŚ 4 T.28 554b13ff, 5 T.28 560c21ff, 6 T.28 568b8ff, 6 T.28 568c21ff.

66. This "combinatory formula" appears in the commentarial exegesis of the traditional scriptural passage on the four applications as a gloss on the term *smṛtiman:* DS 5 T.26 476a20ff. Cf. ŚAŚ 13 T.28 613a10ff and 13 T.28 613c14ff; Rhys Davids, *Vibhaṅga,* pp. 193ff. For this scriptural passage, see note 17. Elsewhere, the *Dharmaskandha* (DS 8 T.26 491c3ff) first defines the praxis-related modes of mindfulness in terms of the four applications and then identifies them with the various processes included in the extended psychological definition.

67. DK T.26 614c20ff. Though the *Dharmaskandha* includes a list of mental factors in its examination of the factors sense sphere (*dharmāyatana*), neither the *Dharmaskandha* nor the *Saṅgītiparyāya* specify *smṛti* as a separate mental factor.

68. See PP 1 T.26 (1541) 627b23, 1 T.26 (1542) 693a18. Cf. PP 2 T.26 (1541) 635a10 and 2 T.26 (1542) 699c17ff, for a longer definition; AARŚ T.28 970b18–19; AHŚ-D 1 T.28 810c6, AHŚ-U 1 T.28 836c23; SAHŚ 2 T.28 881a8; *Sa-p'o-to-tsung wu shih lun* T.28 (1556) 996b3.

69. See ŚAŚ 14 T.28 624a21, 23 T.28 673a25ff, and 13 T.28 613c14ff, for a longer definition.

70. See *Milindapañho* 37. Cf. P. S. Jaini, ed., *Milinda-ṭīkā* (London: Pali Text Society, 1961), p. 10; P. V. Bapat and R. D. Vadekar, eds., *Aṭṭhasālinī,* Bhandarkar Oriental Series 3 (Poona: B.O.R. Institute, 1943), pp. 99–100. See also E. Hardy, ed., The *Netti-pakaraṇa* (London: Pali Text Society, 1961), pp. 28, 54, which gives only *apilāpana* as the defining characteristic of mindfulness (*sati*); and the *Nettipakaraṇa* 15, which refers to "mindfulness in the sense of *apilāpana* in accordance with what has been seen": *yathādiṭṭhaṃ apilāpanaṭṭhena sati.* For a similar definition used by Vasubandhu, see AKB 6.15b p. 342.11: . . . *yathādṛṣṭasyā 'bhilapanāt.*

71. See *Milindapañho* 37. Cf. *Aṭṭhasālinī* 99–100; Max Walleser and Hermann Kopp, eds., *Manorathapūraṇī* (London: Pali Text Society, 1967), vol. 2, p. 52. However, the *Milindaṭīkā* echoes the second interpretation cited next also given in the *Aṭṭhasālinī*(120): see Padmanabh S. Jaini, ed., *Milindaṭīkā* (London: Pali Text Society, 1961), p. 10. It is unclear whether this first interpretation is based on a derivation of *apilāpana* from the root, *lap,* with the addition of a prefix, *api,* or possibly, *abhi;* or whether it should be understood as an extension of meaning from *a-pilāpana* based on the root, *plu* with a privative prefix. The *Critical Pāli Dictionary* records the derivation from the root, *plu:* see Trenckner et al., eds., *The Critical Pāli Dictionary* (Copenhagen: Royal Danish Academy of Sciences and Letters, 1924–48), vol. 1, p. 292; cf. note 72. K. R. Norman argues for the derivation from the causative of the root *lap* with the prefix *api:* K. R. Norman, "Pāli Lexicographical Studies V: Twelve Pāli Etymologies," *Journal of the Pali Text Society* 12 (1988): 50.

72. *Aṭṭhasālinī* 120. Here, it appears that *apilāpanatā* is to be understood as a nominal form derived from the causative of the root *plu,* "to float," to which is added a privative prefix and an abstract suffix, yielding *a-pilāpana-tā,* meaning "the state

of not floating.'' This second interpretation that assumes a privative prefix is supported by the explanation of ''lapsed mindfulness'' (*muṭṭhasacca*) in the *Dhammasaṅgaṇi*(Müller, *Dhammasaṅgaṇi*, p. 232). There the defining characteristics of mindfulness are negated: *apilāpanatā* is replaced with *pilāpanatā*, and *asammusanatā* with *sammusanatā*. *Pilāpanatā* in this passage is also glossed in the *Aṭṭhasālinī* (320) by the same reference to floating gourd vessels. Cf. R. Morris, ed., *The Puggalapaññatti* (London: Pali Text Society, 1883), p. 21.

73. See Vidhushekhara Bhattacharya, ed., *The Yogācārabhūmi of Ācārya Asaṅga* (Calcutta: University of Calcutta, 1957), pp. 60–61: *smṛtiḥ katamā. yatsaṃstute vastuni tatra tatra tadanugābhilapanā. . . . smṛtiḥ kiṃkarmikā. ciracintitakṛtabhāṣitasmaraṇānusmaraṇakarmikā.* See YBŚ 3 T.30 291c2–3 and 291c13–14. Cf. YBŚ 55 T.30 601c22–23, 82 T.30 758a26ff.

74. See AAŚ T.28 982a18–19; Hajime Sakurabe, trans., ''*Nyūabidatsumaron* [Chibetto bun yori no wayaku],'' in *Bukkyō go no kenkyū* (Kyoto: Buneidō, 1975), p. 140. ADV #112 p. 69.6–7 ''Mindfulness has as its form the functioning of the mind. It is the *abhilapana* of the object of the mind and has the characteristic of not losing the accomplishment of what has been, will be, or is being performed'': *cittavyāpārarūpā smṛtiḥ cittasyā 'rthābhilapanā kṛtakartavyakriyamāṇakarmāntāvipramoṣalakṣanā.*

75. AKB 2.24 pp. 54.21–22: *smṛtir ālambanāsaṃpramoṣaḥ*. SAKV pp. 127.32ff: *yadyogād ālambanaṃ na mano vismarati tac cā 'bhilapatī 'va sā smṛtiḥ.* Vasubandhu himself uses the term *abhilapana* in a discussion of the operation of the applications of mindfulness: AKB 6.15b p. 342.11.

76. The *Abhidharmasamuccaya* defines *smṛti* as ''the nonloss of mind events with regard to a familiar object, and its activity is nondispersal.'' See V. Gokhale, ''Fragments from the *Abhidharmasamuccaya* of Asaṃga,'' *Journal of the Bombay Branch of the Royal Asiatic Society* 23 (1947): 16: *smṛtiḥ katamā. saṃstute vastuni cetaso 'saṃpramoṣaḥ. avikṣepakarmikā.* Cf. *Abhidharmasamuccaya* 1 T.31 664b1–2. Sthiramati glosses this ''activity of nondispersal'' as indicating ''the state of the nondispersal of mind events when there is *abhilapana* the object-support of mindfulness once again.'' See N. Tatia, ed., *Abhidharmasamuccaya-bhāṣyam*, Tibetan Sanskrit Works Series 17 (Patna: Kashi Prasad Jayaswal Research Institute, 1976), p. 5: *saṃstutaṃ vastu purvānubhūtaṃ veditavyam. avikṣepakarmikatvaṃ punaḥ smṛter ālaṃbanābhilapane sati cittāvikṣepatām upādāya.* Cf. *Abhidharmasamuccayabhāṣyam* 1 T.31 697b10–13. Sthiramati also uses *abhilapana* in commenting on the definition of *smṛti* in the *Madhyāntavibhāga* and its *bhāṣya* as the ''nonloss of the object-support.'' Gadjin M. Nagao, ed., *Madhyāntavibhāga-bhāṣya* (Tokyo: Suzuki Research Foundation, 1964), 52.4 (*kārikā* 4.5): *ālambane 'saṃmoṣo . . . ;* 52.6 (*bhāṣya*): *smṛtir ālambane 'saṃpramoṣaḥ;* T.31 458c3; T.31 471c22ff. Sylvain Lévi, ed., *Sthiramati, Madhyāntavibhāgaṭīkā* (Nagoya: Librairie Hajinkaku, 1934), 175.7: *smṛtir ālaṃbane 'sammoṣa iti vistarīkṛita ālambanam iti cittasthāpanīyam avavādavastv abhilapanam ity arthaḥ.* Cf. Nagao, *Madhyāntavibhāga-bhāṣya* 52.14 (*kārikā* 4.6): *ālambane 'saṃmoṣā . . .* ; 52.16 (*bhāṣya*): *ālambanāsampramoṣādhi-*

patyataḥ; T.31 458c12; T.31 472a4. Lévi, *Madhyāntavibhāgaṭīkā,* 176.21–22: *ālambanābhilapanalakṣaṇaṃ smṛtindriyam.*

77. Sylvain Lévi, ed., *Vijñaptimātratāsiddhi. Deux traités de Vasubandhu, Viṃśatikā et Triṃśikā,* Bibliothèque de l'École des Hautes Études 245 (Paris: Librairie Ancienne Honoré Champion, 1925), pp. 25–26: *smṛtiḥ saṃstute vastuny asaṃpramoṣaś cetaso 'bhilapanatā.*

78. Unfortunately, Chinese translations other than those by Hsüan-tsang also do not unequivocally establish an interpretation for what would apparently be the equivalent of *abhilapana.* For example, Guṇabhadra and Bodhiyaśas. (PP 1 T.26 (1541) 627b23) adopt a negative expression where Hsüan-tsang (PP 1 T.26 (1542) 693a18) translates "the state of the fixing (or noting) (*ming-chi, *apilapanatā*) of the mind," not employing a negative expression. Dharmaśrī's **Abhidharmahṛdaya* (AHŚ-D 1 T.28 810c6) employs a negative expression, Upaśānta's **Abhidharmahṛdaya* (AHŚ-U 1 T.28 836c23) does not, and Dharmatrāta's **Saṃyuktābhidharmahṛdayaśāstra* (SAHŚ 2 T.28 881a8) employs both. The *Sa-p'o-to-tsung wu shih lun* (T.28 (1556) 996b3) offers the same expression (*ming-chi*) used by Hsüan-tsang.

79. Hsüan-tsang uses five equivalents for **abhilapana: ming-chi* (HTAKB 23 T.29 119a9; cf. PAKB 16 T.29 271a26, which uses *pu-wang*), *ming-liao chi-i* (YBŚ 3 T.30 291c2–3, and 291c 13–14; in a comparable formula, only *ming-chi* is used: YBŚ 55 T.30 601c22); *ming-chi-i* (*Abhidharmasamuccayabhāṣya* 1 T.31 697b10–13), or *chi* (*Madhyāntavibhāgabhāṣya chung* T.31 471c22ff). Hsüan-tsang also appears at times to equate *abhilapana* and *asampramoṣa,* translating *asampramoṣa* by *ming-chi pu-wang,* which combines *ming-chi,* his usual translation of *abhilapana,* with *pu-wang,* a frequent equivalent for *asampramoṣa.* See *Abhidharmasamuccaya* 1 T.31 664b1–2; HTAKB 4 T.29 19a20; cf. PAKB 3 T.29 178b14–15, which uses *pu-wang.* Paramārtha also, however, uses *pu-wang* to translate both *abhilapana* and *asampramoṣa:* see PAKB 3 T.29 178b14, 16 T.29 271a26. The identification of the original for Hsüan-tsang's equivalents is then very difficult. For example, in the definition of *smṛti* in the *Prakaraṇapāda* (1 T.26 (1542) 693a18) Hsüan-tsang uses *ming-chi* where the earlier translation (1 T.26 (1541) 627b23 by Guṇabhadra and Bodhiyaśas) uses *pu-wang.* Cf. PP 5 T.26 (1541) 652b25ff, 7 T.26 (1542) 720b25ff. See also PAKB 18 T.29 283c12–13, which includes a definition of *smṛti* that is not included in Hsüan-tsang's translation or Pradhan's edited Sanskrit text: HTAKB 25 T.29 132b12, AKB 6.68 p. 383.8, and NAS 71 T.29 726c20ff; cf. ADV #446 pp. 360.14ff. Here, Paramārtha defines *smṛti* as *hsin ming pu-wang:* possibly "**abhilapana* and **asampramoṣa* of mind." However, because both *abhilapana* and *asampramoṣa* are attested in similar definitions of *smṛti* extant in Sanskrit, the positive identification of the original term is doubtful.

80. See Shōshin Kuwayama and Noriaki Hakamaya, *Genjō* (Tokyo: Daizō shuppan, 1981), pp. 252ff, which follows *K'ai-yüan shih-chiao lu* 8 T.55 555b27ff.

81. See AKB 6.15b p. 342.11; SAKV p. 530.24: . . . *tathai 'vā 'bhilapyate. smṛtyo 'dgṛhyata ity arthaḥ.* Though Yaśomitra here uses *abhilapyate,* grammatically a passive derived from the root, *lap,* he appears not to support a connection with the

sense of "expression" since he glosses *abhilapyate* with *udgṛhyate*, or "to be sustained."

82. See notes 71 and 72. The possible confusion or difficulty in determining the exact meaning of and relation between the Pāli term *apilāpana*, the Sanskrit term *abhilapana*, and related terms may have had a linguistic impetus. Regardless of the original derivation of *apilāpana*— from the root *plu* with a privative or from the root *lap* with a prefix *api*—a Buddhist Middle Indic *apilāpana* can be assumed to have had the phonetic variant *avilāpana*, due to the common alternation of *v* and *p* (*A Critical Pāli Dictionary*, sub voce, *avilāpanatā*, cites the *Puggalapaññatti* 25. On this variation of *p* and *v*, see Heinrich Lüders, *Beobachtungen über die Sprache des buddhistischen Urkanons*, Abhandlungen der Deutschen Akademie der Wissenschaften zum Berlin, Klasse für Sprachen, Literatur und Kunst, 1952, 10 [Berlin: Akademie-Verlag, 1954] pp. 112ff, and for forms from *plu*, especially 114–115; Oskar von Hinüber, *Das ältere Mittelindisch im Überblick*, Österreichische Akademie der Wissenschaften, Philosophisch-historische Klasse 467, 20 [Vienna: Österreichische Akademie der Wissenschaften, 1986], p. 98; K. R. Norman, "Dialect Forms in Pāli," in *Dialectes dans les littératures indo-aryennes*, ed. Colette Caillat, Publications de l'Institut de Civilisation Indienne 55 [Paris: Institut de Civilization Indienne, 1989], pp. 373ff.) In the case of derivation from the root *plu*, this variation of *v* and *p* might have obscured the derivation and facilitated resegmentation and root reassignment in conversion from Buddhist Middle Indic to Sanskrit. Northwest dialects or Gāndhārī, in particular, exhibit frequent phonetic or graphic alternation between *v* and the Sanskrit *b*, *bh*. (For this alternation, see T. Burrow, *The Language of the Kharoṣṭhi Documents from Chinese Turkestan* [Cambridge: Cambridge University Press, 1937], p. 8; John Brough, *The Gāndhārī Dharmapada*, London Oriental Series 7 [London: Oxford University Press, 1962], pp. 87, 96–97; von Hinüber, *Das ältere Mittelindisch*, p. 101; Oskar von Hinüber, "Origin and Varieties of Buddhist Sanskrit," in *Dialectes dans les littératures indo-aryennes*, pp. 341–67, especially 357–58; Norman, "Dialect Forms," p. 374; for the less frequent alternation of *p* and *bh*, notably, however, in a variation of *api* for *abhi*, see Richard Salomon, "The Inscription of Senavarman King of Oḍi," *Indo-Iranian Journal* 29 [1986]: 261–93, especially 276–77. For evidence that the Sarvāstivādins at one time employed Gāndhārī, see von Hinüber, "Origin and Varieties of Buddhist Sanskrit," pp. 353–54.) Similarly, this dialectical variation may have led to a loss of distinction between forms derived from the prefix *api* and root *lap* and *abhi-lāpa* in the sense of chatter or express. Thus, instead of *a-v(p)ilāpana* or *api-lāpana*, the corresponding form *abhi-lapana* might result, also induced by familiarity with the use of derivatives from *lap* in other contexts. In the Pāli canon *apilāpana* with the sense of "noting or fixing," derived from the prefix *api* or *abhi* and root *lap* or understood by commentators, if only to underscore this distinct meaning, to be derived from the privative *a-* or the root *plu*, occurs alongside numerous forms of *abhilāpa* with the predominant sense of chatter or express. Thus, the Pāli tradition would appear to preserve a distinct semantic use of linguistically distinct derivatives. Accordingly, it is unlikely that Sanskrit redactors would conflate forms that were unequivocally recognized to have distinct meanings. Rather, one might assume that at some point early within the northern Indian Buddhism tradition before its lin-

guistic standardization, terms were merged or distinctions were lost. The enlarged semantic range of *abhilapana* resulting from this merging might later have been retrospectively narrowed by harmonizing commentary and standardizing translation.

83. *Abhilāpa* is clearly interpreted as derived from the root *lap* and is translated consistently in Chinese with some sense of "expression." See, for example, AKB 4.77c p. 247.9, and *yen* in HTAKB 17 T.29 88a28; and *yü* in PAKB 12 T.29 243b12. See also AKB 7.38c–d p. 418.16; *shuo* in HTAKB 27 T.29 142a18; and *yen* in PAKB 20 T.29 293b1; for the same translation of *vāc*, see AKB 7.39b p. 419.3; HTAKB 27 T.29 142b8; PAKB 20 T.29 293b7. See also Nagao, *Madhyāntavibhāga-bhāṣya*, 66.9 (*kārikā* 5.16); *yen* or *yen-yü* in Paramārtha's translation T.31 461c24, 29; *hsi-lun* in Hsüan-tsang's translation T.31 475a20; Lévi, *Sthiramati, Madhyāntavibhāgaṭīkā*, 219.8ff. Though it is not certain that Hsüan-tsang understood *abhilapana* as derived from the root, *lap*, support for this interpretation is found in one passage in his translation of the *Madhyāntavibhāgabhāṣya*, where he uses *chi-yen* as a translation for *asampramoṣa*. This would only be possible if Hsüan-tsang identified *asampramoṣa* with *abhilapana*, as suggested in Sthiramati's commentary and finally understood *abhilapana* as derived from *lap*. See Nagao, *Madhyāntavibhāga-bhāṣya*, 52.4 (*kārikā* 4.5): *ālambane 'saṃmoṣo* . . . ; 52.6 (*bhāṣya*): *smṛtir ālambane 'saṃpramoṣaḥ;* Hsüan-tsang's translation T.31 471c22ff. Cf. Lévi, *Sthiramati, Madhyāntavibhāgaṭīkā*, 175.7ff, 176.21–22. On the meaning in later Mahāyāna texts of *abhilāpa*, used in connection with the terms *prapañca* and *vikalpa* to denote verbal extension or conceptualization, see Lambert Schmithausen, *Der Nirvāṇa-Abschnitt in der Viniścayasaṃgrahaṇī der Yogācārabhūmiḥ*, Österreichische Akademie der Wissenschaften, Philosophisch-historische Klasse 264, 8 (Vienna: Österreichische Akademie der Wissenschaften, 1969), 137ff. For an example of a similar use of *abhilāpa* by Abhinavagupta, in the context of explanations of the verbalizing that in some form always accompanies or constitutes conceptualization or conscious recognition and identification, see K. A. Subramania Iyer, *Bhartṛhari, A Study of the Vākyapdīya in the Light of the Ancient Commentaries*, Deccan College Building Centenary and Silver Jubilee Series, 68 (Poona: Deccan College, 1969), 107, 436.

84. In his various commentaries, Sthiramati appears to accept a relation between *abhilapana* and the various derivatives from the root, *lap*, involving some sense of "expression." For example, in one passage, he identifies *abhilapana* as the teaching that is to be established in the mind. See Lévi, *Sthiramati, Madhyāntavibhāgaṭīkā*, 175.7–8: *smṛtir ālaṃbane 'sammoṣa iti vistarīkṛita ālambanam iti cittasthāpanīyam avavādavastv abhilapanam ity arthaḥ*. In another, he equates mental chatter (*jalpa*) with *abhilapana*, specifically, defining that mental chatter from which attention (*manaskāra*) results as *abhilapana* by the mind and speech. See ibid., 218.17ff: . . . *vāṅmanobhyāṃ yad abhilapanaṃ sa jalpa* . . . This attention resulting from mental chatter is then described as pervaded by expression (*abhilāpa*) and concept (*saṃjñā*). See ibid., 219.11ff: . . . *abhilāpasaṃjñāparibhāvitatvāj jalpamanaskāra ucyata iti*. It is of interest that *jalpamanaskāra* in this discussion is explained as attention resulting from chatter, which is in turn identified with *abhilapana* and finally with *smṛti*. This order echoes the Abhidharma lists of mental concomitants in which *manaskāra* follows *smṛti*.

85. See MVB 16 T.27 79c6ff, 90 T.27 463a20ff, 95 T.27 493c24ff, 145 T.27 745a7ff.

86. Yamada (*Daijō Bukkyō*, pp. 409ff) cites possible scriptural precedents for a classification of mental factors into ten groups (e.g., SN 45–47 *Okkantasaṃyutta, Uppādasaṃyutta, Kilesasaṃyutta* 3: 225ff) and proposes five stages in the development of the Abhidharma classification of mental factors; a listing of discrete mental factors first appears in the *Dharmaskandha* (DS 10 T.26 500c17ff); the term "ten *mahābhūmika* factors" first appears in the *Dhātukāya* (DK T.26 614b14ff) and *Prakaraṇapāda* (PP 2 T.26 (1541) 634a25ff, 2 T.26 (1542) 698c10ff); and the final classification of five groups of mental factors, adopted by later Abhidharma treatises, takes shape in the **Saṃyuktābhidharmahṛdayaśāstra* (SAHŚ 2 T.28 880c29ff). For the ten *mahābhūmika* factors, see MVB 42 T.27 220a2ff.

87. See Saṅghabhadra's detailed treatment of each of the ten *mahābhūmika* factors, NAS 10 T.29 388b25ff.

88. MVB 187 T.27 938b12ff.

89. NAS 10 T.29 389b12ff.

90. Cf. AARŚ T.28 978c7ff, where *smṛti* is explained in terms of attention within the stream of mental events.

91. NAS 10 T.29 384b12ff.

92. Cf. TSŚ 6 T.32 288b7ff, which defines *smṛti* as knowing that which has been previously experienced.

93. NAS 10 T.29 389b19–21.

94. NAS 10 T.29 389b24–25.

95. Cf. P'u-kuang 4 T.41 74b21ff; Fa-pao 4 T.41 527c13ff.

96. Sthiramati, like Saṅghabhadra, accepts nonloss and fixing or noting as the activities of mindfulness, but differs from Saṅghabhadra in his definition of fixing or noting (*abhilapanatā*) as "the repeated retention of the features of the object-support pertaining to a given object grasped previously." Lévi, *Vijñaptimātratāsiddhi*, 26: . . . *pūrvagṛhītasya vastunaḥ punaḥ punarālambanākārasmaraṇam abhilapanatā*. For Sthiramati, fixing or noting is clearly the recursive operation of recollection: that is, grasping once again a previously experienced object. For further discussion of Sthiramati's interpretation, see Paul Griffiths's chapter in this volume. Hsüang-tsang also emphatically limits the activity of mindfulness to past objects; therefore, mindfulness cannot be accepted as functioning in each momentary mental event with regard to a present object. See *Ch'eng wei-shih lun* 5 T.31 28b20ff Cf. K'uei-chi's *Ch'eng wei-shih lun shu-chi 5 pen* T.43 396b23ff For Hsüan-tsang, the proper function of mindfulness is to support concentration (*samādhi*): mindfulness is able to extract concentration because it recollects and retains previously experienced objects causing them not to be lost. See *Ch'eng wei-shih lun* 5 T. 31 28b18ff.

97. These conditions include: a particular state of mind that accords with the concept of the previously experienced object; orientation toward the object to be remembered; a similar or related concept; expectation; obligation; habit; and finally, a corporeal basis free of distraction. See AKB 9 p. 472.16ff; SAKV p. 710.32ff. *Ch'eng wei-shih lun* 5 T. 31 28b24–25. Cf ADV #27 p. 22.2ff. See also the chapter by P. S. Jaini in this volume.

98. MVB 11 T.27 55a16. Cf. AVB 6 T.28 42a12ff.

99. MVB 12 T.27 55c28ff.

100. MVB 12 T.27 57b9ff, 12 T.27 57c22ff.

101. For a discussion of the terms *ākāra* and *ālambana*, see Paul Griffiths's chapter in this volume.

102. This view is attributed to Vasumitra: MVB 12 T.27 57c24ff.

103. See MVB 12 T.27 57c28ff. For an analogous discussion of the process of forgetting, see MVB 12 T.27 58b5ff.

104. MVB 12 T.27 58b26ff. Three reasons for forgetfulness are also given by Vasumitra (MVB 12 T.27 58b24ff): (1) not securely grasping the characteristics of the previous object; (2) the present operation of a dissimilar series; and (3) losing mindfulness.

105. NAS 19 T.29 447c9ff, 19 T.29 448a2ff.

106. Cf. NAS 19 T.29 448a8ff, for a refutation of Śrīlāta's theory of the secondary or subsidiary element (*sui-chieh*, **anudhātu*).

107. AKB 5.2a p. 278.23ff: . . . *anubhavajñānajā smṛtyutpādanaśaktir* . . . Cf. SAKV p. 444.11ff.

108. NAS 45 T.29 597b10ff.

Abbreviations

ADV: Padmanabh S. Jaini, ed. *Abhidharmadīpa with Vibhāṣāprabhāvṛtti*. Tibetan Sanskrit Works Series 4. Patna: Kashi Prasad Jayaswal Research Institute, 1977.

AARŚ: *Abhidharmāmṛtarasaśāstra*. T.28 (1553). Ghoṣaka, trans. anonymous.

AAŚ: *Abhidharmāvatāraśāstra*. T.28 (1554). Attributed to Skandhila(?), trans. Hsüan-tsang.

AHŚ-D: **Abhidharmahṛdayaśāstra*. T.28 (1550). Dharmaśrī, trans. Saṅghadeva.

AHŚ-U: **Abhidharmahṛdayaśāstra*. T.28 (1551). Upaśānta, trans. Narendrayaśas.

AKB: P. Pradhan, ed. *Abhidharmakośabhāṣyam of Vasubandhu*, 2d ed. Tibetan Sanskrit Works Series 8. Patna: Kashi Prasad Jayaswal Research Institute, 1975.

AN: Robert Morris and E. Hardy, eds. *The Aṅguttaranikāya*, 5 vols. London: Pali Text Society, 1885–1890; reprint, 1960.

ASPŚ: **Abhidharmasamayapradīpikāśāstra*. T.29 (1563). Saṅghabhadra, trans. Hsüan-tsang.

AVB: *Abhidharmavibhāṣāśāstra*. T.28 (1546). Trans. Buddhavarman, Tao-t'ai.

DA: *Dīrghāgama*. T.1 (1). Trans. Buddhayaśas, Chu Fo-nien.

DK: *Dhātukāya*. T.26 (1540). Attributed to Pūrṇa (Skt.), Vasumitra (Ch.), trans. Hsüan-tsang.

DN: T. W. Rhys Davids and J. E. Carpenter, eds. *The Dīghanikāya*, 3 vols. London: Pali Text Society, 1890–1911; reprint, 1960.

DS: *Dharmaskandha*. T.26 (1537). Attributed to Śāriputra (Skt.) Mahāmaudgalyāyana (Ch.), trans. Hsüan-tsang.

EA: *Ekottarāgama*. T.2 (125). Trans. Saṅghadeva.

Fa-pao: *Chü-she lun shu*. T.41 (1822). Fa-pao.

HTAKB: *A-p'i-ta-mo chü-she lun*. T.29 (1558). Vasubandhu, trans. Hsüan-tsang.

Kaidō: *Abidatsuma kusharon hōgi*. T.64 (2251). Kaidō.

MA: *Madhyamāgama*. T.1 (26). Trans. Saṅghadeva.

MN: V. Trenckner et al., eds., *The Majjhima-Nikāya*, 3 vols. London: Pali Text Society, 1896–1899; reprint, 1960.

MPPS: **Mahāprajñāpāramitāsūtropadeśa*. T.25 (1509). Attributed to Nāgārjuna, trans. Kumārajīva.

MVB: *Mahāvibhāṣāśāstra*. T.27 (1545). Trans. Hsüan-tsang.

NAS: *Nyāyānusāraśāstra*. T.29 (1562). Saṅghabhadra, trans. Hsüan-tsang.

PAKB: *A-p'i-ta-mo chü-she lun*. T.29 (1559). Vasubandhu, trans. Paramārtha.

PP: *Prakaraṇapāda*. T.26 (1541). Attributed to Vasumitra, trans. Guṇabhadra, Bodhiyaśas. T.26 (1542). Attributed to Vasumitra, trans. Hsüan-tsang.

P'u-kuang: *Chü-she lun chi*. T.41 (1821). P'u-kuang.

SA: *Saṃyuktāgama*. T.2 (99). Trans. Guṇabhadra.

SAHŚ: **Saṃyuktābhidharmahṛdayaśāstra*. T.28 (1552). Dharmatrāta, trans. Saṅghavarman.

SAKV: Unrai Wogihara, ed. *Sphuṭārthā Abhidharmakośavyākhyā: The Work of Yaśomitra*. Tokyo: Publishing Association of the *Abhidharmakośavyākhyā*, 1932.

ŚAŚ: *Śāriputrābhidharmaśāstra*. T.28 (1548). Trans. Dharmayaśas, Dharmagupta.

SN: L. Feer, ed. *The Saṃyutta-Nikāya*, 5 vols. London: Pali Text Society, 1884–1898; reprint, 1960.

SP: *Saṅgītiparyāya*. T.26 (1536). Attributed to Mahākauṣṭhila (Skt.), Śāriputra (Ch.), trans. Hsüan-tsang.

T: Junjirō Takakusu, Kaikyoku Watanabe, and Gemmyō Ono, eds. *Taishō shinshū daizōkyō*. Tokyo: Taishō issaikyō kankōkai, 1924–1932.

TSŚ: **Tattvasiddhiśāstra*. T.32 (1646). Harivarman, trans. Kumārajīva.

VK: *Vijñānakāya*. T.26 (1539). Attributed to Devaśarman, trans. Hsüan-tsang.

YBŚ: *Yogācārabhūmiśāstra*. T.30 (1579). Attributed to Maitreya, trans. Hsüan-tsang.

Chinese Characters

chi 記

chi-yen 記言

hsi-lun 戲論

ming-chi 明記

ming-chi pu-wang 明記不忘

ming-chi-i 明記憶

ming-liao chi-i 明了記憶

pu-wang 不忘

hsin ming pu-wang 心明不忘

shuo 說

sui-chieh 隨界

yen 言

yen-yü 言語

yü 語

Memory in Classical Indian Yogācāra

PAUL J. GRIFFITHS

Prolegomena

Buddhist intellectuals were not particularly interested in giving a systematic account of the process of remembering as a topic of interest in its own right.[1] Their treatment of it was almost always tangential, the product of pressing conceptual and practical concerns in other areas; such discussions of the phenomenon as there are in the texts of the tradition occur almost always in contexts where either meditational practice or the nature of the person are the main focus. This is partly true of Western discussions of memory as well; these too have often occurred in the context of analyses of the nature of the person. But the absence of discussions of memory as a phenomenon in its own right in Indian Buddhist texts is nevertheless striking and often frustrating for the Westerner studying the tradition from outside with an eye to extracting from it "the Buddhist position" on memory and remembering.

In this chapter I shall focus directly on this puzzlement and frustration by exploring three problems. The first is terminological and a problem only for those studying the tradition from without: Buddhist terms for memory and remembering, derived for the most part from the Sanskrit root *smṛ-*, form an uneasy semantic match with English terms for the same phenomenon, and so make understanding difficult; in order for further investigations to be productive it must be acknowledged that very often the semantic range of *smṛ*-terms is very different from that of Western terms for remembering. The second is a conceptual problem, and was perceived as such by the intellectuals of the Buddhist tradition just as much as it is by contemporary Western scholars: what account of memory and remembering can be given if one resolutely and systematically rejects a substantivist theory of personal identity and the continuity of persons through time? And the third problem is one of silence: some vitally important dimensions of the contemporary Western analysis of memory and remembering appear to have no analogue in Buddhism. This is especially true of phenomenological analyses of memory and remembering.

In this chapter I explore each of these three problems as far as possible in terms of the texts of the classical Indian Yogācāra. These texts are relatively little used and little known in the English-speaking world, and this alone is sufficient reason for turning to them. But it is also the case that the development in them of new and sophisticated ideas about consciousness sheds some light on the problems to be discussed. However, the terminological discussions in the next section, although they will use mostly Yogācāra materials, will also have much wider application. I say as much as I do about terminological questions because it seems to me that in the case of terms for memory, as so often in other contexts, our standard translations are often misleading and do not help those interested in cross-cultural philosophizing. What I say about the terminological issues in this first section, then, should be understood to apply fairly generally to all the scholastic traditions in India.

I offer no definitive answers to any of my three problems; this is especially true in the case of the third, where my comments can be only tentative in the face of complete silence from the texts.

Terminology: The Semantic Range of *Smṛti* and *Anusmṛti*

Smṛti is frequently defined as a technical term in the Abhidharma texts of the Buddhist traditions. The Vaibhāṣika view is that it is one of the *mahābhūmikacaittāḥ*, those mental factors present in all states of mind; it is thus not possible to be conscious and not to have memory functioning.[2] Yogācāra works, by contrast, usually do not list *smṛti* as one of the mental factors present in all states of mind. For them, when they do specify to which category it belongs,[3] it is usually said to be a *viniyata [viṣaya]dharma*, a mental event the scope or object of which is restricted and that therefore is present only some of the time.[4] I shall return to the possible significance of this classificatory change below.

The most common definition of *smṛti* says that it consists in the mind not being deprived or not losing track of (*asampramoṣa*) a particular support for cognition (*ālambana*). Typical here is the definition in the *Abhidharmakośabhāṣya* (fourth or fifth century C.E.), which itself is taken from earlier Sarvāstivādin Abhidharma texts.[5] Almost identical formal definitions are found in many Yogācāra texts;[6] for instance, the following definition from the fourth century *Abhidharmasamuccaya:*

> *Smṛti* is the mind's nondeprivation of an object with which it is directly acquainted. Its function is nondistraction.[7]

On this, Sthiramati's commentary (c. sixth century) says:

> "An object with which it is directly acquainted" should be understood to mean a previously experienced object. "Its function is nondistraction"

> means that when one takes note once again of a support for cognition by means of *smṛti*, this is because of the nondistraction of the mind.[8]

A similar definition is found in the *Mahāyānasūtrālaṅkārabhāṣya*.[9]

These definitions make clear that *smṛti* is concerned with attention to some object (*vastu*) or support for cognition (*ālambana*), an object that was experienced at some time in the past. A mind in which *smṛti* is present does not become distracted (*avikṣepa*) from taking note (*abhilap-*) of its intentional object.

This connection of *smṛti* with a verbal, if not actually vocalized, taking note of a particular object was commonly made by Sarvāstivādin Ābhidhārmikas, as well as in the classical Vaibhāṣika texts, and was taken over by the Yogācāra theorists. The idea, briefly and somewhat too simply, is that *smṛti* consists essentially of paying attention to and taking note of objects of knowledge; it is an intentional act of the mind and thus overlaps in meaning considerably with *attention* (*manaskāra*), the eighth in the list of mental factors present in all states of mind as they are usually given, immediately following *smṛti*. The mental/verbal noting of the existence and nature of a particular object of cognition has by itself nothing essentially to do with the remembering of some past object of cognition; it can operate just as well in the present as in the past, and it is perhaps more natural to take its primary sense as having a present reference. The fact that *smṛti* notes (*abhilap-*) these objects, however, makes possible their preservation as objects of consciousness (hence the reference to ''nondeprivation,'' *asampramoṣa*), and thus explains the extension of the term to cover at least some of the same semantic ground as the English word *memory* and its cognates. In other words, I suggest that the basic meaning of *smṛti* and derivatives in Buddhist technical discourse—basic in the sense that this meaning is both temporally and logically prior to other meanings—has to do with observation and attention, not with awareness of past objects.

Perhaps the fullest technical definition of *smṛti* in the texts of the classical Indian Yogācāra is found in the *Triṃśikābhāṣya* (fourth century CE):

> *Smṛti* is the mind's nondeprivation of an object with which it is directly acquainted; it is the mind's taking note of such an object. *An object with which it is directly acquainted* means a previously experienced [object]. The term *nondeprivation* is used because [*smṛti*] is the cause of [the mind] not losing its apprehension of a support for cognition. *Taking note* refers to the repeated memory of the modes of appearance of a support for cognition derived from a previously apprehended object. . . . Further this [*smṛti*] has the function of nondistraction. This means that when the mind is taking note of some support for cognition it is not distracted by other supports for cognition or other modes of appearance.[10]

This definition makes matters still clearer: *smṛti* is the cause, while it lasts, of continuous and unbroken mental attention to some object. For the first time also we find here a useful gloss on *abhilapanatā:* this is a repeated (and presumably also unbroken while it lasts) awareness of the way or ways in which a particular object appears to the mind cognizing it, an awareness that continues after the initial apprehension, the *pūrvagrahaṇa,* of the object has ceased. Sthiramati's definition also introduces the important term *ākāra,* here translated "mode of appearance," and some comments on this will further our understanding of what Yogācāra theorists meant by *smṛti.*

Etymologically, *ākāra* is a nominal form derived from the root *kṛ-,* "to do, to make," together with the prefix *ā-*. In conjunction with verbal forms this prefix can sometimes suggest "back" or "toward"; so *āgacchati* from *ā* + *gam* (a root meaning "to go") often means "to come" ("to go back," "to go toward"). With *kṛ-* the prefix *ā-* sometimes gives the sense "to bring near," or "to confront." This derivation had some effect on the ways in which *ākāra* was used in technical philosophical texts; it often has the sense of "to confront" or "to bring face-to-face with."[11]

In nontechnical Sanskrit *ākāra* often denotes simply something's shape or external appearance: to be *ākāravat* is to be shapely. In Pāli texts the adjectival form *ākāravatī* is often used to modify *saddhā,* an appropriate translation might be "well-formed confidence" and an appropriate gloss "confidence with the right components in the right configuration." A cognate term *ākṛti,* also a nominal item derived from *ā* + *kṛ-,* is extremely important in Mīmāṃsā and Vedānta theories about meaning and reference. A word's *ākṛti* is "a sort of composite class-contour or concrete universal in virtue of which members of a particular class become individuated."[12] It would not, perhaps, be misleading to think of this "concrete universal" as having a shape (*ākāra*) in virtue of which it is the universal it is and not some other. Indeed, based on this use of *ākṛti,* adherents of the Mīmāṃsā regard a word as producing an *ākāra* in its speakers and hearers. This *ākāra,* as Madeleine Biardeau puts it, is "l'objet direct de la perception reconnaitre,"[13] a meaning that, as we shall see, is close in some respects to the technical Buddhist usage.

Among Buddhist uses of *ākāra* the most significant for the purposes of this study is its use in basic Buddhist theory of cognition. It was (and is) one of the termini technici of this theory. In the *Abhidharmakośabhāṣya,* it is defined thus: "*ākāra* is that mode in which all thought, together with its concomitant mental events, apprehends objects."[14] The implication, as the text goes on to state, is that every mental event which has an intentional object also has an *ākāra.*[15] Further, according to the basic theory, every mental event does in fact have an intentional object, variously called *ālambana, viṣaya, vastu,* and so forth.[16] These terms are not synonymous, and it is not possible to explore fully the subtle differentiations among them. The important point for my purposes is that a given mental event's *ālambana* is that which appears in consciousness, and that same mental event's *ākāra* is the mode under which it appears. So if, for example, one adopts an adverbial account of sensory perception, according to which every instance of sensory perception is described as an appearance to a subject of kind K, the *ālambana* of that appearance is its direct object—say, a color patch—and its *ākāra* (or, better, *ākārāḥ*) constitutes the phenomenological characteristic or characteristics, the flavor, of that appearance. An *ālambana* thus often can be thought of simply as a mental image. Every mental event has (or, perhaps better, is) a particular way of appearing to its subject. This is its *ākāra,* its "mode of appearance." Naturally, any given mental event's *ākāra* will be correlated in some more or less precise way with its intentional object.[17]

This view that every mental event has both an intentional object and some phenomenological content (both *ālambana* and *ākāra*) was the subject of much controversy among later Indian Buddhist epistemologists. Notoriously, those later Indian schoolbooks (Buddhist and non-Buddhist) in which the philosophical views of the various sects and schools are schematically set forth for educational purposes, tend to divide Yogācāra thinkers into *sākāravādinaḥ* and *nirākāravādinaḥ.*[18] The latter are those who think that consciousness is essentially pure and without phenomenological content (*ākāra*) of any kind. The former think that consciousness is essentially intentional and that even the consciousness of an awakened being, a buddha, must have phenomenological content (though, of course, not the same kind of phenomenological content as that occurring in most instances of everyday consciousness). However, most of the explicit references to this controversy postdate Śāntideva (eighth century CE) and the most detailed discussions of it are found in the works of Ratnākaraśānti and Mokṣākaragupta (both c. eleventh century) and cannot be entered into here.[19]

Leaving aside this debate about whether consciousness is or is not essentially *sākāra,* "possessed of modes of appearance," Sthiramati's use of the term in his definition of *smṛti* is suggestive. It moves us into the realm of memory's phenomenology because, as I understand it, *ākāra* is essentially a phenomenological term; it refers to the way in which a remembered past object appears in consciousness at the present. Sthiramati does not tell us anything more than or other than that memory does have such phenomenological content and makes no attempt to differentiate, phenomenologically, between a memory-event and other intentional acts of consciousness; and I shall return to the reasons for this in the final section of this chapter.

To summarize what has been said thus far, *smṛti* is an intentional act of the mind, directed often, but not necessarily, toward some past object; although there need not have been an unbroken chain of such awareness connecting the occurrence of some specific memory-event with the experience of which it is a memory, any specific memory-event, while it lasts, does not lose awareness of the phenomenological content of that past experience because it continually "takes note" of it; and while it is so engaged in taking note, no other object of consciousness, past or present, disturbs its awareness of its support.[20]

The leitmotif in all of this is active attention. Remembering is something one actively engages in, not something one passively undergoes. And it is this stress on attention as an activity of the mind which provides the conceptual connection with the most common context for the use of *smṛti* in Buddhist texts: *smṛti* as a type of meditational practice, usually called "the application of *smṛti*" (*smṛtyupasthāna*). In these contexts, the standard English translation of the term has become "mindfulness." When one engages in the practice of mindfulness one pays close attention to whatever one is taking as the object of one's meditational practice;[21] one notes its presence and its nature, allotting it its proper place in the complex category system evolved by Buddhist thinkers to classify the existents that make up the universe, and thus approaches ever more closely to the awareness of things as they really are (*yathābhūtajñānadarśana*). Here too the term *smṛti* carries with it no essential reference to remembering past events, though the very act of paying close attention to the present contents of one's mind makes it possible to recall those contents at some later time.

The goal of meditational practice of this kind is a dispassionate and disinterested observational awareness of the content and nature of each and every mental event (with it intentional subject (*ālambana*) and its phenomenological content (*ākāra*) as it occurs. One clearly cannot translate *smṛti* as "memory" in such contexts, but the fact that the same term is used in these meditational contexts as in the more technical Ābhidhārmika definitions of memory and remembering should make us aware that attention is a more important part of the term's semantic range than is reference to some past event.

A good example of this systematic semantic ambiguity (from an anglophone viewpoint; not, of course, from a Sanskritic Buddhist viewpoint) is found in the *Mahāyānasūtrālaṅkārabhāṣya*. In a lengthy discussion of the sixty aspects of the buddha's speech, one of which is freedom from grammatical error or vulgarity (*apaśabda*), the text says that the buddha does not make such errors because he has no loss of memory or attention.[22] The term used, of course, is *smṛti*, but here, as so often, it covers a good part of the semantic range of both memory and attention in English.

The connection of *smṛti* with meditational practice in fact is very common in Yogācāra texts. For example, the *Vijñaptimātratāsiddhi* repeats the usual definition of memory in terms of the mind's nondeprivation of its object, and then goes on to say that *smṛti* serves as the support for concentration because it continuously preserves and retains the object experienced (*anubhūtārtha?*) and thus makes concentration (*samādhi*) on it possible.[23] Similarly, a significant proportion of the uses of the term in the *Mahāyānasūtrālaṅkāra* corpus place it explicitly in the context of meditational practice, either as a proper basis for the development of dhyāna,[24] or as part of a discussion of the application of mindfulness.[25]

In addition to the use of *smṛti* in such contexts, there is also an associated term, *anusmṛti*, the use of which makes the association of words derived from *smṛ-* with attention and meditation still more evident. I shall provisionally translate *anusmṛti* as "contemplation." The two most common contexts in which it is found are in the compounds "contemplation of the Buddha" (*buddhānusmṛti*) and "contemplation of previous lives" (*pūrvanivāsānusmṛti*).[26] Although the subject matter of these two practices is quite different, the method they employ is very similar. I offer comments here only on the latter.

Contemplation of previous lives is also, essentially, a meditational practice. The basic textual unit describing it runs as follows:

> [The practitioner] contemplates [*anusmarati*] [his] many previous lives: he contemplates one, two, three, four, five, ten, twenty, thirty, forty, fifty, one hundred lives, many hundreds of lives . . . [the practitioner] thinks: "At that time I had such-and-such a name, such-and-such a family, such-and-such a birth, such-and-such nourishment, such-and-such a length of life . . . "[27]

The active verbal form *anusmarati* found in this unit of tradition is often translated "remembers"; although memory is certainly involved here—the mental events that occur meet the technical requirements set forth for a *smaraṇacitta* in the next section—it seems to me that the central element of the exercise, once again, is the active exercise of attention. One turns one's mind toward one's previous lives, paying lingering and detailed attention to the events in each one of them; one can practice this, according to the tradition, and so get better at it. At first it may be the case that one can penetrate back to only a few of one's previous lives, but as one contemplates single-mindedly and undistractedly, one will be able to retrace the causal chain that connects that past person with this present one further and further.[28]

The semantic range of *smṛ-* and derivatives, then, spans that of memory-words and attention-words in English. This is evident in the use of *anusmṛ-* just discussed, but is still clearer in the single most common use of *smṛti* itself, as a label for a certain kind of meditational practice. It would probably be less misleading to translate *smṛti* as "attention" or "advertence" and *anusmṛti* as "contemplation" than to use the currently popular translations.

It would then be necessary to acknowledge that, although *smṛti* does sometimes refer to an advertence whose object is some past event in the life of the adverter, this is not a central or essential part of its semantic range. It follows that, when Buddhists discuss (what we would call) memory and remembering, they do so as part of a broader interest in intentional acts of the mind and with special reference to those psychotropic intentional acts that we call "meditation."[29]

Necessary Conditions for the Occurrence of Memory

Western philosophers, when thinking about memory, have often done so in the context of thinking about what persons are. They have been concerned to set forth those conditions that are individually necessary and jointly sufficient for a particular mental event to be properly classified as an instance of memory, and to use such an account in the service of some theory about what constitutes continuity of personal identity through time. For example, it might be said that a given cognitive state, C, occurring to a particular subject at a particular time is a memory-event if and only if C corresponds, in some more-or-less well-defined sense, to another cognitive state C-prime, which occurred to that same subject at some previous time.[30] Such accounts make ideas about what constitutes memory logically dependent on ideas about what constitutes a person. Conversely, accounts of what constitutes a person are often given in terms of the occurrence of memory. Thus it is often said that some person is the same as another if and only if the former has memories of events belonging to the history of the latter.[31]

Buddhist intellectuals in India also showed considerable interest in giving accounts of memory and remembering within the context of theories about what persons are. They were much exercised by the conceptual problems involved in giving an account of what it is for a given mental event to be a memory-event without thereby presupposing or entailing some substantivist or quasi-substantivist account of what it is to be a person. This issue was forced upon them from without: most non-Buddhist intellectuals in India relied on some more or less substantivist theory of what it is to be a person in developing an account of memory, and one of the most common challenges brought by non-Buddhists against Buddhists in India was that the Buddhist rejection of the idea that persons are substances that endure, coupled with their rejection of the idea that anything whatever endures through time, together make it impossible to give an adequate account of what it is to remember.[32]

The problem, in large part, is one of accounting for unactualized potentialities or capacities. Any account of memory must include some account of how it is a particular subject has the capacity or potentiality to have memories of experiences that he or she is not currently having. Giving such an account is made somewhat easier if one has a substance-attribute ontology, for then capacities can become properties of enduring substances. Things are more difficult if one rejects altogether, as most Buddhist intellectuals did, the idea that there are any property-possessors (*dharmin*) and thus the idea that there are any substances that endure through time. Where, given such an ontology, are the capacities and potentialities for unactualized memories to be located?

These challenges made it necessary for Indian Buddhist intellectuals to give a sophisticated causal account of memory in which the conditions governing the classification of a given mental event as a memory-event, a *smaraṇacitta,* are set forth and defended. In these accounts, the terms employed for "memory" are usually *smṛti* or *smaraṇa,* here used with specific reference to advertence to a past event. These terms are usually connected in such contexts with another: *pratyabhijñāna,* perhaps best translated "recognition." Recognition follows from memory by way of a conceptualized (and perhaps even vocalized) judgment that (*iti*) the experience in question is an instance of memory. Paradigmatically, the judgment in question is of the form *I saw this.*[33] The maker of the judgment identifies, in making it, with the original experiencer of the experiential object, though according to standard-issue Buddhist accounts of the continuity of personal identity through time, she cannot be substantively identical with that original experiencer.

Those who gave such an account were concerned to avoid postulating the existence of an enduring substance as the locus for memory events or the possessor of unrealized potential memories. The version of the account that became standard in the Sarvāstivādin Abhidharma is presented by Vasubandhu in an appendix to the *Abhidharmakośabhāṣya* and is translated elsewhere in the present volume.[34] In that passage, Vasubandhu attempts to show that it is possible to explain all the significant features of what constitutes a person without resorting to substances.

This account can be restated thus: each instance of memory (*smaraṇacitta*) is caused by, arises from, a specific mental event (*cittaviśeṣa*). The mental event in which the original object was experienced and that in which it is remembered must be part of the same mental continuum (*ekasantānika*). The specific mental event in question must be causally related to a previously experienced object (*pūrvānubhūtārtha*) in a nonaccidental way; further, the specific mental event in question must be similar in kind to that produced by the previous experience of the object; and there must be no obstructions, physical, cognitive, or affective, to the production of an instance of memory. These conditions, if met, jointly both allow and guarantee that a particular mental event is an instance of memory.

For example, suppose at some time in the past I heard a baby cry. For a later mental event to qualify as a memory of this original auditory experience it must be the case that the subsequent mental event is causally related to the previous one in that it belongs to the same mental continuum.[35] Then, the subsequent mental event must be similar in kind to that of which it is a memory: it too must be auditory. And finally, there must be no unusual conditions obtaining in my psychophysical organism that might prevent the memory-experience from occurring.

But this account of the causal mechanisms governing the occurrence of memory and its location in particular persons does not meet all the desiderata that caused its construction. It asserts that continua of mental events can be individuated one from another, and that specifiable causal connections can obtain between mental events that will explain the occurrence of memory. But it does not deal directly with the problem of unrealized potentialities; indeed, the account translated above makes no attempt whatever to explain what kind of existence these unrealized potentialities have.

Although a causal account of memory and remembering such as that presented by Vasubandhu was presupposed by the scholastics of the Yogācāra, it was modified and developed by them in an attempt to supply just this desideratum. They applied to it the metaphors of seed (*bīja*) and tendency (*vāsanā*), metaphors associated above all with the store-consciousness (*ālayavijñāna*) and used by Yogācāra thinkers in a variety of contexts to explain those problems of continuity and potentiality left (as they saw it) in need of further elucidation by the scholastics of the Vaibhāṣika and Sautrāntika.[36] The metaphor of seed and growth already had been applied to memory by Sautrāntika thinkers;[37] in their view, seeds exist in every mental continuum (*cittasantāna*) with the capacity (*śakti* or *sāmarthya*) to engender memory-events in that same continuum. These seeds can lie dormant for long periods of time, being planted at the time when the original experience occurred and growing to manifest maturity when the later memory of that original experience occurs.

The use of such an image immediately raises questions: where, for example, are the seeds located while they are ripening? The Yogācāra answer is that they are located in the store-consciousness. Indeed, one of the major epithets applied to this store-consciousness in virtually all Yogācāra texts is "that which possesses all seeds" (*sarvabījaka*)[38]—including, of course, the seeds of memory. The *locus classicus* for the application of this epithet to the store-consciousness is to be found in the *Triṃśikābhāśya:*

> "Here, maturation is that consciousness which is called 'store', the container of all seeds" . . . [the phrase] *which is called 'store'* identifies that consciousness which is known as the store-consciousness with the transformation which is maturation. It is a store because it has the quality of being

> the place in which all defiled seeds are located. *Store* and *place* are synonyms. Alternatively, considered from the viewpoint of effect, [the store-consciousness] is that in which all dharmas are stored up or are organized. Or, considered from the viewpoint of cause, the store-[consciousness] is that which acts as storer and organizer with regard to all dharmas. [The store-consciousness] is an instance of consciousness because it cognizes; it is called ''maturation'' because it has the quality of bringing to maturity good and bad karma among all spheres, destinies, wombs, and births. And it is called ''the container of all seeds'' because it has the quality of being the basis of the seeds of all dharmas.[39]

Memory is not explicitly mentioned in this definitional analysis of the store-consciousness. This absence is entirely typical of Yogācāra texts, and I shall return to some speculations as to the reasons for it in what follows. But it does make clear that the store-consciousness is precisely that ''place'' in which all karmic seeds lie dormant until they mature and come to fruition. The direct application of this complex of ideas about dormant potentialities to the question of memory (though not the latter's connection with the store-consciousness) is made clear in the fourth century *Mahāyānsaṅgraha,* perhaps the single most important foundational text of the Indian Yogācāra:

> What is a ''tendency'' (*vāsanā*)? What is designated by this term? It is something which, following upon the conjoint arising and passing away (*sahotpādanirodha*) of something [with some other thing], is yet the generative cause of that same thing. So, for example, sesame seeds are perfumed by their flowers; the two arise and pass away conjointly; and the seeds are the generative cause (*janakanimitta*) of another scent [like that given them by their flowers]. Also, among passionate people, tendencies towards passion arise and cease conjointly with [those acts of] passion [that engendered them]; but their minds [filled with tendencies towards passion, i.e., with seeds] are the cause of that [future passion]. Also, among the learned, tendencies towards learning arise and cease conjointly with those acts of attention towards what is heard [that engendered them]; but their minds [filled with tendencies towards learning] are the cause of their [future] learned discourse. Because they are suffused with such tendencies, they are called ''apprehenders of the doctrine.''[40]

The key term at issue here is *vāsanā,* translated ''tendency'' in the extract just given. It is derived from a verbal root meaning ''to perfume'' or ''to suffuse with scent.'' Hence the first example given, that of sesame seeds and flowers (*tila* and *puṣpa*). The seeds are given a perfuming tendency by the flowers that produce them and it is this that enables them to later generate flowers that have the same scent as those flowers from which the seeds originally came. So also with passionate people and learned people: the acts of passion and study[41] that make them passionate and learned "perfume" the continua of mental events in which they consist with tendencies to later engage in passionate acts or to produce learned discourse again. The tendencies in question come into being at the same time as the actions that produce them, and thus, given pan-Buddhist ideas about the momentary existence of all things,[42] cease at that same time. They can nevertheless continue in existence as a potency, as a seed that can, given the right conditions, mature into memory.[43]

This is perhaps clearest in the example of learning: suppose I learn the verses, the *kārikā,* of the *Abhidharmakośa,* all 613 of them, and listen for months or years to my teacher expounding their meaning. These actions will "perfume" my mental continuum with the "tendency" to engage in learned discourse of my own on the subject matter of the *Abhidharmakośa;* this tendency will exist passively (as a potential or seed) even when I am not actively engaged in thinking about the *Abhidharmakośa;* it will emerge into activity when the external conditions are right and the proper trigger-mechanisms obtain.

According to the Yogācāra metaphysic, these seeds and tendencies are located not in any of the active consciousnesses (*pravṛttivijñāna*), but rather in the store-consciousness (*ālayavijñāna*), that nonintentional consciousness wherein are stored all seeds, all potencies, and all capacities. The occurrence of a memory-event is thus presented as a process of maturation located within an individual consciousness, for my store is not the same as yours. The metaphor throughout is agricultural.

It is doubtful whether the application of this metaphor, picturesque and vivid though it is, marks much of a conceptual advance in Buddhist treatment of remembering. The store-consciousness, as I have argued in detail elsewhere, is best understood as an ad hoc explanatory category, designed to function just as a substance—an enduring possessor of essential and accidental properties—would in accounting for a large class of problems of continuity and potentiality, but without actually being one.[44] In applying it to memory and remembering Yogācāra theorists assert that potential memories have continuity of existence in an individuated store, but do not effectively explain in what sense the store's possession of these potencies differs from a substance's possession of its properties.

Yogācāra theorists do, of course, consistently deny that the store-consciousness is an enduring substance and that anything endures therein. The store, in the standard account, is no more that the totality of the causal powers of its constituent events. To call it "the possessor of all seeds" (*sarvabījaka*) is not to say that it is anything over and above its seeds. But then the only account of memorial potency that can be given is one that allows each seed to reproduce itself as a potential from moment to moment, without making its potential manifest. Such an account certainly labels the mystery; but it can scarcely be said to solve it.

It is interesting to observe that, even though one can infer from the language that Yogācāra theorists use about the store-consciousness that it is indeed the locus of memorial potency, the texts very rarely make this connection explicit. Certainly, if *smṛti* operates through the mechanisms of seed and tendency, and if the store-consciousness is the locus for the occurrence of all such events, *smṛti* too must be explicable in terms of the store-consciousness. But the texts do not say so. Even in the case of the standard eightfold proof of the existence of the store-consciousness[45] *smṛti* is not mentioned as one of those things whose occurrence needs to be explained by the existence of the store-consciousness. The eight proofs do say that such things as the processes of death and rebirth, the interrelationships among the six sense-consciousnesses, the individual Buddhist's gradual purification through appropriate religious practice, and her final attainment of nirvāṇa, can all be properly explained only by the existence of the store-consciousness. And all of these involve variants on the problems of continuity and potentiality already noted, as also does the problem of memory; and yet memory is not invoked in such contexts.

I suspect that the main reason for this lack of explicitness about the importance of the store-consciousness in accounting for memory has to do with the slightly different place that *smṛti* has in the taxonomy of Yogācāra Abhidharma. I have already noted that, at least in the *Triṃśikā* and its commentaries, *smṛti* is categorized not as a mental factor present in all states of mind, as it was in Vaibhāṣika theory, but as a *viniyata [viṣaya]dharma,* a mental dharma that is not always present and whose object is circumscribed. It may simply be that this limitation made it conceptually unnecessary for Yogācāra Ābhidhārmikas to advert specifically to the problem of memory when discussing the store-consciousness. There are, after all, more mental events whose object is circumscribed than there are mental factors present in all states of mind, and to take particular account of all of them may have been thought supererogatory.

This is speculation; the texts do not say. But it is clear that any causal account of memory within the limits of a Yogācāra metaphysic must be given in terms of the store-consciousness; it also seems clear that the issue of giving such an account was not thought to be a pressing need by Yogācāra theorists.

None of what has been said in this section gives much sense of what a memory-event is like, phenomenologically speaking; it is a causal analysis rather than a descriptive one. The latter is, indeed, very hard to come by in the scholastic texts of the Indian Buddhist traditions, Yogācāra no less than other, and I shall conclude by offering some very tentative suggestions as to why this might be.

The Phenomenology of Remembering

In addition to the broadly logical accounts of what properties a given mental event must have for it to be considered a memory, there has been considerable interest in the West in the phenomenology of remembering, in descriptions of what it is like for a subject to engage in one of the many varieties of remembering. Since Husserl, this interest has led to the development of a nuanced and complex account of what it is to remember, of the flavors of memory. The best recent example of work in this line, Edward Casey's study *Remembering*, shows in great detail just how complex, subtle, and interesting the phenomenon of remembering is.

The Yogācāra account of memory, and indeed Buddhist accounts in general, concentrating as they do on the causal mechanisms operative in memory-events, and placing the whole discussion within a framework of interest in certain kinds of observational meditational technique, have, whatever their conceptual advantages and disadvantages, little to offer those interested in the phenomenology of remembering. It is difficult, for example, to see how a memory-event would differ phenomenologically, in Buddhist terms, from simple propositional knowledge about the past, on the one hand, or direct perception of some event in the present, on the other. Recall the account of attention to previous lives briefly discussed earlier in this chapter. The most obvious reading of it is that the meditator, by contemplating the details of her previous lives—by, presumably, direct visual awareness of her previous bodies, direct auditory awareness of her previous words, direct tactile awareness of her previous lovers, and so forth—has direct sensory awareness of them, and is then able to assent to the truth of certain propositions about the past: "Then I had such-and-such a body" and the rest.

There is nothing in the account of the experience of paying attention to ("remembering") the events of previous lives to suggest that Buddhist theorists were interested in what might differentiate the phenomenological feel of such experience for its experiencer from the phenomenological feel of other sensory experiences that are not instances of memory. Such events differ, of course, in the causal determinants that produce them from occurrences of simple propositional knowledge of past events. When I give assent to some proposition of the form *William the Conqueror invaded England in 1066* I have propositional knowledge of a past event that does not meet any of the causal requirements for being a memory-event set forth in the Buddhist discussions surveyed above. But it is not so clear that, or how, my knowledge of this proposition differs phenomenologically from memories of events in my past, either within this life or across many. If it does so differ the texts are not interested in telling us how.

One reason for this lack of interest in the phenomenology of remembering is clear: a key element in any account of it must be the sense of identification that the subject of the memory feels with the subject of the event remembered. And this sense of identification, this strong feeling that the "I" now remembering the aesthetic pleasure involved in reading Jane Austen for the first time, the feel of the volume—the look of the print, the delights of her remorselessly bitter analysis of motive—am the same person as that fourteen-year-old boy who originally had those experiences, from the Buddhist viewpoint, is a mistake with important negative effects on my possibilities for realizing nirvāṇa in the near future. For this sense of identification with the events of my past almost always will involve some degree of *asmimāna*, of "the conceit 'I am', " the constructed idea that I have a continuing identity through time; it thus also inevitably will bring with it a greater interest in the well-being and doings of that past self than in those of others. Worse, a frequent paying of attention to one's memories is one of the most effective ways imaginable of cementing one's sense of oneself as separate from and other than other sentient beings, and thus a direct hindrance to what "exchange of self and other" (*parātmaparivartana*) advocated in so many Buddhist texts as the principle means of enabling action that accords with Buddhist ethics.[46] Finally, one may note that ancillary emotions often connected with remembering—nostalgia, romantic *sehnsucht*, and the like—are also unambiguously negative, at least as far as salvation is concerned.[47]

Finally, it is Buddhist orthodoxy that the extent to which one is successful at paying attention to and experiencing one's previous lives is linked to one's degree of spiritual advancement. Buddhas, at one end of the scale, have continuous direct awareness of each and every event in all of their previous lives; I, on the other, have no memories of mine whatever. And because the further one is along the path to nirvāṇa the less likely one is to engage in the kind of mistaken emotional identification with one's past that makes remembering a phenomenologically distinctive occurrence, it follows that one is unlikely to find much in the way of interest in this phenomenology in those Buddhist texts whose central concern is with soteriology, with the description and advocation of the salvific path. Remembering is not something that buddhas do; it is, propter hoc, also not something in whose phenomenology Buddhist texts are much interested.

Notes

I am grateful to Janet Gyatso for detailed editorial comments on an earlier version of this paper. Her stern but compassionate editorial eye has made the paper much better than it otherwise would have been. I remain responsible for any conceptual problems and lack of clarity that remain.

DT = Sde-dge Tanjur.

PT = Peking Tanjur.

1. Lambert Schmithausen says laconically that "recollection does not appear to have been a prominent issue in classical Yogācāra philosophy." *Ālayavijñāna: On the Origin and Early Development of a Central Concept in Yogācāra Philosophy* (Tokyo: International Institute for Buddhist Studies, 1987), vol. 2, p. 246, n. 18.

2. This point is made in *Abhidharmakośabhāṣya on Abhidharmakośakārikā* II. 24; Dwārikādās Śāstrī, ed., *Abhidharmakośa & Bhāṣya of Ācārya Vasubandhu* (Varanasi: Bauddha Bharati, 1981), p. 187. The *kārikā* on which this phrase comments lists the ten mental factors present in all states of mind (*ye [caittāḥ] sarvatra cetasi bhavanti*). *Smṛti* is listed as the seventh among these.

3. The Yogācāra texts do not always make such a specification. The *Abhidharmasamuccaya* and *bhāṣya,* for example, list it simply as one of the fifty-two *caitasikadharmāḥ* classified as part of the *saṃskāraskandha*. See V. V. Gokhale, ed., "Fragments from the Abhidharmasamuccaya of Asaṃga," *Journal of the Bombay Branch of the Royal Asiatic Society* 23 (1947): 16; Nathmal Tatia, ed., *Abhidharmasamuccayabhāṣyam* (Patna: K. P. Jayaswal Research Institute, 1976), p. 5.

4. Sthiramati, in commenting on *Triṃśikā* 10bc (*chandādhimokṣasmṛtayaḥ saha / samādidhībhyāṃ niyataḥ*) says *viśeṣe niyatatvād viniyataḥ / eṣāṃ hi viśeṣa eva viṣayo na sarvaḥ*. See Sylvain Lévi, ed., *Vijñaptimātratāsiddhi: deux traités de Vasubandhu: Viṃśatikā (La Vingtaine) accompagnée d'une explication en prose, et Triṃśikā (La Trentaine), avec le commentaire de Sthiramati* (Paris Librairie Ancienne Honoré Champion, 1925), p. 25. The same move is made in the *Pañcaskandhaprakaraṇa*. See Louis de La Vallée Poussin, *L'Abhidharmakoça de Vasubandhu* (Paris: Paul Geuthner, 1923–1931), vol. 1, p. 154, n. 3; English version, Leo Pruden, *Abhidharmakośabhāṣyam* (Berkeley, Calif.: Asian Humanities Press, 1988), vol. 1, p. 335, n. 115. Compare Stefan Anacker, *Seven Works of Vasubandhu* (Delhi: Motilal Banarsidass, 1984), p. 67.

5. *ālambanāsampramoṣaḥ, Ahidharmakośabhāṣya* on *Abhidharmakośakārikā* II. 24; Śāstrī, *Abhidharmakośa,* p. 187. On this Yaśomitra comments *yad yogād ālambanaṃ na mano vismarati tac cābhilapatīva sā smṛtiḥ / Abhidharmakośavyākhyā* on *Abhidharmakośakārikā* II.24b, Śāstrī, *Abhidharmakośa,* p. 187. A useful list of references on this issue to Chinese translations of early Sarvāstivāda sources no longer extant in Indic languages may be found in Collett Cox, "On the Possibility of a Non-Existent Object of Consciousness: Sarvāstivādin and Dārṣṭāntika Theories," *Journal of the International Association of Buddhist Studies* 11, no. 1 (1988): 85, n. 136. See also *cittavyāpārarūpā smṛtiḥ / cittasyārthābhilapanā kṛtakartavyakriyamāṇakarmāntāvipramoṣalakṣaṇaḥ*. P. S. Jaini, ed., *Abhidharmadīpa with Vibhāṣāprabhāvṛtti* (Patna: K. P. Jayaswal Research Institute, 1970), p. 69.

6. See *Madhyāntavibhāgabhāṣya on Madhyāntavibhāga* IV.5: *smṛtir ālambane 'sampramoṣaḥ* / Nathmal Tatia, ed., *Madhyānta-vibhāga–bhāṣyam* (Patna: K. P. Jayaswal Research Institute, 1967), p. 30. Compare the treatment in the *Karmasiddhiprakaraṇa*, where memory is mentioned briefly among problems of continuity: how is it, for example, that one can recall the contents of a text long after

having studied it or the content of a sensory experience long after having first undergone it? What dharma makes this possible, and what causal account can be given of the process by which this occurs? The text reads: *'o na gzung la goms pa na yun ring mo zhig la lon na yang dran pa skye ba dang / mthong ba la sogs pa'i don gzhan la dran pa skye ba gang yin pa de la goms pa de'am mthong ba la sogs pa de gang gis phyis dran pa skye bar 'gyur ba'i chos ci zhig gam / skad cig ma gang la skyed par byed.* Étienne Lamotte, "Le traité de l'acte de Vasubandhu," *Mélanges chinois et bouddhiques* 4 (1935): 192; for a French translation, see p. 231.

7. *smṛtiḥ katamā / samstute vastuni cetaso 'sampramoṣaḥ / avikṣepakarmikā.* Gokhale, "Fragments," 16.

8. *"samstutaṃ vastu" pūrvānubhūtaṃ veditavyam / "avikṣepakarmikatvaṃ" punaḥ smṛter ālambanābhilapane sati cittāvikṣepatām upādāya.* Tatia, *Abhidharmasamuccayabhāṣyam*, p. 5.

9. The context here is a discussion of the "maturity of intelligence" (*medhaparipāka*) in the *paripākādhikāra*. *Smṛti* is defined as "nondeprivation of what has been heard, considered, and meditated upon, and of what has long since been done or said" (*śrutacintitabhāvitacirakṛtacirabhāṣitānām asammoṣatā. Mahāyānasūtrālaṅkārabhāṣya* on *Mahāyānasūtrālaṅkāra* VIII.7c; Sylvain Lévi, ed., *Mahāyāna-Sūtrālaṃkāra: Exposé de la doctrine du Grand Véhicule selon la système Yogācāra* (Paris: Librairie Ancienne Honore Champion, 1907), p. 29.

10. *smṛtiḥ samstute vastuny asaṃpramoṣaś cetaso 'bhilapanatā / "samstutaṃ vastu" pūrvānubhūtam / ālambanagrahaṇāvipraṇāśakaraṇatvād "asaṃpramoṣaḥ" / pūrvagṛhītasya vastunaḥ punaḥ punar ālambanākārasmaraṇam "abhilapanatā" / . . . sā punar avikṣepakarmikā / ālambanābhilapane sati cittasyālambanāntare ākārāntare vā vikṣepābhāvād avikṣepakarmikā. Triṃśikābhāṣya* on *Triṃśikā* 10; Lévi, *Vijñaptimātratāsiddhi*, pp. 25–26. See also Lévi, *Une système de philosophie bouddhique matériaux pour l'étude du système Vijñaptimātra* (Paris: Librairie Ancienne Honoré Champion, 1932), p. 85, for a French translation of this passage; and compare Hermann Jacobi, trans., *Triṃśikāvijñapti des Vasubandhu mit bhāṣya des ācārya Sthiramati* (Stuttgart: Köhlhammer, 1932), p. 26, for a German translation. The comments of Vinītadeva in his *Triṃśikāṭīkā* offer little more than grammatical elucidation. See P. S. Jaini, ed., "The Sanskrit Fragments of Vinītadeva's Triṃśikā-ṭīkā," *Bulletin of the School of Oriental and African Studies* 48 (1985): 478.

11. As, for example, in the *Abhidharmakośabhāṣya: sākārās tasyaivālambanasya prakāreṇa ākaraṇāt. Abhidharmakośabhāṣya on Abhidharmakośakārikā* II.34; Śāstrī, *Abhidharmakośa*, pp. 208–9. See also: . . . *na ca teṣv āmukham anākāratvāt. Mahāyānasūtrālaṅkārabhāṣya on Mahāyānasūtrālaṅkāra* IX.68: Lévi, *Mahāyāna-Sūtrālaṃkāra*, p. 46. In this connection between "confronting," "coming face-to-face with," or "making visible" (*āmukhi-kṛ-*) some intentional object is important when *ākāra* is used in the context of discussing the buddha's "mirrorlike awareness" (*ādarśajñāna*).

12. Julius Lipner, *The Face of Truth* (Albany: State University of New York Press, 1986), p. 20.

13. Madeleine Biardeau, *Théorie de la connaissance et philosophie de la parole dans le Brahmanisme* (Paris: École Pratique des Hautes Études, 1964), p. 75.

14. *sarveṣāṃ cittacaittānām ālambanagrahaṇaprakāra ākāra iti. Abhidharmakośabhāṣya on Abhidharmakośakārikā* VII.13b1; Śāstrī, *Abhidharmakośa*, p. 1062.

15. *sarve sālambanā dharmā ākārayanti . . . Abhidharmakośabhāṣya on Abhidharmakośakārikā* VII.13d; Śāstrī, *Abhidharmakośa*, p. 1062.

16. The *Abhidharmakośabhāṣya*, in discussing the sense in which three important words for the mental (*citta, manas, vijñāna*) all have the same referent (*eko 'rthaḥ*), explains that all mental events share the same basic characteristics: *ta eva hi cittacaittāḥ sāśrayā ucyanta indriyāśritatvāt / sālambanā viṣayagrahaṇāt / sākārās tasyaivālambanasya prakāreṇa ākāraṇāt / saṃprayuktāḥ samaṃ prayuktatvạt. Abhidharmakośabhāṣya on Abhidharmakośakārikā* II.34bc; Śāstrī, *Abhidharmakośa* pp. 208–9. This links the attribute "having an object" with the attribute "having an *ākāra*," both essential to any member of the class-category "mental event" (*cittacaitta, manas, vijñāna*). This necessary coexistence of *ākāra* and *ālambana* is also made clear by Asvabhāva: *dmigs pa dang bcas pa'i chos rnams ni rnam pa dang bcas pa'i phyir dmigs pa dang 'dzin par byed do. Mahāyānasaṅgrahopanibandhana*, DT semstsam RI 267b2. Compare also Sthiramati's denial that consciousness without *ākāra* and *ālambana* is possible: *na hi nirālambanaṃ nirākāraṃ vā vijñānaṃ yujyate. Triṃśikābhāṣya* on *Triṃśikā* 2cd, Lévi, *Vijñaptimātratāsiddhi*, p. 19.

17. For a detailed study of the meaning of *ākāra* in the compound *sarvākārajñatā*, see my "Omniscience in the Mahāyānasūtrālaṅkāra and its Commentaries," *Indo-Iranian Journal* 33 (1990): 85–120.

18. On this debate, see Kajiyama Yuichi, "Controversy Between the Sākāra- and Nirākāra-vādins of the Yogācāra School—Some Materials," *Indogaku Bukkyōgaku Kenkyū* 14, no. 1 (1965): 26–37; "Later Mādhyamikas on Epistemology and Meditation," in *Mahāyāna Buddhist Meditation: Theory and Practice*, ed. Minoru Kiyota and Elvin W. Jones (Honolulu: University of Hawaii Press, 1978), pp. 114–143.

19. Ratnākaraśānti wrote, among other things, an *upadeśa* on the *Prajñāpāramitā;* see Kajiyama, "Controversy," pp. 36–37; Katsura Shoryu, "A Synopsis of the Prajñāpāramitopadeśa," *Indogaku Bukkyōgaku Kenkyū* 25 (1976): 38–41. Mokṣākaragupta was probably a little later than Ratnākaraśānti. His discussion of this issue is found in the Tarkabhāṣā. See B. N. Singh, *Bauddha-Tarkabhāṣā of Mokṣākargupta* [sic] (Banares: Asha Prakashan, 1985), pp. 97–98.

20. It is relevant to note here that one of the properties of a buddha as listed in classical Yogācāra texts is *asaṃmoṣatā*. See *Mahāyānasūtrālaṅkāra* XX–XXI.55 and *Mahāyānasūtrālaṅkārabhāṣya* thereto; Lévi, *Mahāyāna-Sūtrālaṃkāra*, p. 187; the *Mahāyānasūtrālaṅkāraṭīkā* on this verse is especially illuminating: *'di la de bzhin gshegs pa'i mdzd pa thams cad dang / yul thams cad dang / mdzad pa'i thams cad kyi thabs rnams dang dus thams cad la bsnyel ba mi mnga' zhing rtag tu dgongs pa nye*

bar gnas pa gang yin pa 'di ni der bsnyel ba mi mnga' ba'i chos nyid bltar bar bya'o. Mahāyānasūtrālaṅkāraṭīkā on *Mahāyānasūtrālaṅkāra* XX–XXI.55; DT sems-tsam BI 173b5–7. Compare *Mahāyānasaṅgraha* X.22; Étienne Lamotte, ed., *La somme du grand véhicule d'Asaṅga (Mahāyānasaṃgraha)* (Louvain: Bibliothèque de la Muséon, 1938), vol. 1, p. 89. For texts and translations of the commentaries to this section of the *Mahāyānasaṅgraha,* see Paul J. Griffiths et al., *The Realm of Awakening: A Translation and Study of the Tenth Chapter of Asaṅga's Mahāyānasaṅgraha* (New York: Oxford University Press, 1989), pp. 161–62, 329–30.

21. The standard objects are body (*kāya*), feelings (*vedanā*), mind (*citta*), and doctrinal formulae (*dharmāḥ*). A stereotyped description of these four objects of mindfulness is found throughout the Pali *Nikāyas.* See, among many instances, T. W. Rhys Davids and J. Estlin Carpenter, eds., *Dīgha Nikāya* (London: Pali Text Society, 1890, 1903, 1911), vol. 2, p. 290. It is found also in virtually all scholastic compendia. I have given a detailed phenomenological analysis of this type of meditational practice in my "Indian Buddhist Meditation-Theory: History, Development, and Systematization," (Ph.D., dissertation, University of Wisconsin-Madison, 1983), pp. 92–134.

22. *apaśabdavigata smṛtisampramoṣe tadaniścaraṇatvāt. Mahāyānasūtrālaṅkārabhāṣya* on *Mahāyānasūtrālaṅkāra* XII.9: Lévi, *Mahāyāna-Sūtrālaṃkāra,* p. 80.

23. "Qu' est-ce que la Smṛti?—La memoire, le Dharma qui fait que la pensée se commemore (*abhilapanatā, ming-ki,* 72 et 4, 149 et 3, clair-souvenir) d'une chose experimentée, et ne defaut pas (*asaṃpramosa*). [30a] Elle a pour action d' être le support du recueillement (*samādhi, avikṣepa*), car, incessament, elle conserve et tient (*i-tch'e,* 61 et 4, 64 et 6) la chose experimentée de telle sorte qu'il n'y a pas defaillante de souvenir et, par la elle induit la recueillement." Louis de La Vallée Poussin, trans., *Vijñaptimātratāsiddhi: la Siddhi de Hiuan Tsang* (Paris: Geuthner, 1928–1948), pp. 311–12. See also Wei Tat, trans., *Ch'eng Wei-Shih Lun; The Doctrine of Mere-Consciousness* (Hong Kong: Ch'eng Wei-Shih Lun Publication Committee, 1973), pp. 376–77, for the Chinese text and an English translation.

24. Good examples are *Mahāyānasūtrālaṅkāra* XVI.25b, in which it is said that *dhyāna* is "firmly based upon *smṛti* and energy" (. . . *smṛtivīryapratiṣṭhitam* . . . *Mahāyānasūtrālaṅkāra* XVI.25b; Lévi, *Mahāyāna-Sūtrālaṃkāra,* p. 106.) The *Mahāyānasūtrālaṅkārabhāṣya* says that this phrase refers to the cause of *dhyāna,* because that is achieved when the practitioner is not deprived of the meditational object, the support for cognition (*ālambana*): *smṛtivīryapratiṣṭhitam iti hetuḥ / ālambanāsaṃpramoṣe sati vīryaṃ niśritya samāpatty abhinirharāt. Mahāyānasūtrālaṅkārabhāṣya* on *Mahāyānasūtrālaṅkāra* XVI.25b; Lévi, *Mahāyāna-Sūtrālaṃkāra,* p. 106. See also XVIII.53, a verse on the fourfold salvific technique (*upāya*) belonging to wise persons. *Smṛti* and awareness (*samprajanya*) together form the third division of salvific technique; the *Mahāyānasūtrālaṅkārabhāṣya* says that "because through the first [i.e., *smṛti*] the mind does not diffuse itself among [many] objects" (*ekena cittasyālambanāvisarāt. Mahāyānsūtrālaṅkārabhāṣya* on *Mahāyānasūtrālaṅkāra*

XVIII.53c; Lévi, *Mahāyāna-Sūtrālaṃkāra*, p. 143). Compare also the discussions in *Mahāyānasūtrālaṅkārabhāṣya on Mahāyānasūtrālaṅkāra* XVIII.58ab; XVIII.63–65; XIX.67.

25. See *Mahāyānasūtrālaṅkāra* XI.11; XIV.36; XVIII.42–44; XX–XXI.53 and the commentarial literature thereto.

26. There in fact is a number of different lists of contemplations (*anusmṛtayaḥ*), perhaps the most common being a list of six: contemplation of the buddha, doctrine (*dharma*), the monastic community (*saṅgha*), proper ethical behavior (*sīla*), renunciation in favor of others (*tyāga*), and divinity (*devatā*). Sometimes two more are added to these: contemplation of breathing (*ānāpānānusmṛti*) and death (*maraṇānusmṛti*). For a detailed discussion, see Étienne Lamotte, trans., *Le traité de la grande vertu de sagesse de Nāgārjuna (Mahāprajñāpāramitāśāstra)* (Louvain-la-neuve: Institut Orientaliste, 1944–1981), pp. 1329–1430. He translates *anusmṛti* as "Commémoration," meaning thereby not quite the same as the honoring of a past figure or event through a present action discussed at length in Edward Casey's *Remembering: A Phenomenological Study* (Bloomington: Indiana University Press, 1987). Contemplation of one's previous lives is not part of this list, though the same term is used for it.

27. *so 'nekavidhaṃ pūrvanivāsam anusmarati / ekam api jātim anusmarati / dve tisraś catasraḥ pañca daśa viṃśati triṃśataṃ catvāriṃśataṃ pañcaśataṃ jātiśatam anusmarati / anekāny api jātiśatāni . . . amutrāham āsam evaṃnāmā / evaṃgotra evaṃjātir evamāhāra evamāyuḥpramāṇa* . . . Lamotte, *Le traité*, p. 1811. Sanskrit cited from the *Abhidharmakośavyākhyā*. Lamotte's discussion of this pericope is, as always, essential reading (*Le traité*, pp. 1809–77). See also *Mahāyānasūtrālaṅkāra* VII.1 and *Mahāyānasūtrālaṅkārabhāṣya* thereon, Lévi, *Mahāyāna-Sūtrālaṃkāra*, p. 25; *Mahāyānasūtrālaṅkāravṛttibhāṣya* on *Mahāyānasūtrālaṅkāra and Mahāyānasūtrālaṅkārabhāṣya* VII.1; DT sems-tsam MI 82a7ff.

28. On this notion of retracing, see the somewhat idiosyncratic but nevertheless interesting analysis given by Rod Bucknell and Martin Stewart-Fox in *The Twilight Language* (London: Curzon Press, 1986), pp. 51ff.

29. For an excellent discussion of the difficulties involved in using this English word, and the range of indigenous Buddhist terms for which it might stand as a translation, see Alan Sponberg, "Meditation in Fa-hsiang Buddhism," in *Traditions of Meditation in Chinese Buddhism*, ed. Peter Gregory, Studies in East Asian Buddhism vol. 4 (Honolulu: University of Hawaii Press, 1986), pp. 15–21.

30. For an account of this kind see Sydney Shoemaker, "Persons and Their Pasts," *American Philosophical Quarterly* 7 (1970): 269–85.

31. This was the line taken by John Locke, most notably in the *Essay Concerning Human Understanding*, Book 2, Chapter 27.

32. For an intra-Buddhist version of this debate, see Vasubandhu's treatise on the negation of the person (*pudgalapratiṣedha*), included as an Appendix (or ninth

chapter) to his *Abhidharmakośabhāṣya*. The text of the discussion of memory is found in Śāstrī, *Abhidharmakośa*, pp. 1215–18. An excellent translation into English is in Matthew Kapstein, "Self and Personal Identity in Indian Buddhist Scholasticism: A Philosophical Investigation," (Ph.D. dissertation, Brown University, 1987), pp. 261–63. An earlier and less reliable translation is in T. Stcherbatsky, *The Soul Theory of the Buddhists* (Delhi: Bhāratīya Vidyā Prakāśan, 1976), pp. 50–54. See also La Vallée Poussin, *L'Abhidharmakoça*, vol. 5, pp. 273–79. Perhaps the most thoroughgoing non-Buddhist attack on Buddhist attempts to construct an account of memory without postulating an enduring substantive possessor of it is to be found in Udayana's *Ātmatattvaviveka*. See Mahāmahopadhyāya Vindhyeśvariprasāda Dvivedin and Lakṣmaṇa Śāstrī Dravida, eds., *Udayanācārya: Ātmatattvaviveka, With the Commentaries of Śaṅkara Miśra, Bhagiratha Ṭhakkura and Raghunātha Tarkikaśiromaṇī* (Calcutta: Asiatic Society, 1986), pp. 739–946, especially 791ff.

33. Yaśomitra, in his comments on the rather unhelpful *smaraṇād eva ca pratyabhijñānam* from the *Abhidharmakośabhāṣya* says, *tad evedaṃ yan mayā dṛṣṭam iti smaraṇāt*, *Abhidharmakośabhāṣya* IX (appendix); Śāstrī, *Abhidharmakośa*, p. 1217.

34. Śastrī, *Abhidharmakośa*, pp. 1215–16. See pp. 49–51, supra.

35. There are problems involved with the machinery developed by Buddhist scholastics for individuating one mental continuum (*cittasantāna*) from another, but these are beyond the scope of this chapter. For some preliminary discussion, see *Abhidharmakośabhāṣya* and *Abhidharmakośavyākhyā* on *Abhidharmakośakārikā* II.36; Śāstrī, *Abhidharmakośa*, pp. 210–18.

36. Standard treatments of the *ālaya* in Western languages are Étienne Lamotte, "L'Ālayavijñāna: Le receptacle dans le Mahāyānasaṅgraha (Chapitre II)," *Mélanges chinois et bouddhiques* 3 (1934): 169–225; Louis de La Vallée Poussin, "Note sur l'Ālayavijñāna," *Mélanges chinois et bouddhiques* 3 (1934): 145–68; Schmithausen, *Ālayavijñāna;* see also my own *On Being Mindless: Buddhist Meditation and the Mind-Body Problem* (La Salle, Ill.: Open Court, 1986), pp. 91–106, in which the standard arguments for the *ālaya*'s existence are treated.

37. As, for example, in *Abhidharmakośabhāṣya* on *Abhidharmakośakārikā* V.2a. The context here is a discussion of the meaning of the terms *kleśa* and *anuśaya*. The Sautrāntika view, apparently approved by Vasubandhu, is that *anuśaya* refers to *kleśa* in a dormant state (*prasupta*), *kleśa* as a seed (*bīja*) not yet fully manifested (*kā ca tasya prasuptiḥ / asaṃmukhibhūtasya bījabhāvānubandhaḥ*). The text goes on: "What is a 'seed'? It is the capacity to bring forth *kleśas* in a particular person, a power that comes from [previous] *kleśas*. In just the same way there is a power to bring forth memory, a power that comes from [previous] experiential awareness" (*ko 'yaṃ bījabhāvo nāma / ātmabhāvasya kleśajā kleśotpādanaśaktiḥ / yathānubhavajñānajā smṛtyutpādanaśaktiḥ / yathā caṅkurādīnāṃ śaliphalajā śaliphalotpādanaśaktir iti. Abhidharmakośabhāṣya* on *Abhidharmakośakārikā* V.2a; Śāstrī, *Abhidharmakośa*, pp. 763–64).

38. For the use of this image, see, notably, *Mahāyānasaṅgraha* I.2–3, I.14 and the commentaries to it: Lamotte, *La somme*, pp. 175–76, 221–25; Nagao Gadjin, *Shōdaijōron: wayaku to chūkai* (Tokyo: Kodansha, 1982, 1987), vol. 1, pp. 111–16, 133–35.

39. *"tatrālayākhyaṃ vijñānaṃ vipākaḥ sarvabījakam" . . . "ālayākhyam" ity ālayavijñānasaṃjñakaṃ yad vijñānaṃ sa vipākapariṇāmaḥ / tatra sarvasāṃkleśikadharmabījasthānatavād ālayaḥ / ālayaḥ sthānam iti paryāyau / atha vālīyante upanibadhyante 'smin sarvadharmāḥ kāryabhāvena / tad vālīyate upanibadhyate kāraṇabhāvena sarvadharmeṣv ity ālayaḥ / vijānātīti vijñānam / sarvadhātugatiyonijātiṣu kuśalākuśalakarmavipākatvād "vipākaḥ" / sarvadharmabījāśrayatvāt "sarvabījakam." Triṃśikābhāṣya on Triṃśikā* 2cd; Lévi, *Vijñaptimātratāsiddhi*, pp. 18–19.

40. *bag chags zhes bya ba 'di ci zhig / bag chags zhes brjod pa 'di'i brjod par bya ba ni ci zhe na / chos de dang lhan cig 'byung ba dang / 'gag pa la brten nas de 'byung ba'i rgyu mtshan nyid gang yin pa de ni brjod par bya ba ste / dper na til dag la me tog gis bsgos pa til dang me tog lhan cig 'byung zhing 'gags kyang til rnams de'i dri gzhan 'byung ba'i rgyu mtshan nyid du 'byung ba dang / 'dod chags la sogs pa la spyod pa rnams kyi 'dod chags la sogs pa'i bag chags 'dod chags la sogs pa dang lhan cig 'byung zhing 'gags kyang sems ni de'i rgyu mtshan nyid du 'byung ba dang / mang du thos pa rnams kyi mang du thos pa'i bag chags kyang thos pa de yid la byed pa dang lhan oig tu 'byung zhing 'gags kyang sems ni de brjod pa'i rgyu mtshan nyid du 'byung ste / bag chags des yongs su zin pas chos 'dzin pa zhes bya ba ltar kun gzhi rnam par shes pa la yang tshul de bzhin du blta bar bya'o/. Mahāyānasaṅgraha* I.15; Lamotte, *La somme*, vol. 2, p. 9; Nagao, *Shōdaijōron*, vol. 1, p. 23. The comments in the *Mahāyānasaṅgrahabhāṣya* are little more than grammatical elucidations (PT sems-tsam LI 153b2–4), whereas those in the *Mahāyānasaṅgrahopanibandhana* (DT sems-tsam RI 202b6–203a5) are much fuller and more useful.

41. Literally, of "hearing." To be learned is to have heard much. One is *bahuśruta* because all or almost all learning within the Buddhist scholastic traditions in India came from hearing texts and exposition of them. Texts were not read silently.

42. Usually expressed with the tag *yat sat tat kṣaṇikam*. See, for arguments in support of this view, A. Charlene S. McDermott, *An Eleventh-Century Buddhist Logic of 'Exists'* (Dordrecht: Reidel, 1970), pp. 14ff.

43. This is made very clear by Asvabhāva's comments on this passage in the *Mahāyānasaṅgrahopanibandhana: chos de dag [Mahāyānasaṅgraha dang] lhan cig 'byung ba dang 'gags [Mahāyānasaṅgrapha 'gag] pa la brten nas de 'byung ba'i rgyu mtshan nyid gang yin pa de ni brjod pa bya ba ste zhes bya ba ni bag chags sgo bar byed pa de dag dang lhan cig dus gcig tu skye ba dang 'gag pa yun ring du rnyed nas bag chags sgo bar byed pa de dag nye bar ma gyur kyang skye ba 'gyur ba'i rgyu mtshan nyid ni bag chags bsgo bar bya ba yin te. Mahāyānasaṅgrahopanibandhana* on *Mahāyānasaṅgraha* I.15; DT sems-tsam RI 202b6–203a1.

44. See my *On Being Mindless*, pp. 94–96, and Schmithausen's typically cautious endorsement of my phraseology in *Ālayavijñāna*, p. 182 and n. 1172. Schmit-

hausen's study concerns how the concept of the *ālaya* came into being as a key part of Yogācāra theory, and his conclusions are worth noting: "according to my own hypothesis, too, *ālayavijñāna* was derived from a certain yogic state (viz. *nirodhasamāpatti*), but only indirectly, through the medium of additional dogmatical and exegetical factors" (*Ālayavijñana*, p. 182). One of these "additional dogmatical factors" appears to have been precisely the need to give an account of the continuity of the capacity for memory *in potentia*.

45. The complete Sanskrit text and an English translation of this eightfold proof is given in my *On Being Mindless*, Appendix C, pp. 129–38. The proof occurs in both the *Abhidharmasamuccayabhāṣya* and the *Yogācārabhūmi;* full references to the texts and discussions of them are given in *On Being Mindless.*

46. A classical exposition of the exchange of self and other may be found in Śāntideva's *Bodhicaryāvatāra*, VIII.103ff, and in Prajñākaramati's *Pañjikā* thereto. See Louis de La Vallée Poussin, ed., *Bodhicaryāvatārapañjikā: Prajñākaramati's Commentary to the Bodhicaryāvatāra of Çāntideva* (Calcutta: Asiatic Society of Bengal, 1901–1914), pp. 337ff.

47. I offer an analogous argument in connection with *pūrvanivāsānusmṛti*, developed with rather more precision, in "Why Buddhas Can't Remember Their Previous Lives," *Philosophy East and West* 39, no. 4 (1989): 449–51.

Buddhist Terms for Recollection and Other Types of Memory

ALEX WAYMAN

Buddhist texts necessarily go into the theory of memory. Traditional monastic study requires committing basic texts to memory. Also, it is believed that it is theoretically possible to remember previous lives. Further, Buddhist logic considers whether memory has the status of an authority. There appear to be two main types of memory: that of holding in mind, and that involving recollection of what was previously experienced. Both have a fund of material concerning them in Buddhist texts. However, it seems that material on holding in mind is much more abundant, because of the stress on memorization, and because of meditative praxis that involves holding a designated object in mind.

There are various terms for holding in mind, forgetting and not forgetting, and recollection in ordinary human as well as extraordinary manners. For holding in mind there are *smṛti* (''mindfulness''), *anusmṛti* (''remembrance''), *dhāraṇa* (''holding''), *asampramoṣa* (''not forgetting''), and avoiding *vismaraṇa* and *muṣitasmṛti* (both mean ''forgetting''). Because holding in mind as connoted by *smṛti* or by *dhāraṇa* (also *dhāraṇī*) is treated in depth by other chapters in this volume, I will not discuss this type of memory here, except incidentally. My concern is with words distinctly used for recollection. Here the general terms include again *smṛti,* as well as *smaraṇa,* and *parāmarśa.* In addition there is the term *medhā* for a type of reliable memory, *pratyabhijñāna* for a type of unreliable memory, and some others.

It should be conceded that these terms are drawn from the large corpus of Indic terms, the associated literature of which antedates the rise of Buddhism and then develops parallel to Buddhist literature. Nevertheless, Buddhist texts are the main sources for this chapter.

The Remembering of Former Lives

The old formula for the Buddha's remembering his previous lives uses the Pāli phrase *pubbe-nivāsa-anussati-ñāna* (Skt. *pūrva-nivāsānusmṛti-jñāna*), ''knowledge which is recollection of previous abodes.'' However, the term *anussati* (Skt. *anusmṛti*) would presumably compete in usage with a different meaning: the remembrance, or keeping in mind, of the Buddha, and so forth. Thus, in time authors began to refer to the recollective kind of memory of past lives with other expressions, such as the Pāli *jāti-smaraṇa-ñāna,*[1] and the Sanskrit *jāti-smaratā.*[2]

Buddhism has always admitted that the Buddha had recollection of his past lives. However, in general, the Buddhist texts deny that the one who is doing the recollecting is the same as the one who lived in that previous life, otherwise the remembering agent would be permanent. This involves a subtle and much-argued position of Buddhism, which is set forth, for example, in the *Lam rim chen mo* (*vipaśyanā* section) of Tsong-kha-pa (1357–1419), which in part is based on the *Madhyamakāvātara* section on the "invalidity of remembering a life" by Candrakīrti (c. 650).[3] The opponent mentions that the Teacher (i.e., the Buddha) had pointed out (namely, in the *Jātakas*) that in a previous life he was the King Mandhātṛ; but according to this Madhyamaka critique, that self could not be this self. Yet it is valid to posit cause and effect and say that the present self is the result of the previous self and thus they would not be identical. But if one admits such a difference, how does this different self recollect the other, distant self that is its cause (*hetu*)? This problem is akin to that raised, for example, in Nāgārjuna's *Madhyamakakārikā,* I.1.

In Indian Buddhist circles there must have been many discussions of this kind of memory. The *Mahāvastu* twice uses the expression *vāsitavāsana,* rendered by Jones as "has the memory of past lives."[4] Edgerton, by including this term in his *Buddhist Hybrid Sanskrit Dictionary,* takes the position that non-Buddhist texts do not have the term or else not with such a meaning. Because *vāsana,* or more commonly, *vāsanā,* means impressions from former deeds, especially those of former lives, Edgerton interprets the compound expression as meaning *"having impressions* from previous births *duly formed."*[5] Suzuki considers *vāsanā* as being memory itself, saying: "This is the function of the Ālaya [store-consciousness]. It looks into itself where all the memory (*vāsanā*) of the beginningless past is preserved in a way beyond consciousness (*acintya*)."[6] Using Suzuki's interpretation, the compound expression *vāsitavāsana* could be translated, "one whose memory [of the past] has been remembered" or, in other terms, "one whose subconscious memory has been made into a conscious memory."

The *Mahāvastu* also has some other citable passages. The "First Avalokita-sūtra" speaks of when Gautama, the future Buddha, applied his mind (*citta*) to the "knowledge which is recollection of previous abodes" in the middle watch (*madhyama-yāma*) of the night. Then, setting up an introductory remark for his recollecting many different former abodes—each illustrated by a paragraph detailing the particular eon and what he recollected from that life—the text uses the verb *samanusmare.*[7] Here the prefix *sam* should be understood as having the lexical definition of *samanta* ("all," "completely").[8] Thus, the scripture is claiming that the Buddha recollected all of his former lives, his name and family therein, and so on.

The "Second Avalokita-sūtra" has this verse:

> And the monk, having purified morality, being respectively mindful with awareness, recollected his former dwellings during myriads of eons.[9]

The verse alludes to two kinds of memory. Although this chapter will not discuss the theory of mindfulness except incidentally, to appreciate the message of the above verse it is necessary to point out on the basis of Buddhist meditation theory that "being respectively mindful" (*pratismṛta*) constitutes a protective faculty that can bring on an awareness (usually *samprajanya*) that recognizes subtle faults of meditation.[10] Hence meditative mindfulness sets up a "true" situation for the other kind of memory, that of recollection. In short, the text insists that the memory of former lives is possible only in samādhi, which the second instruction (*śikṣā*) of Buddhism goes into, and which in turn requires the first instruction, that of morality. It also requires the "divine eye" of the first watch of the night, which sees forms in past and future.[11]

A final reference from the *Mahāvastu* regarding memory of past lives concerns a different way of bringing in such memory. This is found in the story called "The Royal Umbrellas" (*chatra*). The Lord urges Vāgīśā: "Let the previous association (*pūrvayoga*) between you and the Tathāgata be perfectly clear (*pratibhātu*)!"[12] Then, presumably by virtue of the Buddha's empowerment, Vāgīśā tells in verse the story of a former life in which the Buddha was a certain brahmin and Vāgīśā that one's student.

Medhā

The term *medhā* is mentioned as a word for memory in both the *English-Sanskrit Dictionary* by Borooah[13] and *The Student English-Sanskrit Dictionary* by Apte.[14] The translation into Tibetan of this term is regularly *yid gzhungs pa*. Das's *The Tibetan-English Dictionary* takes the Tibetan expression as meaning such things as prudence, analytic power, honesty, and cleverness in resources, without a suggestion that it could mean memory.[15] However, the three-volume Tibetan-Chinese dictionary *Bod rgya tshig mdzod chen mo* has under the entry *yid gzhungs* the first definition *blo gsal ba'am mkhas pa* ("clear or learned mind"), and the second definition *dran skyen pa* ("nimble memory").[16] With this confirmation that the term *medhā* means a kind of memory in Buddhist texts, and possibly also in general Indian literature, we are enabled to suggest a marked improvement in the translation of the following passages in the Buddhist scriptures.

When setting forth its version of the first sermon, the biography of the Buddha called *Lalitavistara* reports what the Buddha told of what arose in him as he thought of each of the four noble truths. He reports that "knowledge arose, sight arose, clear realization arose, strong thought arose, adroit memory arose, insight arose, light appeared" (*jñānam utpannaṃ cakṣur utpannaṃ vidyotpannā bhūrir utpannā medhotpannā prajñotpannā ālokaḥ prādurbhūtaḥ*).[17] It seems that the passage is going by pairs. That "knowledge arose" and "sight arose" agrees with the well-known Buddhist pair, *jñānadarśana* ("knowledge and vision"). The term *bhūri* seems not to be an important term in later Buddhist literature, and the sense is obscure; but we can take it together with *vidyā,* hence "clear realization arose" and "strong thought arose." Then, taking *medhā* and *prajñā* as a pair, "adroit memory arose" and "insight arose." Finally, that light appeared seems to cover all the previous terms as connoting forms of (metaphorical) light.

The *Laṅkavatārasūtra* pairs *smṛti* and *medhā* in its question section of Chapter 2: "What is mindfulness (*smṛti*)? What adroit memory (*medhā*)?"[18] Although I could not locate the answers to these questions in the sūtra, the two terms also appear as a pair in the *Mahāyānasūtrālaṅkāra* (VIII.7) in a passage that is inaugurated by the remark, "a verse on the maturation of adroit memory (*medhā*)":

> Purity of maturation, no theft of what was heard and so on; understanding of the well said and the badly said, fitness of mindfulness (*smṛti*) to arouse great cognition—these are the characteristics of the maturation of good adroit memory."[19]

On this Asaṅga (c. 375–430 CE) comments:

> Among them, purity of maturation consistent with adroit memory is the instrumental cause. The nature of mature adroit memory is that of mindfulness to which belongs the non-theft of what was heard, pondered, and cultivated, done long ago or said long ago, and the good understanding of the meaning of the well said and the badly said. Its activity is the fitness to arouse supramundane insight (*prajñā*).[20]

Asaṅga's final remark corroborates our pairing of *medhā* and *prajñā* in the above *Lalitavistara* passage. This *medhā* seems to be the kind of memory that in its mundane occurrence comes up with the appropriate passage for the occasion; and it also has a supramundane form as well.

Our last reference for this term is in an evocation of the goddess Mahāsarasvatī wherein she is accompanied by four compassion goddesses, with the names Prajñā ("She the Insight"), Medhā ("She the Adroit Memory"), Mati ("She the Intelligence"), and Smṛti ("She the Mindfulness").[21] The set of four shows the optimal situation for genuine recollection.

Discursive Thought and Recollection

La Vallée Poussin, in his translation of the *Vijñaptimātratāsiddhi,* explains that the recollecting type of discursive thought (*anusmaraṇa-vikalpa*) has for its domain the natures previously experienced.[22] Buddhism predominately uses the term *kalpa* with or without prefix for types of discursive thought. The texts that treat memory in this context usually employ the forms *vikalpa* or *saṅkalpa.*

Vikalpa, with the *vi-* understood in the Vedic usage as the going apart toward objects (as solar rays separate and extend outward),[23] may or may not be the recollecting type. The Abhidharma distinguishes recollecting as one of the three types of discursive thought (*vikalpa*), as in *Dharmasaṅgraha,* CXXXV: the recollecting kind of discursive thought (*anusmaraṇa-vikalpa*); *santiraṇāvikalpa* (presumably = *nirūpaṇa-vikalpa*); and the concomitant kind of discursive thought (*sahaja-vikalpa*).[24] For the meaning of *nirūpaṇa-vikalpa,* there is the help of Bhartṛhari's *Vākyapadiya* (II.60). This text uses the term *nirūpaṇa* practically as a synonym of *pratyaya,* employed here in the sense of the verb form *pratīyate,* as I came to understand it from the beginning of Dharmakīrti's *Nyāyabindu.*[25] Thus, *pratyaya,* ditto *nirūpaṇa* as employed in Bhartṛhari's text, means "cognitive dawning", that is, the initial discursive thought. There is now enough information to treat the discussion by Vasubandhu (c. 400–480 CE) in *Abhidharmakośa,* I.33:

> They [i.e., inquiry (*vitarka*) and cognitive conclusion (*vicāra*)] are free from discursive thought in the sense of the cognitive-dawning and recollecting [kinds of] discursive thought. Those two [i.e., inquiry and cognitive conclusion] are the unsteady insight (*prajñā*) in the mind, and all the mindfulness (*smṛti*) in the mind.[26]

The two, inquiry and cognitive conclusion, presumably constitute the concomitant (*sahaja*) kind of discursive thought; they consist of unsteady insight, but also mindfulness. By translating *smṛti* as "mindfulness" (instead of as "recollection" as per the general Indian usage), one avoids the contradiction of treating it as equivalent to recollection (*anusmaraṇa*) as in the term *anusmaraṇa-vikalpa.*

For the term *saṅkalpa,* we observe that the prefix is the indeclinable *sam.* The invaluable reference work *Avyayakośa* cites Kṣīraswāmi for a long list of definitions of *sam* and then provides examples. Usually the meaning of *sam* changes according to the particular verb root to which it is prefixed. When *sam* is employed in the meaning of "recollection" (*smṛtāu,* showing the locative sign), the examples are *saṃjñānam* and *saṅkalpah.*[27] Both of these terms are important in Buddhist literature, the first in the form *saṃjñā,* the second as cited here. The term *saṃjñā* seems not to have been recognized as a word for memory, except by Nyanaponika Thera whose essay is included elsewhere in this volume. *Saṃjñā* as one of the five personal aggregates (*skandha*) comes right after *vedanā* ("feeling"). In fact it is often the kind of discursive thought that recollects feelings, for example, *Dhammapada* I.3: "He abused me, he struck me, . . . " But it also comes after sense perception, say of blue, with the notion, "It is blue." Such usages of these terms are extensions of its general Indian usage as the naming function.[28] In this sense, every name is a kind of memory. The term *saṅkalpa* means a purpose or resolution, whether virtuous or unvirtuous. It can imply the kind of memory that one bears in mind—which is not my concern in the present essay.

The verbal root *cit,* "to think," might mean with or without discursive thought, as reflected in its finite verbal and nominal forms. The form *cintā* means "anxious thought about," and so does not appear to involve memory. However, the celebrated Indian lexicon *Amarakoṣa* has this line: "There could be *cintā* ("anxious thought"), *smṛti* ("memory"), *ādhyāna* ("regretful or sorrowful remembrance"), *utkanthā* (= a longing for, or missing a person or thing) and *utkalikā.*"[29] The term *utkalikā* has been picked for inclusion in the *nānārtha* lexicons of India, and therein we find it is given the meaning of dalliance; so this term implies a type of sexual memory.[30] Thus *cintā* as an anxious thought implicates a group of words involving the missing of what used to be.

Besides, the *Mahāyānasūtrālaṅkāra* (XIV.6) has six steps of consciousness (*citta*), the first with nondiscursive thought, and the last five, which are forms of discerning (*vipaśyanā*), with discursive thought. According to Sthiramati's (c. sixth century) subcommentary, the only one that seems to involve memory is the fifth; that is, classifying consciousness (*saṅkalana-citta*). Sthiramati explains this as follows: "With whatever insight one possesses for the meaning of the scriptural passages, using judgment, for example, in terms of the twelve classes of scriptures, one knows in which class the passages are to be included."[31] One could substitute for the words "one knows in which class" the alternate words "one adroitly recalls in which class," as the meaning of the passage agrees with the sense previously explored for the term *medhā.*

The foregoing makes it clear that remembering of the ordinary human sort, as well as the special types distinguished in the Buddhist texts, are understood as kinds of discursive thought.

The Challenge to Memory as an Authority in Buddhist Logic

Here we consider some verses in the *pratyakṣa* ("direct perception") chapter of the *Pramāṇavārttika* by Dharmakīriti (c. 650). There is a fund of supporting philological material concerning the issue. In particular, there is the Sanskrit text of the *Pramāṇavārttika*, along with its excellent Tibetan translation; the Sanskrit commentary by Manorathanandin (eleventh century); and the commentary (the *bhāṣya*) by Prajñākaragupta (c. 700) along with its Tibetan translation.[32] For the theory of recognition (*pratyabhijñāna;* Tib. *ngo shes pa*) there is also a rich treatment in the *Tattvasaṅgraha*, which will be referred to later.[33] Because these materials are extensive, only some leading ideas will be discussed here.

But first a few matters must be explained. "Authority" translates the Sanskrit term *pramāṇa*. Asaṅga's "Rules of Debate" (in his *Yogācārabhūmi*) has three authorities: perception (*pratyakṣa*), inference (*anumāna*), and the scriptures of the Master (*āptāgama*).[34] It is well known that Dignāga (fifth century) allows just two authorities, perception and inference. In his *Pramāṇasamuccaya*, he maintains that these two are "results" (*phala*); that is, resulting cognitions of their respective objects, namely, the inherent character (*svalakṣaṇa*) and the generalizing character (*sāmānyalakṣaṇa*).[35] Because "scriptures of the Master" has been left out as an authority, how are Dignaga and the other Buddhist logicians going to deal with the Buddhist critics? For this, I appeal to the great Tibetan commentary of Bu-ston (1290–1364) on Dharmakīrti's *Pramāṇaviniścaya*. Bu-ston cites Dignāga (*Pramāṇasamuccaya, svārthānumāna* chapter, 5ab), for which there is extant the original Sanskrit: *āptavākyāvisaṃvāda-sāmānyād anumānatā*, which I render: "When the state of inference is from a generality [consisting] of the nondeceptive references of the Master." Then Bu-ston points out that Dharmakīrti's *Pramāṇavārttika* (*svārthānumāna* chapter, 216) uses Dignāga's words: *āptavādāvisaṃvādasāmanyād anumānatā / buddher agatyābhihitā parokṣe 'py asya gocare*, which I render: "When the state of inference is from a generality [consisting] of the non-deceptive references of the master, it [the state of inference] is defined [by Dignāga] in the sense of one's domain beyond [the "out of bounds" (*atyantaparokṣa*)] to which the intellect (*buddhi*) cannot go."[36] The passages show that in Dignāga's system the scriptures of the Master are transformed into a kind of object of inference—but of a very privileged kind. Therefore, it was not necessary to consider whether the criterion of nondeceptiveness, which is the criterion for status as an authority, applies to the scriptures, because they are defined as objects of inference, but are not authorities in themselves. And by extension, any remembered object would also not be an authority in itself.

Other arguments also exclude memory from the status of an authority. If it were to be an authority in the Dignāga-Dharmakīrti system, it would have to be the result of the discursive thought of a generalizing character (*sāmānyalakṣaṇa*) that is nondeceptive. Recollective memory has been shown above to be a kind of discursive thought, and memories by and large are not to be called nondeceptive. We saw that for "true" memory a samādhi situation was required, and human inferences, such as those made by logicians, are not conducted while in samādhi.

We are now ready to consider the verses from the *Pramāṇavārttika*. First, there are various verses in the *pratyakṣa* ("direct perception") chapter that differentiate recollection from sense cognition:

> 174. The procedure (*upāya*)[37] of recollecting signs (*saṅketa-smaraṇa*) has the nature of classifying the visible.[38] How could [such a procedure occur] in an eye-cognition which lacks the recollection (*parāmarśa*) of earlier and later?[39]

This argument is carried on by a set of five verses (185–189, which the Tibetan translation and the Manorathanandin commentary do well to elucidate, except for the last verse, which requires special treatment):

> 185. The association [i.e., sequence], with an external entity not depended upon, is from recollection (*smṛti*) of a sign (*samaya;* Tib. *brda*). Likewise, when there is no depending on a sign, the eye-cognition is precisely the "localized power" (*vastuśakti*).[40]
>
> 186. When the form depends on memory (*smaraṇa*) of a sign without depending on sense cognition, no power [is involved]. It is like a sign (*liṅga*) that is just in memory (*smṛti*).[41]
>
> 187. Since that arising [of cognition] is [invariably] connected with that [external entity], there is no sense cognition due to recollection [*smṛti*). It [the sense cognition] would occur at a different time than that [recollection], because the possibility [of recollection] is distracted [impotently] elsewhere.[42]
>
> 188. [Should one believe that] there is [the same] cause for both [sense cognition and recollection] by way of sequence—given that [sense cognition] is earlier—such that they are not different? [Response: Then there is no sequence]. [Should one believe that] the cause of sensory cognition is other than [recollection's]? [Response:] Then recollection is meaningless in that case.[43]

We notice that Dharmakīrti usually uses the term *smṛti* for recollective memory, but he also employs *smaraṇa* when for metric reasons he needs a three-syllabled equivalent, and *parāmarśa* when he needs a four-syllabled one. He also uses *smṛti* in the next verse (189), which needs some discussion prior to its translation. This verse employs the term *samita* in connection with recollection of a sign, and *asamita* for the perceptible of sense cognition. The word *samita* can be taken literally either as *sam-ita* ("come together") or as *asamita* ("measured"). There is commentarial evidence that the former is meant here, in its sense of "delineated."[44]

> 189. [Therefore:] when you (or we) claim that the recollection of a sign is according to the meaning of an [enunciated] proof that has been delineated [with conventional naming], and that a perceptible [for perception] is a difference that has not been delineated [with conventional naming]—what use is recollection in this [latter] case?[45]

The *bhāṣya* especially mentions mental perception (*mānasapratyakṣa*) in regard to this verse.[46] It seems that in this set of five verses Dharmakīrti wishes to contrast the faculty of recollection with sense evidence, first with the five outer senses and finally with mental perception, and to reject the idea that the objects of perception and memory might somehow be identified. Of course, direct perception is an authority in this system, whereas recollection is not.

Later, Dharmakīrti contrasts recollection and sense organs on another ground; that is, with regard to their respective delusion:

> 498. And that which is the identification of similar modes is recollection (*smaraṇa*), a discursive thought deluded by lack of character for difference. It is otherwise in the case of the delusion of the sense organs.[47]

As the Manorathanandin commentary on this verse points out, the sense organs whose cognitions are free from discursive thought can be deluded by such things as a whirling fire brand that creates the illusion of a solid wheel. Furthermore, these sense organs have different fields of operation, the eye seeing forms, ear hearing sounds, and so on. Recollection, on the other hand, is a discursive thought involved in the identification (*ghaṭana*) of similar modes, and so it is deluded by an inability to characterize difference.

This theory of difference and nondifference is discussed under the heading of recognition. Śāntarakṣita (eighth century), in his *Tattvasaṅgraha* (vss. 446–447) compares recognition with sense cognitions in their undeluded condition. Dharmakīrti, in contrast, seems to compare recognition with sense cognitions subjected to falsification of perception (*pratyakṣābhāsa*), or misperception.[48] Those *Tattvasaṅgraha* verses are as follows:

446. You should know (*khalu*) that recognition (*pratyabhijñāna*) is not possibly a direct perception (*pratyakṣa*), because the reality of a given thing (*vastu-rūpa*) is not verbally expressible and it (recognition) is expressed verbally.[49]

447. Recognition is deluded by its nature of positing "non-difference" in the case of a different reality. Direct perception is differentiated from it [i.e., it is not deluded].[50]

We learn from the discussion around these particular verses that the Hindu opponent, especially the Śaiva one, has stressed this recognition theory as a proof of the permanence of the soul, which is in opposition to the theory of momentariness of the Buddhist logicians.[51] It is well also to cite from the *Tattvasaṅgraha* this verse, which maintains the tone of the foregoing:

451. It is not right that it [i.e., recognition] is an authority (*pramāṇa*) because it operates in regard to an object whose practical function is finished, like a recollection (*smaraṇa*), etc., because it abandons the effective object.[52]

For the meaning of this, one may refer back to verse 186 from the *pratyakṣa* (direct perception) chapter of the *Pramāṇavārttika,* translated above. That verse has a sexual implication, perhaps because such imagery can get the point across where abstract discussions make the topic intractable. The verse could be paraphrased: When the woman exists only in memory, the goddess Śakti is not there, comparable to when the male organ (*liṅga*) is just a memory.[53] The Buddhist logicians claim that recognition is of this nature, never directed toward concrete reality, but aiming at the elapsed, the no-longer.

Dharmakīriti's view on recognition is expressed in two verses of the *pratyakṣa* chapter:

236. Because of the engagement of reference and discursive thought by recollection (*parāmarśa*) of what was [previously] seen, the recognition (*pratyabhijñāna* through [again] seeing cows, etc., is to be taken account of.[54]

The Manorathanandin Sanskrit commentary associates this recognition with the words "this one is that one" (*ayam asāu*). So, "he is the person I previously met" and so on. This commentary explains the form *nivārita,* which seems to mean "warded off" or "rejected," to mean "to be taken account of" (*boddhavya*) as we have translated it. If it does mean "to be rejected," it would imply that, although this recognition cannot be denied, the fact is that the object recognized had been changing all the while and so could not be precisely the same thing.

Dharmakīrti's second verse on recognition is this one:

> 503. For in this way the discursive thoughts rightly characterize the sequential occurrence. Thereby, given the perceived entity, one constructs the discursive thought of recognition.[55]

Thus, even though one does not see an object or person for a long time, if one can appreciate the feasible changes, it is reasonable to recognize that old house as the one we lived in many years ago and that person as the one we knew long ago. The denial by Buddhist texts of a permanent agent that performs this recognition, however, already has been discussed with regard to the remembering of former lives.

Finally, we can cite here another definition for authority in Dharmakīrti's *Pramāṇavārttika* (*pramāṇasiddhi* chapter, 5c): "Besides, it reveals the not yet known object-entity (*ajñātārthaprakāśo vā*)." Again, this means that memory cannot be an authority.[56]

The foregoing for this writer has been a fascinating investigation of the Buddhist theory of recollective and other types of memory by way of the words utilized in the texts discussing the topic. Any clarification of the issues found in the present essay must take into account an approach that considers the technical terminology. We learned that there is a reliable memory called *medhā* obtained in the context of samādhi. And we learned that the unreliable memory in normal consciousness could be called, in general, *smṛti,* and in particular, *saṃjñā,* or *cintā,* or *pratyabhijñāna*. Because there is much more to be said about these issues, the present essay could only touch upon certain salient points.

Notes

PT = Peking Tanjur. References are to D. T. Suzuki, ed., *The Tibetan Tripitaka, Peking ed.* (Tokyo and Kyoto: Suzuki Research Foundation, 1956).

1. Paravahera Vajiranana Mahathera, *Buddhist Meditation in Theory and Practice* (Colombo: M. D. Gunasena & Co., 1962), p. 450.

2. In *Mahāyāna-Sūtrālaṃkāra,* XII, 22, ed. Sylvain Lévi (Paris: Librairie Ancienne Honore Champion, 1907–1911), rendered into Tibetan as *tshe-rabs dran-pa.*

3. Alex Wayman, trans., *Calming the Mind and Discerning the Real, from the Lam Rim chen mo of Tsong-kha-pa* (New York: Columbia University Press, 1978), pp. 350–51. For Chandrakīrti's discussion, cf. Louis de La Vallée Poussin, "*Madhyamakāvatāra*," *Le Muséon* 8 (1907): 295.

4. Radhagovinda Basak, ed. *Mahāvastu Avadāna*, vol. 3 (Calcutta: Sanskrit College, 1968), pp. 244.4 and 542.3. J. J. Jones, trans., *The Mahāvastu*, vol. 3 (London: Luzac & Co., 1956), p. 175n, reports that *Suttanipāta*, 1009, also has the expression.

5. Franklin Edgerton, *Buddhist Hybrid Sanskrit Grammar and Dictionary*, vol. 2 (New Haven, Conn.: Yale University Press, 1953), p. 479A, where he says the expression is employed in the good sense.

6. Daisetz Teitaro Suzuki, *Studies in the Lankavatara Sutra* (London: George Routledge & Sons, 1930), p. 190.

7. *Mahāvastu*, vol. 2, p. 390.12.

8. V. Srivatsankacharya, *Avyaya Kosa; A Dictionary of Indeclinables* (Madras: The Sanskrit Education Society, 1971), p. 363.

9. Mahāvastu, vol. 2, p. 485.1–2: *śīlaṃ ca bhikṣu śodhitvā nivāsam purimaṃ smare / kalpakoṭīsahasrāṇi saṃprajānapratismṛto*.

10. Wayman, *Calming the Mind*, p. 118, and other passages.

11. Alex Wayman, "The Buddhist Theory of Vision," in George Elder, ed., *Buddhist Insight; Essays by Alex Wayman* (Delhi: Motilal Banarsidass, 1984), p. 156.

12. *Mahāvastu*, vol. 1, p. 338.4–5: *pratibhātu te vāgīśa tathāgatatasya pūrvayogo*. Cf. Edgerton, p. 366B, where the verb *pratibhāti* is explained: "it is perfectly clear."

13. Anundoram Borooah, *English-Sanskrit Dictionary* (Gauhati: Publication Board, Assam, reprint 1981) s.v.

14. Vaman Shivram Apte, *The Student English-Sanskrit Dictionary*, 3d rev. ed. (Poona, 1920; reprint Delhi: Motilal Banarsidass, 1974), s.v.

15. Sarat Chandra Das, *The Tibetan-English Dictionary* (Calcutta: Bengal Secretariat Book Depot, 1902).

16. Peking: *Mi rigs dpe skrun khang*, 1985. See Gyatso's chapter in this book, p. 211, n.110 for a use of *yid gzhungs* in a mnemonic sense.

17. Cf. Franklin Edgerton, *Buddhist Hybrid Sanskrit Reader* (New Haven, Conn.: Yale University Press, 1953), p. 22.

18. *The Laṅkāvatāra Sūtra*, ed. Bunyiu Nanjio (Kyoto: Otani University Press, 1956), 27.1.

19. *Vipākaśuddhiḥ śravaṇādyamoṣatā praviṣṭatā sūktaduruktayos tathā / smṛter mahābuddhyudaye ca yogyatā sumedhātāyāḥ paripākalakṣaṇaṃ*.

20. *Tatra medhānukūlā vipākaviśuddhiḥ kāraṇaṃ / śrutacintitabhāvitacirakṛta-cirabhāṣitānām asammoṣitā subhāṣitadurbhāṣitārthasupraviṣṭatā ca smṛter medhā-paripākasvabhāvaḥ / lokottaraprajñotpādanayogyatā karma . . .*

21. S. K. Saraswati, *Tantrayāna Art, an Album* (Calcutta: Asiatic Society, 1977), no. 182.

22. Louis de La Vallée Poussin, trans., *Vijñaptimātratāsiddhi. La Siddhi de Hiuan Tsang,* vol. 1 (Paris: Geuthner, 1928), p. 390. Here he also reports that the term *nirūpaṇavikalpa* is explained as having as its domain the idea of natures that are not directly known, whether past, present, or future. This agrees with the initial *vikalpa* as a kind of adumbration, lacking definition.

23. Cf. M. Monier-Williams, *Sanskrit-English Dictionary* (London: Oxford University Press, 1899), under *vi,* indeclinable, "asunder, in different directions."

24. Kenjui Kasawara and F. Max Müller, *The Dharma-Samgraha* (New Delhi: Cosmo Publications, 1981).

25. My attention was called to this verse of the *Vākya-padiya* as it was among the selections from this work that I was reading together with my Sanskrit Text Readings class at Columbia University in Spring 1988.

26. *Nirūpaṇānusmaraṇavikalpenāvikalpakāḥ / tāu prajñā manasi vyagrā smṛtiḥ sarvaiva manasi . . .*

27. Srivatsankacharya, *Avyaya Kosa,* p. 363.

28. Cf. Alex Wayman, "Regarding the Translation of the Buddhist Terms *saññā/saṃjñā, viññaṇa/vijñāna,*" *Malalasekera Commemoration Volume* (Columbo: Kularatne & Co., 1976), pp. 325–35. Also, Louis de La Vallée Poussin, *L'Abhidharmakośa de Vasubandhu,* Chapters 1 and 2 (Paris: Geuthner, 1923), p. 41, concerning *saṃjñā* for "false notions" in general. And, see Masaaki Hattori, *Dignāga, On Perception* (Cambridge, Mass.: Harvard University Press, 1968), p. 26.

29. Among the various editions of the *Amarakoṣa,* for example, *The Amarakoṣa* with a short commentary and footnotes, ed. Nārāyaṇ Rām Āchārya, ninth ed. (Bombay: Nirnaya Sagar Press, 1950), line no. 419.

30. Anundoram Borooah, *Nānārtha-Saṃgraha* (Gauhati: Publication Board, Assam, 1884; reprint, 1969), p. 41.

31. Wayman, *Calming the Mind,* p. 29.

32. I utilize for the *Pramāṇavārttika* the edition with the Manorathanandin *Vṛitti,* ed. Swami Dwarikadas Shastri (Banares: Bauddha Bharati, 1968); for the Tibetan, the text published at Sarnath, Central Institute of Higher Tibetan Studies, 1974; the Prajñākaragupta *bhaṣya* published in Patna, by Rashi Prasad Jayeswal Research Institute, 1953; the Tibetan for the *pratyakṣa* chapter of the *bhaṣya* in PT, vol. 132, pp. 75–216; and the Sanskrit-Tibetan and Tibetan-Sanskrit indexes to the *kārikā, Acta Indologica* (Narita: Naritasan Shinshoji III, 1973, and IV, 1976) by Yūsho Miyasaka.

33. I utilize for the *Tattvasaṅgraha*, the text by Śāntarakṣita with the *Pañjikā* by Kamalaśīla in the Shastri edition (Banares, 1968), 2 vols.; the English trans. Ganganatha Jha, reprint (Delhi, 1986), 2 vols.; *Glossary of the Tattvasaṃgrahapañjikā* by Shoko Watanabe—Tibetan-Sanskrit-Japanese, Part I, *Acta Indologica*, 1985.

34. Alex Wayman, "The Rules of Debate According to Asaṅga," *Journal of the American Oriental Society* 78, no. 1 (1958): 33B.

35. Hattori, *Dignāga*, p. 28.

36. *The Collected Works of Bu-ston*, Part 24 (YA) (Delhi: International Academy of Indian Culture, 1971), fol. 10b.7. The version of *Pramāṇavārttika* with the Manorathanandin commentary has the reading *niṣiddhe* instead of *parokṣe*, found in editions of the *svārthānumāna* chapter with Dharmakīrti's own commentary. The interpretation of *parokṣa* as *atyantaparokṣa* is found, for example, in *Karṇakagomin's Commentary on the Pramāṇavārttikavṛtti of Dharmakīrti* (Kyoto: Rinsen Book Co., 1982), p. 393.15–16.

37. This is neuter here, but Monier-Williams, *Sanskrit-English Dictionary*, knows this term only in the masculine gender.

38. Compare with the "classifying" above, with note 31.

39. *Saṃketasmaraṇopayaṃ dṛṣṭasaṃkalanātmakam / pūrvāparaparāmarśaśūnye tac cākṣuṣe katham.*

40. *Anapekṣitabāhyārthā yojanā samayasmṛteḥ / tathānapekṣya samayaṃ vastuśakty eva netradhiḥ.*

41. Saṃketasmaraṇāpekṣaṃ rūpaṃ yady akṣacetasi / anapekṣya na cec chaktaṃ syāt smṛtāv eva liṅgavat.

42. *Tasyās tatsaṃgamotpatter akṣadhīḥ syāt smṛter na vā / tataḥ kālāntare 'pi syāt kvacid vyākṣepasambhavāt.*

43. *Krameṇobhayahetuś cet prāg eva syād abhedataḥ / anyo 'kṣabuddhihetuś cet smṛtis tatrāpy anarthikā.*

44. Prajñākaragupta, *Bhāṣya*, (Skt. text), p. 276.26–27. The Tibetan translation is *brdar btags-pa*, which the *Bod rgya tshig mdzod chen mo* dictionary defines as *ming gi tha snyad sbyar ba* ("applied the convention of a name"), thus interpreting the term *samita* as *sam-ita*. The large *bhāṣya* on this verse uses the verb form *ullikhyate*, ("delineates") and the noun form *ullekha*, which among its recognized meanings is an astronomical conjunction; this meaning also accords with *sam-ita*.

45. *Yathāsamitasiddhyartham iṣyate samayasmṛtiḥ / bhedaś cāsamito grāhyaḥ smṛtis tatra kim arthikā.*

46. Prajñākaragupta, p. 276.29. It should also be noted that there is a discussion of *smṛti* in the context of *svasaṃvedana*, which the author hopes to analyze at a future date.

47. *Ghaṭanaṃ yac ca bhāvānām anyatrendriyavibramāt / bhedālakṣaṇavibhrāntaṃ smarannaṃ tad vikalpakam.*

48. Cf. Alex Wayman, "A Reconsideration of Dharmakīrti's 'Deviation' from Dignāga on Pratyakṣābhāsa," *Annals, Bhandarkar Oriental Research Institute (Diamond Jubilee Volume)*, 1977–78, pp. 387–96.

49. *Na khalu pratyabhijñānaṃ pratyakṣam upapadyate / vasturūpam anideśyam sābhilāpaṃ ca tad yatah.*

50. *Bhrāntaṃ ca pratyabhijñānaṃ pratyakṣaṃ tadvilakṣaṇam abhedādhyavasāyena bhinnarūpe 'pi vṛttitaḥ.*

51. The argument of the opponents is well developed in R. K. Kaw, *Pratyabhijna Karika of Utpaladeva*, Part I and Part II (Srinagar: Sharada Peetha Research Centre, 1975).

52. *Niṣpāditakriye cārthe pravṛtteḥ smaraṇādivat / na pramāṇam idaṃ yuktaṃ karaṇārthavihānitaḥ.*

53. Cf. Alex Wayman, "O, that Liṅga," *Ramakrishna Gopal Bhandarkar 150th Birth-Anniversary Volume* (Poona: Bhandarkar Oriental Research Institute, 1987), p. 39.

54. *Vṛtter dṛśyaparāmarśenābhidhānavikalpayoḥ / darśanāt pratyabhijñānam gavādīnām nivāritam.*

55. *Tathā hi samyag lakṣyante vikalpāḥ kramabhāvinaḥ / etena yaḥ samakṣe 'rthe pratyabhijñākalpanām.*

56. Cf. Ernst Steinkellner and Helmut Krasser, *Dharmottaras Ezkurs zurs Definition gültiger Erkenntnis im Pramāṇaviniścaya* (Vienna: Österreichischen Akademie der Wissenschaften, 1989), pp. 3–5, and notes, for the cited passage and more information. The present writer can add that this definition has a certain implication which can be exposed in this way: Because the Buddha was referred to at the outset of Dignāga's *Pramāṇasamuccaya* as *pramāṇabhūta*, Dharmakīrti in that second definition must accept the teaching of the *Lalitavistara* (cf. note 17) that the Buddha had turned his mind to natures (or doctrines) not previously heard (*pūrvam aśruteṣu dharmeṣu*).

The *Mātikās:* Memorization, Mindfulness, and the List

RUPERT GETHIN

Nikāya Lists and Mnemonic Technique

Most people coming into contact with Buddhist literature and thought outside traditional Buddhist cultures are probably struck by the fact that it seems to be full of lists. Indeed, nearly all introductory accounts of Buddhism straight away present the reader with two fundamental Buddhist lists: that of the noble eightfold path (*ariyo aṭṭhaṅgiko maggo*) and that of the four noble truths (*ariya-sacca*). This is only the beginning. Very soon one gains the impression that Buddhism has a convenient list for everything: the three jewels, the five aggregates, the five precepts, the eight noble persons, the ten fetters, the ten unwholesome courses of action, and so on.

It is apparent that much of the scriptural sutta material preserved in the four primary Nikāyas can be regarded as exposition based around lists of one sort or another, and that very many suttas might be resolved into and summed up in terms of their component lists. The reason why the noble eightfold path and the four noble truths feature so regularly in introductory accounts of Buddhism is because, according to tradition, these two lists formed the basis of the Buddha's first discourse outside Benares. But why are there so many other lists in Buddhist thought and literature? A number of writers have drawn attention to the usefulness of these lists as mnemonic devices,[1] and it seems clear that the proliferation of lists in early Buddhist literature has something to do with its being an "oral literature"—a "literature" that was composed orally and only subsequently became fixed in the form of written texts. Of course, in the Indian cultural context Buddhist literature is not uniquely or peculiarly "oral," rather Indian culture as a whole is in origin "oral";[2] indeed, a penchant for analyzing something in terms of a neat categorized list is characteristic of much of traditional Indian learning, and the oral origins of Indian learning continued to inform its structure long after its exponents had begun to commit it to writing.

One only has to reflect for a minute on the difficulties of composing a talk or a discourse without the aid of pen and paper, or without access to computers and word processors, to begin to appreciate what a convenient solution the list is. A list immediately imparts to the discourse a structure that makes it more easily remembered by the one giving the talk. At the same time a talk based on lists is easier to follow and remember for those listening. With a list one has a certain safeguard against losing one's way in a talk or forgetting sections of it. Thus if I go to a talk by the Buddha on the noble eightfold path and later find I can only remember five of the eight "limbs," then, provided that I remember that buddhas always talk about *eight*fold paths, I will at least know that I have forgotten something and do not remember the talk in full.

Lists may be a feature of ancient Indian literatures in general, but it is probably true to say that no one makes quite as much of lists as the Buddhists. At this point I should like to try to explore some of the ways in which Buddhist literature forms itself around lists and consider how these lists proliferate and interconnect. An obvious starting point is the list of the four noble truths. The bare statement of this list is as follows:

> The four noble truths: the noble truth that is suffering, the noble truth that is the origin of suffering, the noble truth that is the ceasing of suffering, the noble truth that is the way leading to the ceasing of suffering.[3]

In various places in the Nikāyas this bare and concise statement of the four noble truths is explained:

> This, monks, is the noble truth that is suffering: birth is suffering; growing old is suffering; illness is suffering; dying is suffering; sorrow, grief, pain, unhappiness and weariness are suffering; association with what is not liked is suffering; dissociation from what is liked is suffering; not to get what one wants is suffering; in short the five aggregates of grasping are suffering.
>
> This, monks, is the noble truth that is the origin of suffering: that thirst for repeated existence, accompanied by delight and passion and delighting in this and that, namely thirst for the objects of sensual desire, thirst for existence, thirst for nonexistence.
>
> This, monks, is the noble truth that is the ceasing of suffering: the complete fading away and ceasing of this very thirst, its abandoning, relinquishing, releasing, letting go.
>
> This, monks, is the noble truth that is the way leading to the ceasing of suffering: this noble eightfold path, namely right view, right thought, right speech, right action, right livelihood, right effort, right mindfulness, right concentration.[4]

It is immediately apparent that this explanation of the four truths keys into a number of other Nikāya lists. Thus the first truth is summed up by reference to the list of the five aggregates of grasping (*upādāna-kkhanda*); the second truth is explained in terms of various kinds of "thirst" that, by the close of the Nikāya period, achieve the status of list in their own right—"the three thirsts" (*taṇhā*);[5] the third truth consists in the ceasing of these very same three thirsts; finally the fourth truth is classically summed up as the noble eightfold path. So at the first stage of analysis the list of the four truths links into three further lists.

Having been told that "suffering" is the five aggregates of grasping, we need to know what precisely they are. They are listed in very many Nikāya contexts: physical form (*rūpa*), feeling (*vedanā*), recognition (*saññā*), volitions (*saṅkhāra*), and consciousness (*viññāṇa*).[6] Various definitions of these five categories are offered, definitions that in turn refer to still more Nikāya lists. Thus "physical form" is the four "great essentials," namely, the elements of earth, water, fire, and air;[7] "feeling" consists of the three feelings that are pleasant, painful, and neither-pleasant-nor-painful;[8] "recognition" can be of six sorts, namely, of shapes, sounds, smells, tastes, bodily sensations, and ideas;[9] there are three "volitions," namely, the volitions of body, speech, and mind;[10] depending on the eye, ear, nose, tongue, body, or mind, "consciousness" can be of six sorts.[11] Alternatively, both feeling and volitions can also be of six sorts: feeling born of contact through the eye, ear, nose, tongue, body or mind and volition associated with shapes, sounds, smells, tastes, bodily sensations, or ideas.[12] These explanations by way of six classes based on the six senses tie in with another favorite Nikāya list, that of the six "(sense-)spheres" (*āyatana*).[13] Appropriately enough, the first truth is occasionally summed up, not in terms of the five aggregates, but in terms of these six sense spheres.[14]

Like the first truth, the fourth truth also demands and receives considerable elaboration. The noble truth that is the way leading to the ceasing of suffering is said to consist of eight "limbs." Once more these eight limbs are explained in more detail elsewhere in the Nikāyas, and once more the explanations make free reference to yet more Nikāya lists.[15] Thus right view (*sammā-diṭṭhi*) is knowledge of suffering, its arising, its ceasing, and the way leading to its ceasing—in other words, knowledge of the four truths. Right thought (*sammā-saṅkappa*) is explained in terms of three kinds of thought, namely, thoughts that are free from desire, free from hatred, and free from cruelty; these feature in the *Saṅgītisutta* as "three wholesome thoughts."[16] Right speech (*sammā-vācā*) is speech that refrains from wrong speech, devisive speech, hurtful speech, and idle chatter, and is thus of four kinds. Right action (*sammā-kammanta*) is action that refrains from attacking living beings, taking what is not given, and noncelibacy, and is thus of three kinds. Right livelihood is explained simply as "abandoning wrong livelihood and making a living by means of right livelihood." Right effort (*sammā-vāyāma*) is explained by way of a stock Nikāya formula detailing four kinds of effort that are elsewhere called "the four right endeavors" (*cattāro sammappadhānā*).[17] Right mindfulness (*sammā-sati*) is explained by another stock Nikāya formula detailing the four kinds of contemplation (*anupassanā*) that are usually called "the four applications of mindfulness" (*cattāro satipaṭṭhānā*).[18] Lastly, right concentration (*sammā-samādhi*) is explained by way of the stock description of the successive attainment of the four "meditations" or *jhānas*.

The quest for explanation and exposition may be taken further still, linking in to yet more Nikāya lists. The detailed exposition of the four applications of mindfulness as found in the (*Mahā*) *Satipaṭṭhānasutta* is particularly fruitful ground in this respect. The first application of mindfulness, "contemplation of body with regard to body" (*kāye kāyānupassanā*), consists of various exercises. There is the fourfold practice of mindfulness of breathing (a subject that is itself expanded in other Nikāya contexts).[19] There is the practice of clearly knowing when one is walking, standing, sitting, or lying down; these four postures are elsewhere called "the four ways of going."[20] There is the practice of reflecting on the body as full of different kinds of impurity by way of a stock list of thirty-one parts of the body.[21] There is the practice of reflecting on the four elements. There is the practice of comparing one's body to a corpse in nine different states of putrefaction; this list of nine states, it would seem, is adapted to give a list of ten "uglinesses" (*asubha*) that becomes standard for the canonical Abhidhamma and the commentaries.[22]

The practice of the second application of mindfulness, "contemplation of feeling with regard to feeling" (*vedanāsu vedanānupassanā*), revolves around the contemplation of the three kinds of feeling mentioned above. The exposition of the third application of mindfulness, "contemplation of mind with regard to mind" (*citte cittānupassanā*), although it does not use a standard Nikāya list, does follow a strictly numerical structure based around the distinction of sixteen kinds of mind in eight pairs. Finally, the practice of the fourth application of mindfulness, "the contemplation of Dhamma with regard to dhammas" (*dhammesu dhammānupassanā*), involves the contemplation of such old favorites as the five hindrances (*nīvaraṇa*), the five aggregates, the six sense-spheres, the seven awakening-factors (*bojjhaṅga*), and the four noble truths.

Continuing this pursuit of Nikāya lists, I shall return briefly to the eighth limb of the path, right concentration. Right concentration led us to the stock description of the four meditations (*jhānas*). This appears to be a condensed version of a fuller description that forms the center piece of what probably should be regarded as the classic Nikāya account of the Buddhist path.[23] In this context the attainment of the four meditations is immediately prefaced by the abandoning of the five hindrances; in the *Dīgha* version it is followed by the attainment of what are later known as the six higher knowledges (*abhiññā*), in the *Majjhima* version by what are later known as the three knowledges (*vijjā*).[24] The last of these, in both cases, involves knowledge of what constitutes suffering, its arising, its ceasing, and the way leading to its ceasing; we are back with the four noble truths. Also involved is the mind's being released from defilements in their most radical form, that of the three "influxes" or *āsavas.*[25] So, while the description of the meditations does not obviously subsume any further Nikāya lists, it does lead us to some additional lists by means of strong associations.

I shall conclude this exploration of Nikāya lists to be derived from the four noble truths by citing an *Aṅguttaranikāya* passage. The fourth truth is usually explained by reference to the noble eightfold path; according to the Buddha's first discourse the eightfold path is to be understood as the "middle way" between the extremes of devotion to sensual pleasure and devotion to self-torment. But, says the *Aṅguttaranikāya,* this middle way can also be seen as the four applications of mindfulness, the four right endeavors, the four bases of success, the five faculties, the five powers, or the seven awakening-factors.[26] Together with the noble eightfold path we have here, then, seven sets of items that are classically referred to in the postcanonical literature as the "thirty-seven dhammas that contribute to awakening" (*satta-tiṃsa bodhi-pakkhiyā dhammā*).[27]

The results of this exercise in deriving lists from the traditional treatment of the noble truths can be conveniently summed up with a tree diagram (see Figure 1). It is important to note that this exercise was concluded at a more or less arbitrary point. In principle the process of drawing out lists might have been continued indefinitely; certain avenues were not fully explored, while at several points we arrive back where we started, with the four noble truths, allowing us to begin the whole process again. What this illustrates is how one Nikāya list acts as a veritable matrix for a whole series of further lists. We may begin with one simple list, but the structure of early Buddhist thought and literature dictates that we end up with an intricate pattern of lists within lists, which sometimes turns back on itself and repeats itself, the parts subsuming the whole.

It should perhaps be stressed that we are not immediately concerned here with the chronology of the evolution of the Nikāya lists; what concerns us is how the literature might have looked to an ancient monk around the close of the Nikāya period. Our perspective is thus synchronic; it assumes the existence of the whole Nikāya corpus. However, it seems to me that there are

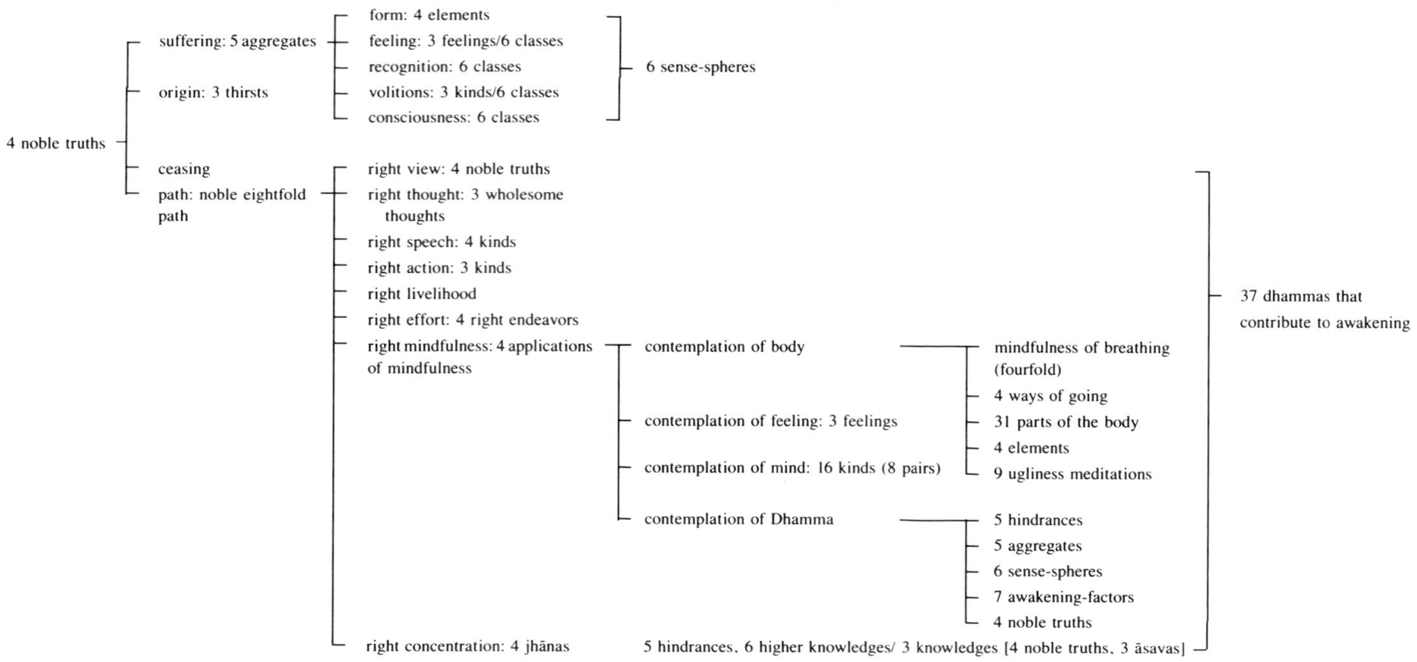

Figure 1. *Tree diagram illustrating the Nikāya use of lists*

two basic ways in which the lists evolved and proliferated. Obviously certain lists—such as the lists of the four truths, the eightfold path, the five aggregates of grasping, and the six sense-spheres—are more fundamental than others. I mean by this that they stand in their own right and for the most part evolved independently of each other. It is only subsequently that they are fitted together in the way I have tried to trace earlier (e.g., the first truth comes to be understood in terms of the five aggregates or the six sense-spheres, the fourth truth in terms of the eightfold path). Other lists appear to evolve out of the practice of taking an item or category in an already existing list and explaining it by way of a carefully structured ''analysis'' (*vibhaṅga*), which in turn can then be conveniently summed up numerically as a list. Thus the ''analysis'' of the eightfold path does not explicitly state that right thought consists of ''the three thoughts,'' rather it simply gives what is in effect a threefold analysis of right thought; nevertheless, as we have seen, an explicit list of ''three wholesome thoughts'' does occur in the *Saṅgītisutta*. Other numerically structured analyses, such as the one found under the heading of the third application of mindfulness, appear never to achieve the status of outright list.

Two general observations can be made at this point by way of summary. First, just by remembering the list of the four noble truths one has a point of access into a vast body of Nikāya teaching on all sorts of topics; in other words, we can see how the lists operate as a basic mnemonic device enabling one to remember a lot of material. There appear to be three principal ways in which the lists do this: (1) a list subsumes another list (e.g., the list of the four truths subsumes the list of the five aggregates under the category of the first truth); (2) one list may be substituted for another in a given context (e.g., under the category of the first truth the six sense-spheres can be substituted for the five aggregates); (3) one list may suggest another list by association in important Nikāya contexts (e.g., the four meditations suggests the five hindrances). There follows from this a second and perhaps more significant point. Using the lists is not merely an aid to learning the Dhamma by rote, as it were; on the contrary, the lists help one to learn the Dhamma with a view to its inner structure and dynamic. For the lists essentially are not just lists to be listed one after another, but fit together to form a pattern. Thus to learn and know the lists is to learn and know how they fit together, how they interconnect to form the structure and pattern of the Dhamma that is ''beautiful in the beginning, beautiful in the middle, beautiful in the end.''

This has certain implications for our understanding of the evolution of both early Buddhist literature and thought. The lists actually inform and to some extent govern the structure of the literature. Taking the example set out above, suppose someone decides to give a discourse on the four noble truths. Various options are open. She could aim to give a full and exhaustive exposition, following through and expanding in full all the subdivisions and secondary and tertiary lists I have indicated. Or she might give a bare and concise account of the four truths. Then again she might decide to focus on and expound in full only one branch, ending up with an expanded talk on, say, the first application of mindfulness (contemplation of body)[28] or the abandoning of the hindrances and the attainment of the first meditation; in such cases the underlying structure of the four truths need not be very obvious or explicit, but it could still serve as a touchstone for the person giving the talk. In this way, it seems to me, the lists not only aid mechanical memorization (learning by rote), but act as a kind of flowchart for the composition of a discourse. They indicate the various paths and themes that the composer can choose to follow and expand as she feels appropriate. The matrix of interconnecting lists provides a form or structure within which she can improvise. Provided she knows the structure well and is endowed with a certain skill, she can be confident she will not lose her way.

The Pāli canon has come down to us as a fixed literary text, but clearly was not always so. Given the model of interlinking lists, one can easily see how there might be a version of a sutta mentioning the four applications of mindfulness as a bare list, and another version mentioning them with a brief exposition, and yet another version that goes on to give a very full exposition. Such a state of affairs highlights the difficulties about entering into arguments about the "original" version of a sutta, for example, in the context of comparative research between the Pāli Nikāyas and Chinese Āgamas.

The *peyyālas* or "repetition" sections of the *Saṃyutta* and *Aṅguttara* Nikāyas are particularly interesting in this respect. Here the texts, as we have them, indicate an initial pattern or formula that is to be applied to various items in succession. The result is a text with quite radical abbreviations. Indeed, it is not always clear from the manuscripts and editions we have just how much we are meant to expand the material to get the "full" text. Perhaps a certain freedom is intended here; the *peyyāla* sections of the *Saṃyutta* and *Aṇguttara* Nikāyas can appear to read more like guidelines for oral recitation and composition than a fixed literary text.

The *Mātikās* and the Development of the Abhidhamma

Early Buddhist literature contains, then, a great number of lists. Clearly certain lists are more significant than others; some lists occur perhaps in only one context, whereas others crop up again and again. In such circumstances it is hardly surprising to find, at a relatively early date, the Buddhist tradition itself focusing on particular groups of lists and drawing up composite lists; that is, lists of lists. Probably one of the earliest such composite lists is the group of seven sets of items, already mentioned, that later came to be collectively known as "the thirty-seven dhammas that contribute to awakening." One might also mention the group comprising the five aggregates, the twelve sense-spheres, and the eighteen elements (*khandhāyatana-dhātu*).[29]

Other early lists of lists include the *Kumārapañha* and the *Mahāpañha*,[30] and, of course, the more extended *Saṅgīti* and *Dasuttara* suttas. In the compilation of these composite lists two methods seem to be employed: (1) in the first place one can make a convenient mnemonic summary of an aspect of the Dhamma by an apposite grouping of lists (e.g., the seven sets of items); (2) in the second place one can make a rather more general summary by employing the principles of numerical association (i.e., bringing together different lists that all comprise the same number of items) and/or numerical progression (i.e., taking a list comprising one item, then a list comprising two items, and so on up to ten or eleven items). Examples where the latter method is employed include the *Saṅgītisutta*, *Dasuttarasutta*, *Kumārapañha*, and *Mahāpañha*. In effect these are also the two methods adopted by the great collections of the *Saṃyutta* and *Aṅguttara* Nikāyas.

These composite lists are no doubt intended to function as succinct compendia of the Dhamma, but at the same time they also appear to be regarded as representing a kind of distilled essence of the Dhamma; the act of reducing suttas to lists was seen, I think, as laying the Dhamma bare and revealing its inner workings. Thus the various composite lists might be viewed as different ways of getting at the structure lying at the very heart of the Dhamma. In undertaking the task of compiling these composite lists the early Buddhist tradition appears to have felt that it was not quite enough simply to list the lists one after another, for, as we have already seen, to understand the lists is to know where they fit in the whole scheme of the Dhamma. Certainly the *Saṅgītisutta*'s method of arrangement appears simply to bring together all lists containing the same number of items, starting with "ones" and ending with "tens," and it is hard to see in this much more than a convenient mnemonic device for remembering a large number of lists. Yet such an exercise as is carried out by the *Saṅgītisutta* is, I think, always looked on as preliminary: it sets out material that is then to be employed and applied in various ways. Significantly the *Saṅgītisutta* is immediately followed by the *Dasuttarasutta*, which, while also using the principles of numerical association and progression, adapts them to produce a system for placing an entire series of lists (100 to be exact) within a structure that precisely indicates the role each plays in the Dhamma as a whole. What is interesting is that if we compare the Pāli version of that text with the corresponding versions of the *Daśottarasūtra* that survive in Buddhist Sanskrit and Chinese translation we find that in a number of places various alternative lists have been slotted in.[31] This seems to me a very good illustration of why we should not think in terms of an "original" or "correct" version of such a text. Rather, what we have here is a mnemonic technique and system of arrangement built around numerical association and progression; this technique and system goes beyond mere learning by rote, yielding a structure within which, provided one knows what one is doing, it is perfectly legitimate to improvise as one feels appropriate.

Towards the close of the Nikāya period we find a rather interesting term being employed in the literature: the term *mātikā*. In the four primary Nikāyas and the Vinaya Piṭaka this term is characteristically found as the first member of the compound *mātikā-dhara;*[32] this in turn always occurs as the third term in the sequence *dhamma-dhara vinaya-dhara mātikā-dhara* that forms part of a stock description of the accomplished monk: he is "one who has heard much, one to whom the tradition has been handed down, learned in the Dhamma, learned in the Vinaya, learned in the *mātikā*."[33] We also find the term *mātṛkā* similarly employed in Buddhist Sanskrit sources.[34] But what exactly is a *mātikā*? Buddhaghosa (fifth century CE) understands *mātikā* in the context of *mātikā-dhara* as referring to the two *pātimokkhas* or the bare lists of rules for fully ordained monks and nuns extracted from their Vinaya context in the *Suttavibhaṅga*.[35] The word *mātikā* is certainly used in this sense by the commentarial tradition and apparently from a relatively early date.[36] However, such an interpretation appears too specific and even anachronistic, and is not supported by the evidence found elsewhere in the texts. The feeling that in the present context the sequence *dhamma vinaya mātikā* ought to correspond to the sequence *sutta vinaya abhidhamma* is backed up by certain accounts of the first Buddhist council surviving in Chinese and Tibetan translation, which relate that after Ānanda had recited the Sūtrānta and Upāli the Vinaya, Mahākāśyapa recited the *mātṛkās*.[37] Accordingly it has been suggested that *mātikā* must be the early name for the Abhidhamma.[38] Although in what follows I certainly do not wish to deny that a relationship exists between the *mātikās* and the development of the Abhidhamma, it seems to me that to suggest any simple equivalence of the two terms must be regarded as a misleading simplification.

The *mātṛkās* Mahākāśyapa is said to have recited comprise the seven sets beginning with the four applications of mindfulness, along with a number of other lists of items. This is one of the reasons that led A. K. Warder to see in this list the basis of the "original" or primary *mātikā* of the Abhidhamma.[39] However, before undertaking a search for the original Abhidhamma *mātikā,* it is worth considering further the actual use of the term in the Pāli sources. Apart from its use in the compound *mātikā-dhara* (where we simply do not know precisely what *mātikā* refers to), the most extensive use of the term *mātikā* in the canonical texts is in the Abhidhamma Piṭaka. Its use here is quite specific and probably constitutes the earliest evidence for the technical application of the term.

In the first place *mātikā* is used to describe the list of twenty-two "triplets" (*tika*) and one hundred "couplets" (*duka*) set out at the beginning of the *Dhammasaṅgaṇi*.[40] Each triplet comprises three categories for classifying dhammas; each couplet comprises two such categories. Essentially the *Dhammasaġaṇi* is an exercise in expounding this *mātikā*, but I shall have more to say on this later. The *mātikā* of the triplets and couplets is also employed by three other canonical Abhidhamma works, namely the *Vibhaṅga, Dhātukathā,* and *Paṭṭhāna*. In addition, the section of the *Dhammasaṅgaṇi* dealing with the analysis of "form" (*rūpa*) begins with its own *mātikā*,[41] which considers form as comprising one, two, three, and so on up to eleven categories; just how this is so is then detailed by the subsequent exposition.

The lists that form the subject of the eighteen "analyses" of the *Vibhaṅga* bear the closest resemblance to Warder's "original" Abhidhamma *mātikā*, but surprisingly the term *mātikā* is not used by the *Vibhaṅga* in this connection; later tradition, however, does appear to have regarded this group of eighteen lists as constituting a *mātikā*.[42] In addition the *Vibhaṅga* does contain four explicit *mātikās*. The Abhidhamma section of "the analysis of the modes of conditioning" opens with a *mātikā* that indicates 144 variations of the dependent-arising formula that are built up systematically around sixteen basic variations (arranged in groups of four), which are each subject to a further nine variations;[43] the exposition that follows begins to apply each variation in turn to the different kinds of consciousness (*citta*) distinguished in the *Dhammasaṅgaṇi*. As a matter of necessity the text stops somewhat short of a full exposition; significantly, what exactly would constitute a full exposition is probably a question of interpretation as it is not entirely clear how many of the *Dhammasaṅgaṇi* variables should be taken into account. In characteristic Abhidhamma fashion a pattern is indicated, but its complete unfolding is left somewhat open; like the scriptural *Saṃyutta* and *Aṅguttara* Nikāyas, the Abhidhamma texts are full of abbreviated repetitions or *peyyālas*. In "the analysis of meditation" (*jhāna*) the Suttanta section opens with a *mātikā*.[44] This is a rather untypical *mātikā;* it is made up of stock Nikāya formulas describing the attainment of the four meditations and four formless attainments. The exposition that follows consists of a straightforward word-commentary. Two further *mātikās* occur at the beginning of "the analysis of the items of knowledge" and "the analysis of minor items," respectively.[45] Both these *mātikās* consist of a schedule compiled (like the *Saṅgītisutta*, the *Dasuttarasutta*, the *Aṅguttaranikāya*, etc.) according to a principle of numerical progression from one to ten. All relevant "ones" are listed, then all relevant "twos," and so on until we reach "tens," the exposition that follows then provides a detailed explanation of all items.

The *Dhātukathā* opens with a rather more complex *mātikā* that falls into four parts: (1) 14 pairs of categories of analysis; (2) 22 sets of items to be analyzed; (3) an indication of the path the analysis is to follow; (4) the 22 triplets and 100 couplets of the *mātikā* from the *Dhammasaṅgaṇi*, which are also to be analyzed. The rest of the *Dhātukathā* takes the form of a relatively concise and restrained working out of this *mātikā*. The *Puggalapaññatti* opens once more with a straightforward *mātikā* that arranges the headings to be discussed in the text according to the system of numerical progression from one to ten. The *Kathāvatthu* and *Yamaka* do not have explicit *mātikās*, although once again later tradition sees fit to describe both the underlying list of discussion points in the *Kathāvatthu* and the aggregate of the ten lists that form the basis of the *Yamaka*'s ten chapters as *mātikās*.[46]

In all there are eight explicit *mātikās* in the texts of the Abhidhamma Piṭaka: two in the *Dhammasaṅgaṇi*, four in the *Vibhanga*, one each at the beginning of the *Dhātukathā* and *Puggalapaññatti*.[47] The term *mātikā* is similarly employed outside the Abhidhamma Piṭaka in the *Paṭisambhidāmagga*, a work of the *Khuddakanikāya*, which consists of thirty "talks" (*kathā*) on various topics; the themes selected and the arrangement of the text are distinctive. The opening "talk on knowledge" starts with a *mātikā*.[48] This lists seventy-three kinds of knowledge that are then explained in the "talk" that follows. As A. K. Warder notes,[49] of the thirty talks the first is by far the longest (constituting about one-third of the whole text), and within this talk only the first of the seventy-three kinds of knowledge gets the full treatment. The *Paṭisambhidāmagga* opens with a *mātikā* and closes with a "talk on a *mātikā*."[50] The *mātikā* in question consists of a series of somewhat miscellaneous terms that appear, from the subsequent exposition, to be intended to constitute fifteen divisions. Again our text is radically abbreviated; great formulas and long lists employed earlier in the work are to be inserted to work out the exposition in full.

It would appear, then, that a *mātikā* can be any schedule or table of items or lists—but especially one built up according to a system of numerical progression—that acts as a basis for further exposition. The commentarial application of the term to the bare list of Vinaya rules hardly stretches this understanding.[51]

At this point it is worth considering how the Sanskrit equivalent, *mātṛkā*, is used beyond the confines of Buddhist literature. A secondary formation derived from the ordinary word for "mother" (*mātṛ*), *mātṛkā* (cognate with English "matrix") is apparently used in the first place again simply to mean "mother," and in addition "grandmother." It is also used figuratively to mean "source" or "origin" in general. In certain kinds of medieval religious literature, such as the *Tāpaniya* Upaniṣads and the Pāñcarātra texts, the term is used to signify "diagrams written in characters (to which a magical power is ascribed)" and also the alphabet employed in this esoteric fashion; in the classical medical texts *mātṛkā* is a name for the eight veins on both sides of the neck.[52]

None of these meanings seems entirely appropriate for the Pāli and Buddhist Sanskrit use of *mātikā/mātṛkā*.[53] Translators of Buddhist texts have often taken the word to mean something like "summary" or "condensed content." Although one would hesitate to say that this is incorrect, it is, strictly speaking, to put things the wrong way round, for it is the underlying meaning of "mother" that seems to inform the use of the term here. A *mātikā* is seen not so much as a condensed summary, as the seed from which something grows. A *mātikā* is something creative—something out of which something further evolves. It is, as it were, pregnant with the Dhamma and able to generate it in all its fullness. Kassapa of Coḷa (fl. c. 1200 CE) explains the word in his *Mohavicchedanī*, a commentary on the *mātikās* of the Abhidhamma, as follows:

> In what sense is it a *mātikā*? In the sense of being like a mother. For a *mātikā* is like a mother as a face is like a lotus. For as a mother gives birth to various different sons, and then looks after them and brings them up, so a *mātikā* gives birth to various different dhammas and meanings, and then looks after them and brings them up so that they do not perish. Therefore the word *mātikā* is used. For in dependence on the *mātikā*, and by way of the seven treatises beginning with the *Dhammasaṅgaṇi*, dhammas and meanings without end or limit are found as they are spread out, begotten, looked after and brought up, as it were, by the *mātikā*.[54]

Kassapa goes on to explain that if the seven canonical Abhidhamma treatises were expanded in full, each one would involve a recitation without end or limit (*anantāparimāṇa-bhāṇa-vāra*). He then concludes:

> Thus the word *mātikā* is used because of the begetting, looking after and bringing up of dhammas and meanings without end or limit like a mother. And looking after and bringing up here are to be understood as the bringing together and preserving of the neglected and hidden meanings of the texts, having distinguished them by following the *mātikā*.[55]

We can sum up by saying that *mātikās* contain the building blocks for constructing an exposition or text. But they are magical building blocks; when combined and used in various ways they can create a palace that is much larger in extent than the sum of the parts.

If the lists and schedules that we have been considering are *mātikās*, then someone who is *mātikā-dhara* or "learned in the *mātikās*" is presumably someone who knows these and similar lists. But that is not all. He also knows what to do with them; in other words, he knows how to expand them and draw out expositions from them. One who is *mātikā-dhara* is not simply someone who can spout endless lists of lists learnt by rote, but a person who can improvise and create through the medium of these lists.

All this certainly suggests some relationship between the *mātikā* and development of the Abhidhamma, but we must, I think, be wary of understanding the earliest *mātikās* in terms of a distinct and separate body of literature existing alongside the Vinaya and Sutta Piṭakas. Rather, the Abhidhamma would appear to evolve out of an already developed practice of taking a list or combination of lists, and then expanding it to produce an exposition. This is a practice that in principle goes right back to the beginnings of Buddhist literature, gradually becoming more formalized as the body of material increased in size and certain lists acquired a special significance. Toward the end of the Nikāya period the way in which lists were being used approaches more and more closely the more formalized Abhidhamma use of *mātikās*. Appropriately enough, the substance of both the *Saṅgīti* and *Dasuttara* suttas is presented not as coming from the mouth of the Buddha but from the mouth of Sāriputta, whose association with the Abhidhamma is very strong in the tradition;[56] and the Sarvāstivādins include the *Saṅgītiparyāya*, a text based on their recension of the *Saṅgītisutta*, among their canonical Abhidharma works.

The works of the canonical Abhidhamma, then, in part are to be seen as the result of a process of drawing up *mātikās* and exploiting them in ways already adumbrated in the sutta literature. If the kind of thing the very earliest of those learned in the *mātikās* were doing was developing suttas such as the *Saṅgīti* and *Dasuttara*, along with treatments like the *Kumārapañha* and *Mahāpañha*, then, as I have already implied, I think we must also discern their activity in the suttas of the two great Nikāyas of the *Saṃyutta* and *Aṅguttara*. The *Aṅguttara* employs the same system of numerical arrangement, while the list of topics focused on in the *Saṃyutta* seems to adumbrate the topics that are so prominent in certain of the canonical Abhidhamma works. A comparison of the Pāli *Saṃyuttanikāya* with what we know of other *saṃyukta* recensions shows that in essence the *saṃyutta/saṃyukta* method consists of compiling and working up a body of sutta material around the following lists: (1) the five aggregates, (2) the six sense spheres, (3) the twelve links of the chain of dependent arising, (4) the four applications of mindfulness, (5) the four right endeavors, (6) the four bases of success (7) the five faculties, (8) the five powers, (9) the seven factors of awakening, (10) the noble eightfold path.[57] In fact, these ten lists appear to constitute a *consistent core element* of the *saṃyutta/saṃyukta* collections, attracting the most attention in the Pāli version and it seems in the recension surviving in Chinese translation. Further, a number of other lists seem to act as important satellites, especially the four noble truths and the four meditations.

This core list of lists continues to be of great importance in the later history of Buddhist thought and literature.[58] We find it expanded and developed as the basis of such canonical Abhidhamma/Abhidharma works as the *Vibhaṅga, Dhātukathā,* and *Dharmaskandha,*[59] and also such later works as the *Arthaviniścayasūtra.* However, attempts to trace the development of this core *mātikā/mātṛkā* are not without their problems.[60] For example, in the canonical works the four truths and the four meditations find a firm place in the core, while the most consistent additions common to all versions appear to be the five precepts and the four immeasurables, neither of which feature at all in the Pāli or Chinese *saṃyutta/saṃyukta* collections.

Of course, focusing on this core *mātikā* in this way tends to the view, as expressed by A. K. Warder, that the earliest Abhidhamma/Abhidharma simply consisted in this *mātikā/mātṛkā,* and that it is the *Vibhaṅga,* in the case of the Pāli Abhidhamma, that represents the earliest and basic Abhidhamma text. According to Warder, the *Dhammasaṅgaṇi,* with its elaborate *mātikā* of triplets and couplets represents a somewhat later refinement. However, in an important but neglected section of the introduction to his edition of the *Abhidharmadīpa,*[61] P. S. Jaini presents a considerable body of material the effect of which is to call into question the adequacy of such a view of the development of the early Abhidhamma. Jaini himself expresses certain doubts in his review of Warder's essay but does not pursue the matter.[62]

It is, however, worth reflecting on the place of the triplet-couplet *mātikā* a little further. What Jaini points out is that the triplet-couplet system of analysis is not peculiar to the Pāli Abhidhamma method, but on the contrary is also fundamental to the dharma analysis of works such as Vasubandhu's *Abhidharmakośa,* Asaṅga's *Abhidharmasamuccaya,* and the *Abhidharmadīpa* itself, except that in these works the number of triplets and couplets employed is somewhat reduced.[63]

But, in fact, as a supplement to Jaini's findings, it is worth noting that the gap between the number of triplets and couplets distinguished in the *Dhammasaṅgaṇi* and in the northern Abhidharma sources perhaps appears greater than it really is.[64] Further, certain triplets already are found in the earlier sutta sections of the Pāli canon.[65] Thus it would seem that the kernel of the triplet/couplet *mātikā* may be very ancient, and to regard either the core *mātikā* beginning with the five aggregates or the triplet/couplet *mātikā* as more fundamental than the other is to misunderstand the basic principle that determines the way in which the Abhidhamma develops out of the use of *mātikās.* The *Dhammasaṅgaṇi* and the *Vibhaṅga,* in the form we have them, are clearly mutually dependent. Although the core *mātikā* beginning with the five aggregates is the *Vibhaṅga*'s starting point, certainly much of the material contained in the "analysis by Abhidhamma" sections assumes and uses the *Dhammasaṅgaṇi* treatment in one way or another. Furthermore, the "question" sections simply collapse without the triplet-couplet *mātikā*. On the other hand, a point often overlooked is that, whereas the triplet-couplet *mātikā* represents the *Dhammasaṅgaṇi*'s starting point, the core *mātikā* is also certainly important to its method of analysis. This is particularly in evidence in the portions of analysis concerned with "sets" (*koṭṭhāsa-vāra*) and "emptiness" (*suññata-vara*). These portions seek to bring out various groupings among the dhammas present in each moment of consciousness; the groupings brought out are for the most part derived from the core *mātikā*.[66]

In considering the *Dhammasaṅgaṇi* and *Vibhaṅga* it is not unhelpful, I think, to see the triplet-couplet *mātikā* and the core *mātikā* as acting like the two axes of the Abhidhamma method. The *Dhammasaṅgaṇi* treats the core *mātikā* by way of the triplet-couplet *mātikā*, and the *Vibhaṅga* treats the triplet-couplet *mātikā* by way of the core *mātikā*. The important point, however, is that the two *mātikās* are fundamental to both texts. Indeed one might suggest that the Abhidhamma method consists precisely in the interaction of the two *mātikās*, and that the Abhidhamma system is actually born of their marriage. Certainly one of the characteristics of the use of *mātikās* in the Abhidhamma is the treatment of one list of categories by the categories of another list. Thus the two lists act like the two axes of a graph table. This is precisely why Abhidhamma material is so susceptible to presentation by charts.[67]

Mātikās, Mindfulness, and Meditation

The starting point of this essay was the profusion of lists in Buddhist literature and the fact that these lists seem to have some sort of mnemonic significance. In the course of my discussion I have suggested that the lists must be seen as something more than crude mnemonic devices. They also acted as a creative medium for Buddhist literature and thought, representing a technique of oral composition as well. Yet, one might ask, what is the point of it all? When we come to these interminable Abhidhamma works with their proliferating lists, has it not all gotten out of control?

Buddhist lists are born out of *vibhaṅga*, "analysis" or, more literally, "breaking up"; that is, into the parts that constitute the whole. This is something dear to the heart of Buddhism. Our disease, suggest the Nikāyas and Abhidhamma, is that we emotionally and intellectually grasp at and fix the world of experience. From something that is essentially fluid and on the move, we try to make something that is inert, static, and solid. Ultimately, our only hope is to see through this state of affairs by undermining and breaking up this apparently solid world. Sometimes the texts suggest the world is to be analyzed and seen in terms of the five aggregates, or the twelve sense-spheres, or the eighteen elements; sometimes in terms of wholesome, unwholesome, and indeterminate dhammas, or in terms of the seven "limbs" of awakening—mindfulness, discernment of Dhamma, energy, joy, tranquillity, concentration, and equipoise—or in terms of the noble eightfold path, and so on. In offering these different methods the texts seem to want to remind one that when the world is broken up into parts, these parts are not to be mistaken for inert lumps; they are moving parts and what is more they are parts that continuously change their shape and color depending on the perspective from which they are being viewed.

Of course, the danger is that when, in our attempts to undo our reifying of the world, we break it up into parts, we might then take the parts as real and begin to reify the world again, if in a different way. This is exactly the danger perceived in certain Abhidharma tendencies by the authors of the Prajñāpāramitā and later spelled out by Nāgārjuna. It seems to me that the early Abhidhamma authors sought to avoid precisely this same danger through the elaboration of the various *mātikās.* Try to *grasp* the world of the *Dhammasaṅgaṇi,* or the *Paṭṭhāna,* and it runs through one's fingers. In short, the indefinite expansions based on the *mātikās* continually remind those using them that it is of the nature of things that no single way of breaking up and analyzing the world can ever be final.

But are not these proliferating lists yet based on, and full of, pedantic, artificial, and ultimately meaningless distinctions? Possibly. However, perhaps this is precisely the point. The Abhidhamma lists largely concern matters of practical psychology, by which I mean to say that their compilers were primarily concerned to distinguish states and processes of mind on the basis of actual observation, rather than to construct an abstract theoretical system as such. At one level the only way to begin to answer the question of why the compilers make the distinctions they do is to confront them in their own terms. Thus when the *Dhammasaṅgaṇi* suggests that a single moment of ordinary wholesome consciousness involves at least fifty-six dhammas,[68] this is at once a reminder of the richness and subtlety of experience, and also a challenge to perceive and investigate that richness and subtlety for oneself. In other words, to take the *Dhammasaṅgaṇi* seriously is to allow it to begin to provoke in one a state of what the texts might call *mindfulness.* It is at this point, I think, that the *mātikās* provide a clue to the relationship between "memory" and "mindfulness" as expressed in the Buddhist conception of *sati/smṛti.*

There is a further dimension to the way in which the *mātikās* serve the purpose of Buddhist meditation. The *Dhammasaṅgaṇi,* like other works of the Abhidhamma Piṭaka, is not really a book to be read beginning at page one, and working one's way through to the end. It is, as I have suggested, more like an abbreviated chanting manual, made up, as the text itself indicates, of a number of "portions of recitation" (*bhāṇa-vāra*). In other words, it is not a book to be read; it is to be performed. The major part of the text is devoted to an exposition of different types of consciousness (*citta*). The full recitation pattern is given only for the first of these—just how many there are in all is not entirely clear; certainly the number runs into the thousands.[69] There are thus considerably more than the convenient summary of eighty-nine major types of consciousness counted by the later Abhidhamma.

Suppose that one has learned to recite the complete scheme for the first type of consciousness. One now sets out to chant it for the second, third, fourth types, and so on. Much is the same, but there are changes—slight from the point of view of the recitation, but significant from the point of view of the Abhidhamma as whole. One must keep awake. If one falls asleep, immediately one will not know where one is in the text: is this the second consciousness or is it the twenty-second? Memory becomes mindfulness. This may sound like a rather dry and sterile mindfulness—like a memory that evokes neither feeling nor emotion. Yet it is to be recollected that for anyone familiar with the Nikāyas, for anyone whose spiritual life has been nurtured by the Nikāyas, the *Dhammasaṅgaṇi* is pregnant with moving and evocative associations.[70] To take but one example, "faculty of concentration" (*samādhindriya*) may sound rather uninteresting and dry, but for the ancient monk—and his modern descendant—the faculty of concentration means the four meditations, and the four meditations mean four vivid and, in the right context, beautiful, and moving similes.[71] And according to the *Dhammasaṅgaṇi*, the seeds of these calm and comforting states of meditation are present in every moment of ordinary wholesome consciousness. Thus at this level, the mindful recitation of a text such as the *Dhammasaṅgaṇi* acts a series of "reminders" of the Buddha's teaching and how it is applied in the sutta. The recitation operates as a kind of recollection of Dhamma (*dhammānusati*), a traditional subject of meditation.[72] The lengthy repetitions themselves contribute to the majesty of the performance;[73] the sheer vastness of the full recitation itself is awe inspiring. Hearing it, one is in the very presence of the Dhamma that is "profound, hard to see, hard to know, peaceful, subtle, outside the sphere of discursive thought, skillful, to be known by the wise."

Conclusion

The earliest Buddhist literature was composed orally and built up around lists. From the ever-growing body of literature, the Buddhist tradition began to abstract lists and to compile composite lists. The development of this process led to the development of the *mātikās* proper. The *mātikās* were seen as encapsulating the essence of the Dhamma; as such they were also seen as sources for the further exposition of the Dhamma. Expositions based on the *mātikās* could reveal the Dhamma in its fullness, and so, in part, the Abhidhamma—the further Dhamma, the higher Dhamma—was born. Especially characteristic of the Abhidhamma proper is the use of the triplet-couplet *mātikā* combined with the core *mātikā* that was the basis of the old *saṃyutta* collection.

The lists and subsequent *mātikās* aided memorization of the Dhamma not only by enabling one to conveniently sum up vast amounts of teaching, but also by helping one to find one's way around it; they provided a map of the Dhamma. The lists also formed a part of the practice of the Dhamma. The recitation and repetition of the lists of the Abhidhamma constituted a meditation exercise in itself that cultivated insight, wisdom, and mindfulness and inspired faith in the teaching of the Buddha. In sum, the *mātikās* seem to combine, in a distinctively Buddhist fashion, elements of memorization, mindfulness, and meditation; from the womb of the *mātikās* these emerge as one.

Notes

BHSD = F. Edgerton, *Buddhist Hybrid Sanskrit Dictionary* (New Haven, Conn.: Yale University Press, 1953).

BSOAS = *Bulletin of the School of Oriental and African Studies*, London.

PED = T. W. Rhys Davids and W. Stede, *Pali-English Dictionary* (London: PTS, 1921–1925).

PTS = Pali Text Society, London.

Abbreviations of Pāli texts are those of *A Critical Pāli Dictionary* by D. Andersen, H. Smith, V. Trenckner, *et al.*, Epilegomena to vol. 1 (Copenhagen: Royal Danish Academy, 1948); references to the *Visuddhimagga* are to chapter and paragraph of the edition of H. C. Warren and D. Kosambi (Cambridge, Mass.: Harvard University Press, 1950), all other references are to PTS editions.

1. S. Collins, *Selfless Persons: Imagery and Thought in Theravāda Buddhism* (Cambridge: Cambridge University Press, 1982), p. 109; L. S. Cousins, "Pali Oral Literature" in *Buddhist Studies: Ancient and Modern*, ed. P. Denwood and A. Piatigorsky (London: Curzon Press, 1983), pp. 1–11 (pp. 3–4).

2. See, for example, E. Frauwallner, *History of Indian Philosophy* trans. V. M. Bedekar, 2 vols. (Delhi: Motilal Banarsidass, 1973), vol. 1, pp. 20–23.

3. D III 277. For the various ways in which the truths are cited in the Nikāyas and the translation problems they pose, see K. R. Norman, "The Four Noble Truths:

A Problem of Pali Syntax'' in *Indological and Buddhist Studies: Volume in Honour of Professor J. W. de Jong on his Sixtieth Birthday,* ed. L. A. Hercus et al. (Canberra: Australian National University Press, 1982), pp. 377–91.

4. S V 421–22.

5. D III 216: *tisso taṇhā. kāma-taṇhā bhava-taṇhā vibhava-taṇhā.*

6. For references and for a fuller discussion of points relating to the five aggregates, see R. Gethin, ''The Five Khandhas: Their Treatment in the Nikāyas and Early Abhidhamma,'' *Journal of Indian Philosophy* 14 (1986): 35–53.

7. M I 185.

8. M I 302.

9. S III 60.

10. M I 301.

11. S III 61.

12. S III 59–60.

13. See in particular the *saḷāyatana-saṃyutta* (S IV 1–204).

14. S V 426.

15. D II 311; M III 251; S V 8–10.

16. D III 215: *tayo kusalā saṃkappā. nekkhamma-saṃkappo avyāpāda-saṃkappo avihiṃsā-saṃkappo.*

17. See in particular the *Sammappadhānasaṃyutta* (S V 244–48).

18. Classically in the *Mahāsatipaṭṭhānasutta* (D II 290–315) and the *Satipaṭṭhānasutta* (M I 55–63).

19. The fourfold practice consists of (1) breathing in and out with a long breath, (2) breathing in and out with a short breath, (3) breathing in and out experiencing the whole body, and (4) breathing in and out tranquilizing the forces of the body. From the point of view of the expanded Nikāya treatment (M III 83–85; S V 329–31, 336–37) this is only the first of what the *Majjhima* commentary calls four ''tetrads'' (*catukka*); the treatment relates the four tetrads to the four applications of mindfulness.

20. S V 78: *cattāro iriyā-pathā.*

21. This list is later expanded to thirty-two parts by the addition of the brain; see Vibh-a 223–48.

22. See, for example, Dhs 55, Vism VI.

23. This account occurs in full (though lost in the abbreviations of the texts) ten times in the first *vagga* of the *Dīghanikāya* (D I 62–84, 100, 124, 147, 157–58, 159–60, 171–74, 206–9, 214–15, 232–33); the accounts in the *Poṭṭhapāda* and *Tevijja sut-*

tas diverge after the description of the fourth meditation (*jhāna*). There is also a briefer *Majjhima* version of this stage-by-stage account of the path (M I 178–84, 267–71, 344–48, III 33–36, 134–37).

24. See D III 279, 275 where the *Dasuttarasutta* calls the six *abhiññās* and three *vijjās* six and three dhammas "to be realized" (*sacchikātabba*); see also PED, s.vv. *abhiñña, vijjā.*

25. See D III 216, which gives the three *āsavas;* there are also lists of four and five *āsavas,* cf. PED, s.v. *āsava.*

26. A I 295–97. The "middle way" here is between "indulgence" (*āgāḷha*) and "burning away" (*nijjhāma*); the terminology here thus differs from that found in the *Dhammacakkappavattanasutta,* where the two extremes are *kāmesu kāmasukhallikānuyogo* and *atta-kilamathānuyoga,* but it is clear from the explanations that the two extremes in both cases correspond.

27. See, for example, Vism XXII 33–43, and also R. M. L. Gethin, *The Buddhist Path to Awakening: A Study of the Bodhipakkhiyā Dhammā* (Leiden: E. J. Brill, 1992).

28. Cf. the *Kāyagatāsatisutta* (M III 88–99).

29. See Th 1255; Thī 43, 69, 103; Ap 563; Nidd I 45.

30. Khp 2; A V 48–54, 54–59.

31. See J. W. de Jong "The Daśottarasūtra," *Kanakura Hakushi Koki Kinen: Indogaku Bukkyōgaku Ronshū* (Kyōto, 1966), pp. 3–25; reprinted in J. W. de Jong, *Buddhist Studies,* ed. G. Schopen (Berkeley, Calif.: Asian Humanities Press, 1979), pp. 251–73.

32. For other uses of the term, see note 53.

33. D II 125; M I 221–23: A I 117, II 147, 169, 170, III 179–80, 361–62, V 15–16, 349, 352: *bahu-ssuto āgatāgamo dhamma-dharo vinaya-dharo mātikā-dharo.* The Vinaya version of this stock phrase (Vin I 119, 127, 337, 339, II 8, 98, 229) adds the words "mature, skilled, intelligent, conscientious, concerned, devoted to the training" (*paṇḍito vyatto medhavī lajjī kukkuccako sikkhā-kāmo*).

34. See BHSD, s.v. *mātṛkā.*

35. Mp II 189, III 382.

36. See K. R. Norman, *Pāli Literature, A History of Indian Literature,* ed. J. Gonda, vol. 7, Fasc. 2 (Wiesbaden: Otto Harrassowitz, 1983), pp. 96, 126; the *parivāra* also appears to use the term in this sense (Vin V 86).

37. I refer to the accounts found in the Mūlasarvāstivādin Vinaya (Tibetan and Chinese) and some versions of the *Aśokāvadāna.* See W. W. Rockhill, *The Life of the Buddha and the Early History of His Order Derived from Tibetan Works in the Bkah-hgyur and Bstan-hgyur* (London: Kegan Paul, Trench, Trübner, 1907), p. 60; J.

Przyulski, *Le concile de Rājagṛha* (Paris: Paul Geuthner, 1926), p. 45; cf. J. Bronkhorst, "Dharma and Abhidharma," BSOAS 48 (1985): 305–20 (p. 320).

38. See PED, s.v. *mātikā*, BHSD, s.v. *mātṛkā;* E. Lamotte, *Histoire du bouddhisme indien* (Louvain: Université de Louvain, 1958), p. 164; Norman, *Pāli Literature*, p. 96.

39. "The Mātikā" in *Mohavicchedanī*, ed. A. P. Buddhadatta (London: PTS, 1961), pp. ix–xxvii (p. xx).

40. Dhs 1–7. This is the *abhidhamma-mātikā;* there is appended a *suttanta-mātikā* consisting of a further forty-two couplets (Dhs 7–8).

41. Dhs 124–33. This is repeated in the *Vibhaṅga* (pp. 12–14) where, however, it is not called *mātikā;* perhaps, this is because here it is regarded as complete in its own right and does not form the basis for a subsequent exposition.

42. As K. R. Norman points out (*Pāli Literature*, p. 100), *Mohavicchedanī* (pp. 116–2, 30) takes the titles of each *vibhaṅga* as forming a *mātikā*.

43. Vibh 138–43.

44. Vibh 244–45.

45. Vibh 306–18, 345–49.

46. See As 4; Kv-a 7; Moh 3, 257, 278; cf. Norman, *Pāli Literature*, pp. 96, 105.

47. Norman's reference (*Pāli Literature*, p. 106) to a *mātikā* at the beginning of the *Paṭṭhāna* appears mistaken.

48. Paṭis I 1–3.

49. *The Path of Discrimination*, trans. Bhikkhu Ñāṇamoli (London: PTS, 1982), pp. xviii–ix.

50. Paṭis II 243–46.

51. Cf. Norman, *Pāli Literature*, p. 96.

52. M. Monier-Williams, *A Sanskrit-English Dictionary* (Oxford: Oxford University Press, 1899), s.v. *mātṛkā*.

53. The term, however, is used in two contexts in the Vinaya Piṭaka in the ordinary figurative sense of "source" or "origin" (a sense not noted in PED, s.v. *mātikā*): there are "eight grounds for the withholding of kaṭhina [privileges]" (*aṭṭha mātikā kaṭhinassa ubbhārāya*) and "eight sources for the production of a robe" (*aṭṭha mātikā cīvarassa uppādāya*); see Vin I 255, 309, III 196, 199, V 136, 172–74. Cf. *Mūlasarvāstivāda-vinayavastu*, Gilgit Manuscripts, ed. N. Dutt, vol. 3, Part 2 (Srinagar, 1942), p. 161: *aṣṭau mātṛkā-padāni kaṭhinoddhārāya saṃvartante* (Edgerton mistakenly translates as "eight summary points," see BHSD, s.v. *mātṛkā*). The word

is also used (only once in the Nikāyas?) to mean "water-course" or "channel" (e.g., A IV 237, As 269).

54. Moh 2: *kenatthena mātikā. mātu-samatthena. mātā viyā ti hi mātikā yathā padumikaṃ mudhan ti. yathā hi mātā nānā-vidhe putte pasavati te pāleti poseti ca evam ayaṃ pi nānā-vidhe dhamme atthe ca pasavati te ca avinassamāne pāleti poseti ca. tasmā mātikā ti vuccati. mātikaṃ hi nissāya dhammasaṅgaṇi-ādi-satta-ppakaraṇa-vasena vitthāriyamānā anantāparimāṇā dhammā atthā ca tāya pasūtā viya pālitā viya positā viya ca labbhanti.*

55. Moh 3: *evam anantāparimāṇānaṃ dhammānaṃ atthānañ ca pasavanato pālanato posanato ca mātā viyā ti mātikā ti vuccati. pālana-posanañ cettha pamuṭṭhānaṃ viraddhānañ ca pāḷi-atthānaṃ mātikānusārena sallakkhetvā samānayanato rakkhanato ca veditabbaṃ.*

56. See, for example, As 1, 16–17.

57. Cf. M. Anesaki, "The Four Buddhist Āgamas in Chinese: A Concordance of their Parts and the Corresponding Counterparts in the Pali Nikāyas," *Transactions of the Asiatic Society of Japan* 35 (1908): 1–149 (pp. 68–126); Bronkhorst, "Dharma and Abhidharma," pp. 316–17.

58. Cf. Warder, "The Mātikā," p. xx.

59. For the *Dharmaskandha*, see J. Takakusu, *Journal of the Pali Text Society* (1905): 111–15.

60. For example, Warder, "The Mātikā;" Bronkhorst, "Dharma and Abhidharma."

61. *Abhidharmadīpa with Vibhāṣāprabhāvṛtti*, ed. P. S. Jaini, Tibetan Sanskrit Works Series, vol. 4 (Patna: Kashi Prasad Jayaswal Research Institute, 1959), pp. 22–49 (pp. 40–45).

62. BSOAS 26 (1963): 438–39.

63. The *Kośa* and the *Dīpa* both use five triplets and fifteen couplets, while the *Abhidharmasamuccaya* uses six triplets and twenty-two couplets; most of these triplets and couplets have their counterparts in the *mātikā* of the *Dhammasaṅgaṇi*, but not all of them.

64. The *Dhammasaṅgaṇi* gains four of its triplets by simply taking four existing triplets and introducing a secondary principle (i.e., the notion of "object" (*ārammaṇa*) of consciousness; thus triplets 9, 13, 19, 21 are variations on 8, 12, 18, 20, respectively). With the couplets the number is brought up to 100 by applying what are more or less the same six principles to ten different lists of unwholesome categories. Of course, since the lists are different, when the resulting couplets are applied, say, in the *Vibhaṅga*'s "question" sections, this can result in significant differences in the answers. Nevertheless there is considerable overlap here, and in the case of the "knots" (*gantha*), "floods" (*ogha*), and "bonds" (*yoga*) there is simple repetition

(see Dhs. 24). One suspects that the purpose in part was simply to reach the number 100. Finally one should also perhaps bear in mind that the northern sources in question are later summary Abhidharma manuals that may have pared down the number of triplets and couplets to essentials; the triplets and couplets are not treated fully in the *Visuddhimagga*, a comparable Pāli summary work.

65. Seven are found in the *Saṅgīti* and *Dasuttara* suttas: triplet 2 (D III 216 19–20, 275 1–3); triplet 6 (D III 217 1–2, 274 25–28); triplet 11 (D III 218 1–2, 219 3–4); triplet 14 (D III 215 23–24); triplet 15 (D III 217 1–2); triplet 18 (D III 216 16–17); triplet 22 (D III 217 22–34). The "within/without/within-without" triplet has an important place in the *(Mahā) Satipaṭṭhānasutta;* in the *Aṅguttaranikāya* we have what appears to be the "small/become great/immeasurable" triplet (A V 63). Thus a total of nine triplets have explicit Nikāya antecedents. Curiously, the triplet that appears to be most basic in both the southern and northern systems, the "wholesome/unwholesome/indeterminate" triplet, is apparently absent from the Nikāyas, but it is found in the Vinaya, though not in the oldest portions (Vin II 91–92).

66. The *koṭṭhāsa-vāra* for the first type of wholesome consciousness belonging to the sphere of the senses states that on the occasions of its occurrence "there are four aggregates, two sense-spheres, two elements, three foods, eight faculties, a five-factored meditation (*jhāna*), a fivefold path, seven powers, three motivations" (Dhs 17). In the treatment of transcendent consciousness the awakening-factors are also brought out (Dhs 60–75, 99–117).

67. Cf. Norman, *Pāli Literature*, p. 107.

68. Dhs 9.

69. This suggests that the complete text could never have been recited in full without any abbreviations (*peyyāla*); possibly sections were singled out for full recitation on occasion.

70. Cf. Cousins, "Pali Oral Literature," pp. 8–9.

71. See, for example, D I 74–76 where the four meditations (*jhānas*) are characterized by the similes of the ball of moist soap powder, the pool fed by a spring, the pool of lotuses, and the man wrapped in a clean white robe.

72. See Vism 68–88.

73. Cf. R. J. Corless, "The Garland of Love: A History of Religions Hermeneutic of Nembutsu Theory and Practice" in *Studies in Pali and Buddhism: A Memorial Volume in Honor of Bhikkhu Jagdish Kashyap*, ed. A. K. Narain (Delhi: B. R. Publishing Corporation, 1979), pp. 53–73 (pp. 63–64).

Letter Magic: A Peircean Perspective on the Semiotics of Rdo Grub-chen's Dhāraṇī Memory

JANET GYATSO

The Buddhist term *dhāraṇī* is ambiguous. In many cases it denotes some sort of curious literal formula,[1] perhaps with "magical" powers. But in other contexts we can see that it also denotes the content held within that formula, as indeed dhāraṇī's etymological connection to the root *dhṛ* ("to hold") itself suggests. A simple case in point is a Prajñāpāramitā sūtra's description of the bodhisattva as one who has "attained the dhāraṇī of nonattachment."[2] This cannot be understood to mean merely that this bodhisattva has finally wrenched some secret mantra[3] from a tight-fisted teacher; clearly, *dhāraṇī* also refers here to the realization of nonattachment that the literal formula somehow stores. This essay will study a number of passages in Buddhist literature that suggest several ways in which the relationship between these two sides of dhāraṇī, its literal surface and its funding store, was understood. Of particular interest shall be the mnemonic character of that relationship. My reflections will draw on key scriptural and commentarial passages, and especially a lengthy study of dhāraṇī by the Tibetan Rnying-ma-pa scholar Rdo Grub-chen 'Jigs-med Bstan-pa'i Nyi-ma (1865–c.1926).[4] I shall also make use of the three basic categories of signs developed by the American philosopher Charles Sanders Peirce (1839–1914), which I find suggestive and appropriate in explicating the semiological issues that passages on dhāraṇī raise—the profound differences in background and intent between Peirce and Buddhist theorists nothwithstanding.[5]

Dhāraṇī can be understood as continuous with several other curious literal formulas in Buddhism. One of its predecessors may be said to be the *mātikā* (Skt. *mātṛkā*), a list of words or statements that summarizes complex Buddhist doctrines.[6] Another relative is the *paritta*, a type of text found in the later strata of the Pāli canon, to which is attributed special magical powers when it is chanted.[7] The mnemonic syllabary, actually a variety of dhāraṇī proper, includes subtypes such as the Sanskrit alphabet itself, and the well-known syllabary that begins with *Arapacana*.[8] Other types of strings of syllables form dhāraṇīs such as those included in their own section of the canon of the Dharmaguptas.[9] Dhāraṇīs are widespread in Mahāyāna scriptures. Mantras, found sporadically in pre-Mahāyāna Buddhism,[10] are common in

Mahāyāna, where they are often closely related to dhāraṇīs;[11] and they proliferate in the Vajrayāna. There is also the single seed-syllable *bīja*, found both in Mahāyāna scriptures and in the Buddhist tantras, and which in its emphasis on the single letter or syllable shows affinity with the dhāraṇī syllabary. Perhaps the most radical member of the group is the *bīja* that itself is broken down into parts, with each part assigned a separate significance.[12]

These various unconventional literal formulas share, in varying degrees, a number of features. One of these is their imputed function to protect. Both the *paritta* and dhāraṇī are said to protect the one who chants them from such dangers as snakes, enemies, demons, and robbers.[13] In the case of the *mātikās*, the one who holds them is himself called a Dharma protector.[14] And the Buddhist mantra, by virtue of a widely cited, albeit false, etymology, protects the mind.[15]

Another shared feature reflects what may be characterized as a decided interest in efficient signifiers. All of these curious formulas are notably efficient and concise in comparison to what they represent, the latter being the Buddhist Dharma in one guise or another—no-self, impermanence, thusness, and so forth. The *mātikā* is tiny compared to the complex Abhidharma teaching that it is supposed to abbreviate. In the case of the syllabary, each letter or syllable is assigned as its meaning a point of doctrine expressed in a phrase that begins with that letter; here a single letter encodes a vast meaning. The tantric mantra is often characterized as signifying aspects of the embodiment and realization of buddhahood. Contemplation of mantric formulas engenders comprehension of the five realizations of the Buddha;[16] the sixteen emptinesses;[17] the dharmakāya, immeasurable in extent,[18] and so forth. The *bīja*, of course, is particularly concise, standing for an entire text or teaching, as does the single letter *A* abbreviate the Prajñāpāramitā teachings that elsewhere are stated in 100,000 verses.[19] The tantric *bīja* most usually condenses a Buddhist deity, or a part of a deity, as do other sorts of mantras that express the deity's "heart."

Related to the formula's conciseness is its ability to exceed its semantic meaning, when and if there is any such meaning (some dhāraṇīs and mantras are composed of a combination of semantically meaningful and meaningless sections;[20] others consist entirely of letters and syllables with no semantic meaning at all). This exceeding might be understood to parallel the manner in which an utterance becomes a speech act, as when a mantra is said to perform a function such as invoking a deity by mentioning its name, or to cause someone or something to be protected, or purified, or killed, or enlightened, and so forth.[21] Even in the case of the *paritta*, which can be entirely semantically conventional, the significance and function of the text far exceeds its size and its denotation, since its primary purpose is not to describe but to engender or invoke a protective power.

One of the ways that the relationship between the concise formula and its vast content is characterized is as a sort of memory. The Buddhist texts that so characterize this relationship suggest at least two forms that such memory takes. When the emphasis is on the literal formula, the memorial relationship is one of reminding: the formula reminds the practitioner of a content that far exceeds the formula's literal surface. When the emphasis is on the other side, that is, that of the content, memory consists in a holding in store. In either case it is dhāraṇī among all of the Buddhist concise literal formulas for which mnemonic features are most often thematized. But it should be noted that the *mātikā* also is clearly mnemonic. And both mantra and *bīja* in some contexts are explicitly defined in terms of *smṛti,* as when the *Mahāvairocanatantra* claims that "through mantra, there is *smṛti* of enlightened awareness,"[22] or when the *bīja* syllable functions to remind the practitioner of the deity she is visualizing.[23]

To get a more precise sense of what sort of memory is meant when Buddhist literal formulas are characterized in mnemic terms, it is necessary first to take a closer look at the types of remembered content the formulas are said to hold in store and remind the practitioner of. We now turn our attention primarily to dhāraṇī, making occasional mention of the other concise formulas.

Memory of What?

Dhāraṇī is often characterized as the holding in memory and lack of forgetfulness[24] of teachings and doctrine. "Attaining dhāraṇī, a door to the light of the Dharma, consists in the retention of what all the buddhas have said," claims the *Lalitavistara.*[25] According to the *Akṣayamatinirdeśa,* "That which is called 'dhāraṇī' is the holding, the complete holding, the not forgetting, the remembering and perfectly holding, of the 84,000 Dharma teachings."[26] In the Prajñāpāramitā dhāraṇī is said to prevent the forgetting of utterances by beings other than the Buddha as well, such as śrāvakas, devas, nāgas, and so on.[27]

A well-known passage in the *Bodhisattvabhūmi* lists four types of dhāraṇī. The first is the "dhāraṇī of Dharma" (*dharmadhāraṇī*). As the passages just mentioned also suggest, this dhāraṇī refers to a recollective memory of the Dharma's verbal formulation that has been heard and then held for a long time.[28] But the descriptions of the other dhāraṇī types listed in the *Bodhisattvabhūmi* make it clear that different sorts of remembered contents may be distinguished as well. The second type, "dhāraṇī of meaning" (*arthadhāraṇī*), is distinguished from the first as the memory of the meaning of those teachings,[29] which would imply that the dhāraṇī of Dharma refers merely to the holding in memory of the specific linguistic formulation of the teachings itself.[30] The *Bodhisattvabhūmi*'s third category, "dhāraṇī through mantra" (*mantradhāraṇī*), refers to a string of syllables that hold certain powers conferred upon them by a bodhisattva while in a state of meditative concentration; this string is then used by the bodhisattva to help sentient beings, for example by averting plagues.[31] Again, the content held in store is not simply a particular memorized formulation, but rather involves a specially marshalled power that is condensed within the formulation. And finally, the *Bodhisattvabhūmi*'s fourth type, "forbearance dhāraṇī" (*kṣāntidhāraṇī*), makes a break with particular formulas and determinant contents of memory altogether. Although it utilizes a literal formula, forbearance dhāraṇī consists in the realization that the ultimate meaning of the dharmas cannot be expressed in such a literal formula. The bodhisattva investigates a mantra that, significantly, is meaningless.[32] When the bodhisattva attains thereby full realization of the inexpressible nature of all dharmas, he attains forbearance dhāraṇī. According to the *Bodhisattvabhūmi*, this attainment involves joyous delight (*prītiprāmodya*), purity of firm resolution (*adhyāśayaśuddhi*), and the stage of aspiration practice (*adhimukticaryābhūmi*).[33]

In the Prajñāpāramitā sūtras, the realization that accompanies dhāraṇī is given even grander soteriological import: for instance, the attainment of dhāraṇī is said to be a sign of the bodhisattva who is "irreversible from the supreme enlightenment."[34] The principal practice of dhāraṇī described in the Prajñāpāramitā sūtras is that of the "dhāraṇī doors." This practice is based on the principle of "letter sameness" (*akṣarasamatā*), a notion akin to the doctrine of emptiness (*śūnyatā*). Here the bodhisattva uses the letters in the dhāraṇī syllabary as mnemonic devices to "remember" the content of enlightenment. I shall explore what might be meant by such a remembering in some depth below. But we need to note here a special feature of the content of this remembering, a feature that also obtains for the *Bodhisattvabhūmi*'s forbearance dhāraṇī. (And we will see that in fact Rdo Grub-chen considers the Prajñāpāramitā syllabary practice to be an example of forebearance dhāraṇī.) In both the Prajñāpāramitā syllabary practice and the *Bodhisattvabhūmi's* forebearance dhāraṇī, the memory involved utilizes particular literal formulas, but its ultimate content transcends such a formulation, consisting instead of the realization of a Buddhist principle such as emptiness, or thusness, or birthlessness, which is not limited by any determination, be it temporal, spatial, or linguistic.

In several further contexts the characterization of the content of dhāraṇī is also something other than a specific recollective memory such as the verbal formulation of teachings that have been heard. When dhāraṇī is connected to meditative absorption (*samādhi*),[35] it would be affiliated with *smṛti* in its sense of meditative mindfulness, a topic explored in several other chapters in this volume. We can note here that dhāraṇī associated with meditative absorption is listed by the *Mahāyānasūtrālaṅkāra* along with the type of dhāraṇī seen in the *Bodhisattvabhūmi* and elsewhere that is the memory of teachings heard. The *Mahāyānasūtrālaṅkāra* distinguishes three dhāraṇī types: that which results from past karma; that which involves a concerted listening to and retaining of teachings; and that which is supported by meditative concentration. It is the last which is considered to be the superior type of dhāraṇī.[36]

Yet another type of dhāraṇī is connected to a faculty attributed to the bodhisattva, namely, the inspired ability to speak eloquently (*pratibhāna*).[37] This refers to the bodhisattva's facility in applying the principles of what he has learned to the contingencies of the moment so as to teach the Dharma effectively.[37] Again, such eloquence is not simply a matter of dredging up specific pat formulas learned in the past—rather, it denotes the bodhisattva's holding in store and fluency in the Buddhist teachings as a whole, a fluency that reflects general understanding more than it does the memory of particular verbal expressions.

In sum, the content of what is asserted to be remembered via dhāraṇī, as well as other literal formulas, may be of a variety of sorts. We have seen some cases in which dhāraṇī is said to store a determinant recollective memory, and others where it holds a more general content. In the following discussion we focus on the type that is the content of the Prajñāpāramitā dhāraṇī door and of forebearance dhāraṇī, two closely related types of dhāraṇī. This content is defined as one or another of the standard expressions for the Buddhist "ultimate truth," such as "emptiness," or "birthlessness," or "thusness," or "letter sameness": in the following discussion I alternate among these terms, which, it will be noticed, themselves are literal formulations. Indeed the Prajñāpāramitā syllabary offers forty-two such verbal expressions, but the presupposition in that and many Buddhist discussions is that the content to which such expressions refer cannot be denoted explicitly. Such a content resists any sort of specification at all. It is not limited to any specific time, and it is said to be the "true nature" of all particular objects everywhere. It is characterized metaphorically in Buddhist discussion as being deep, profound, pervasive, vast.

It is just here, where dhāraṇī is said to hold in store and to remind the practitioner of a vast, unspecifiable content, that the peculiar problem touched on earlier emerges most clearly: how is a literal formula supposed to remind the practitioner of such a content? There is a striking incongruity between the specificity and determinacy of the literal reminder, and the generality and indeterminancy of the pervasive, profound content of which she is reminded. And so in reflecting on this widespread practice in Buddhist texts of reducing and memorializing a vast principle in a skimpy string of letters, I find the skimpy letters to be the most curious and interesting. Scholars already have puzzled a great deal over Buddhist notions of the ineffability, absoluteness, and so forth of the ultimate truth. What shall concern me here is how a little literal formula is supposed to engage, hold in memory, and remind someone of that ineffable immensity.

How? Rdo Grub-chen's Semiotics in Peircean Perspective

Certain Abhidharmic descriptions of conventional recollective memory claim that there is an initial making of an experience into a sign which is crucial to the ability to hold that experience in memory.[38] Discussions of dhāraṇī memory also highlight the manner in which an experience is initially grasped,[39] and the Prajñāpāramitā commentarial tradition is explicit in claiming that this grasping involves signs.[40] According to the *Abhisamayālaṇkāravṛtti* of Ārya Vimuktisena, "By making the letter into a sign (*cihnī*), there is inexhaustible memory (*smṛti*), the cause for giving teachings over many aeons; hence memory, by virtue of holding syllables and their meanings, is [here] called dhāraṇī."[41] As shall be shown in some depth below, Rdo Grub-chen's study of dhāraṇī door practice and its relationship to memory continues in this semiological tradition, depending on the role of the sign as a central element of its analysis.[42]

In general, we might observe that the connection between signification and memory is especially evident in the manner in which reminding occurs. Reminding requires a reminder; a content of which one is reminded; and a remindee, the one who is being reminded. This triad translates into semiological language as the sign vehicle, the signified object, and the interpretant (for which we will substitute the more accessible, if psychologized and less precise, term *interpreter* in this essay). Such terminology can be applied to the theory of forebearance dhāraṇī. The literal formula is a sign vehicle. The signified object is the "profound" content already mentioned, which is held in store by the literal formula, and of which the remindee is reminded. The remindee, or the interpreter, is the practitioner, who is reminded of that content when she understands the signs of the dhāraṇī's literal formula. To take a closer look at these three factors of semiosis as they are represented in Rdo Grub-chen's study of dhāraṇī reminding, I introduce into the discussion at this point Peirce's set of semiological categories, categories that in fact fit remarkably well with Rdo Grub-chen's analysis.

Peirce theorized that the relationship of a sign to what it signifies is of three main varieties: the sign can be an icon of its signified; it can be an index to its signified; or it can be a symbol of its signified.[43] The first of these, the icon, represents its signified object by virtue of being similar to it in some way. Common examples are pictures, diagrams, and metaphors. For Peirce, the icon is the most basic of signifiers, on which all other forms of communication depend.

Iconic Reminding

The literal formula as icon would remind by virtue of something about the formula's being that shares in or resembles what the formula signifies.[44] We can say at once that it is the Vedic tradition which would most readily affirm such a relationship because of the isomorphism that is claimed to obtain, in that tradition, between the word or mantra and ultimate reality, a relation that is considered eternal by the Mīmāṃsakas and others. It is of particular relevance here to note that this eternal relation is understood to be mnemic in nature by the Kashmiri Śaivite philosopher Abhinavagupta (eleventh century) who characterizes both the functioning of mantra and the eternal meaning that it embodies as memory (*smaraṇa*). For Abhinavagupta, memory, even in its mundane occurrences, requires the persistence of a permanent subject, which is both analogous, and allows access, to the underlying eternal, ultimate consciousness.[45]

If the iconic relationship between a verbal formula and its meaning were to be eternal it would be unacceptable to the Buddhists, for most of whom sound and/or verbal expression is produced, conventional, relative, contingent, and not eternal.[46] As could be expected, this is the position taken by Rdo Grub-chen in his characterization of forebearance dhāraṇī memory. But, interestingly, Rdo Grub-chen too ends up by locating this type of dhāraṇī formula's memory power in what can best be characterized as iconic semiosis, albeit in an iconicity that appears to avoid the metaphysical pitfalls of eternalism. And furthermore, as we will see in the last section of this chapter, the iconic semiosis of Rdo Grub-chen's forebearance dhāraṇī has the special property of "self-destructing" at the very moment that it is fully realized. Rdo Grub-chen is also able to find what amounts to indexical and symbolic semiosis in forebearance dhāraṇī practice, but neither of these explain the practice adequately.

This brings us to the details of Rdo Grub-chen's study. Entitled "An Exegesis of the Bodhisattva's Dhāraṇī Ornament: A Well-Spoken Garland Which Beautifies the Queen Mother's Good Body,"[47] the bulk of this 188-page work is focused on what Rdo Grub-chen classifies as forebearance dhāraṇī. Rdo Grub-chen lists three approaches to what he considers to be forebearance dhāraṇī: that of the Prajñāpāramitā sūtras and Nāgārjuna

(c. 200 CE); that of Ārya Vimuktisena (sixth century) and Haribhadra (eighth century); and that of the Yogācāra texts. The Yogācāra school is represented by the *Bodhisattvabhūmi* passage, yet Rdo Grub-chen pays that text relatively scant attention, despite the fact that he has borrowed its basic dhāraṇī classification.[48] Instead, he devotes most of his time to the seminal passage on syllabary dhāraṇī to be found in several Prajñāpāramitā sūtras, a passage that has also received attention from modern Buddhologists. Rdo Grub-chen rarely mentions Nāgārjuna except to associate his name with the Prajñāpāramitā tradition, and he quotes Ārya Vimuktisena and Haribhadra only briefly, citing instead a wide range of Mahāyāna sūtraic and śāstraic sources.

To see how I can claim that Rdo Grub-chen's argument ends up with the position that the literal formula of the syllabary dhāraṇī stores memory and reminds iconically, we need first to consider his comments on the more obvious interpretation of the Prajñāpāramitā's dhāraṇī syllabary; namely, that it reminds indexically.

Indexical Reminding and the Dhāraṇī Door of the Syllabary

An index, according to Peirce, indicates an object by pointing to it.[49] The index accomplishes this pointing because it is somehow connected to its signified object, be the nature of that connection physical, quasi-physical, or conceptual. Examples of indexes are a book used to signify a scholar, or the pole star that indicates which way is north. Because it directs attention to the object to which it is connected, the index can signify that object as such.

At first glance, the dhāraṇī syllabary would seem to be a literal formula that reminds indexically. Consider, for example, *A*, the first letter of the *Arapacana* syllabary, and a highly condensed formula indeed. In the Arapacana syllabary, the letter *A* reminds the practitioner of *anutpannatva* which means "birthlessness," one of the terms that signifies the Buddhist ultimate truth. *Anutpannatva* is what Rdo Grub-chen calls a "defining phrase" (*nges-tshig*); that is, a word or group of words that begins with the letter sign and linguistically expresses, or defines, the meaning that the letter is meant to signify. As the initial element of its defining phrase, the syllabary letter is an index, because it is connected to and thereby leads to the rest of the phrase. It is, to give Rdo Grub-chen's example, like the copper door through which a city is entered.[50] To offer our own example, it is like the first measure of a familiar song that will remind the seasoned listener of the rest of the tune.

The syllabary is considered by Rdo Grub-chen to be the most sophisticated type of dhāraṇī; namely, the dhāraṇī of forebearance. How is this dhāranī practiced? Rdo Grub-chen cites what is widely recognized as the *lo-*

cus classicus for syllabary dhāraṇī practice; that is, the following passage from the Large Prajñāpāramitā:[51]

> Moreover, Subhūti, in this way the dhāraṇī doors are the great vehicle of the bodhisattva, the great being. What are the dhāraṇī doors? The sameness of letters;[52] the sameness of utterances; the letter doors; the letter entrances. And what are the letter doors and the letter entrances? *A* is the door to all dharmas because of their primordial *anutpannatva* ("birthlessness").[53] *Ra* is the door to all dharmas because they are without *rajas* ("dirt"). *Pa* is the door to all dharmas because they teach *paramārtha* ("ultimate truth"). *Ca* is the door to all dharmas because *cyavana* ("passing away") and birth are not apprehended, since dharmas lack passing away and birth. *Na* is the door to all dharmas because they are without *nāman* ("name"), an own-nature of names not being attained nor rejected . . . [etc., through the syllabary down to] *Ḍha* is the door to all dharmas because unsteadiness is not apprehended, and [the dharmas] remain in the final ultimate state, without dying and without birth.[54] There are no letter conventions other than the foregoing.
>
> Why is that?[55] Because there is no name of anything by which [such a thing] can be conventionally designated, spoken, displayed, characterized, or seen.[56] All dharmas, Subhūti, should be understood as being just like space. This, Subhūti, is the entrance into the dhāraṇī door, the entrance into the teaching of the letter *A*, etc.

Unlike most modern editors and translators of this passage, Rdo Grub-chen locates a critical turning point of this passage at the question "Why is that?"[57] He claims that the force of this question is to cast doubt on the manner in which the dhāraṇī doors remind as described in the first paragraph of the passage. *A* might lead one to (or, in Peircean terms, serve as an index to) the meaning of birthlessness when one adds onto it the other letters of its defining phrase; that is, *nutpannatva*. But it is not proper to claim on that basis that *A in general* (*spyi-ldog*) is a door to birthlessness.[58] What follows in Rdo Grub-chen's argument amounts to a demonstration that the indexical dhāraṇī door letter is not absolute:

> To the mere letter *A* it is seen that one can add sounds that will express fire, as in *anala*, or *ayaskantaḥ* [sic] for needle; or *apūpa* for fried bread. If those [words] also are thought to be appropriate to be part of the terminology that expresses birthlessness, then there is the problem that all terms will become terms for emptiness.[59] . . . So even though [the sūtra gives an] explanation using defining phrases, [the sūtra] depends on an approach that does not transgress the principle of letter sameness. The answer that addresses [the preceding problem] is "Because there is no name of anything, etc."[60]

What Rdo Grub-chen is asserting is that the Prajñāpāramitā passage on dhāraṇī doors switches levels, from the conventional to the ultimate. The passage begins with the standard syllabary, which sports an indexical connection between the signifier *A* and its defining phrase *anutpannatva*, and so on through the syllabary. But then a hypothetical questioner, noting that *A* does not always point to its defining phrase *anutpannavta* (and, we might add, *anutpannatva* signifies birthlessness only to those with knowledge of Sanskrit), questions the status of the defining phrase, because the relationship between *A* and *anutpannatva* is but a convention. This, for Rdo Grub-chen, is the force of the question, "Why is that?" And so, in the sentence beginning "Because there is no name of anything," the passage goes on to address the ultimate nature of all things. There is no name or word that actually designates or speaks or makes manifest anything (let alone birthlessness), since all dharmas are empty of such determinations and conventions, like space. In making this statement, Rdo Grub-chen argues, the text is claiming that the manner in which the conventional defining phrase becomes a dharma door ultimately depends on the principle of "letter sameness" invoked at the very beginning of the passage.[61]

As will be evident by the end of this essay, Rdo Grub-chen's discussion of the logic of letter sameness locates the reminding power of the syllabary signs in an iconic relationship to their signified contents; that is, the understanding of birthlessness, and so forth. However, why this is so needs some explanation. We can construct part of such an explanation by considering Rdo Grub-chen's discussion of a practice that he attributes to the Prajñāpāramitā commentarial tradition of Haribhadra and Ārya Vimuktisena. This will supply some of the missing links in the preceding reasoning. In particular, we must ask: how would the principle of letter sameness inform what seemed to be the fairly straightforward indexical semiosis of "*A* is for *anutpannatva*"?

From Letter as Index to Letter as Symbol

According to Rdo Grub-chen's discussion of the Ārya Vimuktisena/Haribhadra tradition, the indexical relationship between *A* and its defining phrase *anutpannatva* is not the basis on which *A* is a dhāraṇī door.[62] Rather, what is required is that the practitioner perform concentration and insight meditation on the Buddhist principles of birthlessness and emptiness. Drawing upon the Prajñāpāramitā tradition, as well as several commentaries, Rdo Grub-chen traces out this practice: the meditator focuses upon the letter *A*, asking, Where did this come from? Where will it cease? How does it abide in its own nature? He then discovers in insight meditation that the letter is birthless and empty, an insight that is also called "letter sameness." When he reaches this realization about the letter, he then takes a second step: he artificially assigns to the letter *A* a superimposed meaning (*sgro-btags;* Skt. *āropa*) so that it can be used to signify this profound emptiness, birthlessness, letter sameness, and so forth. In other words, the letter *A* comes to have assigned to it (*yong-su btags*) as its significatory content the realization of the ultimate principle of emptiness.[63] It should be noted that in this process of making *A* into a dhāraṇī door, a particular defining phrase such as *anutpannatva* has not yet been formulated. Rather, the letter *A* as such, or *in general* (*spyi-ldog*) as Rdo Grub-chen characterizes it, is held as a sign (*mtshan-mar gzung*) of the principle of emptiness.[64]

In this account, Rdo Grub-chen is using the letter *A* as a symbol of emptiness, instead of as an index of it. For Peirce (who, it will be noted, has a very particular definition of the symbol, one that differs from that of many other theorists), a symbol is a sign that represents something by virtue of an established convention or general law.[65] The superimposition or assignation of value we have just seen would be such an established convention. As a symbol, *A in general* (just the aspect of *A* that, as we saw above, was not accounted for and therefore undermined indexicality as the ultimate basis of dhāraṇī door semiosis) is the operative sign, not *A* as attached to any particular defining phrase.[66] For Rdo Grub-chen, *A in general* is what ultimately can become the dhāraṇī door to all dharmas.

However, the defining phrase still has a place in dhāraṇī semiotics, albeit a secondary one. Rdo Grub-chen's account goes on to indicate that after the letter's birthlessness and letter sameness, etc., have been penetrated in insight meditation and the letter has then been assigned the role of symbolizing that insight, the defining phrase is formulated as a further step and applied to the same content in order to signify it linguistically.[67] In other words, the defining phrase is established after the impregnation of the letter with the significatory value of a meditative realization. It is a secondary symbolic label attached to the same realization, one that symbolizes that realization to the practitioner verbally (but note that the phrase is indexically connected to the letter itself).

The Defining Phrase: Dhāraṇī's Back Door

Even though the defining phrase is understood as only a secondary sign, it is employed in many of the scriptural passages that Rdo Grub-chen marshalls to develop the logic of dhāraṇī practice. The letter remains the primary basis of dhāraṇī semiosis.[68] But the defining phrase also has a place.

Rdo Grub-chen refers to the way a defining phrase may be used with a passage from the *Vajramaṇḍadhāraṇīsūtra.* Here the letter *Da,* which is the seventh letter in the *Arapacana* syllabary, and its defining phrase *dama* (control) are the examples:

> "Mañjuśrī, each dharma is a *devadvara* ("god door"). This is the basis of dhāraṇī."
>
> "Bhagavan, how is that the basis of dhāraṇī?"
>
> "Mañjusrī, each dharma abides at the stage of *dama* ("control"). This is the basis of dhāraṇī that is entered through something like *deva* ("god")."[69]

Rdo Grub-chen asserts that this passage suggests a practice whereby all words that begin with the same letter as does a given defining phrase will remind the practitioner of that phrase.[70] Thus whenever the word *deva* is encountered, as well as any other word that begins with *Da,* and indeed all instances of *Da* wherever its place in a word, the practitioner will remember the defining phrase *dama,* and the "profound situation" it symbolizes.[71] In this manner, not only the defining phrase, but all speech and other forms of verbal articulation become dhāraṇī: drawing upon the logic that all verbal articulation is composed of the letters of the alphabet,[72] the practitioner cultivates the ability to perceive those letters as symbols of profound religious content through the practices described above, and then each letter in everything he hears or reads or thinks, and so on, will serve to remind him of that content. The sequence of that reminding goes like this: the letter he hears reminds him of the defining phrase he has assigned to it, and the defining phrase in turn reminds him of the emptiness that he has assigned the letter *in general* to symbolize, an emptiness with which he is familiar based on meditatively cultivated insight.

It should be noted that the practice that Rdo Grub-chen and his scriptural sources are describing here does not use the syllabary as a mnemonic list of defining phrases that the practitioner memorizes and then chants in order to remind himself of the empty, birthless nature of all dharmas. Rather, the practice suggested by the *Vajramaṇḍadhāraṇīsūtra* begins with and focuses upon conventional language and speech. In other words, instead of concentrating on a list of memorized letters and defining phrases, the practitioner concentrates on everyday speech. The syllabary is but a device, a list of preestablished symbolically imbued letters and indexically related phrases with the same symbolic value, to help the practitioner achieve the larger goal of learning to engage all language in dhāraṇī mnemonics.

It is important to keep in mind that the defining phrase is but a secondary device in the scenario worked out by Rdo Grub-chen in his analysis of the

Vajramaṇḍadhāraṇīsūtra passage. We can imagine a practice where it was not employed at all: the practitioner would simply establish all letters as symbols of emptiness and then attempt to perceive them as such every time he encountered them. The role of the defining phrase is simply an extra facilitator in this process, operating, as just suggested, both indexically between the letter and the defining phrase, and symbolically between the phrase and its linguistic signification. It might help to characterize the defining phrase as a back door, as it were, because it ushers the letters employed in everyday language back into their ultimate (or rather penultimate) significance; for example, from *A* as in *apple* to *A* is for *anutpannatva*. The defining phrase is thus a special linguistic symbol that is employed to mediate between conventional linguistic symbols and the extralinguistic signification of the letter meditatively imbued with the value of birthlessness. But it is still the letter that, as discussed, is used as the primary signifier of birthlessness or letter sameness, and so forth. In this practice the letter has a twofold role: (1) it is a clearing station that connects all words that contain it to the defining phrase,[73] and (2) its primary value of emptiness and letter sameness, meditatively realized as the nature of all letters, informs the linguistic meaning of the defining phrase devised to express it. It is for these reasons that Rdo Grub-chen can maintain that it is the letter, the ''empty letter door that displays emptiness,''[74] that remains as the basis for the practice, even in the *Vajramaṇḍadhāraṇīsūtra* passage, which seems at first glance to trade on the force of the defining phrase. The defining phrase is being used only as an intermediary symbol linking everyday language with the ultimate principle of emptiness/letter sameness. And the manner in which the defining phrase performs that intermediary function hinges on the lubrication provided by the letter itself, which in turn mediates between everyday language and the defining phrase. We might note that such lubrication is possible precisely because the letter's intrinsic letter sameness frees all literal symbols from being tied to any one particular conventional meaning.

Dhāraṇī Seal: Why Letters?

In functional terms, both the letter and the defining phrase serve as signs to remind the practitioner of a Buddhist principle such as emptiness. But as we have already seen, the letter is priviliged in dhāraṇī practice. Furthermore, only the letter, and not the defining phrase, can serve as the iconic reminder that ultimately becomes, for dhāraṇi practice, the best reminder of emptiness. To appreciate why this is so, we need to focus for a moment on several additional points developed by Rdo Grub-chen which place the letter at the center of the practice sketched out above.

"To put all the words for dharmas into one word is the skillful way to condense all dharmas," writes Rdo Grub-chen. "It is to apply the dhāraṇī seal to all sounds."[75] It will be recalled that early in this chapter we observed conciseness to be a prominent feature of dhāraṇī as well as other types of Buddhist literal formulas. The condensation of many symbols into one via the principles of dhāraṇī practice is called "dhāraṇī seal" (*dhāraṇīmudrā*), a term known in a variety of Mahāyāna texts.[76] Rdo Grub-chen describes the dhāraṇī seal practice as having two aspects. The first is the making of the letters of the alphabet into seals, which means the deliberate imbuing of letters with meditatively realized meaning, after which they are assigned defining phrases as described above. The second aspect of dhāraṇī seal practice is the application of the seals to all instances of language, as illustrated in the *Vajramaṇḍadhāraṇīsūtra* passage also discussed above.[77]

The operative principle by which a seal acts is as a reduced signifier, serving to represent something in condensed form. Different from the nail, or pin, another metaphor that is sometimes used in Buddhist texts for the literal formula's function to focus the mind on a single point in meditation,[78] a seal can be applied anywhere and to all phenomena. By virtue of this generalized applicability, a seal holds great power and empowers the one who holds it. To translate this into the dhāraṇī door metaphor, we might say that the seal functions like a passkey that allows, nay virtually compels, all phenomena (that is, all verbal articulation) to enter into emptiness.[79] To remain with the seal metaphor, we can think of a king's seal, a single emblem that is imposed upon all documents, thereby subordinating all issues to the authority of the king; in this context, the seal wields power over everything that occurs in the land.[80] The practice of dhāraṇī seal might also be related to the variety of other senses in which *mudrā* is understood in Buddhist thought and practice, particularly in Mahāmudrā ("The Great Seal"), a tradition too vast to be explored here. In the case of the dhāraṇī seal, a concrete and tangible emblem, namely, the letter and/or defining phrase, is employed to seal all phenomena. And if we consider the dynamics of how such a concrete emblem would function in dhāraṇī mnemonics, it will become evident why the letter is more crucial than the phrase.

Conciseness: The Letter as the (Pen)ultimate Condenser

"From every letter (*yig-'bru*) there is the unobstructed power to remember teachings that were given over many eons."[81] In statements such as these we can recognize a number of other reasons, beyond the basic logic of letter sameness, why it is the letter that becomes the primary dhāraṇī seal.

An essential characteristic of a seal is that it is singular. One emblem (even if there are many tokens of it) is applied to a variety of phenomena. The briefer the seal, the more efficient and handlable. Thus, although both letter and defining phrase are concise, the letter of course is the more concise of the two. According to Rdo Grub-chen the defining phrase merely verbalizes the meaning of the letter, similar to a commentary which is condensed by its root text.[82]

The advantages of compactness and efficiency for memory are doubtless the primary reason why Buddhist literal formulas are typically concise. As Rdo Grub-chen writes, "If one is to hold a vast magnitude, one condenses it into a bundle in order to hold it easily—this is a widely practiced technique."[83] By virtue of such a bundle, a great variety of details can be remembered without regard to sequence.[84] Instead of holding a doctrine or principle in drawn-out narrative form, the dhāraṇī letter condenses everything into a single element.

In the course of Rdo Grub-chen's discussion, not only is singularity shown to be efficient, it is also shown to eliminate the possibility of confusion. If one attempts to remember many terms and classifications without employing the condensing dhāraṇī method, Rdo Grub-chen claims, memory is "stolen" because of the multiplicity and becomes mixed up. On the other hand, to penetrate the meaning of letter sameness and then to make that into a single sign greatly facilitates the agility of memory. And so, with the special awareness that penetrates profundity, one ties up all of what one has to remember so that it does not become separated (*mi-phyed-par bsdams*).[85] Thus is it better for *A* to signify the realization of birthlessness directly and through immediate memory (*thod-rgal-du dran-pa*), without the intervention of the defining phrase.[86]

The Sanskrit word for "letter" itself, *akṣara,* which means "imperishable," suggests another advantage of the letter over the phrase: dependability. Rdo Grub-chen claims that the phonic value of a letter that is conventionally in force (*brda-dbang*) remains constant,[87] much more constant, we might add, than the words of a defining phrase that also have conventionally established meanings but that alter more easily according to varying contexts.[88] Presumably for Rdo Grub-chen this does not imply that the phonic value of a letter is eternal; rather, his point is that the phonic value of a letter is a relatively stable building block on which complex linguistic articulations rely.

That the efficiency of the concise letter allows instantaneous and dependable memory suggests to Rdo Grub-chen yet another advantage of the letter over the defining phrase for dhāraṇī seal practice, quite apart from the avoidance of confusion. This is based on the supposition that letters tend not to distract the practitioner. The manner in which letters avoid becoming distractions is not related to their conciseness, however, but to other aspects of the nature of letters.

Letters as Empty Signifiers, Apart from Saṃsāric Woes

This point is only minimally developed by Rdo Grub-chen, but it deserves attention. It is drawn from a passage in the *Sāgaranāgarājaparipṛcchā:*

> Letters have no greed, no aversion, no delusion; but in coming to master letters children become greedy, angry, and deluded.[89]

In other words, letters carry no emotional value themselves. They are merely symbols, pure signifiers that do not partake of what they signify. One could make the same argument for other sorts of verbal symbols as well. In this section of his analysis Rdo Grub-chen does not himself rigorously distinguish letters from words, phrases, and other forms of verbal articulation. His point is that whatever emotional problems are associated with any verbal form, they are extra and superimposed, not inherent to the verbal form itself. Thus letters and words would be excellent symbols in the Peircean sense. To the extent that they are symbols, they are free-floating agents, empty signifiers; that is, empty of any intrinsic meaning of their own. Unlike the icon and the index, which resemble or are part of what they signify, the Peircean symbol has nothing in its nature in particular that makes it a sign of what it signifies. Again from the *Sāgaranāgarājaparipṛcchā:*

> Letters express the obscuring afflictions, but that does not make them obscuring affliction. They express wholesomeness, but that does not make them wholesome.[90]

Letters are only signifiers, pure signifiers, not partaking in any way in that which they purport to signify. Making the same point about words is this statement from the *Samādhirājasūtra:*

> The wise one is an utterer of words, but his mind is not stolen by words. Words are like rocks on the mountain. Therefore one should never become attached to words.[91]

Words in themselves are nothing, just dry rocks lying around on a mountain.[92] The basic message is a common one in Buddhist literature, and many passages illustrating a similar point could be identified. With regard to dhāraṇī itself, we might recall here a definition found in the *Mahāprajñāpāramitāśāstra* concerning "the dhāraṇī that enters [the true nature of] articulated sounds" (*ghoṣapraveśadhāraṇī*), one of three types of dhāraṇī classified there. Here "articulated sounds" refers in particular to verbal speech, the point in this context being that the bodhisattva needs to understand that sounds are impermanent, in order to avoid being either insulted or flattered by what people say, unlike average people who lack such understanding. The logic, again, is that words themselves are like echoes, empty, without agency, and so forth.[93]

These points refer to all forms of language, whether in writing, speech, or thought, and the implications for Buddhist practice, to be discussed briefly below, are considerable. But we might observe, even though Rdo Grub-chen and other Buddhist writers do not themselves make it clear, that the claim that a verbal signifier is a pure signifier is best illustrated by letters. This is because inherent meaning is less likely to be attributed to letters than to words. Words and names and phrases suggest particular lines of thought—and emotion. They remind us of meaning, if not by iconic similarity, then by indexical connection, in the form of association and suggestion via memory itself, as well as by conventionally assigned symbolic value. Letters, because they stand only for sounds, are less likely to be associated with arbitrary and distracting meaning. Thus they would be better suited for holding memory as dhāraṇī, tending less to confuse memory with their own, irrelevant meaning than would mnemonic words and phrases.

In any case, the notion that linguistic signifiers, and especially letters, are empty of inherent "own-nature" amounts to a valorization of language for Buddhist soteriological purposes. If language is in itself disassociated from the emotional and metaphysical additives that tend to be superimposed on it, then language as pure convention becomes just the right medium for the skillful means of the bodhisattva. It is flexible—and discardable. Ironically, what is seen as the ultimate meaninglessness of verbal expression makes it become, in certain Buddhist traditions, an ideal tool for teaching the ultimate truth, avowals of the inexpressibility of that truth notwithstanding. Thus it is not surprising that Rdo Grub-chen can find passages from both the Prajñāpāramitā[94] and Yogācāra texts[95] to illustrate the role of verbalization in the teaching of ultimate truth.

The other dimension of this valorization of language, one that is brought out by the use of alphabets or other syllabaries for dhāraṇī practice, once again focuses on the letter in particular. This is the notion that an alphabet encapsulates the totality of possibilities for writing, speech, and especially teaching. This was already suggested in the statement "There are no letter conventions other than the foregoing" from the Prajñāpāramitā passage cited earlier.[96] Once it is granted that verbal expression is an appropriate Dharma tool, then it follows that the alphabet, which lists all of the basic elements of verbal expression, is a primary source of the Dharma. Rdo Grub-chen writes, "Even though the teachings are infinite, they are all the same to the extent that they are composed solely of letters."[97] And from the

Sāgaranāgarājaparipṛcchā, "There is no dharma that is not contained within letters, and similarly there is no dharma that is not contained within enlightenment (*bodhi*).[98] The same sūtra can even claim, "Only letters teach bodhi. Only letters tell bodhi. Only letters touch bodhi."[99]

But this last point is a very radical one indeed. For us to see the very neat feat of semiological acrobatics that the letter-as-empty-signifier can perform, we might have recourse once more to Peircean semiotics.[100]

Signs of the Signless: Conflating Symbol with Icon

To return to the same passage from the *Sāgaranāgarājaparipṛcchā:*[101]

> O, Master of Nāgas! For example, in the same way that letters are inexhaustible, the teachings of all dharmas are inexhaustible.

Thus begins a series of analogies between letters and all dharmas.

> Letters arise from nowhere, neither body nor mind. In the same way, dharmas arise from nowhere. . . . Letters have no form and arise without being demonstrable. In the same way, dharmas have no form and are not demonstrable, arising from mental projection. Letters are instantaneous things, insubstantial, hollow, and false things, all of which have no maker. In the same way all dharmas are instantaneous, insubstantial, hollow, and false, all of which have no maker.

That dharmas have no arising, no ceasing, go nowhere, and have no essence is the familiar logic of the Prajñāpāramitā. But the notion that letters have no essence, and so on raises an interesting point for semiotics, one that might have interested Peirce. In the particular case of dhāraṇī semiotics, when the letter as symbol signifies the true nature of all phenomena—which for Buddhism are empty, and lacking in own-nature and inherent meaning—the letter as pure symbol becomes icon. Why? What the dhāraṇī letter is symbolizing is the lack of inherent meaning. But its lack of inherent meaning is just what made the letter a pure symbol in the first place. The nature of letters is such that they can mean anything, and anything and everything, according to the Prajñāpāramitā, is emptiness. In this way the dhāraṇī letter, as it is developed in the Prajñāpāramitā sūtras and commentaries, shares the character of that of which it reminds. Hence it functions as an icon of the Buddhist reality.

And so this is the logic that Rdo Grub-chen has in mind when he invokes the principle of "letter sameness" in his exegesis of the classic

Prajñāpāramitā passage on dhāraṇī syllabary. The use of the letter to symbolize emptiness and so forth is grounded in the letter's own emptiness. Indeed, this emptiness is what the entire dhāraṇī practice has been constructed to help the practitioner realize. Thus the semiotics by which the letter and the defining phrases of the syllabary are employed in that passage, though ostensibly indexical in reminding the practitioner that *A* is for *anutpannatva,* draw upon, as well as remind, the practitioner of an ultimately iconic relationship between the letter and the emptiness that it is being used to signify.

It should be noted that the literal formula in the *Bodhisattvabhūmi* passage on forbearance dhāraṇī is also being used to signify the Buddhist truth iconically. The formula that the *Bodhisattvabhūmi* gives is the nonsense mantra "*iṭi miṭi kiṭibhiḥ kṣāntipadāni svāhā.*"[102] It is precisely the formula's lack of any conventional meaning that is its meaning.[103] This meaning is "thusness" (*tathatā*), the meaning of which lacks linguistic expressibility, according to Rdo Grub-chen, in Yogācāra thought. Again, as the mantric formula itself has no linguistically expressible meaning, it resembles the thusness that it is signifying, and so it can be employed as an iconic sign. But note that unlike the Prajñāpāramitā syllabary, in this case there is no attempt to assign any conventional linguistic meaning to the formula whatsoever. And unlike the dhāraṇī seal, the literal formula of the *Bodhisattvabhūmi,* here called a mantra, is a particular group of letters, not any and every letter.

Rdo Grub-chen argues that the *Bodhisattvabhūmi* portrayal of dhāraṇī practice differs from the Prajñāpāramitā approach in the important respect that it reflects a Yogācāra doctrine that the imagined (*parikalpita*) natures of things, which are represented by words, are unreal.[104] By meditating on the mantra *iṭi miṭi* . . ., the bodhisattva comes to reject the usual denial (*apavāda*) and/or exaggerated superimposition (*āropa*) entailed by conventionally meaningful speech[105]—just the superimposition we earlier saw to be gainfully employed in the Prajñāpāramitā technique of assigning symbolic and linguistic value to the letter *A*. Unlike the Prajñāpāramitā dhāraṇī tradition, the *Bodhisattvabhūmi* passage has little interest in establishing (i.e., superimposing) a conventional meaning. "Having penetrated exactly the meaning of the true [inexpressible] nature of all dharmas, the bodhisattva does not look further for other meanings."[106] Reflecting this lack of interest in the conventional is the *Bodhisattvabhūmi*'s lack of a device like the dhāraṇī seal or syllabary that carries the realizations of dhāraṇī memory into all instances of conventional language. Nonetheless Rdo Grub-chen does claim that the dhāraṇī practice described in the *Bodhisattvabhūmi* will lead the practitioner to the same result as does the Prajñāpāramitā method.[107] I would like to suggest that the reason that he ultimately equates the two practices is their shared fundamental feature, namely, their use of iconic semiosis.

Iconic Memory and Enlightenment

It is not difficult to forget what an index points to: *A* is for . . . what? Similarly, it is easy to forget a symbolic assignation. One can tie a string around one's finger to remind oneself to do something, and then forget what that something is. But in the case of the iconic sign, the aspect of the signified object that makes the sign an icon of it is present in the sign itself. This suggests a feature of the iconic sign as reminder that can be exploited for mnemonic purposes, a feature that is especially advantageous if the particular type of signified content that is to be remembered is a Buddhist principle such as emptiness.

In this final section I would like to explore briefly some of the special semiological features of the icon when it is employed in forebearance dhāraṇī to hold in store and remind the practitioner of emptiness. I would also like to consider the soteriological implications, in the Buddhist context, of this special semiology. First, as just suggested, the icon offers certain advantages as a reminder. It is unlike the index, insofar as the index requires some sort of move from the sign to the signified to which it points. It is also unlike the symbol, whose relationship to its signified is purely arbitrary, and which, like the index, requires a sort of conceptual move from the sign to its symbolized content. In contrast—and let us note this is especially true in forebearance dhāraṇī practice where the signified object is the Buddhist principle of emptiness—the icon can be said already to *be,* in an important sense, its signified. Such an identification could not be made in the case of a symbolic sign of emptiness, since the signification is based only upon convention.[108] Moreover, such an identification would not be made when an icon stands for a specific thing; for example, a diagram that is a representation of a temple floor, or the letters in some mystical forms of Islamic calligraphy that are pictograms of particular objects.[109] In those cases the icon clearly is not the same as the thing that it is signifying. But the sign that achieves iconicity of the Buddhist principle of emptiness achieves that iconicity precisely because that sign is not different from its signified; form is emptiness, and emptiness is form, as a famous saying from the Prajñāpāramitā *Heart Sūtra* goes. I will return to this special relationship that emerges between the forebearance dhāraṇī icon and its signified content in a moment, as it is a relationship that ultimately will call into question the place of semiosis in Buddhist soteriology altogether. Let us first note some of the special advantages that are asserted regarding the content of which the forebearance dhāraṇī sign reminds.

The fact that Rdo Grub-chen considers forebearance dhāraṇī to be the most sophisticated type of dhāraṇī is surely to be expected, given that its content, which is an ultimate Buddhist principle such as emptiness or suchness and so forth, is that upon which turns the entire basis, path and fruit of Buddhist soteriology, much more so than any particular verbal formulation as such. But we should further note here another reason that Rdo Grub-chen finds to privilege a ''profound content'' such as emptiness, which he asserts on several occasions. The memory cultivated in the practice of forebearance dhāraṇī, according to Rdo Grub-chen, will also have as its side effect the development of a good memory for specific objects: it will automatically give the practitioner the ability to memorize particular linguistic expressions, sermons, and so forth, a memorization that will occur without any special effort.[110] Rdo Grub-chen does not make the basis on which he asserts this entirely clear; the principal explanation that he offers seems to be simply that the content of the memory of the Buddhist ultimate truth, by its very nature, is such that it clears the head and increases overall astuteness and memory power. However, his point may also be that the indexes of the syllabary can be used as ordinary mnemonic devices, which presumably would be especially efficacious for one whose head has appropriately been cleared:

> If one studies only letters with concealed (*saṃvṛti*) meaning, one's mental power to remember is small. To attain the sort of memory and insight power that has been discussed, one needs to depend upon letters that teach subtlety, since the mode in which ultimate truth abides is profound. As a result of being attached to establishing individual definitions of the expression and the expressed since beginningless time, one has been mixed up, one's head confused with the memory of the dense thicket of the variety of categories of distinctions of words and phrases, such that when one is in a situation, one is not able to attain [clear memory]. One needs to attain the great appearance of awareness and meditative equipoise concerning the thusness of those words and phrases, in a manner that is like a single honey taste.[111]

And so for Rdo Grub-chen, remembering emptiness even has the effect of increasing memory of specific things, the meager soteriological benefit of such a specific memory notwithstanding. But let us return to the soteriological benefits of remembering emptiness itself, as well as the semiology of that remembering when it is engendered by an iconic sign.

That emptiness is the true nature of all things means that not only all letters, but all things, share that nature and therefore could be employed as icons of that emptiness.[112] For the Buddhist practitioner of forebearance dhāraṇī trained in the rigorous technique of perceiving all letters as icons of emptiness, it would be a relatively easy augmentation of the practice to regard everything else that appears as not only appearing as themselves, but also, simultaneously, as transparent icons of the Buddhist principle of emptiness.

But this merits more consideration. If a practitioner were to perceive a letter, or anything, as an icon of emptiness, what would be happening, because of the very special type of iconic semiosis that obtains when the signified content is something like emptiness, is that actually the icon would cease to be a sign altogether. Or put more accurately (since the letter in such a case is indeed being used *as* a sign), there would be no difference between the sign and its signified content. Now this is not to claim that just because something can be an icon of emptiness—for example, a letter, which we showed to be a particularly apt icon of emptiness—that any perception of it would be tantamount to a perception of emptiness. All perceivers of a letter do not necessarily perceive its "nature" as that has been defined in Buddhist theory. As has been discussed, the type of reminding that occurs in forebearance dhāraṇī practice requires the meditative cultivation of a variety of conventions, from general Buddhist teachings on emptiness to the special dhāraṇī semiotics employing letters and defining phrases. But once the letter is directly perceived as an icon of emptiness (a directness, or immediacy, that is allowed both by Buddhist theory as well as in accounts of Peircean iconicity), the conventions and mediations would become redundant. The manner in which the icon would operate as a signifier would be immediate, or what might be called "sudden": it would engender the memory of emptiness at once. In other words, the very special type of semiosis that would operate in Rdo Grub-chen's dhāraṇī practice is such that when the sign reaches full iconicity, semiosis self-destructs (or, better, attains a "zeroed semiosis.")[113]

One of the implications, in Buddhist soteriological terms, of the immediacy of the dhāraṇī's reminding power and the ultimate identity of the iconic sign and its signified emptiness, is that the realization of emptiness thereby engendered would cease to be tied to the practitioner's earlier realization of emptiness while she was meditatively investigating the nature of the letter. If a practitioner were to be reminded of emptiness by a letter because that letter *is* empty, this memory would transcend the particular techniques established to facilitate it, as well as the particular moment when it was "first" realized. This feature of the iconic dhāraṇī sign reveals its critical function: the iconic dhāraṇī sign would free the practitioner from her own conventions, precisely, as Rdo Grub-chen indicates, so that she could make everything into an iconic reminder of emptiness, and precisely so that the emptiness of which everything reminds her would not be limited temporally, or in any other way, to any particular course of training.

A further implication of the conflation of sign and signified, when the sign is an icon and the signified is emptiness, is that whatever is perceived as an icon of emptiness simultaneously becomes an icon of itself. If emptiness is the true nature of everything, then when everything becomes an icon of emptiness, it follows that everything, self-reflexively, becomes a sign of itself.

In these last points it appears that our semiological analysis may have arrived somewhere near to what Rdo Grub-chen meant by "a single honey taste." But before we finish this increasingly arcane analysis, let us turn for a moment to the third member of the semiological triad, the interpreter, the practitioner of forebearance dhāraṇī. When considered in terms of what the practitioner's experience is supposed to be, the conclusion that "everything is a sign of itself" is not the mere tautology that it would seem.

To remind is to bring to mind, to re-present what is forgotten. For the Buddhists practicing dhāraṇī, the assumption is that deluded sentient beings forget the "profound situation" of emptiness and birthlessness. As we have seen, the process of restoring that memory through the technique of dhāraṇī reminding is described as a gradual one; it involves establishing and becoming accustomed to indexical and symbolic signs that come to be understood as icons of that birthless truth—and that ultimately are no longer signs at all. But as the practitioner becomes less dependent on these constructed indexical and symbolic signs, and more conversant with the art of seeing everything as an icon of the emptiness that everything is, her practice, as mentioned earlier, is more aptly described as "sudden." The icon would cease to be for her anything different from what it signifies, and everything would directly and immediately be realized as empty. And this means that the interpreter herself would have to share in the iconicity of the dhāraṇī signs of emptiness. To remember the pervasive emptiness that makes possible the high-speed conflation of sign and signified requires that the practitioner remember herself as empty as well.

In other words, memory takes on a special character if what is being remembered is the general, pervasive, empty nature of all dharmas. It is a radically different sort of memory from that of a particular, determinant content that requires effort to be remembered precisely because that content is separate and distinct from the rememberer, as well as from whatever signs have been employed to remember it. In contrast, if the content of memory is understood to be the nature of everything, then such content would subsume or engulf all of the rememberer's being and experience, and it would do so at the very moment the remembering occurs. In short, the iconically reminded rememberer of emptiness would simultaneously be remembering the emptiness of herself. And since by remembering the emptiness of herself she would have remembered what in Buddhism is identical with the content of enlightenment, it follows that to remember iconically the content of enlightenment would be, in Buddhist theory, to become enlightened oneself.

The claim that the use of a literal formula would enlighten its user is in some ways continuous with the other, relatively less ambitious claims made for these formulas concerning protection, purification, power, and so on. All such claims presuppose that a radical, totalistic change of world-view would effect a radical change in one's world. This is a notion that underlies much of Mahāyāna doctrine and practice, but now with the special feature that letters can encode and then evoke in the user this transformative power. Of course, the slaying of enemies and the amassing of wealth are of questionable soteriological merit, unless the practitioner's "skillful means" are truly superlative. Such dubious powers are not infrequently ascribed to mantra and its tantric cohorts, and have led both traditional Buddhist and modern Buddhological scholars to label mantric practice as "magical," thereby dismissing with this convenient term the whole ludicrous proposal that spells could be efficacious.[114] But there seem to be at least two issues here, that of charlatanism and that of ethics. Surely with regard to the latter some of the worldly or destructive effects attributed to the tantric mantra more than deserve the perjorative implication that "magic" can connote. But with regard to the former issue, which concerns whether the literal formula could possibly be efficacious, and particularly in the case of those formulas that are invested with the power to enlighten, the issues at stake are somewhat different. Perhaps a closer look at the near-magical semiotics of a letter that is made to signify the signless will allow a more nuanced appreciation of how that magical moment of enlightenment is thought, in some Buddhist circles, to come about.

Notes

I would like to express my appreciation to Rdo Grub-chen 'Jigs-med Bstan-pa'i Nyi-ma for his brilliant and stimulating study of dhāraṇī to which the following essay owes so much. Much gratitude is also due to Tulku Thondup, who first introduced me to Rdo Grub-chen's work, reputedly one of the most difficult texts in the indigenous Tibetan philosophical tradition; to Mkhan-po Dpal-ldan Shes-rab, who generously devoted much time and effort in assisting me to understand it; and to Jay Garfield, Ron Davidson, Matthew Kapstein, and David Ruegg who made helpful comments on earlier drafts of this essay.

PT = Peking Tanjur. References are to D. T. Suzuki, ed., *The Tibetan Tripitaka*, Peking ed. (Tokyo and Kyoto: Suzuki Research Foundation, 1956).

DT = Sde-dge Tanjur. References include Toh. numbers from H. Ui et al., *A Complete Catalogue of the Tibetan Buddhist Canon* (Sendai: Tohoku Imperial University, 1934).

1. N.B. The word *literal* in this essay will be used to mean "having to do with letters," rather than its more widely used sense of "being in conformance with a word's explicit or primary meaning." Note too that *letter* in this essay denotes an al-

phabetic symbol representing a sound, not the written character as such, and that in both Sanskrit and Tibetan convention, all consonants are cited with the vowel *a*.

2. *Asaṅgadhāraṇīpratilabdha*, along with many other attributes of the bodhisattva listed in *Pañcaviṁśatisāhasrikā Prajñāpāramitā*, ed. Nalinaksha Dutt (London: Luzac & Co., 1934), p. 4.

3. I am using *mantra* here to refer to the literal side of dhāraṇī, following the *Bodhisattvabhūmi*'s definition of forebearance dhāraṇī in which mantra is the literal formula upon which the bodhisattva concentrates to obtain forebearance (*tathāgatabhāṣitāni bodhisattvakṣāntilābhya mantrapadāni*) (see below for discussion of the *Bodhisattvabhūmi* passage.)

4. *Byang chub sems dpa'i gzungs kyi rgyan rnam par bshad pa rgyal yum lus bzang mdzes byed legs bshad phreng ba*, in *The Collected Works (Gsuṅ-'bum) of rDo Grub-chen 'Jigs-med-bstan-pa'i-ñi-ma*, reproduced photographically from blockprints and manuscripts from the library of the Ven. Dujom Rimpoche by Dodrup Chen Rimpoche (Gangtok, 1974), vol. 1, pp. 1–188. Hereafter abbreviated *Gzungs*.

5. For a useful selection of his semiological writings, see Charles S. Peirce, "Logic as Semiotic: The Theory of Signs," in *Semiotics: An Introductory Anthology*, Robert E. Innis (Bloomington: University of Indiana Press, 1985), pp. 4–23. Peirce's semiology is being utilized increasingly in a variety of fields. An example of his influence on anthropological study is E. Valentine Daniel, *Fluid Signs: Being a Person the Tamil Way* (Berkeley: University of California Press, 1984).

6. For a study of *mātikā*, see Gethin's chapter in this volume. In his discussion of the mnemonic signs of the dhāraṇī formula, Rdo Grub-chen uses the term *mātṛkā* (Tib. *ma-mo*) widely to refer to the smallest literal unit. The Tibetan term *yig-'bru* seems to be a synonym. The originary, maternal connotation is retained in both the Pāli/Sanskrit and Tibetan terms, and both refer also to a class of extremely vicious female deities (natch); but I have resisted the temptation to coin the term "mamory" in this article. For further gender-related speculation, we can note that dhāraṇī itself is feminine in gender, and also that the Tibetan *gzungs-ma* denotes a female yogic consort.

7. On *paritta*, see Ernst Waldschmidt, "Das Paritta: Eine magische Zeremonie der buddhistischen Priester auf Ceylon," *Baessler-Archiv* 17 (1934): 139–50 (reprinted in *Von Ceylon bis Turfan: Schriften zur Geschichte, Literatur, Religion und Kunst des indischen Kulturraumes von Ernst Waldschmidt* [Göttingen, 1967].) For an account of the ritual involved in the reading of a *pirit* in 1828, see R. Spence Hardy, *Eastern Monachism* (London: Williams and Norgate, 1860), pp. 240–42; L. A. Waddell, "The Dhāraṇī Cult in Buddhism, Its Origin, Deified Literature and Images," *Ostasiatische Zeitschrift* 1 (1912–1913): 159 and 163 et seq. See also Étienne Lamotte, *Le Traité de la Grande Vertu de Sagesse de Nāgārjuna* (*Mahāprajñāpāramitāśāstra*) (hereafter *Traité*) (Louvain-la-neuve: Université de Louvain, Institut Orientaliste, 1949–1981), vol. 4, pp. 1860–61. The festival for the recitation of the *Ratanasutta paritta* was instituted in Polonnaruva during the reign of Sena II.

8. John Brough, "The Arapacana Syllabary in the Old Lalita-Vistara," *Bulletin of the School of Oriental and African Studies* 40, no. 1 (1977): 85–95, cannot identify the origins of the *Arapacana*, but speculates that its syllables are abbreviations of words that began the verses or paragraphs of an important text, which were then further reduced to letters. For further speculation on the origin of the *Arapacana*, see Sylvain Lévi, "Ysa,"in *Feestbundel uitgegeven door het Koninklijk Bataviaasch Genootschap van Kunsten en Wetenschappen bij gelegenheid van zign 150 jarig bestaan 1778–1928* (Weltevreden, 1929), vol. 2, pp. 100–8; Sten Konow, "The Arapacana alphabet and the Sakas," *Acta Orientalia* 12 (1934): 13–24; F. W. Thomas, "A Kharoṣṭhī Document and the Arapacana Alphabet," in *Miscellanea Academica Berolinensia: Gesammelte Abhandlungen zur Feier des 250-jährigen Bestehens der deutschen Akademie der Wissenschaften zu Berlin*, II/2 (Berlin: Akademie-Verlag, 1950), pp. 194–207; and most recently, Richard Salomon, "New Evidence for a Gāndhārī Origin of the Arapacana Syllabary," *Journal of the American Oriental Society* 110, no. 2 (April–June 1990): 255–73. Lamotte connects the development of the condensed teaching to the development of new forms of propagation during the Śaka-Pahlava period. Étienne Lamotte, *Histoire du Bouddhisme Indien, des origines à l'ère Śaka* (Louvain: Bibilothèque du Muséon, 1958), pp. 546 et seq. But see Edward Conze, *The Prajñāpāramitā Literature*, (The Hague: Mouton & Co., 1960), p. 11, for aspects of the syllabary that point to a Southern Indian origin. Lamotte, *Traité*, p. 1868n, notes that the *Arapacana* alphabet is also found in the Dharmaguptaka Vinaya. Note that in the *Gaṇḍavyūha*, Sudhana is taught an *Arapacana* syllabary that is not indexically semiotic; that is, the explanatory phrases do not begin with the syllabary letter: Daisetz Teitaro Suzuki and Hokei Idzumi, eds., *The Gaṇḍavyūha Sūtra* (Tokyo: Society for the Publication of Sacred Books of the World, 1949), pp. 448–50. The *Mahāvairocanatantra*, DT, rGyud-'bum, vol. Tha, f. 170b. et seq. (Toh. 494) contains a syllabary based on the Sanskrit alphabet rather than the Arapacana.

9. See Paul Demiéville, "L'origine des sectes bouddhiques d'après Paramārtha," *Mélanges chinois et bouddhiques* 1 (1931–1932): 61. Lamotte, *Traité*, p. 1862, notes that Hsüan-tsang saw an Aśokan stūpa that marked the spot where the Mahāsāṅghikas compiled a *mantrapiṭaka*, not a *dhāraṇīpiṭaka* as the Chinese *kin-tcheou-tsang* is usually translated. (Cf. Samuel Beal, trans., *Buddhist Records of the Western World* [London: Kegan Paul, Trench, Trübner & Co. Ltd., 1906], vol. 2, p. 164.)

10. Some listed by *Lamotte*, Traité, p. 1860n.

11. *Mantra* and *dhāraṇī* are sometimes used interchangeably in general discussion, in both sūtraic and tantric contexts. Examples: Kūkai, *Hannya shingyō hiken*, trans. Yoshito S. Hakeda, *Kūkai: Major Works* (New York: Columbia University Press, 1972), pp. 273 et. seq.; Praśāstrasena, Āryaprajñāpāramitāhṛdayaṭīkā (PT 5220,) vol. 94, p. 296.2–3, referring to the *Heart Sūtra* mantra as a dhāraṇī, as cited by Donald S. Lopez, Jr., "On the *Heart Sūtra* Mantra," typescript, p. 4, a different version of which was published in *History of Religions* 29, no. 4 (May 1990): 351–72. When precise distinctions are made, either seems to be a candidate for being a subcategory of the other. *Mantra* is not necessarily the more general term, as David

Snellgrove claims, *Indo-Tibetan Buddhism* (Boston: Shambhala Publications, 1987), vol. 1, p. 122. *Mantradhāraṇī* is a subtype of dhāraṇī in the *Bodhisattvabhūmi*, along with *dharmadhāraṇī, arthadhāraṇī,* and *kṣāntidhāraṇī* (discussed below). Mantra is also a subtype of dhāraṇī, here along with word (*pada*), meaning (*artha*), and seal (*mudrā*), *in the Āryanāmasaṅgītiṭīkāmantrārthāvalokinī* (PT 3356, vol. 74, 194.2.8) a commentary to the *Mañjuśrīnāmasaṅgīti* by Vilāsavajra, as mentioned by Ronald M. Davidson, "The *Litany of Names of Mañjuśrī:* Text and Translation of the *Mañjuśrīnāmasaṃgīti,*" in *Tantric and Taoist Studies in Honour of R. A. Stein,* ed. Michel Strickmann, *Mélanges chinois et bouddhiques* 20 (1981): 23n. (Note Rdo Grub-chen's use of the term *dhāraṇīmudrā* in reference to *kṣāntidhāraṇī,* as discussed below.) As mentioned by Alex Wayman in "The Significance of Mantras, From the Veda down to Buddhist Tantric Practice," *Indologica Taurinensia* 3–4 [1975–1976]: 490), Jñānavajra's *Vajravidāraṇanāmadhāraṇīpaṭalakramabhāṣyavṛtti-pradīpa* (PT 3511, vol. 78, p. 169–4.3) lists *vidyāmantra* and *guhyamantra* as the two types of dhāraṇī. On the other hand, a widely used distinction in Tibetan Buddhism makes dhāraṇī one of the three types of mantra, along with *guhyamantra* and *vidyāmantra*. See, for example, Alex Wayman, *The Buddhist Tantras: Light on Indo-Tibetan Esotericism* (New York, 1973), pp. 64–65, citing the *Mi ṭa dang rdo rje 'phreng ba'i dbang chen skabs kyi sngon 'gro'i chos bshad,* which in turn cites the *Vajraśekharatantra*. Often four types of mantra, *bīja, mūla, hṛdaya,* and *upahṛdaya,* are listed, as in Kazi Dawa-Samdup, trans., *Shrīcakrasambhāra Tantra* (London and Calcutta: Luzac & Co. and Thacker, Spink & Co., 1919), pp. 59–60. On the distinction between dhāraṇī and mantra, see also Hiromi Yoshimura, "How to Interpret Dhāraṇī in Early Mahāyāna Buddhism and How Buddhists Interpreted Mantra," *Ryūkoku Kiyō,* 9, no. 1 (1987): 1–16. The history of the relationship between mantra and dhāraṇī requires systematic research; the above-cited classifications are but random examples of the many schemes to be found.

12. As, for example, in Kazi Dawa-Samdup, *Shrīcakrasambhāra Tantra,* pp. 4 et seq.

13. An often-cited *paritta* that is a protector (*rakkhā*) from snakes is found in *Cullavagga* V.6, *The Vinaya Piṭakaṃ,* ed. Hermann Oldenberg, vol. 2: *The Cullavagga* (London: Luzac & Company, Ltd., 1964), p. 110 (the rhythmic symmetry of the incantation is not fully preserved in the translation by Henry Clark Warren, *Buddhism in Translations* [reprint New York: Atheneum, 1987], pp. 302–3.) A protector (*rakkhā*) against *yakkhas,* in the form of extended verses that offer praise to various heroes in the four quarters, is presented in *Āṭānāṭṭiyasuttanta,* ed. T. W. Rhys Davids and J. E. Carpenter, in *Dīgha-Nikāya,* 3 vols. (London: Henry Frowde, for the Pali Text Society, 1890–1911), vol. 3, pp. 195 et seq. Dhāraṇīs are often given by the Buddha as protectors from danger to those who themselves "retain" the content of a sūtra: see, e.g., *Saddharmapuṇḍarīkasūtra,* ed. H. Kern and Bunyiu Nanjio, Bibliotheca Buddhica 10 (St. Petersburg: Académie Impériale Des Sciences, 1912) Chapter 21 (this and the following chapters are a later addition to that sūtra). For the more general notion that the presence of a Buddhist scripture makes a place a protective sanctuary, and the larger context of such an idea, see Gregory Schopen, "The Phrase *'sa pṛthivipradeśaś caityabhūto bhavet'* in the *Vajracchedikā:* Notes on the Cult of the

Book in Mahāyāna," *Indo-Iranian Journal* 17 (1975): 154ff. For a variety of scriptural references to dhāraṇīs placed inside of caityas/stūpas see Mkhas-grub-rje's *Rgyud sde sphyi'i rnam gzhag* (Wayman and Lessing, *Introduction*, pp. 107 passim).

14. *Dhammarakkha*. The *dhammadhara* and the *vinayadhara* are also so designated: *The Milindapañho*, ed. V. Trenckner (London: The Royal Asiatic Society, 1928), p. 344 (trans. I. B. Horner, *Milinda's Questions*, 2 vols., [London: Luzac & Company, Ltd., 1969], vol. 2, pp. 193–94.)

15. Cf. *Guhyasamājatantra* XVIII.69b–70a: ed. S. Bagchi, (Darbhanga: Mithila Institute, 1965), p. 126. The Fourteenth Dalai Lama Tenzin Gyatso understands this to mean that mantra protects the practitioner from "ordinary appearances"; i.e., appearances that are not that of the buddha/deity: Tsong-ka-pa, *Tantra in Tibet: The Great Exposition of Secret Mantra* (London: George Allen & Unwin, 1977), pp. 47–48. The *Guhyagarbhatattvaviniścaya* is said to portray mantra as protecting against subject-object dichotomy, by virtue of evoking ecstatic bliss: Herbert Guenther, *Matrix of Mystery: Scientific and Humanistic Aspects of rDzogs-chen Thought* (Boulder, Colo., and London: Shambhala, 1984), p. 213, n. 10, citing Yon-tan rgya-mtsho's commentary to the *Yon tan mdzod*. Note that the *Bodhisattvabhūmi* passage on dhāraṇī defines mantra dhāraṇī as the bodhisattva's empowerment (*adhiṣṭhāna*) of mantric formulas through meditative consecration, so that these mantras can be used to abate plagues. See note 31. Mantras and *bījas* are also used extensively to construct visualized protective fences around the meditator; see, e.g., Kazi Dawa-Samdup, *Shrīcakrasambhāra Tantra*, p. 13.

16. See Mkhas-grub-rje, *Rgyud sde spyi'i rnam gzhag*, trans. Wayman and Lessing, *Introduction*, p. 28 et seq.

17. Ibid. *raṅ gi sems kyi chos ñid stoṅ pa ñid bcu drug raṅ bźin rnam dag mtshon paḥi āli bcu drug*, etc.

18. See Kūkai, *Ungi gi (The Meanings of the Word Hūṃ)*, in Hakeda, *Kūkai*, pp. 246 et seq.

19. Conze, *The Prajñāpāramitā Literature*, p. 21; Benoytosh Bhattacharyya, *An Introduction to Buddhist Esoterism* (Banares: Chowkhamba Sanskrit Series Office, 1964), p. 56, notes that *praṃ* reduces the goddess Prajñāpāramitā, who in turn stands for the Prajñāpāramitā literature in its entirety.

20. See, for example, R. O. Meisezahl, "The *Amoghapāśahṛdaya-dhāraṇī*," *Monumenta Nipponica* 17 (1962): 265–328.

21. Cf. Agehananda Bharati's distinction between description and the effects of mantra: *The Tantric Tradition* (London: Rider and Co., 1965), pp. 102 et seq. The issue of whether mantra is a speech act or not is discussed at length with reference to the Brahmanic tradition in Harvey P. Alper, ed., *Mantra* (Albany: State University of New York Press, 1989).

22. "*Sngags pas byang chub sems dran zhing...*" DT, Rgyud-'bum vol. Tha, f. 176a (Toh. 494). The *Mahāvairocana*'s entire statement on the nature of mantra deserves further study.

23. For example, *dang po dran rdzogs lha bskyed ni/ hūṃ/ bdag nyid dpal chen he ru ka* ("First, the arousal of the deity that is complete as soon as remembered is: Hūṃ. I am the great glorious heruka," and so forth) in *Stobs ldan phur pa nag po'i hūm sgrub*, from the *Bla med yang phur gva'u dmar nag* cycle by Rtsa-gsum Gling-pa, ms. in my possession. On sādhana traditions that inaugurate the visualization of the deity with a *bīja* syllable, see Davidson, "The *Litany of the Names of Mañjuśrī*," p. 2. The phrase *dran-rdzogs* seems to be used when the memory of self as the deity is produced by virtue of an instantaneous visualization, as opposed to a gradual building up of its parts. Kaḥ-thog Dge-rtse Paṇḍita Tshe-dbang Mchog-grub, in *Bskyed pa'i rim pa cho ga dang sbyar ba'i gsal byed zung 'jug snye ma*, offset ms., n.p., n.d., f.18b, makes this explicit: *skad cig dran rdzogs su gsal gdab pa sogs spros med kyi bskyed rim*. Herbert Guenther, in his translation of this text, renders *dran-rdzogs-su gsal-gdab* as "lucid understanding": *The Creative Vision* (Novato, Calif.: Lotsawa, 1987), p. 86. Where Tshe-dbang Mchog-grub continues to characterize the practitioner's understanding of the elements of the visualization as a *dag-pa'i dran-pa* ("remembering of purity"), Guenther avoids all mnemic connotations of the term *dran-pa*, translating the phrase as "understanding" or "keeping before the mind," pp. 101 et seq. He thereby loses what I think is a critical mnemic dimension in the visualizer's recognition and appreciation of symbols. See Tshe-dbang Mchog-grub's discussion of *dag-dran* on f. 27b.

24. *Asampramoṣatva. Daśabhūmikasūtra*, ed. Johannes Rahder, (Louvain: J.-B. Istas, 1926), p. 71 (re: the eighth *bhūmi*).

25. Ed. P. L. Vaidya, Buddhist Sanskrit Texts No. 1 (Dharbhanga: The Mithila Institute of Post-Graduate Studies and Research in Sanskrit Learning, 1985) p. 25.16: *Dhāraṇīpratilambho dharmālokamukham sarvabuddhabhāṣitādhāraṇatāyai saṃvartate.*"

26. PT 842, p. 71.4.4–5: *Gzungs shes bya ba ni . . . chos kyi phung po brgyad khri bzhi stong 'dzin pa dang / kun 'dzin pa dang / mi brjed pa dang / dran pas yang dag par 'dzin pa ste.* Cited by Jens Braarvig, "*Dhāraṇī* and *Pratibhāna*": Memory and Eloquence of the Bodhisattvas," *Journal of the International Association of Buddhist Studies* 8, no. 1 (1985): p. 18.

27. Edward Conze, in *The Large Sutra on Perfect Wisdom* (Berkeley, Los Angeles, and London: University of California Press, 1975), p. 403.

28. *Tatra dharmadhāraṇī katamā / iha bodhisattvas tadrūpāṃ smṛtiprajñābalādhānatāṃ pratilabhate yayā śrutamātreṇaivānāmnātān vacasā, aparicitān nāmapadavyañjanakāyasaṃgṛhītān, anupūrvacaritān, anupūrvasamāyuktān, apramāṇān granthān apramāṇam kālaṃ dhārāyati.* Cf. *Bodhisattvabhūmi*, ed. Unrai Wogihara (Tokyo, 1930–1936), pp. 272–74; see also *Bodhisattvabhūmiḥ* by Nalinaksha Dutt (Patna: K. P. Jayaswal Research Institute, 1966), pp. 185–86. Translated by Lamotte, *Traité*, pp. 1858–59, who consulted also the Chinese translations. In this and the following notes, I have cited the Sanskrit from Lamotte.

29. *tatrārthadhāraṇīkatamā / pūrvavat tatrāyaṃ viśeṣaḥ / teṣām eva dharmāṇām apramāṇam artham anāmnātam, aparicitaṃ manasā, apramāṇaṃ kālaṃ dhārayati.*

30. And we would note that this means that the *Bodhisattvabhūmi*'s dhāraṇī of Dharma is not strictly speaking a concise formula at all; its content is the specific literal signs themselves. The passages cited in the previous paragraph are ambiguous and do not indicate in what form the memory is held.

31. *tatra mantradhāraṇī katamā / iha bodhisattvas tadrūpāṃ samādhivaśitāṃ pratilabhate yayā yāni mantrapadānītisaṃśamanāya sattvānām adhitiṣṭhati tāni siddhāni bhavanti paramasiddhāny amoghāny anekavidhānām ītīnāṃ saṃśamanāya / iyam ucyate bodhisattvasya mantradhāraṇī.*

32. *Sa eṣāṃ mantrapadānām evaṃ samyakpratipanna, evam arthaṃ svayam evāśrutvā kutaścit, pratipadyati tadyathā nāsty eṣāṃ mantrapadānāṃ kācid arthaparinișpattiḥ / nirarthā evaite / ayam eva caiṣām artho yad uta nirarthatā / tasmāc ca paraṃ punar anyam arthaṃ na samanveṣate / iyatā tena teṣāṃ mantrapadānām arthaḥ supratividdho bhavati.*

33. . . . *udāraṃ ca tasyārthasya prativedhāt prītiprāmodyaṃ pratilabhate. . . . tasyāś ca lābhāt sa bodhisattvo nacirasyedānīm adhyāśayśuddhiṃ pratilabhate / adhimātrāyām adhimukticaryābhūmikṣāntau vartate.* For the role of *adhimukti* preceding *bodhicittotpāda,* see Har Dayal, *The Bodhisattva Doctrine in Sanskrit Literature,* (reprint Delhi: Motilal Banarsidass, 1970, 1975), pp. 50 et seq. (See Gustav Roth's correction of Dayal's claim that *adhimukti* occurs only in the later sections of the *Bodhisattvabhūmi:* "Observations on the First Chapter of Asaṅga's *Bodhisattvabhūmi,*" *Indologica Taurinensia,* 3–4 [1975–1976]: 410–11). Conze, *The Prajñāpāramitā Literature,* p. 107 attributes to Haribhadra the view that *adhimukticaryābhūmi* is associated with the *prayogamārga;* such a view is also represented by Rdo Grub-chen (see note 48). But Lamotte places his discussion of the entire *Bodhisattvabhūmi* passage, as well as his discussion of the Prajñāpāramitā notions of *akṣarasamatā,* inexpressibility of ultimate nature etc., in the category of "weak" dhāraṇī, for reasons that are not entirely clear: why does he import into these contexts the classification of weak dhāraṇī that he has taken from the *Mahāyānasūtrālaṅkāra,* where it refers to bodhisattvas who have not yet entered the impure stages (*aśuddhabhūmi*) of the path? Lamotte considers the practices of dhāraṇī that occur in the *Daśabhūmika*'s first to seventh *bhūmis* to be illustrations of the *Mahāyānasūtrālaṅkāra*'s "medium" dhāraṇī, and those practiced on the eighth and ninth *bhūmis* to be illustrations of the "superior" type.

34. Conze, *The Large Sutra,* p. 403.

35. See, e.g., *Abhidharmasamuccaya,* ed. Pralhad Pradhan (Santiniketan: Visva-Bharati, 1950), p. 97: *jñānapariśuddhiḥ katamā / dhyānaṃ niśritya yathākāmaṃ dhāraṇīmukhasandhāraṇasamṛddhau yaḥ samādhiḥ prajñā śeṣaṃ pūrvavat; Daśabhūmikasūtra,* p. 73 (re: the ninth *bhūmi*); *Saṃdhinirmocana Sūtra,* ed. Étienne Lamotte (Louvain and Paris, Université de Louvain and Adrien Maisonneuve, 1935), IX.3.3; 4.3. The *Mahāprajñāpāramitāśāstra* (Lamotte, *Traité,* p. 1875) compares *samādhimukha* and *dhāraṇīmukha* at some length. Their difference consists in samādhi's required association with mental states (*cittasamprayukta*), whereas dhāraṇī can be either associated or not associated with mental states (*cittaviprayukta*).

This means that samādhi disappears when distraction arises and at death, but that dhāraṇī, once attained, persists through all successive states, following its holder like a shadow follows the body, or like a vow that causes its holder to maintain certain disciplines. Samādhi without wisdom is here compared to an unfired pot, whereas more sophisticated samādhi engenders the attainment of dhāraṇī, which enables the practitioner to hold his realization like a well-fired pot holds water. Note also that the first of the *Mahāprajñāpāramitāśāstra*'s three types of dhāraṇī, namely, the retaining of what one has heard (*śrutadhāraṇī*), is said to employ samādhi and "the liberation exempt from forgetting" (*asampramoṣavimokṣa* to aid in the memorization of particular words and teachings: see Lamotte, *Traité*, p. 1865.

36. Ed. Sylvain Lévi (Paris: Librairie Honoré Champion, 1907 and 1911), 2 vols., XVIII.71: *vipākena śrutābhyāsāt dhāraṇyapi samādhinā / parīttā mahatī sā ca mahatī trividhā punaḥ*. The superior type of dhāraṇī is again classified into three varieties: weak, medium, and strong. XVIII.72: *apraviṣṭapraviṣṭānāṃ dhīmatāṃ mṛdumadhyamā / aśuddhabhūmikānāṃ hi mahatī śuddhabhūmikā* (see note 33).

37. See Braarvig, "*Dhāraṇī* and *Pratibhāna*."

38. See especially Nyanaponika's chapter in this volume, regarding the "making of marks." The role of signs is equally in evidence in accounts of the later remembering of the experience, as for example in the *Pramāṇavārttika*, *pratyakṣa* chapter, vss. 174 and 185–86; see Wayman's chapter in this volume. See also note 43.

39. Especially as dhāraṇī practice is interpreted by Rdo Grub-chen, e.g., *Gzungs*, p. 64: (in the context of a discussion of *kṣāntidhāraṇī* memory): *Dran pa'i 'jug tshul ni sngar gyi myong ba'i rjes su byed pas phyis dran pa skye lugs khyad par can de lta bu 'ong ba yang dang po'i 'tshul la thug go.*

40. Rdo Grub-chen identifies the absence of discussion of the role of signs in the *Bodhisattvabhūmi* description of forebearance dhāraṇī practice as the main factor that distinguishes that tradition from the dhāraṇī practice recommended by the Prajñāpāramitā commentarial tradition: See note 107.

41. Ārya Vimuktisena's full statement on dhāraṇī in the context of the Prajñāpāramitā syllabary practice: *Dhāraṇīsambhāro yad āha: punar bodhisattvasya mahāyānaṃ yad uta dhāraṇīmukhāni ta‹t punar› akāro mukhaṃ sarvadharmāṇām anutpannatvāt / repho mukhaṃ rajo 'pagatvāt / pakāro mukhaṃ paramārthanirdeśād iti vistaraḥ / tena tenākṣaracihnīkāreṇānalpakālpadharmadeśanāhetoḥ smṛter aparyupayogāt / smṛtir hi vyañjanārthadhāraṇārthena dhāraṇīti kṛtvā.* Corrado Pensa, ed., *L'abhisamayālaṃkāravṛtti Di Ārya-Vimuktisena: Primo Abhisamaya* (Rome: Istituto Italiano Per Il Medio Ed Estremo Oriente, 1960), pp. 101–2. Cf. Haribhadra, *Abhisamayālaṃkār'ālokā Prajñāpāramitāvyākhyā*, ed. Unrai Wogihara (Tokyo, Toyo Bunko, 1932–1935), Part I, p. 98.1–4: *mārgânvitasy' a-kāro mukhaṃ sarva-dharmāṇām ādy-anutpannatvād ity ādinā tena-tenâkṣara-citrīkāreṇânalpa-kalpa-dharma-deśanā-hetoḥ smṛter aparyupayogāt. Smṛtir hi granthârtha-dhāraṇena dhārayatîti kṛtvā dhāraṇī-sambhāra iti. Gzungs*, p. 63, glosses Tib. *ri-mor byed-pa* with *mtshan-mar byed-pa*. Rdo Grub-chen attributes the same notion concerning the

use of signs in dhāraṇī practice to Abhayākaragupta's *Munimatālaṅkāra* and the *Śuddhamatī* by Ratnākaraśānti.

42. Rdo Grub-chen identifies forebearance dhāraṇī in particular as "the dhāraṇī that makes letters into signs" (*Gzungs*, p. 63: *Yig 'bru la mtshan mar byed pa'i gzungs de bzod pa'i gzungs su bshad do.*)

43. Peirce delineates two other triads as well, one that lists three characters of the sign itself (qualisign, a mere quality; sinsign, an actual existent; and legisign, a general law), and another that names the ways that the interpretant represents the sign (as a rheme, a possibility; a dicisign, a proposition of fact; and argument, a reason). The varying combinations result in at least ten classes of signs and numerous subdivisions. Still, the trichotomy of icon, index, and symbol remains at the basis of semiosis. See Peirce, "Logic as Semiotic." It is of considerable interest to note that two alternative conditions for recollective memory identified by Vasubandhu in the *Abhidharmakośabhāṣya* are that either the present mental event (*citta*) should bear resemblance (*sādṛṣya*) to the past object, or it should have a relation (*sambhanda*) to the past object. Resemblance is clearly analogous to iconicity, and relationship, exemplified by Vasubandhu as the remembrance of fire aroused at the sight of smoke, is largely indexical, although if convention were allowed as a type of relationship it could be symbolic as well. See Jaini's chapter in this book, pp. 49–50.

44. N.B. The notion of iconic reminding, or "iconic memory" developed in this chapter is to be distinguished from the phenomenon noted by George Sperling and others, also labeled "iconic memory." The latter refers to the registration of incoming sensory stimuli in memory before their categorization in linguistic terms; see Robert G. Crowder, *Principles of Learning and Memory* (Hillsdale, N.J.: Lawrence Erlbaum Associates, 1976), Chapter 2. In contrast, the phrase in this chapter refers to the iconic relationship between remembered concepts and principles, and specially developed reminders in the form of letters and other external objects.

45. See André Padoux, *Recherches sur la symbolique et l'énergie de la parole dans certains textes tantriques* (Paris: Éditions de Boccard, 1975), pp. 323 et seq. See also Chapter 1 and throughout for a survey of the metaphysics of the primordial word in the Vedas and the identity of mantra with the energy of the deity and/or essence of the universe.

46. For the Sarvāstivādins, a word is a force not associated with mental states (*cittaviprayukta*), a view critiqued by the Sautrāntikas who claimed that words are material (*rūpa*), with meaning established by convention. For an excellent summary of this debate as presented in the *Abhidharmakośa*, as well as of precedents in Theravādin works, the views expressed in the *Abhidharmadīpa*, and relations to Mīmāṃsaka and Sphoṭavādin theories, see P. S. Jaini, "The Vaibhāṣika Theory of Words and Meanings," *Bulletin of the School of Oriental and African Studies* 22, no. 1 (1959): 95–107. For a summary of the views of Dignāga and Śāntarakṣita on *śabda* as that which is arbitrary and a conceptual construction that does not denote a real thing, see Masaaki Hattori, *Dignāga, On Perception, being the Pratyakṣapariccheda of Dignāga's* Pramāṇasamuccaya *from the Sanskrit fragments and the Tibetan ver-*

sions (Cambridge, Mass.: Harvard University Press, 1968), n. 1.27. But some Buddhist tantric traditions retain traces of doctrines that posit some sort of eternal status of either verbal expression itself, or its meaning, or both. The *Mañjuśrīnāmasaṅgīti*, vs. 12, suggests that its own verbal formulation is eternal when it claims that it will be repeated in past, present, and future (Davidson, "The *Litany of Names of Mañjuśrī*," p. 50). The *Mahāvairocanatantra* posits a supra-buddhaic, eternal, and primordial ground for mantra, here analogized to *dharmatā: 'Di ltar de bzhin gshegs pa rnams byung yang rung / ma byung yang rung / chos rnams kyi chos nyid de ni ye nas gnas pa ste / de yang 'di ltar gsang sngags rnams kyi gsang sngags kyi chos nyid do.* (Toh. 494, f.170b). Directly related to the *Mahāvairocanatantra* tradition are the works on the nature of word and mantra by Kūkai. Kūkai allows an invariable connection between word and sound and real object (see Hakeda, *Kūkai*, pp. 236–37) and traces words to the vibrations of the elements: "the five great elements . . . are the original substance, and the sounds or vibrations are their functions" (p. 240). And, "The word is, indeed, created by the suprarational power and the natural grace of the Tathāgata" (p. 262). Kūkai also portrays the word as structurally similar to the general structure of reality: "In the sermons delivered by the Buddha, a single word contains the teachings of the five vehicles . . . these words are comparable to the diagrams on the back of a tortoise, or the divination stalks which bear the signs of all phenomena, the endlessly interrelated meshes of Indra's net" (p. 265). Note also that mantras are the "true words" (p. 241). An operative notion here is that a permanent, indestructible substratum underlies phenomenal reality: "Even if Mount Sumeru blocks the sight of the Milky Way . . . that space thereby is not decreased is an attribute of great space. . . . Such is the ultimate meaning of the letter Ū." And, "The raging flames of negation of the Mādhyamika . . . may reduce to ashes, with nothing remaining, the dust of attachment . . . but the Three Mysteries [body, speech, and mind of the dharmakāya] are not thereby decreased. They are like a fabric made from the fur of a certain rat that lives in fire—they become pure as they burn" (pp. 250–51). Kūkai's *Shōji jissō gi ("The Meanings of Sound, Word, and Reality")*, and the *Ungi gi ("The Meanings of the Word Hūṃ")*, from which these statements are taken, deserve further study.

47. See note 4.

48. We can say, however, that Rdo Grub-chen's use of the rubric *kṣānti* to refer to the Prajñāpāramitā dhāraṇī syllabary practice would also invoke a notion such as *anutpattikadharmakṣānti*, for reasons that will be evident below, or *sarvadharmasamatākṣānti* as in *Çatasāhasrikā-Prajñā-Pāramitā*, ed. Pratāpacandra Ghoṣa, Bibliotheca Indica, New Series Nos. 1006–1378 (Calcutta: Asiatic Society, 1902–1913), p. 4, which, as we will see, links up with the notion of *akṣarasamatā*. It should also be noted that Rdo Grub-chen associates the *kṣānti* involved in *kṣāntidhāraṇī* with the *kṣānti* of the *prayogamārga*, citing as evidence the *Bodhisattvabhūmi* identification of *adhimukticāryabhūmi* with *kṣāntidhāraṇī: Gzungs*, p. 157 (see note 33).

49. "[An index is] a sign . . . which refers to its object not so much because of any similarity or analogy with it, . . . as because it is in dynamical (including spatial)

connection both with the individual object, on the one hand, and with senses of memory of the person for whom it serves as a sign, on the other hand.'' See Peirce, ''Logic as Semiotic,'' pp. 12 et seq., for a variety of examples of indexes.

50. P. 65: ''*Ming dang tshig gi bye brag ji lta bu zhig la dran pa 'jug kyang / dang po gang nas 'jug pa'i grong khyer gyi srang sgo lta bu ni rang gi thog ma na yod pa'i yi ge nyid yin pas.*''

51. I use this appellation following Conze; similar versions of the passage are found in the *Pañcaviṃśatisāhasrikā* and the *Śatasāhasrikā* Prajñāpāramitās. Cited by Rdo Grub-chen, *Gzungs*, pp. 67 et seq., which closely follows the Peking Tibetan *Śatasāhasrikā* (PT 730) vol. 13, pp. 94.2.1 et seq. Cf. *Çatasāhasrikā-Prajñā-Pāramitā*, ed. Ghoṣa, Chapter 9, pp. 1450–53; and *Pañcaviṃśatisāhasrikā*, ed. Dutt, pp. 212–14. The passage is translated by Conze, in *The Large Sutra*, pp. 160–63; and Lamotte, *Traité*, pp. 1867–68, both of whom construct a reading based on several recensions. The translation given here is mine. In the first paragraph I largely follow the *Śata*, using Ghoṣa's Sanskrit and the Peking Tibetan. I insert an ellipsis at the same point as does Rdo Grub-chen. In the second paragraph I have favored Dutt's *Pañca*.

52. *Akṣara* (Tib. *yi-ge*) can be translated as ''letter'' or ''syllable.'' In his following discussion, Rdo Grub-chen distinguishes *yi-ge ma-mo* and *yi-ge 'bru*, both of which refer specifically to single letters.

53. The Peking Tibetan *Śata* and Rdo Grub-chen lack the equivalent of *ādi* (''from the beginning''), which is found in both Dutt's *Pañca* and Ghoṣa's *Śata*.

54. See Conze, *The Large Sutra*, p. 162, n. 15. He was unable to determine the word that begins with *Ḍha* that has this meaning.

55. I insert a paragraph break here, differing from Conze, Lamotte, and Dutt who insert the paragraph break before ''There are no letter conventions other than the foregoing.'' They do so because they interpret the question ''Why is that?'' to refer to that sentence; that is, the fact that the syllabary just listed represents all of the letters in conventional use. (Ghoṣa makes no paragraphs at all in this passage). But Rdo Grub-chen gives more weight to the question, interpreting it to refer to the more general proposition that letters are doors to all dharmas. See the discussion below.

56. This is a problematic sentence; every one of the versions I have at hand is different. I have largely followed Dutt's *Pañca* in my translation of this passage: *Tathāhi na kasyacinnāmāsti yena saṃvyavahriyeta yena vābhilapyeta yena nirdiśyeta yena lakṣyeta yena paśyet.* Cf. Peking Tibetan *Śata: De ni 'di ltar gang la yang gang gis tha snyad du bya ba dang / gang gis brjod pa dang / gang gis bstan pa dang / gang gis bri ba dang / gang snang ba dang / gang klag par bya ba de lta bu'i ming gang yang med do.* Ghoṣa's *Śata* introduces, among other things, the phrase *kiñcid anyan: Tathāhi na kasyacit kiñcidanyannāmavyavahriyate yena 'bhilapyeta / yena nindayyate yallikhyeta dṛśyeta vācyeta.* Lamotte picked up the *Śata's kiñcid anyan*, translating ''*Parce qu'aucun autre nom n'est employé grâce auquel quoi que ce soit pourrait être exprimé, désigné, caractérisé, aperçu.*'' Conze's translation: ''For no word that is not

composed of them is used when anything is conventionally expressed, talked about, pointed out, written about, made manifest, or recited.''

57. (For the readings of several modern Buddhologists, see notes 55 and 56.) The following paragraph paraphrases, with a bit of Peircean terminology, Rdo Grub-chen's discussion in *Gzungs*, pp. 69–70. Rdo Grub-chen refers to the interpretations of Śāntipa and the *Yum gsum gnod 'joms* in locating at the question ''Why is that?'' a transition from a conventional interpretation of the syllabary's *indicatum* to an interpretation that equates the *indicatum* with *tathatā*.

58. *Gzungs*, pp. 69–79: *A zhes pa de nutpana* [sic] *bsnan pa'i nges tshig gis bshad na skye med kyi don la 'jug pa yin yang / de tsam gyis a yig spyi ldog nas skye med kyi chos skor bshad mi nus te.*

59. Note that in fact this comes to be demonstrated as true in the ultimate sense (see following discussion). But it is not true in conventional terms.

60. *Gzungs*, p. 70: *A yig tsam zhig ni me brjod pa'i don du anala dang / khab long brjod pa la ayaskantaḥ dang / snum khur la apūpa zhes sgra sbyor ba lta bur yang mthong bas / de dag kyang skye med rjod pa'i ngag gi cha shas su 'dod rigs par 'gyur la / de lta na / ngag thams cad stong nyid rjod pa'i ngag tu thal ba'i phyir ro / . . . de la nges tshig gis ji ltar bshad kyang yi ge mnyam pa nyid kyi chos nyid las mi 'da' ba'i tshul la brten nas de ltar bshad ches lan mdzad pa ni / 'di ltar gang la yang zhes sogs te.* I have adjusted the last line of my translation to match my translation of the original passage above.

61. Note that the *Mahāprajñāpāramitāśāstra*, attributed to Nāgārjuna, makes a similar switch from an indexical/conventional account of syllabary dhāraṇī practice, to an explanation of the practice from the standpoint of ultimate truth. After describing the Arapacana syllabary indexical mnemonics in its section on *akṣarapraveśadhāraṇī*, the third and highest class of dhāraṇī in this text, it states: ''*Le Bodhisattva pratiquant cette Dhāraṇī, dès qu'il entend le phonéme A, pénètre aussitôt le fait que tous les dharma sont, dès le début, non-nés*, etc. (Lamotte's translation, from *Traité*, p. 1868).

62. *Gzungs*, pp. 77–78: *'On kyang mdo las ni a dang ra dang pa yig sogs yi ge bsnan pa'i nges tshig gi steng nas skye ba med pa dang / rdul dang bral ba dang / don dam pa sogs ston byed du bshad nas de'i rgyud mtshan gyis chos thams cad kyi skor 'gyur bar gsungs pas mi 'grigs.*

63. The preceding summarizes *Gzungs*, pp. 76–77 et seq. The terms *sgro btags* and *yongs su btags* are from the *Yum gsum gnod 'joms*, cited by Rdo Grub-chen on p. 76.

64. *Gzungs*, p. 79: *A yig lta bu la mtshon na / ming tshig so so'i ma phye ba'i a yig spyi ldog de la mtshan mar bzung ba yin gyi / skye med ston pa'i nges tshig gis bye brag tu byas ba'i a yig ni ma yin te.*

65. See Peirce, ''Logic as Semiotic,'' pp. 16 et seq. Unlike indexes, symbols do not represent an individual thing, but rather a general thing or a class of things.

66. *Gzungs*, p. 79.

67. Ibid., p. 78: *Sdud tshul ni / a zhes bya ba ni ma bskyes ba'i phyir chos thams cad kyi sgo'o / zhes sogs gong du drangs pa ltar / adyanutpana [sic] la sogs pa'i nges tshig gis bsgrubs pa'i 'og tu sdud ba yin te.*

68. When Rdo Grub-chen says, *Gzungs*, p. 78, that "*yi ge de dag bshad gzhir bzung / tshig de dag 'chad byed du byas*, he is even claiming that the letter, because of its association with emptiness that has been forged in insight meditation, becomes in a certain sense the signified, and the defining phrase expresses it linguistically. In any case, it is clear that Rdo Grub-chen considers the following practice from the *Vajramaṇḍadhāraṇīsūtra* to be based entirely upon the letter: he introduces the whole discussion by stating: "*yi ge tsam las stong pa nyid kyi don nges par 'char thub pa ni* (p. 114).

69. Ibid., pp. 114–15 (= PT 807, p. 222.3.1–2). See also the discussion in *Gzungs*, p. 128.

70. Ibid., p. 114: *Rdo rje snying po'i gzungs mdo las yi ge de rnams ngag gang gi sngon du dmigs kyang stong nyid ston pa'i nges tshig dran byed kyi sgor 'gyur bar.*

71. Ibid., p. 115: *lha'i ming thog mthong ba na dul ba'i nges tshig gi tshul gyis zab mo'i gnas lugs dran par gsungs so.* The "profound situation" being referred to here is presumably the act of controlling and taming one's saṃsāric tendencies in the course of the Buddhist path.

72. Ibid., p. 64.

73. As stated, e.g., in ibid., p. 115: *da yig thun mong du yod pas.*

74. Ibid., p. 116: *stong pa nyid ston pa'i yi ge'i sgo nyid.*

75. Ibid., p. 128: *de 'dra'i chos tshig mtha' yas pa tshig gcig tu 'jug pa ni chos thams cad bsdu ba la mkhas pa ste. . . . sgra thams cad gzungs kyi phyag rgyas 'debs pa ste.*

76. *Mahāvyutpatti* 4297, ed. R. Sakaki (Kyoto 1916–1925), 2 vols.; *Vimalakīrtinirdeśa* ("*dhāraṇīsūtrāntarājamudrāmudrita*") in Étienne Lamotte, trans., *L'Enseignement de Vimalakīrti*, (Louvain: Publications Universitaires & Institut Orientaliste, 1962), p. 378; *The Laṅkāvatāra Sūtra*, ed. Bunyiu Nanjio (Kyoto: Otani University Press, 1956), p. 160. Cf. "*akarādyakṣarapraveśamudrā*," *Śatasāhasrikā*, ed. Ghoṣa, p. 1452; or "*akarādyakṣaramudrā*," *Pañcaviṃśati*, ed. Dutt, p. 213.

77. *Gzungs*, p. 120. The second aspect of *dhāraṇīmudrā* seems similar to "the dhāraṇī that turns on skill with regard to all uttered sounds" (*sarvarutakauśalyāvartā dhāraṇī*) mentioned in *Saddharmapuṇḍarīka*, ed. H. Kern and Bunyiu Nanjio, p. 475.

78. Instances of the literal formula as nail, reminding by pinning down: *Guhyasamājatantra* XVI.66–67A, as given in Alex Wayman, *Yoga of the Guhyasamājatantra: The Arcane Lore of Forty Verses* (reprint Delhi: Samuel Weiser,

Inc., 1980), p. 209: the practitioner imagines himself gored by mantric syllables in the form of arrows piercing his cakras, which allows him to remember "the highest peak" (*khavajramadhyagataṃ cintet mañjuvajraṃ mahābalam / pañcabāṇaprayogena mukuṭāgraṃ tu saṃsmaret / pañcasthāneṣu mantrajñaḥ krūravajra pātayet*). The eighteenth century Tibetan Buddhist visionary 'Jigs-med Gling-pa calls his "not-forgetting remembering dhāraṇī" a six-nailed key (*mi brjed dran pa'i gzungs / gzer drug gnad kyi lde mig* in *Ḍakki'i gsang gtam chem mo*, in *Klong-chen snying-thig: Treasured rNying ma pa precepts and rituals received in a vision of Klong-chen-pa Dri-med 'od-zer by 'Jigs-med gling-pa Rang-byung Rdo-rje mkhyen-brtse'i 'od-zer* [New Delhi: Ngawang Sopa, 1973], p. 13). Rdo Grub-chen, *Gzungs* p. 127, in the course of discussing forebearance dhāraṇī, calls it "the single nail key for holding the signs of endless Dharma teachings."

79. Cf. Peirce's description of the action of indexical signs: "they direct the attention to their objects by blind compulsion." "Logic as Semiotic," pp. 12 et seq.

80. The example is Mkhan-po Dpal-ldan Shes-rab's, offered in June 1989 in Amherst.

81. *Gzungs*, pp. 63–64.

82. Ibid., p. 78.

83. Ibid., p. 64.

84. Ibid., p. 125: *go rim gyi nges pa la mi ltos par dran pa.*

85. The foregoing sentences paraphrase Rdo Grub-chen's discussion in ibid., p. 126; cf. p. 156: *sdom du mtshan mar byed.*

86. Ibid., p. 82.

87. See ibid., p. 64. See discussion of *akṣara* and its Vedic creative powers in Padoux, *Recherches*, pp. 26 et seq.

88. On the question of constancy, cf. Lamotte, *Traité*, pp. 1876–77, where Nāgārjuna claims that the śrāvakas reject the notion of dhāraṇī because all dharmas are impermanent, and therefore there is nothing to be retained. To this the Mahāyāna reply is that both production and destruction are unreal. To retain past dharmas is not a defect; the bodhisattva needs dhāraṇīs to retain good dharmas, etc.

89. PT 820, vol. 74, p. 104.3.6–7. Cited by Rdo Grub-chen, p. 122.

90. PT 820, vol. 74, p. 104.2.7–8.

91. PT 795, vol. 72, p. 24.1.1–2.

92. Here I cannot resist a comment, based on much observation of rocks during a recent trip to Tibet. I cannot say if Tibetans are attached to rocks, but they certainly do seem to be obsessed with them. I am thinking of the teetering piles of auspiciously stacked stones and pebbles around stūpas, and on mountain passes—not to mention the megatons of rocks inscribed with mantras and dhāraṇīs all over Tibet. On a climb

of lCags po ri in Lhasa, I noticed in amazement that large portions of the mountain itself are virtually covered with inscribed letters.

93. See Lamotte, *Traité*, p. 1866.

94. In addition to some of the others already mentioned, Rdo Grub-chen, in *Gzungs*, p. 152, quotes Dignāga's *Prajñāpāramitāpiṇḍārtha*, vs. 53 (cf. G. Tucci, "Minor Sanskrit Texts on the Prajñâ-pâramitâ. 1. The Prajñā-pâramitâ-piṇḍârtha of Diṅnâga," *Journal of the Royal Asiatic Society*, [1947]: 53–75): *De nyid rig pas ming rnams kun / don ji lta bar yang dag tu / dmigs pa med nyid de yi phyir / sgra 'di zlog par byed ma yin* (Skt: *Naivopalabhate samyak sarvanāmāni tattvavit / yathārthatvena tenedaṃ na dhvaner vinivāraṇaṃ:* "The one who realizes the truth does not perceive words actually to be in accordance with their meanings, but does not thereby reject [the use of verbal] sounds").

95. Rdo Grub-chen, *Gzungs*, p. 153, quotes a passage from the *Bodhisattvabhūmi:* "Thus if dharmas in their actual nature are inexpressible, then why are expressions used? Even if in that way inexpressible, the inexpressible *dharmatā* is explained to others. It is not able to make itself heard, but the inexpressible actual nature will not be understandable without words and hearing. Thus for the purpose of making heard and understood, expressions are used."

96. It was this statement that was seen as key to the Prajñāpāramitā dhāraṇī theory by Conze and Lamotte; see note 55 above and the ensuing discussion. The totality of the alphabet or syllabary, and the necessary presence of at least some of its members in any given linguistic expression, is certainly an important reason why the alphabet becomes a powerful dhāraṇī or mantra, but as we have shown here there are other important reasons as well.

97. *Gzungs*, p. 64.

98. PT 820, p. 104.3.8–4.1: *Chos gang yang yi ge rnams kyis ma bsdus pa med pa de bzhin du chos gang yang byang chub kyis ma sdus pa med de.*

99. Ibid., p. 104.4.2–3: *Yi ge rnams kho nas byang chub ston par byed do / yi ge rnams kho nas byang chub gleng bar byed do / yi ge rnams kho nas byang chub la reg par byed do.*

100. According to Mkhan-po Dpal-ldan Shes-rab, the claim that only letters touch bodhi, etc., cannot be understood without recourse to tantric doctrine concerning the somatic basis of *bīja* letters. Interview, Amherst, June 1989.

101. The following two sets of quotes extracted from *Gzungs*, pp. 121–23 (= PT 820, p. 104.2.6–3.5.)

102. As given by Dutt, *Bodhisattvabhūmiḥ*, p. 185.

103. As argued in the passage quoted in note 32. But at least *kṣāntipadāni*, meaning "words of forebearance," which would seem to be a sort of descriptive title for the rest of the mantra, would have semantic meaning. Wogihara, *Bodhisattvabhūmi*, p. 273, gives " . . . *bhikṣāṃti padāni* . . . which would mean

something like "they desire words." According to Wogihara the Tibetan Sde-dge translation gives " . . . bhiḥ kānti. . . . " The Peking Tibetan translation gives " . . . *bhikṣanati / padani* . . ." *Gzungs* p. 150, gives " . . . *bhiḥ kṣantir trāni*. . . . "

104. *Gzungs*, p. 153.

105. Ibid., pp. 133–34.

106. From Lamotte, *Traité*, p. 1858: *Sa evaṃ sarvadharmāṇām svabhāvārthaṃ samyak pratividhya tasmāt param arthaṃ na samanveṣate.*

107. Gzungs, pp. 156–57: *Gzhung 'dir [= Bodhisattvabhūmi] ming tshig thams cad yi ge'i ma mo la bsdus nas 'dzin pa dngos su ma bshad kyang / 'dir bshad pa ltar bsgrubs nas grub pa na / de ltar yang 'dzin nus par gsal te / de ltar sdud pa'i gnad du yum las gzungs pa'i gtso bo dag 'dir yang snang ba'i phyir ro / . . . thog ma'i yi ge la sdom du mtshan mar byed mi byed kyi khyad kyis gzungs kyi sgo sgrub lugs gnyis su 'gyur bar bshad pa yin gyi / grub pa'i gzungs mi 'dra ba gnyis yod par ston pa min no.*

108. We have seen several symbols of emptiness in our preceding discussion. I do not believe it is possible for an index to signify emptiness, however. In the case of the indexical syllabary, the index signifies merely the word *birthlessness*, and so forth.

109. For an excellent study of the former case, see Annemarie Schimmel, *Calligraphy and Islamic Culture* (New York: New York University Press, 1984). In many other cases these letters signify profound contents akin to the Buddhist emptiness as well.

110. Ibid., p. 118: "By holding [in memory], through the technique of making those letters and sounds, with which one was not previously familiar, equal to the language of birthlessness, they will all be condensed into the meaning of the phrase *birthlessness* which is within the *A*. This will happen without making a second effort at purifying and becoming accustomed. . . . Having cultivated the memory of how those letters become doors for entering into forebearance, all other sounds will also be placed into the box of letter *mātṛkās* and held. This is the special intelligence (*yid-gzhungs*) that catches (*lo-bskyen*) and holds quickly." Similar claims are made with reference to the use of dhāraṇī seal on p. 120, which seem to trade on a distinction between Dharma (the Buddhist teachings) and dharma (a conventional phenomenon): "Two methods have been taught clearly: the method of establishing all letters as dhāraṇī seals, and then having accomplished that, there is the method of applying it to all sounds. The first is the way in which one never forgets the symbols of the profound Dharma (*zab-mo'i chos-kyi brda rnams*). The second is, through the means of the first, to quickly hold other symbols of the dharmas (*chos-kyi brda gzhan*), which having been understood, then this dhāraṇī becomes the way for holding [i.e., remembering] karma and obscuration and persons etc., all sorts of sounds for objects." We can understand the first of these practices to mean that the practitioner reinforces the linguistic meaning of a term for the profound Dharma, such as *emptiness* or

birthlessness, with a meditative insight into that principle, this being in consonance with a general Buddhist idea that once one has such a meditative insight one never loses it. Once the two, the linguistic signifier and the meditative insight, are thus connected, the practitioner would remember the "meaning" of that signifier with ease. As for Rdo Grub-chen's second aspect of dhāraṇī seal practice, we can note an interesting ambiguity: what does it mean to hold the other signs? Does it mean that their particular literal formulation and/or conventional meaning is remembered, or does it mean that the practitioner "remembers" the ultimate meaning of those signs as being empty, as are all signs? On pp. 119–20 it is claimed that the remembering of mundane terms does not contradict the principle of letter sameness: "Forebearance dhāraṇī is classified as holding the meaning of the profound word, but the memory of many other symbols for objects (*gzhan-pa'i brda'i yul-can gyi dran-shes*) is also included therein. One does not only hold the plethora of symbols referring to obscuration and enlightenment. By merely condensing a plethora of [other] signs into the letter door that enters into thusness and holding them, they go in the direction of holding the profound word, and so there is no contradiction."

111. *Gzungs*, pp. 65–66.

112. Of course, all things could also be made to be symbols of emptiness, but to the degree that something remains a symbol (i.e., as long as its symbolism is not conflated with iconicity by a logic akin to that associated with the forebearance dhāraṇī letter), it does not allow the identification of sign and signified that engenders the instantaneousness, as asserted below, of the iconic reminding of emptiness.

113. The phrase *zeroed semiosis* was suggested to me by David Ruegg in a personal communication. For a contemporary Pericean account of the perception of the icon, see Joseph Ransdell, "On Peirce's Conception of the Iconic Sign," in *Iconicity: Essays on the Nature of Culture, Festschrift for Thomas Sebeok on his 65th birthday*, ed. Paul Bouissac et al (Tübingen: Stauffenburg Verlag), 1986, especially pp. 68–73. I read Ransdell's article after writing this essay and was interested to find much there that concurs with my semiological analysis of the dhāraṇī icon (without, of course, the soteriological dimension, and without a consideration of a signified content such as emptiness). Note Ransdell's comments on the question of immediacy, and his consideration of ways in which the iconic sign is independent of convention. For Rdo Grub-chen's remarks on the immediacy of dhāraṇī memory see, for example, the passage referred to in note 86 above. I have used the term *sudden* in the preceeding passage only to suggest a loose connection between the practices discussed here and the notion of "sudden enlightenment" in Buddhism. Rdo Grub-chen's term is *thod-rgal* which implies a type of "leap," but is not to be equated with sudden enlightenment. See David Ruegg, *Buddha-nature, Mind and the Problem of Gradualism in a Comparative Perspective: On the Transmission and Reception of Buddhism in India and Tibet* (London: School of Oriental and African Studies, 1989) pp. 164–175 for a discussion of two senses of leaping (*thod-rgal* translates Skt. *avaskanda(ka), viskanda(ka)* or *vyutkrānta(ka)*) that can be identified in Buddhist texts.

114. Lamotte's use of the term *magical* in his translation of the *Bodhisattvabhūmi* passage on dhāraṇī in *Traité* seems inconsistent. To the degree that

he renders both *mantrapadāni* and *dhāraṇīpadāni* as ''magical syllables'' (e.g., *Tena bodhisattvena pratilabdhā tāni dhāraṇīpadāny adhiṣṭhāya bodhisattvakṣāntir vaktavyā* from the *Bodhisattvabhūmi* is translated by Lamotte ''*La [conviction] ainsi conquise par ce Bodhisattva sur la base des syllabes magiques doit être appelée Conviction de Bodhisattva*''), he appears to be discounting the crucial role of *adhiṣṭhāna* in the practice of dhāraṇī. *Adhiṣṭhāna* was also referred to in the *Bodhisattvabhūmi*'s previous section on mantra dhāraṇī, where indeed Lamotte does translate *adhitiṣṭhati* as ''*consacre*'', i.e., the bodhisattva's act of consecrating the mantra syllables so as to make them efficacious. Both the *Bodhisattvabhūmi* and the Prajñāpāramitā doctrines on dhāraṇī rest on the notion that the bodhisattva can imbue the words or letters of a mantric formula with meaning, an imbuing, or consecration, said to be possible through the application of realizations gained in meditation. Such a lofty interpretation of the force of a mantric formula would seem to be recognized by Lamotte in his following discussion, pp. 1859–60, where he records the *Daśabhūmika* claim that an infinite number of dhāraṇīs are composed by the bodhisattva on the ninth *bhūmi*, a level on the Buddhist path that Lamotte surely did not think was considered to consist of a mere reliance on magical spells. Lamotte also grants, on p. 1867, that the forty-two letters of the Prajñāpāramitā dhāraṇī practice are not thought to have magical power but are simply used as mnemonic devices to remember points of doctrine. As for traditional ambivalence toward spells, see, e.g., the *Aṣṭasāhasrikā*'s description of the irreversible bodhisattva as one who rejects spells [mantras], etc., ''which are the work of women.'' Conze, *The Perfection of Wisdom in Eight Thousand Lines*, p. 205.

Commemoration and Identification in *Buddhānusmṛti*

PAUL HARRISON

Introduction

No study of the place of memory in Buddhism would be complete without some discussion of the theory and practice of *buddhānusmṛti,* usually translated into English as "recollection," "remembrance" or "commemoration of the Buddha," "calling the Buddha to mind," or "meditation on the Buddha." For over two and a half millennia of Buddhist history this technique has enjoyed wide currency, spawning a host of derivative practices and being itself transformed beyond recognition. Who, for example, would discern in the rather abstract and bloodless *buddhānusmṛti* so meticulously analyzed in the work of the fifth-century Theravādin monk Buddhaghosa the ancestor—or perhaps we should say previous incarnation?—of the *nembutsu,* the ritual invocation of the Buddha Amitābha that twentieth-century Japanese laymen and laywomen utter with such fervent piety? Who for that matter would read in those same lines a foreshadowing of the Tibetan practice of "deity yoga," regarded as one of the most distinctive characteristics of tantric or Vajrayāna Buddhism? Such connections may not be immediately obvious, but they are far from tenuous. This chapter will attempt to lay them bare by sketching[1] the historical development of *buddhānusmṛti* in the various texts devoted to it or to its derivatives, by describing the functions it is believed to perform, and by asking what sort of "recollection" or "remembrance," if any, it involves.

Buddhānusmṛti in the Mainstream Buddhist Traditions

Previous general treatments of Buddhist meditation have not given much weight to *buddhānusmṛti* and its companion techniques. Including these techniques under the category of "devotional exercises," Conze characterizes them as "rather sober and restrained, without great emotional fervour,"[2] and interprets them primarily as antidotes to specific unwholesome states. In his detailed study of Theravāda meditation, King devotes less than a page to what he calls the eight "thematic recollections" or "items to be brought to mind," which he also describes as "preliminary low-level subjects . . . in which one's mood is set favourably toward the meditative process but that produce no recognised level of higher awareness.''[3] Another recent study of early Buddhist meditation by Vetter[4] does not mention the topic at all. Was *buddhānusmṛti* then originally little more than a devotional preliminary, a relatively insignificant ''ground-clearing'' practice?

This is a question that can be answered only by reference to the Pāli Nikāyas of the Theravādin school, extant in their entirety, and to the Sanskrit Āgamas of various other ''Mainstream''[5] schools, most of which survive only in Chinese translation. Although the status of the different Buddhist canons is a contentious issue, we can be reasonably sure that the Pāli scriptures in particular provide evidence of a relatively early stratum of Buddhist belief, however out of reach the bedrock may remain. Their testimony is also conveniently distilled for us by two voluminous Pāli commentaries, the *Visuddhimagga* (''Path of Purification'') of Buddhaghosa, dated to the fifth century CE,[6] and the *Vimuttimagga* (''Path of Liberation'') of Upatissa, of roughly the same date.[7]

In the suttas (''discourses'') of the Pāli Nikāyas *buddhānussati* (the Pāli form of the Sanskrit *buddhānusmṛti*) seldom occurs alone, but usually as one of a series of three, four, five, six, or ten *anussati* or ''recollections.'' It is the tenfold series that is set forth in the two commentaries as a component of their standard lists of thirty-eight or forty subjects of meditation: *anussati* directed toward (1) the Buddha, (2) the Dhamma, (3) the Sangha, (4) morality, (5) liberality, (6) deities, (7) respiration, (8) death, (9) the parts of the body, and (10) peace (i.e., nibbāna). Of these ten the first three form an obvious group, but the four- and sixfold series also seem well attested in all Nikāyas except the Majjhima.[8] We are therefore dealing with a fairly old set of practices, arranged in various groupings in very early sources. The tenfold classification was probably the last to emerge, as is suggested by the *Visuddhimagga* itself, which sets the first six *anussati* or recollections proper off as a group[9] and also uses the term *sati* (Skt. *smṛti*), in the sense of mindfulness, for numbers 7–9.

What is the actual content of this seemingly heterogeneous series? If we confine ourselves to the first six, we find that each *anussati* consists of the recitation of a short formula, the text of which displays very little variation across a wide range of sources. By performing this recitation in a meditational context, practitioners are encouraged to recall or call to mind (1) the virtues of the Buddha, (2) the superiority and profundity of the Buddhist teaching, (3) the merits and worthiness of the Buddhist order, (4) the superiority of their own moral training (in the sense of the excellence of the Buddhist precepts they have adopted), (5) their own commitment to a spirit of generosity, and (6) those qualities such as faith, learning, liberality and so on by which the deities have attained their exalted rebirths and to which the practitioners themselves also aspire. If there is any unifying theme here it is the deliberate focusing on what is accounted spiritually wholesome and beneficial. The six *anussati* then are a kind of exercise in the power of positive thinking, but of the most abstract kind.

We can see this if we look, for example, at the wording of the first *anussati,* which is the one that directly concerns us here. The Pāli formula runs as follows:

> *Iti pi so bhagavā arahaṃ sammāsambuddho vijjācaraṇa-sampanno sugato lokavidū anuttaro purisadammasārathi satthā devamanussānaṃ buddho bhagavā ti.*
>
> This Lord is indeed the Arhat ("Worthy One"), the Correctly and Fully Awakened One, Perfected in Knowledge and Conduct, the Sugata ("Well Gone"), the Knower of the World, the Supreme One, the Trainer of Men [sic] Amenable to Training, the Teacher of Devas ("gods") and Humankind, the Buddha, the Lord.

This formula is commonly known as the "ten epithets" (*adhivacana*) of a buddha. The Sanskrit version found in the Āgamas differs substantively only in adding the term *Tathāgata* ("Thus Come" or "Thus Gone" = "Reality Realizer") before *Arhat,* consequently reading *anuttaraḥ puruṣadamyasārathiḥ* as one epithet (i.e., "the Supreme Trainer of Men Amenable to Training") to keep the number at ten.[10] In both versions, then, what we have is essentially a listing of titles or attributes of the Buddha of a more or less creedal nature. The formulas dealing with the Dharma and the Sangha are equally reminiscent in tone of the Apostles', Nicene, and Athanasian Creeds of the Christian tradition. They can be seen, in the first place, as a confession of faith that functions on the same level as the celebrated triple refuge formula; that is, by encapsulating the core beliefs and defining the identity of a particular religious community.[11]

When we turn to the alleged results of the rehearsal of the ten epithets, however, the similarities with the Christian tradition may be less apparent, for all the *anussati* seem to have served—initially at least—an expressly psychotropic purpose; that is to say, they were seen as producing an alteration in consciousness. The testimony of various Pāli suttas is conveniently condensed for us by Buddhaghosa, who describes the benefits of *buddhānussati* first in terms of mental purification and preparation for advanced trance meditation (Skt. *dhyāna,* Pāli *jhāna*).[12] Contemplation of the virtues of the Buddha displaces the "three poisons" of lust, hatred, and delusion and overcomes the five hindrances or obscurations (sensual desire, illwill, sloth and torpor, excitation and guilt, and doubt) so as to permit "applied" and "sustained" thought on those virtues. Such thought produces rapture, rapture leads to tranquility (in the sense of the disappearance of any physical or mental discomfort), tranquility to bliss, and in that state of bliss, concentration of the mind on the Buddha's virtues is achieved. In this way the five components (or "limbs") of meditation are produced; that is, contemplation of the virtues has laid down a foundation of psychological stability for the advanced trance meditations. According to the *Visuddhimagga*, the state of concentration achieved in this way is known as *access* or *neighborhood* (*upacāra*), not full absorption or ecstasy (*appanā*), because of the plural nature and profundity of the meditation subject.[13]

Whereas all this is in line with the basic characterization of *buddhānusmṛti* advanced by Conze and King, Buddhaghosa goes on to list other benefits that begin to point in a different direction:[14]

> And the monk who is devoted to this recollection of the Buddha is respectful and reverent to the Teacher; reaches an abundance of faith, mindfulness, wisdom and merit; is always full of zest and joy; overcomes fear and dread; is able to bear pain; obtains a sense of intimacy with the Teacher; and his body which has embodied this recollection of the Buddha is, like a shrine, worthy of worship; his mind steers in the direction of Buddhahood; when he is confronted with reprehensible situations, a sense of shame and a dread of blame are set up in him, as though he saw the Teacher before him. Even if he does not penetrate any further, he is at least bound for a happy rebirth.[15]

Similar results are claimed for the other five *anussati*, and at the end of the section Buddhaghosa recapitulates the purificatory properties of the six with reference to various canonical texts,[16] noting that their practice is open to ordinary persons (*puthujjana*) as well as "noble disciples" (*ariya-sāvaka*); that is, the initiated.[17] Consultation of these and other canonical sources indicates that many of the properties listed by Buddhaghosa were ascribed to the *anussati* at an early date. For example, the *Dhajaggasutta* (S i 218) relates how Gautama prescribed the practice of the first three *anussati* (Buddha, Dhamma, and Sangha) to his disciples as a specific remedy against fear when meditating in wild and solitary places. Thus, like the meditation on loving kindness or the recitation of the short texts known as *parittas*, the practice of *buddhānussati* must have assumed quite early on the nature of an apotropaic technique, providing its practitioners with general protection, or at least a sense of this. There are revealing illustrations of the extent of this development in the commentary to the *Dhammapada*, the *Dhammapadaṭṭhakathā*, where, for example, King Kappina the Great gets himself and his thousand mounted courtiers dryshod across three impassable rivers by performing in turn the *anussati* on the Buddha, the Dhamma, and the Sangha: "While thus engaged in meditation the king and his retinue dashed over the surface of the river on their thousand horses, the Sindh horses springing upon the surface of the river as on a flat rock, without so much as wetting the tips of their hoofs.''[18] This fable indicates the great power eventually thought to inhere in these simple formulas; as the text itself makes abundantly clear,[19] their recitation has the magical force of an ''act of truth'' (Skt. *satyakriyā*, Pāli *saccakiriyā*). In the same work, in the story that provides a commentary on *Dhammapada* 296–301,[20] the Buddha remarks that ''Meditation on the Buddha is not the sole means of protection, but those whose thoughts have been well disciplined by any of the Six Forms of Meditation have no need of any other protection or means of defense, nor of spells or herbs.''[21] In this way a creedal statement with a psychotropic function has come to be used as an apotropaic incantation, rather like the Christian Lord's Prayer.[22] And this is indeed a dominant use of the first three *anussati* in Theravādin societies today: recitation of the virtues of the Buddha, the Dhamma, and the Sangha is a popular ritual device for ensuring safety in battle, the successful cure of illness, or release from prison, and routinely occurs in liturgy to confer general protection.[23]

Although Buddhaghosa's *Visuddhimagga* presents *buddhānussati* solely in terms of the ten epithets, clearly the original core of the practice, the *Vimuttimagga* indicates that a considerably amplified form was known in Theravādin circles at around the same time. Beginning with the ten epithets, it goes on to add the various moral perfections exemplified in the former life-histories (*jātaka*) of the Buddha, key episodes in his last life as Gautama, his ten powers (*bala*), his fourteen kinds of buddha-knowledge, his eighteen qualities exclusive to a buddha, and various other virtues.[24] Here too all the qualities to be called to mind are rather abstract, but in another important departure from the *Visuddhimagga*, Upatissa writes ''if a man wishes to meditate on the Buddha, he should worship Buddha images and such other objects.''[25] Although it is likely that this is merely a reference to a meritorious preliminary practice, as nowhere else in the text is there any suggestion that the Buddha's physical form should be visualized, it is still a tantalizing clue, because, as we shall see, the incorporation of this kind of visualization was a crucial development in the practice of *buddhānusmṛti*. One further such clue occurs in the *Visuddhimagga*, where, in a discussion of the mindfulness of death, Buddhaghosa uses an alternative formula to refer to the Buddha, one that makes explicit reference to his physical form.[26] Yet this formula plays no part in his exposition of *buddhānusmṛti* itself.

Moving now to other Mainstream sources outside the Theravādin tradition, we find in the Chinese translations of the Sanskrit Āgamas (belonging to the canons of several different schools) many passages dealing with *buddhānusmṛti* that have no counterpart in the Pāli Nikāyas.[27] One of these passages in particular, *Ekottarāgama* III, 1 (T. Vol. 2, pp. 554a7–b9), propounds *buddhānusmṛti* as the one practice for realizing all spiritual goals and recommends that practitioners contemplate the image of the Buddha without taking their eyes off it, that they call to mind the body and the countenance of the Buddha and then his moral and mental qualities, arranged under the traditional rubrics of morality, meditation, wisdom, liberation, and the cognition and vision of liberation (*śīla-samādhi-prajñā-vimukti-vimuktijñānadarśana*).[28] In this canonical text of indeterminate date (the translation is late fourth century) there is no mention of the ten epithets, but clear reference to visualization of the Buddha's physical form, and a suggestion that one should have recourse to an image of the Buddha to assist this. Other Mainstream sources, however, include both the ten epithets and a considerable number of physical details in a more developed listing of the Buddha's attributes. The best example of this is the *Mahāvastu,* a text belonging to the Lokottaravādins, a subsect of the Mahāsāṃghikas, which is extant in Sanskrit.[29] It seems quite likely that the wide currency of such formulas would have lead to their early incorporation in the practice of *buddhānusmṛti* by Mainstream Buddhists.

Buddhānusmṛti in the Mahāyāna

In fact, although the evidence of the *Vimuttimagga* and the Chinese Āgamas is more suggestive than decisive, there can be no doubt that by the second century CE some Buddhists were indeed practicing a form of *buddhānusmṛti* that did employ these expanded formulas, included detailed visualization of the physical body of the Buddha, and was accompanied by the use of images. The principal evidence for this is provided by a Mahāyāna sūtra called the *Pratyutpanna-buddha-saṃmukhāvasthita-samādhi-sūtra* (hereafter *PraS*), the first Chinese translation of which was made by the Indo-Scythian Lokakṣema in 179 CE.[30] This text describes in great detail and sophistication a meditation technique known as the *pratyutpanna-buddha-saṃmukhāvasthita-samādhi,* or "*samādhi* ("meditation," "concentration") of direct encounter with the buddhas of the present," which is clearly a developed form of *buddhānusmṛti;* in fact, in some sources it is referred to as the *buddhānusmṛti-samādhi.* To be sure, the buddhas who are being called to mind here are not Śākyamuni (i.e., the "historical" Buddha Gautama), but the myriad buddhas of the present, of whom Amitābha is the preeminent example, but these buddhas are simply idealized clones of Śākyamuni transposed to different world-systems. The purpose of the *pratyutpanna-samādhi,* very briefly, is to enable practitioners to have audience with these buddhas and hear their teachings in this very life, and, secondarily, to achieve rebirth in their buddha-fields on their death. The primary focus is on vision and hearing, that is, on an authentically transformative experience of a reality that must be taken seriously but at the same time subjected to the thoroughgoing critique of the "perfection of wisdom" (*prajñā-pāramitā*) approach with its core doctrine of universal "emptiness" (*śūnyatā*). As interesting as this approach is—in twentieth-century terms it is like trying to collapse the Newtonian and quantum universes into one—what concerns us here is the precise form of the practice itself. The detailed directions given by the *PraS* in Chapters 3, 4, and 8[31] indicate a combination of the traditional prescriptions for *buddhānusmṛti* with the lore pertaining to Mahāyāna cosmology. Choosing a particular buddha of the present, practitioners seat themselves in a quiet place, orient themselves to the quarter in which that buddha resides and visualize him teaching the Dharma surrounded by his disciples in his world-system. The precise form of the visualization is laid out in terms of *buddhānusmṛti* in Section 3F (Amitābha is speaking):

> What then, sons of good family, is the calling to mind of the Buddha [*buddhānusmṛti*]? It is when one concentrates on the *Tathāgata* in this way: "He, the *Tathāgata*, *Arhat*, Correctly and Fully Awakened One, Perfected in Knowledge and Conduct, the *Sugata*, the Knower of the World, the Trainer of Men Capable of Training, the Supreme One, the Teacher of *Devas* and Humankind, the Buddha and Lord, endowed with the Thirty-two Marks of the Great Man and a body with a colour like gold, resembling a bright, shining, and well-set golden image, and well adorned like a bejewelled pillar, teaches the Dharma in the midst of an assembly of disciples, that is, teaches to the effect that nothing perishes. What does not perish? Earth does not perish. Water, fire, air, beings (Skt. *bhūta*), the *Devas*, Brahmā and Prajāpati do not perish. Form does not perish. Feelings, perception, predispositions, and consciousness do not perish;" and one does not misconceive, does not objectify, does not fixate on, does not falsely perceive, does not falsely imagine, does not falsely discriminate, and does not review the *Tathāgata*: when in this way one obtains the *samādhi* of emptiness by concentrating on the *Tathāgata* without objectification, that is known as the calling to mind of the Buddha.[32]

If one persists in this practice for seven days and seven nights then one is guaranteed a vision of the buddha in question, either in the waking state or in a dream (see *PraS*, 3B).

Here we see, then, that the visualization of the physical form of the Buddha has been added to the original core component of *buddhānusmṛti*, the mental rehearsal of the ten epithets. That visualization is effected primarily through the contemplation of the thirty-two marks of the Great Man (*dvātriṃśad mahāpuruṣa-lakṣaṇāni*), a well-known list of physical characteristics supposedly possessed by universal emperors (*cakravartin*) and buddhas alike, and found in both Pāli and Sanskrit sources. Ranging from the ordinary to the fantastic, and deriving in some cases from the conventions of sculpture, they include such features as the mark of wheels on the soles of the feet, webbed fingers and toes, arms that reach down as far as the knees, a penis concealed in a sheath, a golden color, a nimbus of light, forty teeth so closely spaced that they appear to form a single mass, a tongue so large that it can cover the whole face, blue eyes, a protruberance on the crown of the head, and a white tuft of hair between the eyebrows.[33] To aid this detailed iconographical visualization, practitioners are encouraged to imagine the Buddha's body as resembling an image; elsewhere in the text there are other clear references to the use of images, either two- or three-dimensional (see, e.g., *PraS* 4D). Lastly, the Buddha is to be imagined as teaching the Dharma in the midst of an assembly of followers; that is, as the center of a complex picture. However, as vivid and realistic as this picture might be, practitioners are instructed not to perceive it in an inappropriate way, not to "objectify" it (Tib. *dmigs pa;* Skt. *upa-*√*labh*), but to realize it as empty (*śūnya*) or devoid of independent existence. In this way the Buddha as meditation object is seen not as an end in itself, but as a means to a correct understanding of the true nature of phenomenal reality.

Additional instructions for the practice are given in Chapter 8 of the *PraS:*

> Bhadrapāla, how then should *bodhisattvas* and *mahāsattvas* cultivate this *samādhi?* Bhadrapāla, just as I am at present sitting before you and teaching the Dharma, in the same way, Bhadrapāla, *bodhisattvas* should concentrate on the *Tathāgatas, Arhats* and Perfectly Awakened Ones as sitting on the Buddha-throne and teaching the Dharma. They should concentrate on the *Tathāgatas* as being endowed with all the finest aspects, handsome, beautiful, lovely to behold, and endowed with bodily perfection. They should look at the bodies of the *Tathāgatas, Arhats* and Perfectly Awakened Ones with their Marks of the Great Man, each one of them produced by a hundred merits. They should also apprehend the external features (or "signs," Skt. *nimitta*)[of the Marks]. They should also check [?] the invisible crown of the head.[34] Having checked it, they should also once more apprehend the external features of the Marks of the Great Man.[35]

Once again it can be noticed how the traditional prescriptions for *buddhānusmṛti* have been supplemented by a detailed iconographical visualization based on the thirty-three marks and—probably somewhat later—the eighty minor characteristics. But what is more significant is the place the practice has assumed in the Mahāyāna scheme of things, even if it is still directed to a goal beyond itself; that is, the realization of the truth of universal emptiness.[36]

By the second century CE, then, the vision of the Buddha (*buddha-darśana*) and the accompanying hearing of the Dharma (*dharma-śravaṇa*) are represented as a transformative experience of decisive importance for practitioners, be they renunciants or householders. The centrality of this kind of experience to the early Mahāyāna has already been highlighted by others; one could refer for example to the work of Beyer, who convincingly equates *anusmṛti* with bhakti, and speaks of a "wave of visionary theism sweeping over the whole of northern India,"[37] or that of Rawlinson, who claims that the essence of the Mahāyāna is a single experience of direct encounter with the Buddha in which the vision, sound/voice, and cognition of the Buddha are simultaneously present.[38] Rawlinson's thesis deserves more careful study, but the significance of the notion of darśana (literally "seeing" or "vision") to Indian religion as a whole has been convincingly underscored by Diana Eck,[39] and the relationship between bhakti and darśana is certainly a close one, as Beyer has suggested. Bhakti, usually translated as "devotion," has the connotation of sharing or participation, which suggests something more momentous than the pious adoration of a distant "other." In a stimulating essay on Hindu darśana,[40] Lawrence Babb has shown that Hindus not only wish to see their deities, they also wish to be seen by them. Further, the benefits which they believe flow to them from this process of mutual visual interaction rest on a particular conception of seeing, one in which darśana is almost construed as a transmission of fluids:

> In the Hindu world "seeing" is clearly not conceived as a passive product of sensory data originating in the outer world, but rather seems to be imaged as an extrusive and acquisitive "seeing flow" that emanates from the inner person, outward through the eyes, to engage directly with objects seen, and to bring something of those objects back to the seer. One comes into contact with, and in a sense becomes, what one sees. . . . Under the right circumstances, then, seeing and being seen by a deity is valuable because it permits the devotee to gain special access to the powers of a superior being.
>
> But I think even more is involved than this. If seeing itself is carried outward as flow, then what the gazing devotee is receiving, at least by implication, is an actual exteriorized visual awareness, one that is superior to his own. This means that quite apart from its more general benefit-bestowing characteristics, darshan has important potential soteriological implications, for by interacting visually with a superior being one is, in

> effect, taking into oneself a superior *way* of seeing, and thus a superior way of knowing. Given the premises of the system, this makes available to the devotee the symbolic basis for an apprehension of himself as transformed. Since he himself is an object of his lord's seeing, by mingling this seeing with his own he can participate in a new way of seeing, and thus of knowing, himself.[41]

The interpretation Babb has so lucidly developed on the basis of contemporary Hindu material may be applied with equal force to the Buddhist data under scrutiny.[42] It is certainly the case as far as the Mahāyāna is concerned that the essence of the darśana or "seeing" process—and of *śravaṇa* or "hearing" as well—is not the passive experience of a remote or separate "other," but a direct encounter leading to self-transformation in the image of that "other," and to a radically new way of seeing.

However one understands their purpose, there is no doubt that techniques for visualizing particular buddhas or their realms are referred to in passing or expounded at length in scores if not hundreds of texts translated into Chinese during the early centuries of our era;[43] but though the buddhas proliferate in staggering numbers throughout the ten quarters of the universe, and the names of the samādhis differ considerably, in essence it is the same developed form of *buddhānusmṛti* that we find in the *PraS*. Many of the contributions to the recent volume on Chinese Buddhist meditation edited by Peter Gregory[44] testify to the key role played by this type of practice in the Mahāyāna (there is no reason to believe that its popularity was exclusive to China), as well as to the philosophical sophistication with which it was interpreted. Whether referred to as *buddhānusmṛti-samādhi, pratyutpanna-samādhi*, or *eka-vyūha-samādhi* ("one-practice" samādhi—the three are in fact barely distinguishable—the crucial point that the canonical sources and the commentaries repeatedly emphasize is the use of the visualization as a gateway to the realization of emptiness; that is, to supreme and perfect awakening itself. All of this is a far cry from the supposedly preliminary purification practice of the early Pāli sources.

However, we should take care that our feet do not leave the ground at this point. The practice of visualizing the buddhas of the present in this way was soon extended to other figures, chiefly the so-called celestial bodhisattvas of the Mahāyāna, and although this extension seems to have been motivated by a variety of factors, the apotropaic element attested for the basic form of *buddhānusmṛti* is very much in evidence. In the famous Chapter 24 of the *Saddharmapuṇḍarīkasūtra*, for example, the manifold benefits and advantages of calling to mind the bodhisattva Avalokiteśvara are set out in lavish detail. The catalogue of dangers to life and limb—fire, flood, shipwreck, attack by wild beasts, execution and imprisonment, lightning strike, the malice of supernaturals, banditry, snakebite, and so on—is alarmingly comprehensive, but calling on Avalokiteśvara saves one from them all. However, the text must be read carefully, for it does not say that Avalokiteśvara himself saves the faithful from their particular peril, by seeing to their rescue in person. It is tempting to construe the material in this way, and thereby assimilate the cult of the "celestial bodhisattvas" to the Christian cult of the saints, but the way in which Avalokiteśvara's salvific function is conceptualized seems to be rather more complex. Sentient beings *in extremis* are indeed advised to call on Avalokiteśvara for help (Skt. *ā-√kram-*), but mostly they are promised relief if they hear or "bear in mind" the name of the great bodhisattva. The precise sense of "bearing the name in mind" (Skt. *nāmadheyaṃ √dhṛ-*) is problematical,[45] but it is often coupled with or replaced by the performance of homage or salutation (*namaskāra*) to Avalokiteśvara; that is, with the formula *"Namo namas tasmai abhayaṃdadāyāvalokiteśvarāya bodhisattvāya mahāsattvāya,"* "Hail, hail to the bodhisattva and *mahāsattva* Avalokiteśvara, bestower of safety!"[46] It therefore seems to refer both to the remembering and to the recitation of the name. This is confirmed by the substitution for it of the verb *√smṛ-* throughout the verses of Chapter 24. The crucial point is that it is the *calling to mind* of Avalokiteśvara that does the trick, presumably by generating a vast amount of merit or, as we might put it, by producing a psychotropic effect, or an alteration in consciousness. In this respect one might note the lexical slippage of Skt. *bhaya* from "fear" to "danger" and of *abhaya* from "fearlessness" to "safety," one that surely is germane to our concern here. The power of the mind is obviously paramount, in that the elimination of fear in one's own mind cancels external dangers. How it is supposed to do this is not entirely clear; although such psychotropic effects are held to be transmittable to other minds,[47] this does not explain how they affect inanimate sources of danger. Nevertheless, we can see that the invocation of the great bodhisattvas has the same protective benefits that some of the Pāli sources claim for *buddhānusmṛti*, being especially useful as a specific against fear.[48]

Vajrayāna and Pure Land Expressions

This rich tradition of iconographic visualization, growing out of *buddhānusmṛti* and developed and employed for a variety of purposes, must have been the matrix for what is now known as "deity yoga" in the Vajrayāna or tantric Buddhist tradition. Like the use of sexual imagery, deity yoga is regarded as one of the distinguishing characteristics of tantric Buddhism; it is in fact one of its richest and most elaborate features. The deities in question are the various buddhas and bodhisattvas we have been discussing, as well as other mythic figures symbolizing different aspects of human consciousness, all in their manifold wrathful and benign forms. Two basic types of practice are taught, visualization of the chosen deity in front of oneself ("generation in front") and visualization of oneself as the chosen deity ("self-generation").[49] Although the first type is very similar to that propounded in the *PraS*,[50] what supposedly marks tantric deity yoga off from the Mahāyāna techniques we have been discussing—apart from the complexity of its ritual and its exegesis—is the process of subjective identification with the visualized deity of the second type. In fact, however, even this is not too far removed from the kind of approach propounded in the *PraS* and in other Mahāyāna sūtras, where the understanding of emptiness is supposed to dissolve the perception of the object of visualization as a real or substantial entity, as something separate from one's own mind (the same bright lens of wisdom is also to be turned on one's own self). Apart from this, which is the essence of the problem for tantric commentators as well, there are other suggestions in these early texts of a process of subjective identification. For example, following the instructions in Chapter 8A of the *PraS* previously cited, the text goes on to say:

> Having apprehended them [the external features of the Thirty-two Marks] they should train themselves in this way:
>
> "Oh how marvellous the beauty of those *Tathāgatas*, *Arhats* and Perfectly Awakened Ones! I too at a future time shall be endowed with such bodily perfection. I shall perfect such marks. I too shall be endowed with such morality. I shall be endowed thus with *samādhi*, thus with wisdom, thus with emancipation, and thus with the cognition and vision of emancipation. I too shall in the same way become fully awakened to supreme and perfect awakening. And once I am fully awakened I shall expound the Dharma to the four assemblies and the world with its *devas*!"
>
> —thus should they train themselves.[51]

However, in Chapter 3 (Sections L–O), practitioners reviewing their experience of the *pratyutpanna-samādhi* are said to ask themselves the question, Did these tathāgatas come from anywhere? Did I go anywhere? Pondering this,

> they understand that the *Tathāgatas* did not come from anywhere. Having understood that their own bodies did not go anywhere either, they think: "Whatever belongs to this Triple World is nothing but thought. Why is that? It is because however I imagine things, that is how they appear. . . .
>
> By thought is the Buddha produced;
> And by thought alone is he seen.

The Buddha is only thought for me,
Thought alone is the *Tathāgata*."[52]

Here, then, the object of visualization becomes an object of both emulation in the outer sense ("I shall become a buddha") and identification in the inner sense ("Buddha is nothing but my mind"). Whereas the former is clearly the central thrust of the Mahāyāna—the bodhisattva path and the aspiration to buddhahood—the latter embodies a more subtle conception of this undertaking, one that the Vajrayāna has inherited and continued to develop. In a sense the Vajrayāna has only made explicit what is already implicit in the Mahāyāna. Its contribution has been in effect to expose the underlying dynamics of the developed form of *buddhānusmṛti* by collapsing the I with the Thou, by placing the process of identification with the "deity" in the forefront of the practitioner's consciousness. This it has done while at the same time making the visualization and vocal ritual accompanying the practice dizzyingly rich and elaborate. But in Tibet, as in the rest of the Buddhist world, this baroque level of ritual detail was only one end of a spectrum of practice that ran all the way to the bare invocation of the name or the mantra of the "deity" for the purposes of protection and blessing, and it is at this other end of the spectrum that the distinction between the I and the Thou looms largest.[53]

This is most apparent in China and other parts of East Asia, where increasingly simplified forms of the *buddhānusmṛti* technique were evolved, chiefly by reducing the central text to the bare name of the Buddha (usually Amitābha). In this way the formula *namo 'mitabhāya buddhāya* (Chinese *nan-wu emituo-fo,* Japanese *namu amida butsu*) came to serve for the earlier much more complex recitation with its attendant visualizations.[54] This trend was pushed further and further by various Chinese, Korean, and Japanese Pure Land masters who sought to emphasize the importance of total surrender to Amitābha as an antidote to the concern with self, the elimination of which has always been the principal aim of Buddhist endeavor.[55] The resulting practice is still called *buddhānusmṛti,* which in Chinese is *nian-fo,* thinking of or calling to mind (*nian*) the Buddha (*fo*); the Japanese pronunciation of this term is *nembutsu.* Here the Chinese character *nian,* in which the graphemes for "now" and "heart-mind" are juxtaposed vertically, has the primary sense "to think of," but later it also came to mean "to read (out loud)." Whether or not this is relevant, *nian-fo/nembutsu* came increasingly to be understood as the recitation of the Buddha's *name,* as it is through the medium of the name that one calls the Buddha to mind. This can best be seen as a radical shortening of the "text" through which *buddhānusmṛti* had always been effected, thus paralleling the development and use of the formula *namo tassa* bhagavato arahato sammāsambuddhassa in Theravādin circles, which can also be seen as a kind of stripped-down *buddhānusmṛti.*

All Buddhist traditions, then, continue to promote a mental focusing on buddhas and other exalted figures for the purposes of salvation, even if the precise nature of these figures and their relationship to the practitioner remain problematical issues for Buddhist thinkers. The practice may be peripheral or central, plain or elaborate, restricted or open, and the salvation sought through it may be from the immediate perils of this life or the suffering of conditioned existence in general, but the entire complex can be seen to have evolved from *buddhānusmṛti* and from its simple purificatory logic, that concentration on the good dispels the bad.

Theoretical Considerations

Our discussion to this point has tended to focus on the objective referent of *buddhānusmṛti* and the various ends for which it is employed. It is now time to say a few words about the nature of *anusmṛti* itself. What is *anusmṛti,* and what is its relation to memory as we understand it? The verb *anu-√smṛ* does mean basically "to remember" or "to recollect," and is compounded of the prefix *anu-* (of which the dominant senses here seem to be "after" and "repeated") and the verb *√smṛ,* which means both "to remember," "to recollect," and "to bear in mind," "be mindful of." *Smṛti* in the sense of mindfulness or continuous attentiveness is a well-known element of Buddhist self-cultivation; at the same time the word stands for memory in general, for its personification, the goddess Memory herself, and for the corpus of sacred Hindu tradition (passed down by memorization). It is not surprising therefore to find *anusmṛti* sharing the same wide range of meanings. But if we look at the traditional subjects of *anusmṛti,* we can see quite clearly that personal recollection of past experience is not involved. This can hardly be the case for the *anusmṛti* of death, for example, which not only urges practitioners to consider the deaths of figures who died eons ago (as well as the deaths of those known to them) but also advises them to bear in mind their own inescapable demise as well.[56] The general interchangeability of *smṛti* and *anusmṛti* (as in the *Dhammapada* passage cited above) also suggests that we are dealing with a "calling to mind" rather than recollection in the strict sense, which, as far as *buddhānusmṛti* is concerned, would clearly have been impossible within a generation of Gautama's death.

There is, however, one type of "remembering" which seems to come very close to *buddhānusmṛti,* and that is commemoration; for in acts of commemoration we frequently "remember," call to mind or focus our attention on people whom we cannot personally recollect, or on events we did not ourselves experience. In New Zealand, for example, on April 25 every year we observe Anzac Day in commemoration of a suicidal landing by a joint force of Australian and New Zealand troops on the beaches of Gallipoli in 1915 during World War I. This military disaster, which is supposed to have helped form our national identity, is publicly remembered in dawn parades, church services, and wreath-laying rituals throughout the country, even though, some seventy-five years on, there remains only a handful of survivors who can still recall the event. Nevertheless, all participants, young and old, recite the solemn words of the service together: "They shall not grow old as we who are left grow old. Age shall not weary them, nor the years condemn. At the going down of the sun, and in the morning, we shall remember them." In Edward Casey's classic study of memory this kind of commemoration is characterized as a form of remembering which is intensified by the use of text and ritual, does not involve any personal recollection of the object, and has necessarily a social or communal aspect: "nothing effected by oneself alone is adequate to the task of commemoration. . . . commemorating is an essentially *inter*personal action . . . undertaken not only in relation *to* others and *for* them but also *with* them in a common action of communalizing."[57]

How then does *buddhānusmṛti* square with this characterization? While the indispensability of language or "text" in the broad sense to any act of commemoration seems especially relevant, as *buddhānusmṛti* in all its varied forms relies on some kind of "script," at first sight it lacks the social or communal aspect that Casey deems essential, being performed as a rule in the context of solitary meditation. However, particularly in its later forms, it has striking affinities with what Casey sees as a possible form of commemoration that is noncommunal and not mediated by text, something he labels "intrapsychic memorialization," a process of identification involving psychical incorporation of another person.[58] For our purposes the most important aspect of intrapsychic memorialization is precisely this refashioning of identity by means of identification with the other. As Casey puts it, "to identify with someone in Freud's rich sense of the term is to merge not only with that person's mental or psychic being. It is also to assimilate his or her corporeality in its full emotional resonance."[59] These words seem especially relevant to a deeper understanding of the psychotropic or transformative function of the Buddhist practice under review and of the course of its later development. Yet, although an absent other is indeed interiorized in *buddhānusmṛti,* the process is definitely mediated by text (the ten epithets, various visualization prescriptions, etc.) and ritual (the ritual of meditation or recitation); it is repetitive and conscious.[60] Thus *buddhānusmṛti* appears to lie halfway between Casey's "overt ritualistic commemoration" and "intrapsychic memorialization" and to contain elements of both.

However, the communal element is definitely present, for although *buddhānusmṛti* was normally to be performed alone, the ritual and text connected with it were the shared property of the community that transmitted them, and their performance, even in solitude, marked one off as a participant in that community.[61] Is this not the property of all creeds, that, even when recited in private, they are essentially instruments of communion and co-participation; that is to say, they affirm one's identity as a member of a particular religious group? Indeed this, it seems to me, is the principal function of all acts of commemoration, such as the Anzac Day observance referred to earlier. Even after all the veterans have passed on, the ''memory'' of Gallipoli will remain in the minds of New Zealanders, placed there not by personal experience of the event itself, but through the mediation of text in the broad sense (the services and rituals, the monuments and inscriptions in stone, the newspaper articles and television programs).[62] Further, the significance of that memory lies precisely in the fact that it is communal: it evokes (or is intended to evoke) a sense of communal identity, involving—among other things—mourning, gratitude, and responsibility. We cannot recollect the fallen, but in remembering them in this way we make them part of our past all the same, and thus see ourselves in a new light. In this sense ''overt ritualistic commemoration'' and ''intrapsychic memorialization'' share the same function of re-creating identity. This is crucial to our understanding of what we may now call *commemoration of the Buddha.*

In his concluding remarks on darśana in Hinduism, Babb observes that:

> it may be that darshan finally and essentially is a way of utilizing the internal deposit of social experience as a way of changing and confirming certain special kinds of self-identity. In treating an ''image'' of a deity or guru as a superior being to be ''taken from,'' the devotee may be simply realizing possibilities for self-transformation that are, whatever their origins in social experience, already internalized as part of his personality structure; creating for himself, and from himself, a frame of reference that is superior to—and for the moment perhaps ''realer than'' (Geertz 1966)—all normal frames of reference. The deity would then be a point of focus for an internalized version of Mead's ''generalized other,'' and darshan would be a powerful mirror with the potential to transform the viewer.

We have seen that from the outset the purpose of *buddhānusmṛti* and its derivatives has been personal transformation, however differently that transformation has been conceived—as purification of consciousness, understanding of emptiness, elimination of terror, awakening in this very life. This transformation rests ultimately on the close relationship between memory and identity.[63] In the act of commemoration, in the uttering of the memorized text, the practitioners of *buddhānusmṛti* establish a communal identity that links them to other members of the Buddhist faith. But at the same time they call forth a relationship between two persons, themselves and the Buddha, capable of being profoundly catalytic, to the extent that distinctions of self and other dissolve in its luminosity and a new identity comes into existence, purified, omniscient, fearless, and awakened.

Notes

A = *Aṅguttara Nikāya* (Pāli Text Society Edition).

S = *Saṃyutta Nikāya* (Pāli Text Society Edition).

Skt. = Sanskrit.

SP = P. Vaidya, ed., *Saddharmapuṇḍarīkasūtra*. Darbhanga: Mithila Institute, 1960.

T. = Takakusu Junjirō and Watanabe Kaikyoku, eds., *Taishō shinshū daizōkyō*, 100 vols., Tokyo: 1924–34.

1. The word *sketch* is used advisedly. Many of the issues raised in this chapter deserve a far more detailed treatment than I have been able to give them.

2. Conze, *Buddhist Meditation*, p. 28; see also pp. 14–15 and 45–52.

3. King, *Theravāda Meditation*, p. 33; see also p. 38.

4. Vetter, *The Ideas and Meditative Practices of Early Buddhism*.

5. I employ the term *Mainstream Buddhism* to avoid using the more customary *Hīnayāna*, which has pejorative connotations.

6. Translated by Pe Maung Tin as *The Path of Purity*.

7. See Ehara, Soma Thera, and Kheminda Thera, trans., *The Path of Freedom*. Although the *Vimuttimagga* survives only in Chinese translation, for the sake of convenience we may still refer to it as one of the Pāli sources.

8. See Lamotte, *Traité*, vol. 3, pp. 1329ff, for detailed references.

9. See, e.g., Pe Maung Tin, *Path of Purity*, p. 261.

10. For a detailed exposition of the ten *adhivacana*, see Lamotte, *Traité*, vol. 1, pp. 126–44 and vol. 3, pp. 1340–42.

11. Cf. the article on creeds in Eliade, ed., *Encyclopedia of Religion*.

12. See Pe Maung Tin, *Path of Purity*, p. 245; Conze, *Buddhist Meditation*, pp. 48–49.

13. Although Ehara *et al.*, *Path of Freedom*, p. xlv, assert that the *Vimuttimagga* holds a different opinion on this, their claim is not clearly substantiated by the text

(ibid., p. 148) nor by the *Mahānāmasutta* quoted in note 3. According to the *Visuddhimagga*, only two of the ten *anussati* (those on respiration and the body) produce anything more than access concentration.

14. Translation from Conze, *Buddhist Meditation*, pp. 48–49.

15. Such hyperbole—the ascription of a host of desirable effects to something originally intended to produce only one—is a standard feature of Buddhist literature of all schools, and should not strike us as at all strange, familiar as we are with toothpastes that not only clean one's teeth but also render one irresistibly attractive to members of the opposite sex, or soft drinks the thirst-quenching properties of which are complemented by their ability to produce states of intense euphoria and manic hyperactivity. But it raises a serious question: could this propensity for hyperbole itself have been responsible for a progressive extension of the range of these exercises?

16. These are the *Mahānāma Sutta* (A iii 284), the *Gedha Sutta* (A iii 312), the *Sambādhokāsa Sutta* (A iii 314), the *Uposatha Sutta* (A i 206), and the *Ekādasanipāta* (A v 329, 333).

17. Pe Maung Tin, *Path of Purity*, pp. 261–63.

18. Burlingame, *Buddhist Legends*, vol. 2, pp. 169–76.

19. Ibid., p. 174.

20. Ibid., vol. 3, pp. 179–81.

21. The list of six in the *Dhammapada* is not standard: mindfulness (here *sati* instead of *anussati*, presumably *metri causa*) directed toward Buddha, Dhamma, Sangha, and the body, and a mind that delights in harmlessness (*ahiṃsā*) and self-cultivation (*bhāvanā*). See Carter and Palihawardana, *Dhammapada*, pp. 325–27.

22. Cf. the brief but perceptive remarks about the confessional, purificatory, and apotropaic functions of creeds in van der Leeuw, *Religion in Essence and Manifestation*, pp. 441–43. I am indebted to my colleague Colin Brown for this reference and others to the Christian tradition.

23. See, e.g., Spiro, *Buddhism and Society*, pp. 212 and 263–64. For an illuminating extended discussion of this aspect of contemporary Buddhism, consult in particular Tambiah, *Buddhism and Spirit Cults*, pp. 195–222. Here the Christian parallels are especially striking; in discussing the situation in medieval England, for example, K. Thomas writes: "The Church itself recommended the use of prayers when healing the sick or gathering medicinal herbs. Confessors required penitents to repeat a stated number of Paternosters, Aves and Creeds, thereby fostering the notion that the recitation of prayers in a foreign tongue had a mechanical efficacy. . . . The medieval Church thus did a great deal to weaken the fundamental distinction between a prayer and a charm, and to encourage the idea that there was virtue in the mere repetition of holy words. . . . This had not been the teaching of the medieval Church, for prayers, though necessary, were not intended to be effective without medical treatment. But the clergy had claimed that the recitation of prayers could afford protection

against vermin or fiends; and without the Church's encouragement of the formal repetition of set forms of prayer the magical faith in the healing power of Aves and Paternosters could never have arisen'' (*Religion and the Decline of Magic*, pp. 46–48).

24. Ehara *et al.*, *Path of Freedom*, pp. 140–48.

25. Ibid., p. 141.

26. Pe Maung Tin, *Path of Purity*, pp. 269–70.

27. See Harrison, ''*Buddhānusmṛti*,'' pp. 36–38.

28. See ibid., pp. 37–38, for the full text.

29. See, e.g., Jones, *Mahāvastu*, vol. 3, p. 426.

30. For a preliminary discussion of the content of this sūtra, see Harrison, ''*Buddhānusmṛti*.'' An ''edition'' of the Tibetan text has been published (Harrison, *Tibetan Text*), my English translation of the earliest Chinese version is in print (for the *English Translation of the Chinese Tripitaka*, being prepared under the auspices of the Bukkyō Dendō Kyōkai), and my English translation and study of the Tibetan version has recently appeared as *The* Samādhi *of Direct Encounter with the Buddhas of the Present*. All translations from the *PraS* are taken from the latter work.

31. Reference to the *PraS* is to the chapter and paragraph divisions of the Tibetan text.

32. Harrison, *Direct Encounter*, pp. 37–38.

33. For a list of these ''marks'' and a review of the literature on them, see Lamotte, *Traité*, vol 1, pp. 271–81. See also Thomas, *Life of the Buddha*, pp. 220–23. The thirty-two marks were at some point supplemented by the eighty minor characteristics (*anuvyañjana*), which in a sense form a commentary on them (see Lamotte, *Traité*, vol 1, p. 271, n. 2; vol 3, p. 1346, n. 1).

34. ''Invisible crown of the head,'' Skt. *anavalokitamūrdhatā*, refers to the fact that one cannot look down upon the top of a buddha's head. This is one of the eighty minor characteristics. However, with regard to what the practitioner is actually supposed to do at this point, the text is not entirely clear. What exactly is intended by Tib. *yongs su zhu ba* (usually Skt. *pari-$\sqrt{}$prach*, ''to question''), which I have translated here as ''check''? Is one supposed to review mentally the eighty *anuvyañjana*, starting with the *anavalokitamūrdhatā*, which is the first of them according to some sources? The Chinese translations of the *PraS* are no clearer, but a process of mental review seems to be intended. In this regard one might note the detailed instructions given by the Chinese monk Zhiyi (538–597) for the *pratyutpanna-samādhi*, which appear to reflect this section. The critical passage (as summarized in Stevenson, ''Four Kinds of Samādhi,'' p. 59) is: ''The meditative discernment itself centers around the visualization of the thirty-two major marks and eighty minor excellent qualities of the Buddha Amitābha. This practice is performed repeatedly, 'in reverse order from the thousand-spoked wheels on the soles of his feet to the indiscernible *uṣṇīṣa* on the crown of his head, and then in the normal order from the crown of the head back to

the thousand-spoked wheel.' " Zhiyi cannot have got this level of detail from the Chinese translations of the *PraS*, so he must have derived it from some other source.

35. Section 8A; see Harrison, *Direct Encounter*, pp. 68–69.

36. The increasing importance of *buddhānusmṛti* in Mahāyāna circles in North India was already noted by Demiéville, "*Yogācārabhūmi*," pp. 354–63.

37. Beyer, "Notes on the Vision Quest," p. 337.

38. See Rawlinson, "Visions and Symbols."

39. See Eck, *Darśan*.

40. "Glancing: Visual Interaction in Hinduism." I thank my colleague Bo Sax for bringing this article to my attention.

41. Ibid., pp. 396–97.

42. It enables us, for example, to make sense for the first time of the numerous passages in the *PraS* and other Mahāyāna sūtras that promise practitioners that they will be seen *by* the buddhas, bodhisattvas and other exalted beings; see, e.g., *PraS*, Section 14H.

43. See especially the so-called Pure Land texts, such as the *Sukhāvatī-vyūha* and the *Amitāyur-dhyāna-sūtra*, translations of which may be found in Max Müller, *Buddhist Mahāyāna Texts*. Pas's article "*Kuan-wu-liang-shou Fo-ching*" provides a helpful general discussion of some representatives of the genre. See also the section on *buddhānusmṛti* in the *Śikṣā-samuccaya* (Bendall and Rouse, trans., pp. 285–88), where Śāntideva quotes a hymn of praise to the Buddha from the *Rāṣṭrapāla-paripṛcchā*, which can be seen in part as a poetic restatement of the liturgy accompanying the developed Mahāyāna practice.

44. Gregory, ed., *Traditions of Meditation*.

45. In this context *nāma[dheya]dhāraṇa* seems to refer to the uttering of the name, not merely the "holding" or remembering of it in the mind, because it can be performed just once as a single act (see *SP*, p. 251.23–24), and appears to be interchangeable with *nāma[dheya]grahaṇa* ("uttering the name") and *namaskāra*. Clearly it would not be enough simply to remember the name in the sense of storing it away in the mind: one has to perform an operation with it, in the other sense of the English word *remember;* i.e., to retrieve it by "uttering" it. Whether this uttering is mental or oral is not clear.

46. *SP*, p. 250, 1.31.

47. Relevant here are the supposed benefits of the cultivation of loving kindness (Skt. *maitrī*, Pāli *mettā*), which protects one against snakes, beasts of prey, etc. by imbuing them with the same feeling; see, e.g., Tambiah, *Buddhist Saints of the Forest*, pp. 86–90. The idea that animals sense fear or its absence and respond accordingly is of course widespread.

48. One might compare Chapter 24 of the *SP* with the extract from the commonplace book of Robert Reynys, a fifteenth-century church reeve in Norfolk, England, quoted in K. Thomas, *Religion and the Decline of Magic*, p. 48: "Pope Innocent hath granted to any man that beareth the length of the three nails of Our Lord Jesus Christ upon him and worship them daily with five Paternosters and five Aves and a psalter, he shall have seven gifts granted to him. The first, he shall not be slain with sword or knife. The second, he shall not die no sudden death. The third, his enemies shall not overcome him. The fourth, he shall have sufficient good and honest living. The fifth, that poisons nor fever nor false witness shall grieve him. The sixth, he shall not die without the sacraments of the Church. The seventh, he shall be defended from all wicked spirits, from pestilence and all evil things."

49. See, e.g., Bstan-'dzin rgya-mtsho, *Deity Yoga*; Lessing and Wayman, *Introduction to Buddhist Tantric Systems*, esp. pp. 159–87; and the comments by Snellgrove in *Indo-Tibetan Buddhism*, pp. 130–31, 235–43.

50. In fact the literal sense of *saṃmukhāvasthita* in the title of that text, which I have translated rather loosely as "direct encounter," is "standing face-to-face," or "standing in front."

51. See Harrison, *Direct Encounter*, p. 69.

52. *PraS*, Chapter 3, Section 3L and 3O, verse 1; see Harrison, *Direct Encounter*, pp. 42–44. This verse appears as prose in the first Chinese translation of the sūtra (179 CE). The same idea is expressed in the *Amitāyurdhyānasūtra;* see F. Max Müller, *Buddhist Mahāyāna Texts*, p. 178.

53. A full treatment of tantric deity yoga and its evolution from Mahāyāna visualization techniques lies beyond the scope of this chapter, in which I can do little more than suggest a few connections and continuities.

54. This is similar to the invocation of Avalokiteśvara propounded in Chapter 24 of the *SP*, for whom a detailed visualization practice was also taught.

55. See, e.g., the entry on "Nien-fo" by Fujiwara in Eliade, ed., *Encyclopedia of Religion*.

56. See Ehara *et al.*, *Path of Freedom*, p. 67: "And again, one subject of meditation is of the future, namely, recollection of death." Cf. also Lamotte, *Traité*, vol. 3, p. 1422.

57. Casey, *Remembering: A Phenomenological Study*, p. 225. Casey takes the equivalent observance in the United States, Memorial Day, as the basis for many of his remarks on commemoration.

58. Ibid., pp. 239ff.

59. Ibid., p. 246.

60. Cf. ibid., pp. 239 and 250.

61. As we have seen, *buddhānusmṛti* did assume in its later developments more of the nature of a public ritual, as for example in the group recitation of the *nembutsu* (or its derivative, the *daimoku*) by Japanese Buddhists or the liturgical use of the "virtues" in Theravādin worship.

62. In fact, if there is any "recollective consciousness," to use Casey's term, it is of these forms of text and their affective associations.

63. Cf. in particular Casey's comments in *Remembering*, pp. 243–45.

Bibliography

Babb, Lawrence A. 1981. "Glancing: Visual Interaction in Hinduism." *Journal of Anthropological Research* 37: 387–401.

Bendall, Cecil, and W. H. D. Rouse, trans. 1971. *Śikshā-samuccaya: A Compendium of Buddhist Doctrine*, reprint ed. Delhi: Motilal Banarsidass.

Beyer, Stephan. 1977. "Notes on the Vision Quest in Early Mahāyāna." In Lewis Lancaster, ed., *Prajñāpāramitā and Related Systems: Studies in Honor of Edward Conze*, pp. 329–40. Berkeley, Calif.: Berkeley Buddhist Studies Series.

Bstan-'dzin-rgya-mtsho (H. H. the XIVth Dalai Lama). 1987. *Deity Yoga in Action and Performance Tantra*, trans. and ed. Jeffrey Hopkins, reprint ed. Ithaca, N.Y.: Snow Lion.

Burlingame, E. W., trans. 1921. *Buddhist Legends*, 3 vols. Cambridge, Mass: Harvard University Press; reprint ed., Luzac & Co.: London, 1969.

Carter, John Ross, and Mahinda Palihawadana. 1987. *The Dhammapada*. New York: Oxford University Press.

Casey, Edward S. 1987. *Remembering: A Phenomenological Study*. Bloomington: Indiana University Press.

Conze, Edward. 1956. *Buddhist Meditation*. London: Allen & Unwin.

Demiéville, Paul. 1954. "The *Yogācārabhūmi* of Saṅgharakṣa." *Bulletin de l'École française d'Extrême-Orient* 44, no. 2: 339–436.

Eck, Diana. 1985. *Darśan: Seeing the Divine Image in India*, 2d ed. Chambersburg, Pa.: Anima Books.

Ehara, N. R. M., Soma Thera, and Kheminda Thera. 1961. *The Path of Freedom*. Colombo: Roland D. Weerasuria.

Eliade, Mircea, ed. 1987. *The Encyclopedia of Religion*, 16 vols. New York: Macmillan.

Gregory, Peter N., ed. 1986. *Traditions of Meditation in Chinese Buddhism*. Honolulu: University of Hawaii Press.

Harrison, Paul. 1978a. "*Buddhānusmṛti* in the *Pratyutpanna-buddha-saṃmukhāvasthita-samādhi-sūtra.*" *Journal of Indian Philosophy* 6: 35–57.

———. 1978b. *The Tibetan Text of the Pratyutpanna-Buddha-Saṃmukhāvasthita-Samādhi-Sūtra,* Studia Philologica Buddhica, Monograph Series I. Tokyo: Reiyukai Library.

———. 1990. *The* Samādhi *of Direct Encounter with the Buddhas of the Present.* Studia Philologica Buddhica, Monograph Series V. Tokyo: International Institute for Buddhist Studies.

Jones, J. J. 1949, 1952, 1956. *The Mahāvastu,* 3 vols. London: Pali Text Society.

King, Winston L. 1980. *Theravāda Meditation: The Buddhist Transformation of Yoga.* University Park: Pennsylvania State University Press.

Lamotte, E. 1949. *Le traité de la grande vertu de sagesse de Nāgārjuna (Mahāprajñāpāramitāśāstra),* Vol. 1. Louvain: Université de Louvain; reprinted 1966.

———. 1970. *Le traité de la grande vertu de sagesse de Nāgārjuna (Mahāprajñāpāramitāśāstra),* Vol. 3. Louvain: Université de Louvain.

Lessing, F. D., and Alex Wayman. 1980. *Introduction to the Buddhist Tantric Systems,* 2d ed. Delhi: Motilal Banarsidass.

Max Müller, F., ed. 1894. *Buddhist Mahāyāna Texts.* Sacred Books of the East, 49. Oxford: Oxford University Press; reprint ed., Delhi: Motilal Banarsidass, 1965, 1968, 1972.

Pas, Julian F. 1977. "The *Kuan-wu-liang-shou Fo-ching:* Its Origin and Literary Criticism." in Leslie Kawamura and K. Scott, eds., *Buddhist Thought and Asian Civilization: Essays in Honor of Herbert V. Guenther on His Sixtieth Birthday,* pp. 194–218. Emeryville: Dharma Publishing.

Pe Maung Tin. 1971. *The Path of Purity,* 3 vols. in 1, reprint ed. London: Routledge & Kegan Paul.

Rawlinson, Andrew. 1986. "Visions and Symbols in the Mahāyāna." In Peter Connolly, ed., *Perspectives on Indian Religion: Papers in Honour of Karel Werner,* pp. 191–214. Delhi: Sri Satguru Publications.

Snellgrove, David. 1987. *Indo-Tibetan Buddhism: Indian Buddhists and Their Tibetan Successors,* London: Serindia.

Spiro, Melford E. 1970. *Buddhism and Society: A Great Tradition and its Burmese Vicissitudes.* Berkeley: University of California Press.

Stevenson, Daniel B. 1986. "The Four Kinds of Samādhi in Early T'ien-t'ai Buddhism." In Peter N. Gregory, ed., *Traditions of Meditation in Chinese Buddhism,* pp. 45–97. Honolulu: University of Hawaii Press.

Tambiah, S. J. 1970. *Buddhism and the Spirit Cults in North-east Thailand.* Cambridge: Cambridge University Press.

———. 1984. *The Buddhist Saints of the Forest and the Cult of Amulets.* Cambridge: Cambridge University Press.

Thomas, Edward J. 1949. *The Life of the Buddha as Legend and History,* 3d ed. London: Routledge & Kegan Paul.

Thomas, K. 1973. *Religion and the Decline of Magic: Studies in Popular Beliefs in Sixteenth- and Seventeenth-Century England.* Harmondsworth: Penguin Books.

van der Leeuw, G. 1963. *Religion in Essence and Manifestation,* 2 vols., trans. J. E. Turner. New York and Evanston: Harper Torchbooks; 1st English ed., London: Allen & Unwin: 1938.

Vetter, Tilmann. 1988. *The Ideas and Meditative Practices of Early Buddhism.* Leiden: E. J. Brill.

The Amnesic Monarch and the Five Mnemic Men: "Memory" in Great Perfection (Rdzogs-chen) Thought

MATTHEW KAPSTEIN

Preliminary Orientations

In the literature of the Great Perfection (Rdzog-chen) traditions of the Rnying-ma-pa school of Tibetan Buddhism, the words *dran-pa,* "memory" (= Skt. *smṛti, smaraṇa*), and *dran-med,* "freedom from/loss of memory, unconsciousness, inattentiveness" (= Skt. *vismṛti, asmṛti*) are encountered very frequently, among other terms formed on the lexeme *dran-,* "to remember." Though no systematic exegesis of the use of these terms within the tradition itself has yet come to my attention, it appears nonetheless possible to attempt a tentative account of the role of certain basic terms relating to memory in a few distinctive contexts.[1]

Something must be said at the outset about the way in which "distinctive context" is to be understood here. The literature of the Great Perfection developed in some respects in a fluid relationship with other branches of Tibetan religion and culture:[2] on the one hand, for instance, we find the colloquializing tendencies of Tibetan biographical and popular literature informing the diction of those writing on the Great Perfection; whereas on the other hand, normative uses of Indian Buddhist scholastic materials are also well represented. Thus such monumental products of doctrinal speculation and systematization as the *Wish-Fulfilling Treasury* (*Yid-bzhin mdzod*) or the *Great Chariot* (*Shing-rta chen-mo*) of Klong-chen Rab-'byams-pa (1308–1363) involve the deliberate effort to disclose the Great Perfection as fully harmonized with, in fact the culmination of, the Indian Buddhist inheritance of theory and practice.[3] To survey the occurrences of *dran-* derivatives in such works would require the repetition of a great amount of material gleaned from Indian Abhidharma and Yogācāra sources, which in any event are examined elsewhere in this volume.

Nonetheless, the superabundance of texts of the Great Perfection traditions that have become available during the past two decades do reveal a unique system, in which a substantial portion of the technical terminology is not shared by other Buddhist schools; for example, *rtsal,* "expressive power"; *ka-dag,* "primordial purity"; *cog-bzhag,* "total presence." And many terms common elsewhere are also found in Great Perfection writings used in special senses or with peculiar connotations; for example, *rig-pa*, ''awareness''; *rol-pa* ''(dis)play''; or *thugs-rje* ''compassion/spirituality.''[4] The question we should ask about *dran-* derivatives then is: in those texts not especially concerned with harmonizing the Great Perfection with scholastic norms, but instead present it as a distinctive way of thought and practice, do we find evidence to suggest that these terms were regularly used in a peculiar manner, that possibly extends beyond the parameters of normal Tibetan colloquial and Buddhist technical usage?

It is clear that this question must be answered affirmatively, though the volume of extant Great Perfection texts precludes a thorough survey of the relevant material at the present time. My discussion therefore will concern selected themes in just one well-defined group of texts, whose authority within the tradition provides some assurance that the conclusions reached will characterize the perspective of the Great Perfection traditions more broadly than such a narrow sampling might otherwise suggest.

The texts chosen for consideration here are all drawn from the rediscovered ''treasures'' (*gter-ma*) of Rig-'dzin Rgod-kyi ldem-phru-can (1337–1408), founder of the important Rnying-ma-pa suborder of the ''Northern Treasure'' (*byang-gter*), so called because the original site of these treasures' revelation was Zang-zang lha-brag, a sacred mountain in the wilds of Tibet's Northern Plain (*byang-thang*).[5] Among the many treasures forming the corpus of Rig-'dzin Rgod-ldem's rediscoveries, the Great Perfection is treated expansively in the two closely related cycles of the *Penetration of the Intention of Samantabhadra* (*Kun-tu bzang-po'i dgongs-pa zang-thal*) and *Primordial Purity, Self-Emergent and Self-Arisen* (*Ka-dag rang-byung rang-shar*), which in fact are often transmitted as a single corpus.[6] They are marked by an unusual clarity and precision of diction, in which it may be possible to detect some affinity with the Great Perfection writings of Klong-chen Rab-'byams-pa. And, what makes them most suitable for present purposes, *dran-* derivatives seem to receive a remarkable degree of emphasis throughout.

In the discussion that follows, I shall set forth a preliminary analysis of the use of words generated from the lexeme *dran-* as they occur in a single text of the *Primordial Purity, Self-Emergent and Self-Arisen* collection, the *Intention of Buddha Vajrasattva, the Wide-Open Tantra of Universal Liberation* (*Sangs-rgyas rdo-rje sems-dpa'i dgongs-pa: kun-grol yangs-pa'i rgyud*).[7] To bracket out irrelevant connotations stemming from the use of the English words *memory, recollection, forgetting,* and so forth, I shall use derivatives of the Greek root *mnā-* ''to remember, be mindful'' (= Skt. *smṛ*) for all Tibetan terms formed on *dran-*. Thus, for *dran-pa* I shall use the phrase ''mnemic engagement''; for *dran-med,* ''amnesis''; for *dran-rig,* ''mnemic awareness'' (i.e., acts of awareness involving mnemic engagement); and for *dran-pa'i mi*, "mnemic man" (the sense of this allegorical phrase will become clear later). Where *dran-* is best treated as a verb it will be necessary unfortunately to employ some wordy constructions, like "to practice mnemic engagement," but this still seems preferable to the introduction here of English verbs the connotations of which might sometimes be even more misleading. *Memory* and *remembering* seem to be for us terms preeminently referring to the representation of the past, so that our preunderstanding as determined by them may sometimes obscure the significance of *dran-* in the present discussion.[8]

Whereas the preliminary analysis of the concept of mnemic engagement in Great Perfection thought will have a markedly phenomenological coloring to it, it would be an error to suggest, as some recent writers perhaps have done, that the tradition of thought and practice considered here is to be distinguished as a sort of phenomenology par excellence. This is plainly incorrect. Indeed, it will be precisely to avoid this misapprehension that we shall turn, in the latter sections of this chapter, to study the doctrines considered here as they are employed within the cycle of the *Penetration of the Intention of Samantabhadra* in allegory and in the practice of prayer. The issue of paramount concern for the Great Perfection thinker is salvific praxis, praxis that must open up a passageway mediating between "ordinary" experience and the rich domain of symbolic forms, and between the latter and that primordial reality which stands in the final analysis beyond temporality and symbolic mediation. Our discussion, accordingly, will seek broadly to introduce the theme of mnemic engagement as it pertains to each of these three worlds, proceeding from its function in "introducing" the timeless realm of the dharmakāya, to its symbolic representation in allegory, to its role in the transfiguration of the ordinary through the ritual practice of prayer.[9]

Mnemic Engagement in the *Wide-Open Tantra of Universal Liberation*

The *Wide-Open Tantra of Universal Liberation* does not use all of the terms just listed. To comprehend more clearly the contextual background for the occurrences of *dran-* we do find there, it will be useful to have come conception of the text overall, as this will supply a brief Baedeker to the particular system of the Great Perfection involved here. A short work, its nine chapters treat, first of all, the nature of the primordial ground, and the manner in which the original Buddha Samantabhadra and bewildered sentient beings have both arisen from it.[10] The second chapter concerns the characteristics of bewilderment, which obstructs the potential to encounter and realize the teachings whereby the freedom of buddhahood may be achieved. This is followed by "The Introduction to Awareness as the Dharmakāya." "Introduction" (*ngo-sprod/-sprad*), as used in this third chapter in its technical sense, refers to instruction that, if skillfully delivered to an appropriately receptive disciple by an appropriately qualified master-,catalyzes an immediate intuitive grasp of the instruction's content. This need not be so mysterious as it may seem: when a tennis pro points out what's wrong with your serve with the result that there is a flash of recognition, you exclaim, "got it!" and then deliver one that screams past Martina, you have just become the fortunate recipient of an "introduction." But here we are concerned not with the contact of racket and ball, rather with the primordial relationship between the essential nature of mind and the ground of its origination. It is this third chapter that first uses *dran-*, though elsewhere Rgod-ldem does use it in connection with subject matter similar to that of the earlier chapters of this particular text; for example in the *Prayer of Great Power* (translated in the appendix).

The fourth and fifth chapters, respectively, survey false assumptions about the nature of apparent reality and the manner in which these generate continued bewilderment, and the essential elements of practical instruction on meditation that accords with the teachings given in the preceding chapters. For the purposes of the present discussion, it is the sixth chapter that is perhaps the most important: "On Circumstantial Proximity to the Dharmakāya." This describes the recovery of the realization of the dharmakāya under the varied circumstances to which ordinary experience subjects us, such as birth and death, waking consciousness, sleep and dream.

The two following chapters conclude the actual teaching of the *Wide-Open Tantra of Universal Liberation* by providing practical details regarding the appropriate times at which the various meditational practices of the Great Perfection are to be undertaken, and the means by which buddhahood may be realized during the intermediate state following death. Because this is a "rediscovered treasure" (*gter-ma*), the ninth and final chapter presents a discourse on the concealment of the text, with prophecies of its recovery.[11]

In its small span of ten folios, then, the *Wide-Open Tantra of Universal Liberation* provides a remarkably thorough account of the central features of Great Perfection cosmology, phenomenology, and soteriology, describing the most essential elements of both theory and practice. The fact that a given term does not occur in a particular context, of course, should not be taken as evidence that the term does not so occur elsewhere. But the very brevity of the text permits, at least, the isolation of a relatively small range of characteristic occurrences of the technical terms found therein. The instances of *dran-* occurring in the *Wide-Open Tantra of Universal Liberation* are given here in full, beneath the headings of the chapters in which they are found and in the order of their occurrence.

Chapter Three: The Introduction of Awareness as the Dharmakāya

137.5 "One ought to attend to the example and its significance, with unwavering mnemic engagement."[12] This occurs in the beginning of the chapter and is offered as an injunction preceding the "introduction" itself. "Mnemic engagement" in this instance means roughly, "mindful attentiveness"; that is, to the content of the teachings about to be conferred.

138.3 "Concerning this mind that is bewildered at present, from the time of one's birth until now, mnemic engagement [reflecting] whatever one's done [has been and] is [karmic] residue."[13] The topic under discussion is the bewilderment arising from the universal ground in its conditional aspect (*sbyor-ba rkyen-gyi kun-gzhi*). Here "mnemic engagement" is a determination of the "bewildered mind," referring to *my* continuously renewed construction of *my* past and to the particular acts of consciousness that inform that construction. It is not uncommon, in similar contexts, to see it closely related to *bag-chags* (Skt. *vāsanā*), residual dispositions generated by previous action, *karman*.

138.6–139.1 "Just *that* is the self-presenting awareness that is the dharmakāya. By continuous mnemic engagement in it, one well investigates and establishes it."[14] This passage concludes the "introduction" given in Chapter Three. Reference to "mnemic engagement" here involves a double entendre. On the one hand, the "it" (*de*) that in the second sentence indicates the object of the act in question may refer to the propositional content of teaching just given (that "thus-and-such is the self-presenting awareness that is the dharmakāya"). In this case, "mnemic engagement" must mean roughly "mindful attentiveness" that is directed on that teaching. On the other hand, the object must also be understood to *be* the "self-presenting awareness that is the dharmakāya," so that "mnemic engagement" must also refer to the reflexive disclosure of that awareness to the meditator who has grasped the point of the teaching; that is, who has genuinely realized the "introduction." "Investigation" in this case cannot be the discursive analysis of ideas or their contents. Rather, it is the self-disclosure of the meditator's awareness qua dharmakāya. The double entendre here is, I think deliberate, precisely marking the passage from a preliminary intentional relationship between the disciple's thought and the content of the "introduction" she has been granted, to the disciple's nonintentional, reflexive recovery of the self-presenting awareness that is the dharmakāya. This act of recovery is in a sense the objective of a secondary intention; for it is the intention of the teaching whose content is the intention of initial reflection. In the terminology of normative scholastic Buddhism, this passage would be analogous to the movement from "discernment born of thought" (*cintāmayī prajñā*) to "discernment born of meditative cultivation" (*bhāvanāmayī prajñā*).[15]

Chapter Five: The Teaching of the Conduct of the Path

141.2–3. ''At that time, when one is in meditative equipoise, then, neither passing into amnesis, which follows after [discursive thoughts, imagining,etc.,] proceeding one after the next, nor passing, withdrawn, into sleep and oblivion, awareness is essentially self-clarifying.''[16] ''Amnesis'' is here the engagement in discursive thought that militates against those forms of ''mnemic engagement'' that favor or are constitutive of the realization of the goals of the path. A few lines later the latter conception is further elaborated.

141.3–4. ''The wide-open universal ground is dharmakāya-as-mother, and uncontrived awareness is dharmakāya-as-son. If the son's mnemic engagement is not lost, then, meeting with the mother, bliss is won.''[17] And later in the same chapter we are told the following.

142.6. ''When the five poisons [stupidity, passion, hate, envy, and pride] adventitiously arise, the least [of disciples] perceives the essence of beginning-and-end [i.e., determines the emptiness of the ''poisons'' in terms of their coming-into-being, abiding, and perishing], the middling [disciple] perceives the appearance of objects as apparition; and the best, through mnemic engagement, perceives self-presenting awareness.''[18] The continued use of the verb ''to look/gaze/perceive'' (*lta*) throughout this passage, which accords with the Tibetan stylistic love of verbal parallelism, should not obscure the nonintentional character of the practice attributed to the best disciple here, as contrasted with the two preceding (though it must also be noted that the Great Perfection traditions make abundant use of ocular imagery). To clarify somewhat the notion of non-intentional presentation, consider those instances in which we have a ''sense-memory'' or the memory of a mood, not in the propositional sense of remembering that we were once in the mood in question, but in the sense of *being* in a certain mood and re-cognizing it, as part of that experienced state of being. ''Memory,'' in such cases, is the palpable *recovery* of a state of being or affect, and thus in a peculiar sense is no more intentional in its phenomenological character than were the apparently recovered experiences when they originally occurred. It is a secondary act of awareness that determines that the act in question is a memory of a prior experience, and this secondary act is, of course, an intentional one. It is, however, an act of awareness that one is experiencing a type of memory and not the memory itself.

Chapter Six: On Circumstantial Proximity to the Dharmakāya

This chapter makes plentiful use of *dran-* and, most significantly, closes by making explicit a distinction of usage that has been presupposed throughout the preceding discussion. Rather than enumerate each occurrence in this chapter separately, it will be clearer to present them in two groups, abridging the text somewhat in the first instance.

144.3–6. "This arising of awareness as anything whatever, by dissolving into the dharmakāya itself, [results in] sleep's being a self-emergent im mobility. When dream-appearances arise, suffering fades away immediately following mnemic engagement. . . . Thus, the many bewildered appearances of dream are just mind's own light: manifesting shimmeringly, they dissolve into [that] itself. By mnemic engagement alone, [the dualistic modes of] apprehended object and apprehender are released. Therefore, swiftness of mnemic engagement is supreme."[19] The modes of mnemic engagement involved in the meditational discipline of the dream state appear to be essentially similar to those already considered: there may be a mindful attentiveness to the content of received teaching, leading to an immediate "fading away" of phenomenal suffering, or the non-intentional recovery of mind's ground, aroused by the recognition that the "bewildered appearances of dream are just mind's own light," and involving the "release" of subject and object.

145.1–4. "The trio of womb, sleep and the intermediate state, are envisioned as one in essence: this is repeatedly envisioned [through] mnemic engagement, in which the succession of discursive thought has not arisen. If one thinks that mnemic engagement becomes discursive thought [reading here *rtog* for *rtogs*], then [in response to that objection it may be affirmed that] discursive thought is that successive mnemic engagement that pursues external objects. The genuine mnemic engagement associated with the dharmakāya is not lost in succession and is free from obsessive attachment. It is self-emergent and is pristine cognition, the view of the equanimity of the dharmakāya, awareness that is self-clarifying pristine cognition."[20]

Chapter Seven: The Teaching of the Time of Realization

146.2. "Even if a bewildered mind does arise with respect to appearances, it is reined in immediately by mnemic engagement. The self-emergent body of essential reality (= Skt. *svābhāvikakāya*) being comprehended, realization is at hand when objects arise."[21] The reflexive mnemic engagement of mind in its ground is not to be construed as a sort of transic oblivion. Emergent objects are neither forgotten nor forsaken, but now are revalued as reminders, signaling mind's potential straying into bewilderment to mind itself, and thus continually arousing its capacity for genuine mnemic engagement.

Chapter Eight: The Attainment of Buddhahood during the Intermediate State

147.2–3. "As soon as you part from this physical body, then just as darkness is dispelled at dawn, you become mnemically engaged in the esoteric precepts of the three temporal phases of the intermediate state. Attaining stability in the appearance of pristine cognition, visionary clarity emerges in the self-presenting awareness that is dharmakāya."[22] *Dran-* here operates much as it had in passages 137.5 and 138.6–139.1, though the occasion is now the intermediate state (*bar-do*) intervening between death and rebirth, and not the state of ordinary waking consciousness.[23]

The foregoing survey provides, I believe, sufficient evidence to suggest that, in the doctrines of the Great Perfection as represented by Rig-'dzin Rgod-ldem, *dran-* derivatives are used in some clearly delineated senses, which will be found below to occur with remarkable consistency throughout the textual corpus under consideration, despite the genre differences of particular texts. In the absence of a formal treatise explicitly devoted to *dran-*, we therefore are entitled to maintain that the texts under consideration do present a relatively well-formed doctrine of "memory." The occurrences of *dran-* found here may be gathered into four primary categories, summarized below, enumerating the passages that I believe represent the uses in question. The first of these categories is quite general. Passages listed under more than one heading include either several distinctive occurrences of the terms under consideration, or, in a few instances involving uses B and C, seem reasonably subject to either interpretation.

A. Mnemic engagement (*dran-pa*) = mnemic acts (i.e., memory, recollection, recognition, etc.) that are determinations of the domain of mundane possibilities, or saṃsāra: 138.3, 145.1–4.

B. Mnemic engagement (*dran-pa*) = mindful attentiveness (directed to whatever contributes to advancement on the path): 137.5, 138.6–139.1, 141.3–4, 144.3–6, 145.1–4, 147.2–3.

C. Mnemic engagement (*dran-pa*) = immediate recovery of the self-presenting awareness of the dharmakāya: 138.6–139.1, 141.3–4, 142.6, 144.3–6, 145.1–4, 146.2.

D. Amnesis (*dran-med*) = negatively valued engagement in discursive thought, oblivion with respect to primordial awareness. [Let us note that *dran-med*, as the negation of B and, especially, C, refers to discursive engagement constituting the bewilderment of saṃsāra, so that in one sense D *dran-med* is equivalent to A *dran-pa*. As the *Prayer of Great Power* also makes clear, amnesis marks a drifting away from the original ground of awareness on the part of sentient beings): 141.2–3.

We may note too that in some contexts *dran-med* may be said, quite oppositely, to characterize the practice of the path, referring in this case, it seems, to contemplative "oblivion" marked by freedom from discursive thought (= A *dran-pa*). Rgod-ldem in fact uses *dran-med* in this fashion in several passages I have located, though not in the tantra considered here.[24] We shall refer to this as:

E. Amnesis (*dran-med*). (Because this is not much emphasized in the texts we are considering, it is bracketed in Figure 1.)

In further elaborating our account it seems essential that we address at once an important objection; for we have not yet shown that the various significations of the *dran-* derivatives found here do indeed have some common semantic or conceptual core. It may be objected that we are dealing not with a unified conception, but with the use of a single lexeme to refer to a number of genuinely distinct concepts that, for one reason or another, often are accidentally associated with one another. The association of both memory and mindfulness with the Sanskrit root *smṛ-* is often thought of as an instance of just such a phenomenon. I believe that, in this instance, the objection will not hold, that *dran-* in Great Perfection thought represents a univocal, but highly abstract concept, with reference to which the various *dran-* derivatives surveyed here may all be understood.

To see how this is so, let us consider the three fundamental significations of *dran-pa* just noted, and the two of *dran-med*, in their relationships to one another and to the categories of ground (*gzhi*), path (*lam*), and result (*'bras-bu*). We may further distinguish between two process categories, termed *cosmogonic* and *soteriological*. Cosmogonic process embraces, in classical Buddhist terms, the truths of suffering and its origin, whereas soteriological process pertains to the extinction of suffering, nirvāṇa, and the path whereby that is achieved. The interrelationships among the terms and categories with which we are concerned may be illustrated schematically as in Figure 1.

The arrow indicates a very weak relationship of conditionality: A→B means here that A is possibly a necessary condition for the occurrence or realization of B. Of course, in some cases a stronger relationship may also be affirmed: the primordial awareness of the ground is the condition sine qua non for all modes of awareness, for example; and A *dran-pa* is certainly a necessary condition for B *dran-pa*, which is to say only that there must be some mnemic intentions present for there to be any soteriologically valuable mnemic intentions. The weak relationship of possible necessary conditionality is useful in that it permits one to plot out a sequential ordering of the cosmogonic and soteriological processes—the ways of bewilderment and liberation (*sems-can 'khrul-lugs, sangs-rgyas grol-lugs*)—that well accords with what in fact is set forth in traditional expositions. This is first and foremost a matter of exegetical convenience, providing a generalized and idealized map of the path.

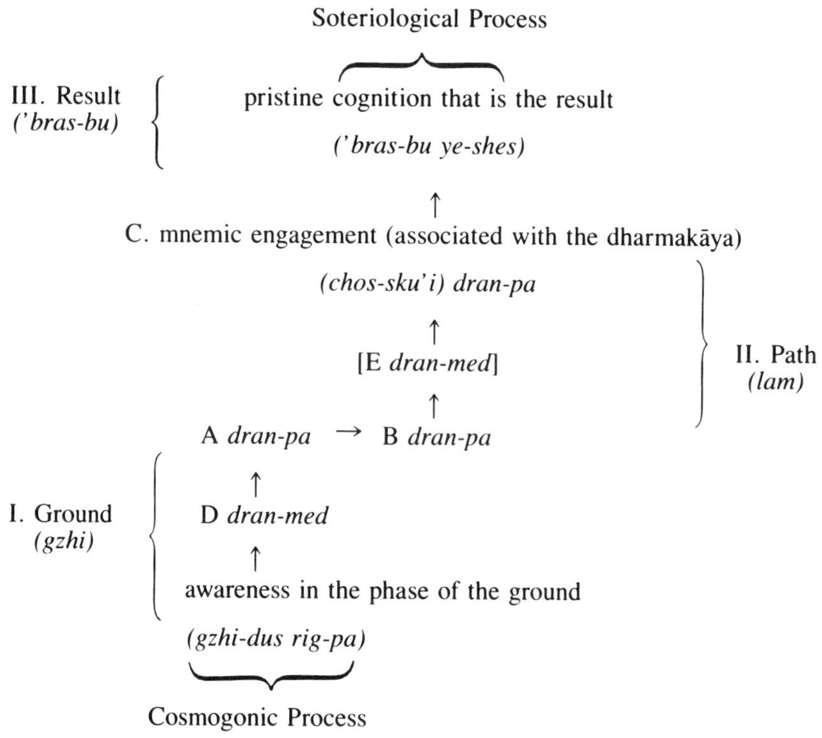

Figure 1.

The proposed schematization, whatever its other defects may be, does suggest an observation of some consequence here, emphasizing what we may designate the *primacy of amnesis.* Amnesis (D *dran-med*), as the loss of, or deviation from, the primordial awareness of the ground, must be regarded as the first of all mnemic phenomena. This determines a proper understanding of mnemic engagement (*dran-pa*), for we must now say that all acts of mnemic engagement involve the apparent *recovery* or *retention*, that is to say *nonloss*, of a causally or temporally precedent psychic or experiential condition by an act of awareness. Memory, for instance, is now determined to be the mind's recovery or retention of, and is presumed to be causally related to, the content of prior experience; recognition, the cognition that one has recovered the object of prior perception; recollection, the recovery of knowledge acquired earlier; memorization, the deliberate retention of knowledge; mindfulness, the retention of awareness's specifically appropriate engagement in a given act or experience. (In this last case, what counts as "specifically appropriate" will necessarily vary according to the nature of the act or experience concerned: a chainsaw operator's mindfulness will involve a rather differently specified sort of engagement than will that of a practitioner of *ikibana.*)

Recovery, retention, and *loss* here are, admittedly, metaphorical terms, but this seems not to present grave difficulties in the present context. For loss may be understood phenomenologically as the alienation of the subject from any of its apparent properties, and recovery and retention together determine its contradictory. Regarded in this way, it appears not at all strange that memory and mindfulness have often been gathered together under a single lexical head—for example, *mnā-*, *smṛ-*, or *dran-* —and rather odd that this convention has sometimes been thought to be problematic. Although the normal temporal reference of memory to the past is sometimes not a feature of the codesignated phenomena in question, we nonetheless find in these cases a relatively straightforward analogy of intention.

To the foregoing considerations, our sources further suggest that when awareness turns not to the ground of any particular act, but to the ground of all possible acts of awareness, it reaches its end in the reflexive recovery of the pristine cognition of the ground-of-all (*kun-gzhi'i ye-shes*) that is dharmakāya in its noetic aspect. Here the analogy with "memory" as we ordinarily conceive of it is found solely in the phenomenon of recovery, but the character of the act in question has neither the temporal nor the intentional properties of the quotidian concept. In its most characteristic sense, then, *dran-* in Great Perfection thought as represented by Rig-'dzin Rgod-ldem refers to awareness qua awareness orienting itself to its proper ground. Its primary "referent," the "object" of this act of retention/recovery, is the self-presentation of awareness as dharmakāya; and it is by analogy that all mnemic acts, by virtue of their orientation to their proper ground or some part thereof, counteracting "loss" or "deviation," are equally *dran-pa.*

An Allegorical Re-presentation

The *Penetration of Samantabhadra's Intention* and its allied literature are, on the surface at least, extremely repetitive compilations, the topics we have seen surveyed in the brief tantra just discussed being variously restated, with more or less elaboration, in many of the texts forming the corpus of the *GZT.* The repetitiveness of these works, however, betokens no want of ingenuity on the part of the redactor; for this represents in part a carefully crafted effort to clarify and reinforce the vision of the Great Perfection. Repetition, in short, functions *mnemotechnically.*[25] As the preceding section makes clear, it is part of the soteriological strategy of the Great Perfection to arouse mnemic engagement of a type that, indirectly or immediately, recalls, calls one back to an object of loss, the revelation of the dharmakāya quo self-presenting awareness. The mnemotechnics, to borrow a term from Nietzsche, of the literature and practice of the Great Perfection must be seen as contributing to the formation of such soteriologically valued mnemic engagement. In this and the section that follows, we examine two aspects of the mnemotechnic strategies that are employed here: allegorization and ritualization.

The *Wide-Open Tantra of Universal Liberation* well represents the character of much abstract Great Perfection discourse; like certain aspects of Indian Buddhist Abhidharma, it employs what in many respects is a sort of phenomenological language, whose operating terms are to be understood as signifying empirical phenomena that are revealed and clarified only when one becomes engaged in appropriate types of contemplative abstraction.[26] One of the functions of allegory, of course, is to render an abstract message more *memorable*, by recasting it in terms of the concrete relationships portrayed as holding among fictitious agents.[27] Allegorical narrative, like mythic and historical narrative, may seek to overcome the atemporal character of more highly abstracted modes of discourse, disclosing to us what that discourse had situated outside of time in an abode phenomenologically rather like that of human temporal experience. Ironically, therefore, allegorical narrative, "the figure of false semblance" as it was known to the Renaissance, may be employed as a corrective to a distortion inseparable from much philosophical language—we may say, to a *lie* of philosophical language, the lie of timelessness.[28]

The teaching of the *Penetration of Samantabhadra's Intention* is given allegorical expression in the sixth chapter of a tantra entitled *The Tantra of the Eradication of Bewilderment* (*'khrul-pa rtsad-gcod-kyi rgyud*), whose importance in the corpus as a whole is signaled by the description of the text as "the first of all tantras of the esoteric instructions of the Great Perfection."[29] The chapter that interests us here is called "The Symbolic [i.e., Allegorical] Teaching of the Authentic and Real Introduction to the Abiding Nature of Mind and the Approach to the Path of Purification."[30] Because, for reasons argued above, the attempt to separate the particular symbolic figures met here from their narrative context would necessarily miss the very point of their employment in narrative, the chapter is presented in its entirely. Readers may find this text to be confusing in parts, but, bewilderment being precisely an aspect of experience that it seeks to underscore, it would be, I think, very misleading to attempt to clarify it through editorial abridgement or alteration.

The Lord of Secrets petitioned the Teacher Vajrasattva: "O Body of Perfect Rapture! Teacher Vajrasattva! Concerning the so-called 'mind of sentient being,' is it the case that, even though other names be attributed to it, it comes into being from the ground of arising because of varied agitations? And is it the case that there is a difference between the mind autonomously engaged in the afflicted states and the mind of the individual who has embarked on the path of the bodhisattva?"

In response, [Vajrasattva] declared: "This so-called 'mind' is most exceedingly miraculous! Its potencies and enumerations are inconceivable, beyond speech. Nonetheless, this so-called 'mind' is spontaneously present, though of indeterminate material cause. The contributory condition is ignorance. Its essential characteristic is such that it can become anything. At first, when the appearance of twofold apprehension [of subject and object] is vaguely set in motion, one may speak of 'precedent intellectual cognition,' or 'doubtful thought,' or 'pride-generating sensation.' Then, when that has coarsened, there is the bifurcation of outer and inner, the vessel [of the world] and its contents [sentient beings]. When the residues have extensively developed one may speak of ' the intermediate state of imaginative cognition,' 'dualistic bewilderment,' or 'the ramification of the residues of action.' Thence proceeds saṃsāra. When the body of a sentient being is acquired, one speaks of 'the mind that constructs all bewildered appearance.' It is that which apprehends bewildered appearance as an autonomous continuum. That is the King of All Bewilderment.

"Though he performs many deeds, without associates he remains at leisure. He has five ministers, the greatest of whom is stubborn, speaks indistinctly, is derisive toward all, and obscure. His name is Stupidity. When that minister and the king enter into consultation, the whole country is thrown into blackness. Following him, there is one [characterized by] clear mnemic engagement, who rushes about to and fro. Evilly motivated, he's a clever talker. His name is Desire. When that minister and the king enter into consultation, he teaches deceit toward all, ensnarement through the appearance of truth. Following him, there's one who looks after himself, not others, and ruins both. He holds himself dear, but has no thought for any other. His name is Hatred. When he and the king enter into consultation, they wreck everything they see, touch, or otherwise handle. Following him, there's one with great words and little skill. He brings about self-regard and blame of others. His name is Pride. When he and the king enter into consultation, disregarding subjects and property, there's only self-regard. The last causes only selfish desire. He takes everything he sees to be an enemy, and accords with no one. His name is Envy. When he and the king enter into consultation, everyone becomes an enemy. Those are the five afflictions. Serving under those five ministers are 84,000 slaves who conform with them. They are called 'the host of adventitious afflicted thoughts.' They emanate from the mind that is an autonomous continuum of affliction.

"Now, if a fortunate individual emerges who enters into [the cultivation of] the enlightened mind, then the so-called 'inception of pure pristine cognition' occurs.

"At some interval, when the five ministers are not in the presence of the Omnicreative King of Mind, a man may come forth to teach in symbols the purification involving mnemic engagement [pertaining to] desire for and subjective apprehension of what may be (*srid-pa chags-'dzin dran-pa'i dag-pa*), saying, 'You, King, were alone even before the first origins of what may be. When you fell asleep and became bewildered you met with an associate [who arrived] from here and there. That one altered your mind, making the King as you are today, by affirming the being of what is not. Therefore, through the power of deeds, you've been made to consult with the five ruinous ministers. Now many incompetent functionaries have assembled, one such as yourself is present, and these evil courtiers have transformed you, so that you've fallen, without autonomy, into unbearable suffering. You must wake up! Being deceived by me, you must go off without associates. What can you do with a retinue like this? If you listen to me, you'll just abandon this ruinous retinue. There's the one called the "Friend who is a Pure Antidote," into association with whom I'll place you. Joining forces will him, without separation, run off with your thoughts bent on the Three Gems Blazing with Light that are found in the upper valley. That way, O king, you'll be happy both immediately and ultimately. Then waking up, you'll come to be undeceived.'—So he spoke.

"Then the king, freeing his mind, renounced all the retinue and his ministers, and, undetected by anyone, joined together with the Friend who is a Pure Antidote. Directing his thoughts to the Gems at the head of the valley he fled and, though pursued by his servants and ministers, escaped in an instant. Such is the entranceway according to the lower vehicle. So it is that in the lower vehicle, the king whose mind has given birth to an attitude of renunciation, has only the single friend, Pure Antidote.

"In entering upon the path of the higher vehicle, there are, just as described above, the king of the mental continuum, with his servants and ministers. At some time an adviser comes forth and addresses him as follows: 'O king, listen to me. Formerly, in the city of Vaisālī, the universal ground, there was a prince called "Luminous Essence." He had a wish-fulfilling gem from which all desired qualities naturally emerged. At some point that great city was destroyed, there was the terrifying roar of a thousand thunders, and all was scattered to the wind. The tornado that demolished the palace took the form of a brilliant conflagration and the Prince became senseless, lost his composure, and, terrified, fled in a state of oblivion. Arriving in a district in a neighboring land, he met an old woman with cataracts. The old woman took the prince to her home and dressed him in thick garments. The prince, exhausted, fell asleep, and the old woman stole the precious gem that he wore beneath his shirt. That thief then fled into the darkness, where she met up with five men. The old woman got to talking with them and lost the gem to those five men, who couldn't hold on to it either, and so sold it in the six cities of deeds. There, in the desire to worship the gem without the prince, the six cities shared it; but when the desired objects failed to appear in [those] six dungeons, it was abandoned.

" 'At that time the prince awoke and, the old woman not having returned, he was amazed and ran out the door. Meeting a man named "Self-Manifest Bewilderment," the two conversed. [The prince's] mind, unaccustomed, entered into dualistic apprehension, whereupon many motivational bandits arrived and kidnapped the prince. Selling him in a city of perversity, which was princeless, the prince was appointed lord of that land. At that one adviser came forth and said, "I've come to give you a message, for I've heard about your incessant suffering, due to the five ministers who ruined everything, along with the 84,000 subjects who created meaningless pain. At that time you were the king. Now, what is it that you're doing?"

" 'The prince made his previous pain an object of mnemic engagement, and wept until he was exhausted. "Alas, alas! I have no friends," he cried. At that the adviser said, "At first you were the owner of the precious gem. So it is impossible that you're without a pouch for the gem, or perhaps some garment that came into contact with the gem. Examine your body!"

" 'The prince found that there was a cord for the gem around his neck, reaching his heart. Cutting it into five pieces, he made the gem an object of mnemic engagement and prayed to it, whereupon, by the blessing of the gem, five heartlike men came forth. The adviser spoke as follows: "The eldest of the five men should be appointed to be the 'Guardian of Inseparable Menemic Engagement' (*dran-pa 'bral-med-kyi so-pa*). Without separation from him, whatever you do will be easy. Next, there is one called 'Impermanence that Reveals the Fault of the Round' (*'khor-ba'i mtshang-'don-gyi mi-rtag-pa*). Without separation from him, you needn't wander in evil abodes. This next one is called the 'Person who is the Self-Clarification of Cognition' (*shes-pa rang-gsal-gyi skyes-bu*). Without separation from him, whatever you do is delightful to the mind. The next one is called the 'Sentinel of Mnemic Engagement and Mindfulness Revealing the Fluctuations of One's Evil Residues' (*bag-chags ngan-pa'i yo-lang 'don-pa-la dran-pa shes-bzhin-gyi byar-ba*). Without separation from him, whatever you do will come out well. The youngest one is called the 'Messenger of the Connection between Saṃsāra and Nirvāṇa' (*'khor-'das mtshams-sbyor-gyi phrin-pa*). Without separation from him, you and I will meet repeatedly. Never let yourself be separated from these five mnemic men! Now you must change your name. You have parted ways with the retinue of ruin. As for the manner in which misery arose so long as you were alienated from your original homeland, you must continually practice mnemic engagement with respect to the heartfelt advice I've now given to you. May you bear the name 'Youth of Awareness!' "

" 'When he had spoken thus the youth and the five mnemic men became constant companions. They captured the five thieves and imprisoned them. They vanquished all the retinue and subjects. They demolished the six cities and stole back the gem. They killed the old woman with cataracts. Having returned to his former land, the prince, together with the five mnemic men, were united with the precious gem. In the pinnacle of the castle the first of the five mnemic men was appointed watchman. The next was appointed guard at the door to the royal apartments. The next one, accompanying the prince and the gem, was appointed to reside at the center of the fortress and became inseparable from them. The next was assigned to be a hero, a tamer of enemies. The next was assigned to be a fleet-footed messenger, incessantly arranging for princely audiences with the gracious adviser. So it was that the prince's land achieved a stable ground, and the various desires were fulfilled.

" 'It is said that afterwards there was nothing to fear in that land. And it is said that sometimes messengers were dispatched, to guide men who wished to reach that land on the path.'

"That is the manner of entry into the higher vehicle. Such is the allegory concerning the need of the Youth of Self-Presenting Awareness for the five self-emergent associates who are mnemic engagement." So he said.

Thus the sixth chapter of the tantra of bewilderment and mind, which teaches as an allegory the genuinely meaningful introduction to the abiding nature of mind, and the manner of entry into the pure path.

The allegory in its two versions, pertaining to the "lower" and "higher" vehicles,[31] involves considerable complexity of detail, so that remarks here must be limited to address only a few elements that are especially pertinent in the present context. The *Prayer of Great Power,* translated below, will provide a key that, I believe, together with some knowledge of the classical Buddhist doctrine of dependent origination (*rten-cing 'brel-bar 'byung-ba, pratītyasamutpāda*) and the material presented in the previous section, will help the reader to decipher many of the particular symbolic allusions.

Both versions of the allegory emphasize a reorientation involving mnemic engagement, a reorientation aroused by the appearance of a benevolent adviser at the decisive turning point of the monarch's troubled career: starting here, the increasingly ramified network of affliction begins to become undone. The narrative fulcrum of the allegories therefore is found at the point at which soteriologically valuable mnemic engagement (B *dran-pa*) is born within the obscure domain of bewilderment (*'khrul-pa*). Deception, as these allegories well illustrate, must therefore be part and parcel of the inception and development of the path. The notion of deception (*bslu-ba*) that we find here is notably similar to the concept of *upāyakauśalya*, "skillful means," famously revealed in the *Lotus Sūtra*'s "Parable of the Burning House."[32]

Given the essential constitution of the round of saṃsāra as bewilderment, determined throughout by amnesis, it seems clear that this concession to deception in fact is required: honest acknowledgment of the limitations of ordinary discourse, as that is conceived here, and not cynical manipulation of the faithful, demands such a concession. With this in mind, the purpose of the apparently strange *emboîtement* of several speakers' discourses in the second allegory becomes clear; for, without explicit reference to deception, the inclusion of allegory within allegory self-referentially betokens the text's own deceptiveness, so that one need be no longer deceived by it.[33] The technique of allegorical *emboîtement*, generating the functional equivalent of a metalanguage, permits the disclosure of deception to take place without involving the obvious circularity of the liar paradox. The narrative's allegorized self-reference further reinforces the allegorical passage from lower to higher vehicle, in which the self-referentiality of awareness itself is disclosed and characterized as the inalienable possession of mnemic engagement, embodied now as the Self-Clarification of Cognition, third (and so central) among the mnemic men. Thus allegory recapitulates the course we have previously traversed in preeminently doctrinal terms and, in so doing, reminds us that the actual path will be disclosed symbolically; for the intentional character of symbolic discourse is at once the mark of bewilderment and the conveyance of the antidote for it.

Mnemic Engagement in the Practice of Prayer

Although the study and practice of the Great Perfection traditions emanating from Rig-'dzin Rgod-ldem have been traditionally maintained among lineages of highly trained religious specialists within particular branches of the Rnying-ma-pa sect, including both laypersons and celibate clergy, one short litany derived from the *Penetration of Samantabhadra's Intention* is known and practiced throughout the Tibetan Buddhist world. This is the *Prayer of Great Power* (*smon-lam stobs-po-che*), a text without parallel in Tibetan Buddhist literature, the peculiar popularity of which was perhaps part of its intention from the beginning. The text, translated in the appendix, aims to reveal the manner in which the awakened intention of the original buddha Samantabhadra literally penetrates the universe of sentient beings, and in its original context the *Prayer of Great Power* occurs not as a self-contained work, but rather as the penultimate (and so possibly culminating) chapter of a very extensive tantra.[34] The title of the chapter in which it is given is "The Teaching of the Inability of Sentient Beings Not to Become Buddhas, on Reciting the *Prayer of Great Power.*"[35]

The *Prayer of Great Power* is of interest in part because it recasts several of the fundamental elements commonly attributed to prayer, while at the same time conforming to normative conventions in important respects. How this is so may be made clear with reference to the brief phenomenology of-prayer suggested by Gerardus van der Leeuw,[36] who begins his account by-considering the relationship between prayer and magical formulas, the efficacious recitation of which always demands that they be repeated with perfect accuracy. Their power may be enhanced by additional factors, too, especially the introduction of what van der Leeuw terms the *magical antecedent,* often a mythical narrative invoking the past efficacy of the formula concerned. Again, we find incorporated in prayer exclamations that originally served to summon the deity, or "to remind the god of the pact that had been concluded," and even to "compel the presence of divine Power."

Prayer, properly speaking, emerges "[w]hen man recognizes first of all Form, and later Will, within Power." These are among the key terms of van der Leeuw's phenomenology of religion, and elsewhere he explains that "in the three terms *Power, Will,* and *Form,* there lies practically the entire concept of the Object of Religion"; that is, whatever object is deemed "sacred."[37] The recognition of Form and Will here gives rises to the characteristically dialogic aspect of prayer: "it is an address from man to the Will which he knows to be above him, and the reply of this Will." Finally, in mystical faith, prayer may lose its dialogic character and become "a monologue saturated with religious energy," a "merging in God." "[P]rayer attains its highest form in *submersion,* while the dialogue type of supplication, on the other hand, always remains word and entreaty, practical demonstration of Will to will, even when it prays in *its* highest form: 'not my will, but thine, be done.' "

It will be seen at once that the phenomena of prayer are thoroughly bound up with mnemonics: perfect accuracy of recitation necessitates perfect recall; the "magical antecedant" involves the recollection of past events; the exclamatory summoning of the deity requires both summoner and summoned to remember their compact; dialogic prayer presupposes the petitioner's recollection of the object of faith; and mystical prayer, the exercise of mindful self-collection. In the *Prayer of Great Power* all of these elements, with interesting variations, are in evidence. Moreover, the prayer traces a path through the cosmogony and soteriology of amnesis and mnemic engagement.

The relationship of the prayer we are considering to magical power is made explicit even in its title, and is further asserted in its concluding passage, in which the most propitious times for recital are described. The "magical antecedent," a remembrance of mythical events, is incorporated into the main body of the text itself, which details the manner in which the awakening of the primordial buddha and the amnesis of sentient beings have originated in a common ground. The exclamations *ho!* and *aho!* used throughout Tibetan religious poetry and prayer, are always intended to recall a sense of awe and wonderment, and the ejaculation *tsitta ā!* with which this prayer is introduced, uniquely recalls the primordial purity (*ka-dag*) of the Great Perfection.

Where the *Prayer of Great Power* curiously departs from the examples examined by van der Leeuw, however, is in its remarkable simultaneous instantiation of both dialogic and mystical paradigms: the petitioner reestablishes a primordial relationship with the buddha Samantabhadra by *becoming* Samantabhadra. The mnemonics of prayer are thus called upon to reawaken one's original affinity with the dharmakāya; that is to say, to arouse the reflexive mnemic engagement of the dharmakāya, to introduce a convergence of will and Will. According to its own logic, then, all beings are indeed powerless not to become buddhas on reciting this prayer; and *that* is its magic and power.

By Way of Conclusion

The foregoing reflections on *dran-pa* in Great Perfection thought suggest that we indeed find here a distinctive doctrine of "memory," which is by no means a simple reiteration of classical Indian Buddhist materials. It is equally clear, however, that this doctrine does not represent a decisive break with the earlier tradition. In this respect, the Great Perfection treatment of *dran-pa* is consistent with many of the other elements incorporated into Great Perfection thought: the resonances of Indian Buddhist teachings are deliberately appropriated, and particular nuances are carefully refined, but in such a manner that the passage from normative Buddhist sources to the particular realm of Great Perfection is rendered quite seamless. It is precisely in virtue of this strategy that the various attempts to forge a scholastic synthesis founded on the Great Perfection tradition, for example, in the writings of Karma Pakshi and Klong-chen Rab-'byams-pa, are genuinely syncretic and not merely eclectic.[38] To this, however, the adherents of the Great Perfection would add that their strategy works so well precisely because Great Perfection thought gets us closer to the bedrock of Buddhist insight than do its competitors, and so best comprehends the genuine insights of particular Buddhist traditions.

It remains a peculiar feature of the Great Perfection approach to "memory" that it emphasizes above all a type of psychological act that stands quite apart from both the intentional character and the temporal reference we usually attribute to memory. And this, we have seen, goes far beyond the appropriation of mindfulness to memory terms, for in such cases the analogical rapport of the intentionality of the former act with that of properly mnemic phenomena seems relatively clear. The puzzlement that is occasioned for us by the Great Perfection transposition of the phenomenological heart of the mnemic act to the reflexivity of awareness is deepened, perhaps, when we remark that the Great Perfection tradition has not been alone in its execution of this striking maneuver.[39] Consider in this respect the argument of Augustine:

> But some one will say, That is not memory by which the mind, which is ever present to itself, is affirmed to remember itself; for memory is of things past, not of things present. For there are some, and among them Cicero, who, in treating of the virtues, have divided prudence into these three—memory, understanding, forethought: to wit, assigning memory to things past, understanding to things present, forethought to things future; which last is certain only in the case of those who are prescient of the future; and this is no gift of men, unless it be granted from above, as to the prophets. And hence the book of Wisdom speaking of men, "The thoughts of mortals," it says, "are fearful, and our forethought uncertain." But memory of things past, and understanding of things present, are certain: certain, I mean, respecting things incorporeal, which are present; for things corporeal are present to the sight of the corporeal eyes. But let any one who denies that there is any memory of things present, attend to the language used even in profane literature, where exactness of words was more looked for than truth of things, "Nor did Ulysses suffer such things, nor did the Ithacan forget himself in so great a peril." For when Virgil said that Ulysses did not forget himself, what else did he mean, except that he remembered himself? And since he was present to himself, he could not possibly remember himself, unless memory pertained to things present. And, therefore, as that which is called memory in things past which makes it possible to recall and remember them; so in a thing present, as the mind is to itself, that is not unreasonably to be called memory, which makes the mind at hand to itself, so that it can be understood by its own thought, and then both be joined together by love of itself.[40]

And a contemporary Augustine scholar comments that:

> Augustine extends the scope of *memoria* so as to include all that we are capable of getting to know explicitly that does not come to us through sense-experience. This includes, for Augustine, knowledge of self, of the truths of reason, of moral and other values, of God. Hence *memoria* loses all refer-

> ence to the past, except in the case of knowledge derived from sense experience, since the content of this is only in the mind if the experience has in fact occurred at some previous time; otherwise, *memoria* is not confined to past experience but embraces all that is latent and *present* [emphasis in the original] as such in the mind.[41]

The redescription of memory as all that is present as such in the mind, or as the mnemic engagement of the dharmakāya and thus standing outside of time, despite the manifold differences between Augustinian thought and that of the Great Perfection traditions with respect to perhaps most matters of "theology,"[42] serves in each case to ground the role of "memory" in a religious epistemology, in part by short circuiting the doubts frequently raised about the relationship between memory and knowledge: memory is here revealed to be *the most natural thing in the world* and, hence, absolutely authoritative. One may well be tempted to suppose that Augustine and the masters of Great Perfection were indeed on to something here, that their assertion that memory is so very much more than a doubtful relationship between an evanescent present and a forever lost past is a real insight, in fact a discovery. In fact, I am inclined to think that it is plausible to view matters in this way; but, still, philosophical scruples require that the most skeptical objections be heard. Let us consider the terrible words of Nietzsche on the subject of memory:

> [P]erhaps indeed there was nothing more fearful and uncanny in the whole prehistory of man than his *mnemotechnics*. . . . Man could never do without blood, torture, and sacrifices when he felt the need to create a memory for himself; the most dreadful sacrifices and pledges (sacrifices of the firstborn among them), the most repulsive mutilations (castration, for example), the cruelest rites of all the religious cults (and all religions are at the deepest levels systems of cruelties)—all this has its origin in the instinct that realized that pain is the most powerful aid to mnemonics.
>
> In a certain sense, *the whole of asceticism belongs here:* [italics added] a few ideas are to be rendered inextinguishable, ever-present, unforgettable, "fixed," with the aim of hypnotizing the entire nervous and intellectual system with these "fixed ideas"—and ascetic procedures and modes of life are means of freeing these ideas from the competition of all other ideas, so as to make them "unforgettable."[43]

Nietzsche perhaps did not perceive the highest degree of subtlety to which mnemotechnics have aspired: with the insight that memory is *the most natural thing in the world* we may dispense with all mnemonic torture; the bond linking pain and memory may at last be severed.

A genuine discovery, then, or the most exquisite possible refinement of *ascesis?* According to what principle is *this* puzzle to be resolved? I shall have to leave it for the reader to ponder; for possibly this will serve as an invitation to *memoria*, to genuine *dran-pa*.

Appendix: The Prayer of Great Power

Tsitta Ā! [Heart-mind Ā!]

Then the original buddha Samantabhadra recited this special prayer, concerning the powerlessness of sentient beings in the round not to become buddhas:

Ho! All phenomenal possibilities—the round and transcendence—
One ground, two paths, two results—
A miracle of awareness and unawareness!
By the aspiration of the Omnibeneficent
May the buddhahood of all be perfectly disclosed
In the fortress of reality's expanse.
The ground-of-all is unconditioned,
A self-emergent, open expanse, ineffable,
Without even the names of both "round" and "transcendence."
Being aware of just that is buddhahood,
While sentient beings, unaware, wander the round.
May all sentient beings of the three realms
Be aware of the ineffable significance of the ground.

For I, the Omnibeneficent,
Am the significance of the ground, without cause or condition.
Awareness, self-emergent from the ground that's just that,
Imputes no fault, outer or inner, by exaggeration or depreciation.
It is free from the dark taint of amnesis,
And so unsullied by self-manifest fault.
In abiding in self-presenting awareness,
There is no terror though the three worlds be afraid;
There is no desire for the five sensual pleasures.
In nonconceptual cognition, self-emergent,
There are neither concrete forms nor the five colors.
The unimpeded radiant aspect of awareness
Has the five pristine cognitions in its sole essence.
As the five pristine cognitions mature,
The original buddhas of five families emerge.

The horizon of pristine cognition expanding thereafter,
Forty-two buddhas emerge.

The expressive power of the five pristine cognitions arises,
And the sixty blood-drinkers emerge.
So the ground-awareness experiences no error.

Because I am the original buddha,
By reciting my aspiration,
May the sentient beings of the round's three realms
Know the face of self-emergent awareness
And expand the horizon of great pristine cognition.

My emanations are incessant,
Radiating inconceivably by hundreds of millions,
Variously revealing how each is trained according to need.
By the aspiration of my compassion,
May all sentient beings in the round's three realms
Be set free from the six classes' abodes.

At first, sentient beings, in error,
Awareness of the ground not arising,
Suffer total amnesis and oblivion.
Just that is unawareness, the cause of error,
Overcome by which, as in a faint,
Cognition, in terror, wanders intoxicated.
Thus dividing self and other, enmity is born.
As its residues develop by stages,
The round emerges in evolutionary sequence;
The five poisonous afflictions expand therefrom;
The activity of the five poisons is incessant.
Therefore, because error's ground within sentient beings
Is amnesic unawareness,
By my aspiration as a buddha,
May all sentient beings of the three realms
All know by themselves their own awareness.

Coemergent unawareness
Is cognition in amnesic oblivion.
Imputative unawareness
Is the apprehension of self and other as two.
Coemergent and imputative unawareness together
Form error's ground for all sentient beings.
By my aspiration as a buddha,
May all sentient beings in the round
Find the thick darkness of amnesis dispelled,
Dualistic cognition removed,
And then know the proper face of awareness.

Dualistic intellect is doubt.
When subtle obsessive attachment arises,
Its residues densely ramify in sequence.

Food, wealth, clothing, abode, and friends,
The five sensuous objects and loving relations—
You are tormented by passionate desire for what pleases.
These are worldly errors;
Apprehended, apprehender, and act have no final end.
When the fruit of obsessive attachment matures,
Embodied as a ghost wracked by craving,
You are born to terrible hunger and thirst.
By my aspiration as a buddha,
May sentient beings engaged in desire and obsessive attachment
Neither renounce the torment of desire,
Nor adhere to desire and obsessive attachment,
But, by letting cognition relax in its proper domain,
May they seize the proper domain of awareness,
And acquire all-comprehending pristine cognition.

Directed to the appearance of outer objects
There proceeds a subtle, frightened cognition;
When the residues of hatred spread forth,
Coarse enmity and violence are born.
When anger's result has matured,
You suffer in the inferno of hell.
By the power of my aspiration as a buddha,
May all sentient beings of the six destinies,
Whenever fierce anger is born,
Neither adhere to nor reject it, but relax in their proper domain,
And by seizing the proper domain of awareness,
May they acquire clarifying pristine cognition.

When your mind becomes inflated,
There's the thought to debase, in competition with others.
The thought of fierce pride being born,
You suffer combat between self and other.
When the result of that action matures,
Born a god, you are liable to fall and to die.
By my aspiration as a buddha,
May self-inflated sentient beings
Relax cognition in its proper domain,
And by seizing the proper domain of awareness
Acquire equanimity's pristine cognition.

Owing to ramified residues of dualistic grasping,
There are tortured deeds of self-praise, blame of others;

Violent competitiveness develops
And you are born in the murderous antigods' abode:

The result, a fall into hellish abodes.
By the power of my prayer as a buddha,
May those born competitive and violent
Not engage in enmity, but relax in their proper domains,
And by seizing the proper domain of awareness
Realize the pristine cognition of unimpeded enlightened activity.

The result of amnesis, apathy, and distraction,
Oblivion, dullness, forgetfulness,
Unconsciousness, laziness, and stupidity
Is to roam as an unprotected beast.
By my aspiration as a buddha
May the luster of mnemic clarification arise
In the darkness of insensate stupidity,
And bring acquisition of nonconceptual pristine cognition.

For all the sentient beings of the three realms
Are equal to me, the buddha of the universal ground.
Amnesic, they have drifted into bewilderment's ground,
And so now are engaged in meaningless deeds:
The six deeds are like the bewilderment of dreams.
I am the original buddha:
To train the six destinies by my emanations,
By my aspiration as the Omnibeneficent,
May all sentient beings, none excepted,
Become buddhas in reality's expanse!

Aho!
In the future a powerful yogin,
With unbewildered awareness, self-clarified,
Will recite this powerful prayer,
And all sentient beings who hear it
Will disclose buddhahood within three lives.
During solar or lunar eclipse,
At times of thunder or earthquake,
During the solstices or at New Years,
He will recreate himself as Samantabhadra.
If this is uttered so that all may hear,
Then all the sentient beings of the three realms,
Because of that yogin's prayer,
Will be successively released from suffering
And swiftly attain buddhahood!

From *The Tantra which Teaches the Great Perfection, the Penetration of Samantabhadra's Intention,* the nineteenth chapter, which teaches the powerlessness of sentient beings not to become buddhas, on reciting the *Prayer of Great Power.*

Figure 2. Samantabhadra, the first of all buddhas, the dharmakāya in the embrace of self-radiance (*rang-'od*).

Notes

I am grateful to Columbia University's Council on Research in the Humanities and Social Sciences for generous assistance in support of this research.

1. The conception of this paper owes a great deal to a series of conversations in December 1987 and December 1988, that I was privileged to conduct with the Ven. Tulku Urgyen Rinpoche of Nagi Gompa, Nepal, one of the leading contemporary exponents of the Great Perfection. Rinpoche's reflections on *dran-pa* revealed a rich vein of Great Perfection thought centering on this topic and supplied me with the point of departure for the investigation of the texts considered here. The actual form and content of this paper, however, represent only my own attempt at understanding the

texts explicitly discussed, and so do not seek to provide a documentary record of Rinpoche's observations.

2. The historical study of the Great Perfection tradition in both its Bon-po and Rnying-ma-pa guises has recently been given a solid foundation in Samten Gyaltsen Karmay's *The Great Perfection: A Philosophical and Meditative Teaching of Tibetan Buddhism* (Leiden: E. J. Brill, 1988), the bibliography of which, pp. 234–38, well documents earlier scholarship in this area.

3. On Klong-chen-pa and his contributions to Great Perfection thought, see especially: Herbert V. Guenther, *Kindly Bent to Ease Us*, 3 vols. (Emeryville, Calif.: Dharma Publishing, 1975–76); Tulku Thondup Rinpoche, *Buddha Mind: An Anthology of Longchen Rabjam's Writings on Dzogpa Chenpo*, ed. Harold Talbott (Ithaca, N.Y.: Snow Lion, 1989); H. H. Dudjom Rinpoche, *The Nyingma School of Tibetan Buddhism: Its Fundamentals and History*, trans. Gyurme Dorje and Matthew Kapstein (London and Boston: Wisdom, 1991), vol. 1, pp. 575–96.

4. The most important of the distinctive Great Perfection classifications and concepts, as emphasized in Rnying-ma-pa texts, are surveyed in Dudjom Rinpoche, *The Nyingma School*, vol. 1, pp. 294–345.

5. The life of Rig-'dzin Rgod-ldem and his contributions to Rnying-ma-pa Buddhism are summarized in Dudjom Rinpoche, *The Nyingma School*, vol. 1, pp. 780–83. For a more extensive biography in Tibetan, see Sūryabhadra (Ñi-ma-bzaṅ-po), *Sprul sku rig 'dzin rgod kyi ldem 'phru can gyi rnam thar gsal byed ñi ma'i 'od zer: The Biography of Rig-'dzin Rgod-kyi-ldem-'phru-can* (Paro, Bhutan: Lama Ngodrup and Sherab Drimey, 1985). From a traditional standpoint Rgod-ldem is, of course, the discoverer and *not* the author of his treasures. But, because this entailed his being their redactor, i.e., the individual responsible for the precise verbal form in which they have come down to us, I have not insisted on making a distinction that would have no practical role in the context of the present discussion.

6. The edition referred to throughout the present essay is the A-'dzom chos-sgar xylograph, published in facsimile as *Rdzogs pa chen po dgoṅs pa zaṅ thal and Ka dag raṅ byuṅ raṅ sar*, 5 vols., Smanrtsis Shesrig Spendzod Series vols. 60–64 (Leh, Ladakh: S. W. Tashigangpa, 1973), abbreviated hereinafter as *GZT* followed by roman volume number and arabic plate numbers, including the line number where relevant. *GZT*, V is in fact the *Ka dag rang byung rang shar* collection.

7. *GZT*, V.131–49.

8. Compare, for instance, the conclusions of the next section with the influential analytic philosophical account of memory given in C. B. Martin and Max Deutscher, "Remembering," *Philosophical Review* 75 (1966): 161–96.

9. It is not possible in the space of this chapter to examine the difficult doctrines concerning the dharmakāya (*chos-kyi sku*, the "body of reality") and its disclosure as the primordial buddha Samantabhadra. For a detailed discussion see Dudjom Rinpoche, *The Nyingma School*, vol. 1, book 1, part 2.

10. The Tibetan titles of the chapters are (1) *'khor 'das gnyis byung tshul* (*GTZ*, V.132.2–135.6); (2) *skal med man ngag 'di dang mi 'phrad pa* (135.6–137.1); (3) *rig pa chos skur ngo sprad pa* (137.1–139.2); (4) *lta ba'i gol sa bcad pa* (139.2–140.5); (5) *lam gyi spyod lam bstan pa* (140.5–143.3); (6) *rkyen gyis chos sku la nye ba* (143.3–145.4); (7) *rtogs pa'i dus bstan pa* (145.4–146.6); (8) *bar dor sangs rgyas thob pa* (146.6–147.5); (9) *gtad rgya* (147.5–148.6); colophons (149.1–6).

11. In this context we must recall the fundamental role of mnemonic concepts in connection with the entire phenomenon of *gter-ma*. See, especially, Janet Gyatso, "Signs, Memory and History: A Tantric Buddhist Theory of Scriptural Transmission," *Journal of the International Association of Buddhist Studies* 9, no. 2 (1986): 7–35.

12. *ma yengs dran pa'i dpe don blta*. Note that ambiguity in the use of the "genetive" *-'i* and the "instrumental" *-s* is very common in the texts considered here, a characteristic that these works share with Tibetan vernacular literature. In this respect compare the biographies edited and translated in David Snellgrove, *Four Lamas of Dolpo*, 2 vols. (Oxford: Cassirer, 1967).

13. *da lta 'khrul pa'i sems 'di la: mngal nas skyes nas da lta 'i bar: ci byas dran pa bag chags yin.*

14. *de nyid rang rig chos sku yin: de la rgyun du dran pa yis: legs par brtag cing gtan la dbab.*

15. The puzzlement about reflexivity and its relationship to reference involved here has enjoyed a remarkably long history in the writings of the Indian contemplative traditions and their offshoots. Cf. my remarks on some Upaniṣadic references to reference in "Indra's Search for the Self and the Beginnings of Philosophical Perplexity in India," *Religious Studies* 24: 239–56, esp. p. 244.

16. *mnyam par bzhag pa'i dus nyid na: 'phros te snga ma phyi ma yi: rjes 'brang dran med ma song ba: byings te gnyid rmugs ma song ba'i: rig pa rang gsal ngo bo nyid.*

17. *kun gzhi yangs pa chos sku'i ma: bcos med rig pa chos sku'i bu: bu yi dran pa ma shor na: ma dang 'phrad nas bde ba thob.*

18. *dug lnga thol gyis skyes pa'i tshe: tha mas thog mtha' ngo bor lta: 'bring gis yul snang sgyu mar lta: rab kyi dran pas rang rig lta.*

19. *rig pa cir yang 'char ba 'di: chos sku nyid la thim pa yis: gnyid ni rang byung g.yo med yin: rmi lam snang ba shar ba'i tshe: dran ma thag tu sdug bsngal yal: . . . de ltar rmi lam 'khrul snang mang: sems kyi rang 'od tsam yin te: za zir gyur cing rang la thim: dran pa tsam gyi gzung 'dzin grol: de phyir dran pa myur bar mchog.*

20. *mngal dang gnyid dang bar do gsum: ngo bo gcig tu gsal thebs pa: snga phyi'i rtog pa ma shar ba'i: dran pa yang yang gsal btab bo: dran pa rtogs par 'gyur snyams na: phyi rol yul gyi phyir 'brang ba'i: snga phyi'i dran pa rtog pa yin: snga*

phyir ma shor zhen pa med: yang dag chos sku'i dran pa de: rang byung yin la ye shes yin: chos sku mnyam nyid lta ba yin: rig pa ye shes rang gsal yin.

21. *snang bar 'khrul pa'i sems shar yang: de ma thag tu dran pas zin; rang byung ngo bo nyid kyi sku: go ba yul shar rtogs par nye.*

22. *rdos pa'i lus 'di bral ma thag: dper na nam langs mun sangs bzhin: bar do dus gsum man ngag dran: ye shes snang bar brtan pa thob: rang rig chos skur gsal bar byung.*

23. Compare, too the passages cited from Chapter Six. The investigation of the *GTZ* collection so far has not revealed any special signification to the phrase "three temporal phases" (*dus-gsum*) as it is used in this context; so that the ordinary sense of "past, present, and future" may well be all that is intended here. Moreover, one interesting passage (*GTZ*, IV.367.5–6) concerning the *bar-do* contains the only reference I have found in this material to the canonical doctrine of the *rjes-su dran-pa drug*, the "six recollections" (*anusmṛti*), which are not listed in the ordinary manner, but rather as recollections of the deity (*lha*), path (*lam*), birthplace (*skye-gnas*), meditative concentration (*bsam-gtan*), precepts of the guru (*bla-ma'i man-ngag*), and dharma (*chos*). I believe that this enumeration in fact strengthens my interpretation of *dran-pa* (B.) as mindful attentiveness to the conditions for advancement on the path.

24. For example, *GTZ*, III.120–21: "Mnemic engagement is the ground; amnesis is the path. . . . Mnemic engagement is appearance; amnesis is emptiness. . . . Mnemic engagement is the precept (*gdams-ngag*) of the waking state; amnesis the precept of sleep." Some interesting observations on *dran-med* in Indo-Tibetan meditational literature may be found in David Seyfort Ruegg, *Buddha-nature, Mind and the Problem of Gradualism in a Comparative Perspective* (London: School of Oriental and African Studies, 1989), pp. 94, 99, 115, 155, 160, 183, 202, 207.

25. Knowledge of the importance of repetition as a dimension of soteriological strategy was well-established within the Rdzogs-chen tradition. Thus, for example, Zhabs-dkar Tshogs-drug rang-grol (1781–1851), *'Od gsal rdzogs pa chen po'i khregs chod lta ba'i glu dbyangs sa lam ma lus myur du bgrod pa'i rtsal ldan mkha' lding gshog rlabs* (xylographic edition, Bkra-shis-ljongs), folio 37a, insists that the disciple *repeatedly* receive guidance in the teaching in order for it to be firmly impressed on the mind (*yang yang khrid nas yid la 'byor ba dgos*). This, I hope, will answer the reviewer of the manuscript who expressed some doubts regarding the role of repetition as I have described it here.

26. For a theoretically provocative attempt to characterize Abhidharmic discourse and analyze the role of such discourse, see Paul Griffiths, "Denaturalizing Discourse," in Frank Reynolds and David Tracy, eds., *Myth and Philosophy* (Albany: SUNY Press, 1990).

27. Neither is it uncommon for the fictitious agents so portrayed to represent dimensions of a single psyche. Cf. Jon Whitman, "From the *Cosmographia* to the *Divine Comedy:* An Allegorical Dilemma," in Morton W. Bloomfield, ed., *Allegory, Myth, and Symbol*, Harvard English Studies 9 (Cambridge, Mass, and London:

Harvard University Press, 1981), pp. 63–86, esp. p. 85: "The figures Dante meets are potentialities of his own soul, possibilities which he briefly activates in his personal vision."

28. The reflections on narrative and philosophy roughly sketched out here will be found more fully developed in M. Kapstein, "Samantabhadra and Rudra: Two Philosophical Myths of Tibetan Rnying-ma-pa Buddhism," to appear in Frank Reynolds and David Tracy, eds., *Discourse and Praxis* (Albany: SUNY Press, 1992).

29. *rdzogs-pa chen-po man-ngag-gi rgyud thams-cad-kyi thog-ma. GZT,* III.49–81.

30. *sems kyi gnas tshul dang: dag pa'i lam du 'jug tshul yang dag pa don gyi ngo sprod brda ru bstan pa. GZT,* III.69.5–79.4.

31. The text, of course, does not make it entirely clear how we are to understand this division. I suspect that "lower vehicle(s)" (*theg-pa 'og-ma*) in this case refers to all eight vehicles that, according to the nine vehicle system of the Rnying-ma tradition, are ranked below the Great Perfection, or Atiyoga, whose teachings constitute the "higher vehicle(s)" (*theg-pa gong-ma*). See, for instance, the extraordinary passage from the *All-Accomplishing King* (*Kun-byed rgyal-po*) quoted in Dudjom Rinpoche, *The Nyingma School,* vol. 1, pp. 295–97, in which the first eight vehicles are criticized in turn for obscuring, through their false projections, the genuine nature of things.

32. Leon Hurvitz, trans., *Scripture of the Lotus Blossom of the Fine Dharma* (New York: Columbia University Press, 1976), Chapter 3. See, too, the rather neglected monograph by Michael Pye, *Skillful Means: A Concept in Mahayana Buddhism* (London: Duckworth, 1978).

33. Note the similarity between the revaluation of deception, as characterized here, and that of *māyā,* so often thought of as an evil deception, in Buddhist yogic literature. The yogic evaluation of *māyā* is considered in some detail in M. Kapstein, "The Illusion of Spiritual Progress," in R. Buswell and R. Gimello, eds., *Paths to Liberation* (Honolulu: University of Hawaii Press, 1992).

34. The tantra in question (*GZT,* IV.81–181) in fact has several titles, of which the one used in the chapter colophons best illustrates the centrality of this work in the *GZT* corpus overall: *Rdzogs pa chen po kun tu bzang po'i dgongs pa zang thal du bstan pa'i rgyud, The Tantra Teaching the Great Perfection, the Penetration of Samantabhadra's Intention.*

35. *smon lam stobs po che btab pas: sems can sangs mi rgya ba'i dbang med par bstan pa, GZT,* IV.171.5–177.6. There are many minor variations in the text of this prayer, particularly in its countless vulgate editions. The translation given in the appendix strictly follows the text as found in *GZT,* however, and is given in its entirety so as to give some indication of the way in which the topics under consideration are actually distributed in typical passages of *GZT.* An earlier English translation, with accompanying Tibetan text, may be found in Taklung Tsetul [Pema Wangyal] Rim-

poche and Kunzang Tenzin [Keith Dowman], *Ornaments of Illumination, The Sacred Path of Omniscience* (Darjeeling: Keith Dowman, 1970), pp. 20–27. The woodcut of Samantabhadra illustrating the present article was also reproduced there.

36. G. van der Leeuw, *Religion in Essence and Manifestation,* trans. J. E. Turner (Princeton, N.J.: Princeton University Press, 1986), Chapter 62. All uncited quotations in this and the following paragraphs may be found in this chapter.

37. Ibid., p. 87.

38. M. Kapstein, "Religious Syncretism in 13th Century Tibet: *The Limitless Ocean Cycle,*" in B. N. Aziz and M. Kapstein, eds., *Soundings in Tibetan Civilization* (Delhi: Manohar, 1985), pp. 358–71.

39. We should note, too, that the emphasis on reflexivity we find here is entirely consistent with an emphasis on reflexive acts that runs throughout Great Perfection thought. Cf. M. Kapstein, "Mi-pham's Theory of Interpretation," in Donald S. Lopez, Jr., ed., *Buddhist Hermeneutics* (Honolulu: University of Hawaii Press, 1988), pp. 158, 164.

40. *De Trinitate,* XIV.xi, trans. Arthur West Haddan in Philip Schaff, ed., *A Select Library of the Nicene and Post-Nicene Fathers of the Christian Church,* vol. 3 (New York: Charles Scribner's Sons, 1905), p. 191.

41. R. A. Markus, "Augustine," in D. J. O'Connor, ed., *A Critical History of Western Philosophy* (New York and London: The Free Press, 1964), p. 90.

42. Nor should we ignore, in a more thorough comparative study, the historical and doctrinal roots of the concepts concerned, and the manner in which these contextual considerations may alter our initial understanding of them. Augustine's theory, of course, must be studied in connection with the whole Platonic legacy of speculation on *anamnesis.*

43. Friedrich Nietzsche, *On the Geneology of Morals, Ecce Homo,* ed., with commentary, Walter Kaufmann (New York: Vintage Books, 1969), p. 61.

Remembering Resumed: Pursuing Buddhism and Phenomenology in Practice

EDWARD S. CASEY

> *I admit no memory in your sense of the word . . . Whatever we come on that is great, beautiful, significant, cannot be recollected. It must from the first be evolved within us, be made and become a part of us . . . There is no Past that we can bring back to us by the longing for it, there is only an eternally new Now that builds and creates itself out of the elements of the past as the past withdraws.*
>
> —Goethe, conversation of November 4, 1823

I

The series of studies making up this volume, all of which concern the place of memory in Buddhism, is a remarkable feat of memory in its own right. By this I mean that this book remembers traditions of thought whose meditations on memory might otherwise be forgotten—or perhaps never known at all—in the West. To accomplish this is not to remember in the usual sense of calling back to mind what is already known. Indeed, for scholars of the Buddhist tradition to call their knowledge back to their own minds would be an exercise in futility: it would be remembrance as mere repetition.

Something else is happening in this text: remembering is occurring in a special practice that might be called *remembering-for*. The authors are remembering for—remembering in the place of—the considerable variety of Buddhist texts and practices they treat. They are standing in for material that is not only difficult to grasp but, in certain cases, virtually inaccessible to Western readers. They are in effect memorial emissaries of this material, acting as its delegates in the minds of many of its readers—not excepting *this* reader. In just this regard, however, the authors are doing what every engaged rememberer does: actively recasting the past in the changing terms of the present. Thus remembering-for also means standing in *for the reader* by virtue of accomplishing what the benighted reader, not knowing the texts or practices under discussion, cannot do unassisted. If the first form of remembering-for has to do with representing various exoteric and esoteric doctrines, the second form remembers for the reader what the reader cannot, in the absence of appropriate knowledge, adequately represent to herself or himself.

I begin with this self-referential remark to indicate that writing and reading at the level of scholarly practice immerse us from the start in matters of memory. But much more than the practice of interpreting and reading is at issue in the essays here set forth. The practice in question is Buddhist practice, most notably a meditative practice that includes as well the devotion, prayer, visualization, recounting of myth, and other exercises the Buddhist engages in as part of the path to enlightenment. Reflecting on such practices gives rise to a primary paradox addressed by a number of authors in this volume. On the one hand, memory is deeply ingredient in meditational exercise. On the other hand, when it comes to questions of theory—including the theory of meditational practices themselves—memory is rarely acknowledged as such. Consider only the fact that, in many of these practices, lists of things to be remembered are considered indispensable. As Rupert Gethin shows in his contribution, these lists aid practitioners to remember many items for which they form a concise summation; and as these lists must themselves be memorized, those who use them are engaged in a double rememoration that expands exponentially.[1] Yet the significance of "listing" as a phenomenon in its own right is taken for granted. Furthermore, even in detailed epistemological discussions of human mental activity, Buddhist theorists tend to neglect memory. As P. S. Jaini puts it, "despite the extraordinary preoccupation of the ancient Buddhists in explaining the process of cognition, memory is conspicuous by its absence in the long list of mental events and concomitant mental factors."[2] In Buddhist texts, memory is often subordinated to "mindfulness" (*smṛti*), that pervasive posture of practice which is as easily assimilated to attention as it is to memory. As Paul J. Griffiths writes:

> it is this stress on attention as an activity of the mind which provides the conceptual connection with the most common context for the use of *smṛti* in Buddhist texts: *smṛti* as a type of meditational practice, usually called 'the application of *smṛti*" (*smṛtyupasthāna*). In these contexts, the standard English translation of the term has become "mindfulness." When one engages in the practice of mindfulness one pays close attention to whatever one is taking as the object of one's meditational practice . . . the term *smṛti* carries with it *no essential reference to remembering past events*, though the very act of paying close attention to the present contents of one's mind makes it possible to recall those contents at some later time.[3]

Memory is here regarded as something secondary to meditational practice—what one does *after* the primary activity of mindful attending. This is to split off memory from mindfulness. Other authors, however, insist on the pervasiveness of memory to meditational exercises and, indeed, to mindfulness itself. (*Memor* in Latin connotes both "mindful" and "remembering"—as do the ancient Greek root *mnā* and the Sanskrit *smṛ*, the stem of *smṛti* itself.)[4] On this immanentist view, memory is not only essential to practice but coextensive with it. Collett Cox, for example, quotes Pāli Abhidhamma texts such as the *Dhammasaṅgaṇi* and the *Vibhaṅga:* "mindfulness . . . is reflection, recollection; mindfulness . . . is retentiveness, the state of supporting the state of nondrifting (or fixing), the state of nonlosing."[5] Similarly, Matthew Kapstein argues that "mnemic engagement" is at work *in every stage* of the practice of the Great Perfection: "from its function in 'introducing' the timeless realm of the dharmakāya, to its symbolic representation in allegory, to its role in the transfiguration of the ordinary through the ritual practice of prayer."[6] For Cox and Kapstein, memory is everywhere in Buddhist practice, inseparable from it and essential to it.

Given such disparate views, what are we to think? A clue may come from a very different practice, that of phenomenology. I invoke this last discipline, my own, with some hesitation, given that several authors in this book expressly disavow any phenomenological purport of Buddhist practice, at least as this practice bears on memory. Griffiths claims, for instance, that "the Yogācāra account of memory, and indeed Buddhist accounts in general . . . [have] little to offer those interested in the phenomenology of remembering."[7] Granting for the moment that this may be so, it does not follow that a phenomenological treatment of remembering could not, despite the odds, illuminate Buddhist accounts of memory. This illumination might take place even if it is the case (as Griffiths attempts to demonstrate) that such accounts are concerned primarily—when they are concerned with memory at all—with "the causal mechanisms operative in memory-events."[8]

A first instance of such illumination bears on one of Griffiths's own contentions: namely, that Buddhist practice is concerned with attention *rather than with* memory. Here, however, I would ask: is there any act of attention, including that involved in concentrated mindfulness, that is *not* saturated with memory? Not necessarily with recollective memory; if this were the only choice, Griffiths's skepticism would be merited. But Edmund Husserl, the founder of phenomenology, distinguished another, equally important, form of memory: "primary memory." This is the memory of the just-elapsed event *even as it is elapsing*. Because attention bears on what is happening just *now,* it also bears on what has just now *happened*—which is to say, on the just-vanished or still-vanishing event (whether mental or perceptual). If this is so, attention not only can but *must* include primary memory. Still more strongly, it *depends* on it, for if attention could not remember what has just happened it could not grasp what is now happening *as it is now happening*.

(What is now happening is not only a causal consequence of what has just happened; it depends on knowing that what has just happened is continuous with that to which we are now attending.) Primary memory, far from being an after-event, is always already in the forefront of attention. As William James (who coined the term) wrote: the object of primary memory "comes to us as belonging to the rearward portion of the present space of time."[9] Indeed, it figures not only into "mindful attentiveness" (i.e., Kapstein's "B mnemic engagement") but also into "the immediate recovery of the self-presenting awareness of the dharmakāya" (Kapstein's description of "C mnemic engagement"). A central characteristic of primary memory or "memory of the present" is its capacity to apprehend the immediate present itself, even as it begins to recede from the refined focus of the now-point. To put the point somewhat differently, the immediate moment is *distended* in primary memory. Instead of being allowed to vanish altogether, it is encouraged to linger on: "an object of primary memory is not thus brought back [as in recollection]; *it never was lost;* its date was never cut off in consciousness from that of the immediately present moment."[10] James's words are reminiscent of a formula cited by Jaini from Sthiramati's commentary to the *Trimśikā:* "the nondropping of a familiar entity," with "familiar entity" glossed as "a previously experienced object."[11] Jaini also refers to Theravādin descriptions of an expanded immediate present, in which the cognition of an object is maintained for seventeen moments.[12] This expanded present depends upon primary memory as surely as does attention. It does not undermine the momentariness that is central to Buddhist ontology; it shows instead the considerable range of what can count as "the moment" if the ingrediency of primary memory is taken into account.

Husserl vacillated between regarding primary memory as a form of *memory* and as a form of *perception.* As Derrida has demonstrated, Husserl ended up opting for *both:* as bearing on an elapsing event, it is memorial; as intuitive in its grasp of that event, it is perceptual.[13] This elective affinity between memory and perception (Bergson held that "there is no perception that is not full of memories"[14]) is demonstrated in several studies in this book. For example, Nyanaponika Thera focuses on "the reminiscent function of perception" whereby memory can be seen as part of perception itself. Perception (*saññā*) is "the taking up, the making, and remembering of the object's distinctive marks."[15] Regarded as a modification of perception, such memory comes close to being *memory of the present:* it "refers to an event so close to the present that in normal parlance it is not called 'memory', though it is not essentially different from it."[16]

It follows, then, that if Husserl and James are correct—if all attention, beginning with that elicited by perception, involves primary memory—the practice of meditation is memorious through and through. To engage in such a practice is *never not to remember.* Thus it is not just a matter of admitting memory *into* meditational practice but of realizing that it has *already been there* from the start. Memory and mindfulness, if not one and the same activity, are at least inseparably conjoined in such practice. This practice brings them together as forcefully as certain theories attempt to hold them apart.

We may go even further and ask whether the ubiquity of primary memory—there is such memory of/in every experience, including perception, all forms of cognition, and even other kinds of memory—does not aid in resolving a basic question raised by several authors in this volume: is *smṛti* a universal feature of mental life, or is it just an occasional occurrence? If *smṛti* can be construed as primary memory, then Husserl and James would hold that it is active in every mental event. This position is consonant with the Kāśmīri Sarvāstivādin school, which considers *smṛti* to be one of the ten constant factors of experience—one that "performs the functions of retention, noting or fixing, and stabilizing that are requisite for recollection."[17] James would certainly agree with the claim of the *Mahāvibhāṣā* that, thanks to *smṛti,* "*the object is not lost,* enabling one to give rise to both specific and general activities with regard to it."[18] If *smṛti* is indeed responsible for the nonloss of objects of experience—and if, as for the Sarvāstivādin school, it is singled out as such—it becomes difficult to resist the view that memory, at least in the minimal and primal form of "retention" (a term that Husserl regarded as equivalent to primary memory), is everywhere presupposed and everywhere active.

On a first point, then, phenomenology illuminates the paradox of Buddhism's immersion in, and yet neglect of, memory. Phenomenology's own very different practice—it is arguable that retention or primary memory was Husserl's first discovery in practicing phenomenology—uncovered a type of memory that underlies a variety of meditative practices in the Buddhist tradition. Precisely because it *under*lies these practices, it is not always noticed, much less named, as such. As James said, "namelessness is compatible with existence."[19] But whether such memory is acknowledged or only presumed, it can be argued that it pervades such practices, making each of them possible (including the attention that is central to them all). For how can we meditate on anything whatsoever unless we are able to bear in mind, and thus hold in memory, that on which we are meditating—even, at the limit, emptiness itself?

II

One basic purpose of remembering is to prevent loss. It is precisely because objects of experience *are* lost so often, and in so many ways, that they must be regained and retrieved in memory. One of the most impressive things about the essays in this book is that, taken together, they exhibit the remarkable range of the kinds of memory that are at play in Buddhist practices and texts. In this very respect, they rejoin a phenomenology of memory. For phenomenology, building on primary memory as a proto-phenomenon, has been adept at picking out a spectrum of memorial acts, ranging from "secondary memory" (i.e., recollection) to recognition, from reminding to commemorating. In the essays in this collection we find expositions of just these act-forms—as well as certain others not taken up by phenomenologists, such as the memorizing of lists of items, the invocations of prayer, the recognition of oneself as a buddha, and the use of mnemonic dhāraṇī signs. In the end, the reader is treated to an arborescent display of the many branches of memory—branches dividing into yet other branches as surely as the lists cited in the *mātikās* ramify into still other lists.[20]

In this phase of my remarks I want to focus not on memorial multiplicity as such but on three questions that are raised by this multiplicity itself. Is there a privileged form of memory? Must memory have a sensuous content? Is all significant remembering mental in character?

It is certainly tempting to presume that some one form of remembering is privileged. I have come close to making this presumption myself in my discussion of primary memory as it functions in phenomenological self-scrutiny and in Buddhist meditational practices. But it is one thing to claim that such memory is always present and quite another to say that it is especially privileged in the sense of "most important" or "the only form of memory worth exploring." Let me make it clear, then, that the primariness of primary memory alludes only to its ingrediency in all acts of mind; it is there from the first and, indeed, always there; but this is not to maintain that it matters most compared with other types of memory. These other types may all presuppose it as their epistemological and ontological condition without its being more significant than they in the ongoing life of the remembering subject. In fact, other kinds of remembering are more determinative of the direction and pursuit of this subject's interests. Think only of the extent to which any practice of meditation relies on the remembering of certain ways to proceed that one has previously learned. Such remembering-how or "procedural memory," though dependent on primary memory at every step, differs from primary memory decisively by being at once skillful and adaptable to any number of different situations.[21] But, again, it would be a mistake to hold that as a result of its importance for meditational practices remembering-how is thereby privileged over other forms of memory. It is certainly not privileged when it comes to the question of *what* a person is remembering or is supposed to remember, on any given occasion. What are my former lives like, or, indeed, what is my own life like in the last few moments? Such questions cannot be answered by the deliverances of remembering-how, which has to do with my life regarded as habitual and habituating—as a nexus of learned procedures.

When we begin to look for the "what" of memory, that is, its content, we are once again tempted to privilege a certain form of memory. I refer to "recollection," that memorial action by which we summon to mind particular past events in sensuous display. So powerful is the attraction of recollection that it bids fair to be considered memory *tout court* in the West since at least the era of Plato. That it has comparable power in Buddhist thought is suggested in the ideal of remembering previous lives—a remembering that, if fully successful, would involve the recall of sensuously experienced items from these lives: "thus I remembered various former abodes *in all their modes and details.*"[22] Both Plato and the Buddha seem to merge metempsychotic, transmigratory remembrance with recollection—a word that is often chosen to translate Plato's technical term *anamnesis.* This is perfectly understandable if a recollected object is, in James's description, "one which has been absent from consciousness altogether, and now revives anew."[23] To revive is to come back from from "death's dateless night."[24] Quite apart from special difficulties with the doctrines of *anamnesis* and transmigration—and whether these difficulties are logical or practical[25]—we need to wonder at the tendency, to which thinkers in the West as in the East subscribe, to identify translife (and much of ordinary intralife) remembering with recollection.

If we wonder long enough, we discover two reasons for this identification. One is that recollection *delivers quasi-sensuous content;* the other is that recollection is held to be exclusively *an act of mind.* A double privilege, thus doubly difficult to refuse. On the one hand, the directness and immediacy of sensuous content, perceived or remembered, induces an attitude of epistemic certainty: how can I doubt that which, reviving in such a discrete and concrete format, brings the past back before me in vivid display? What Merleau-Ponty has called "the primacy of perception"[26] is all the more captivating when sensuous qualities appear to inhere in remembered content: as if such qualities were appointed representatives of a perceptual past from which I am otherwise disconnected! On the other hand, the fact that I recapture the past not only in a quasi-sensuous presentation but in an act of my own mind lends seemingly incontrovertible authority even to the most ordinary act of recollection. For if my own mind—about which I am presumably as certain as I am about anything—is bringing back before itself items identical (or at least quite continuous) with those I once experienced *in propria persona,* how can I doubt my apprehension of these items? Not just adequacy but apodicticity appears to be built into the recollective act, especially insofar as it is regarded as an act of a mind that is transparent to itself.[27] No wonder, then, that it is so tempting to imagine that recollection enjoys a privileged standing among acts of remembrance.

And yet this standing is only imaginary—as imaginary as is the perceiving or recollecting self according to Buddhism. To begin with, sensory contents, whether perceived or recollected, can be misleading and are thus subject to doubt at any moment. (Such dubitability is dramatized by Descartes in his *Meditations on First Philosophy,* a text that opens by underlining the unreliability of sensory experience.) There is nothing in being sensory as such that requires belief; on the contrary, the sensory should occasion our doubt (or, in phenomenological parlance, the "suspension of belief"). This is a move familiar to Buddhists of many persuasions, even though the application to recollection may not have been effected as emphatically as is called for. Moreover, to be enacted in a conscious mind brings with it no further certainty. Its own pretensions notwithstanding, the conscious mind is not at all times diaphanous to itself. The certainty supposedly generated by consciousness on a Cartesian model is disputed by Freud, who rejects the epistemic certainty of conscious mind as vigorously as Descartes himself doubts the epistemic certainty of the senses. This is not to say that Freud is right in the matter; it is only to say that he calls into question any undisputed privilege of consciousness in matters of self-knowledge. But to question the privilege of conscious mind is at the same stroke to question the privilege of recollection—a privilege erected upon the twin pillars of consciousness and perception. Once these pillars are discovered to be made of clay, the edifice of epistemic certainty they support begins to crumble into dust.

Does this mean that the object of memory is always irretrievably lost? Assuredly not! It means only that no one such object can be assumed to be continually reliable—not even, indeed perhaps least of all, the object of recollection. Other objects of memory are at least equally trustworthy: for instance, the nonsensuous contents of "remembering-that." (Remembering-that occurs when I recall *that* I once visited Yellowstone Park when I was very young, even though I cannot summon up any concrete details of this experience.[28]) Still other objects of memory prove to be more reliable than either recollection or remembering-that. In "semantic memory," I remember certain items of information, such as historical facts or scientific laws, that are entirely independent of my own experience: say, the Pythagorean theorem, or the date of Descartes's death. I recall them without recollecting them.[29]

By pointing to such alternative forms of remembering, we rejoin from a Western phenomenological perspective a recognition of the importance of decidedly nonsensuous, nonmentalistic, and nonautobiographical forms of memory. Some of the most important of these involve recalling names or formulaic groups of words. I refer in particular to Paul Harrison's chapter as it bears on remembering names. Harrison shows that the elaborate visualization practices of the Vajrayāna or tantric Buddhist tradition may give way to the sheer recitation of a name, such as "Avalokiteśvara," in an appropriate formula. Or, still more extreme, the recitation of the Buddha's name alone in *nien-fo* and *nembutsu* practices in China and Japan comes to be the unique memorial vehicle. In these latter cases, "it is through the medium of the name that one calls the Buddha to mind."[30] Closely allied to this tendency is the condensation of a larger text into a single letter or brief formula—most notably, dhāraṇī of the sort studied in depth by Gyatso. A dhāraṇī letter offers a species of *emboîtement,* a technique that also operates in allegory as Kapstein demonstrates.[31] Unlike a list or an allegory, however, the dhāraṇī of the Prajñāpāramitā syllabary practice condenses in a nonserial manner.[32] The effect is, as it were, a pointillism of memory: memory in the now-point of a name or even just a syllable: "the single letter *A* abbreviate(s) the Prajñāpāramitā teachings that elsewhere are stated in 100,000 verses."[33] In dhāraṇī memory, it is as if remembering sought the magical zero-point where the verbal (typically extended in diachronic display on the horizontal, syntagmatic axis of language) and the imagistic (suspended on the vertical, paradigmatic axis) coincide. This is the point at which memory's imagistic-verbal "dual processing" (as cognitive psychologists call it) suddenly loses its parallel structure by intersecting at a single but momentous point.

Something like this occurs whenever the mere pronunciation of a single proper name or place name evokes an entire shimmering store of memories: as does "Nehru" for contemporary Indians, or as did "Combray" for Proust's narrator in *The Remembrance of Things Past.* Illustrated here is the truth in Wayman's remark that "every name is a kind of memory."[34] What dhāraṇī memory—and other especially efficacious forms of remembering such as the Great Perfection allegories and prayers analyzed by Kapstein—add to this familiar (but often unnoticed) memorial phenomenon is the promise of special efficacy: by their pronunciation and repetition, indeed by their bare perception, I can attain emptiness. These potent vehicles not merely gesture toward such emptiness—as might a metaphysical "cipher script"[35]—they concretely *remind* their practitioners of it. Such extraordinary reminding occurs by means of what I have elsewhere called "remembering-through."[36] *Through* the perception and use of words (or syllables or letters) as reminders, I enable certain realizations to occur. In effecting these realizations, I am not recollecting particular presences. But I am remembering. I am reaching out beyond recollection—or, more exactly, *before* it—to come into the remembered presence (or rather, nonpresence) of that of which I am being reminded.

III

A dhāraṇī letter is like a seed of memory, and it is to the notion of "seed," mentioned by several authors (e.g., Griffiths, Gethin, Cox, Jaini, and Gyatso), that we need next to turn. It is a natural place to go, considering that at some point every rememberer must confront the question: what keeps and conveys memories, given that they pass in and out of consciousness? (Were memories to remain constantly *in* consciousness, they would be intolerable, constituting a memorial overload of the sort from which Luria's subject "S," cited by Lopez, suffered so acutely.[37])

Of various candidates for keeping—the brain is favored by modern neurology, landscape features by Western Apaches and Australian aborigines—the seed has the special advantage of being neither inertly material (it is organic and, literally, seminal) nor sheerly mental (the mind bringing with it distortion and distraction). As a borderline entity, with a status akin to that of the Abhidharmic category of "forces disassociated from mind," or *citta-viprayukta-saṃskāra,*[38] the seed can serve many interests (*inter-esse* means, literally, "being-between"): those of individual rememberers and collective traditions, of the sentient world (each member of which has evolved from a seed of some sort), and of semiological systems ("symbols grow" said Peirce).[39] Precisely as a being of the borderline, the seed also plays a deconstructive role to which I return in Section IV.

But first we need to determine how "seed" operates in Buddhist accounts of memory. Both Jaini and Griffiths quote the following seminal passage from Vasubandhu's *Abhidharmakośabhāṣya:*

> What is a "seed"? It is the capacity to bring forth *kleśas* in a particular person, a power that comes from [previous] *kleśas.* In just the same way there is a power to bring forth memory, a power that comes from [previous] experiential awareness.[40]

If passions (*kleśas*) thus endure in dormant form as seeds, the same is true of memories.[41] Vasubandhu posits that such a "seed of memory," like a dormant passion, calls for a substratum disassociated from the series of consciousnesses (*citta-viprayukta-saṃskāra*). But Jaini makes it clear that this line of thought, intriguing as it is, is not further developed by Vasubandhu.[42] Whatever the resolution of this particular debate may be, it is evident that the primary problem to be addressed is that of *continuity over time:* how do the seeds of memory endure as recognizably the same through a sequence of merely momentary acts of consciousness?

At least three Buddhist answers to this question were proposed. Two of these are particular hallmarks of the Yogācāra school. Of these two, the first and most metaphoric is that of "perfuming." Closely related to the allied metaphor of impregnating, perfuming entails the exuding of odors that are incorporated from flowers into seeds which, once effloresced, will pass the perfume onto yet other seeds, and so on indefinitely. Without attending to the subtleties of the perfuming process,[43] I would only like to note the appropriateness of invoking the process of perfuming. The power and persistence of aromatic memories is known to every human rememberer—not just to Proust or to "S"—and its basis in the rhinencephalon, the most ancient "reptilian" part of the brain, is suggestive. It is precisely what Vasubandhu, commenting on the *Mahāyānasaṅgraha* of Asaṅga, calls the "nondefinite" (*avyākṛta*) character of perfume that allows it to play this extraordinary role.[44] It is the altogether definite in memory that is, paradoxically, the most fragile: to remember it at all, one must remember it in its exact original contour. If this contour is lost, "the object is lost." But if there is no precise shape to start with—as is certainly the case with most sensations of smell—then one can reconnect with it through a broad range of comparably diffuse shapes when remembering it.[45] Thus, on both empirical and theoretical grounds, the choice of perfuming as a model of seed-memory is promising. Its shortcoming is found in the simple fact that many memories—notably, semantic and mantric memories—depend on precision throughout. Nor will it do to circumvent this objection by considering "perfuming" to be shorthand for "tendency" (*vāsanā*). To say that "the seeds are given a perfuming tendency by the flowers that produce them"[46] is only to displace the problem by positing an ad hoc disposition, a "dormitive virtue" à la Molière, in place of a genuine mechanism of conveyance.

A second model of seed-perdurance can be distinguished from the perfuming model. This is the Yogācāra idea of a "store-consciousness," a veritable "storehouse of all seeds," including those of memory. Such a notion of a memory storehouse is hardly restricted to Buddhist thought. It is espoused by John Locke in *An Essay Concerning Human Understanding*.[47] Neurologists have followed suit; for example, the McCullough-Pitts hypothesis that entire memories are stored unchangingly in particular micro-areas in the brain.[48] But skeptics have abounded, East and West, and for good reasons. Freud insisted that memories exist only *between* discrete neurones; that is, in the "facilitating pathways" between "seed neurones."[49] The most effective counterargument in the Buddhist context is offered by Griffiths, who maintains that a store-consciousness is a quasi-substance which is impossible in principle to distinguish from the notion of substance elsewhere rejected by Yogācāra theorists themselves: these theorists "do not effectively explain in what sense the store's possession of [memory-seeds'] potencies differs from a substance's possession of its properties."[50] In this spirit, let us say that the idea of a memory-store is at once factitious and fictitious. It is manufactured to resolve what Dewey liked to call a "problematic situation," and yet it is itself problematic. Indeed, it is an imaginary construct: has anyone, including the most discerning neurologist, ever *seen* such a store?

A third model for the preservation of memory-seeds has not been thematized by Buddhist theorists, but I find it to be suggested at several key points. This is the idea of "mark." This term (or its semiotical equivalent) is discussed by the majority of authors in this volume, including Nyanaponika, Harrison, Cox, Gyatso, Jaini, and Wayman. Cox emphasizes the way in which certain Buddhist texts, earlier than the Yogācāra writings that advocate the idea of *bīja* ("seed"), recommend fastening the mind onto worthy marks as a primary means of avoiding distraction. The marks in question may be marks of the mind itself: "the skillful monk . . . grasps the marks of the mind, experiences concentration of the mind and, thus, abandons defilements."[51] But it would be unduly psychologistic to confine marks to the mind, as if they were only signs *of* the mind. "Memory-seeds" themselves, in any case, cannot be so confined.

How may seed, mark, and memory be brought together more fruitfully? Jaini, commenting on certain Theravādin themes, makes the following pertinent remark:

> Under certain circumstances there arises a mental event called "having the same object" (*tadārammaṇa*) before the series [of mental events] is terminated. This regrasps the object for a moment before the object is lost, the series is terminated, and the *bhavaṅga* [i.e., "constituent of becoming"] instantaneously reemerges. It is conceivable that this having-the-same-object mental event could perform, in addition to reregistering the object, the function of passing on the mark (*nimitta*) of the vanishing object to the *bhavaṅga* consciousness where it could be stored.[52]

This passage offers a crucial clue. It proposes that the way in which marks are apprehended is by a special action of regrasping a vanishing object—a refocusing within the stream of consciousness, however momentary the stream itself may be. Just as the primary memory or "retention" of a particular object is fading out, yet short of a complete elapsing (to remedy which would require wholesale recollection), there is a phase of reconnection with the content of what we have experienced. This intermediate memorial moment was described by Husserl as "still-retaining-in-grasp" (*noch-im-Griff-behalten*) and is to be considered as "a kind of *passivity in activity.*"[53] What we regrasp beyond sheer retention is something that is subject to what Husserl calls "explication," which consists in "a developing contemplation, a unity of articulated contemplation."[54] It is striking that Husserl regards such explicative contemplation as a sense-giving moment out of which the most basic logical categories arise; it is the moment of "pre-predicative synthesis";[55] that is, of associative connection between the apprehended and the still-retained object.

Let us put together these two convergent lines of thought, the one from the Theravādins and the other from the phenomenologists. If regrasping "the same object" amounts to a "passing on the mark of the vanishing object," the still-retaining-in-grasp of this object, thanks to an unfolding contemplation, can achieve an "explicative coincidence" wherein the overlapping of explicated aspects is such that *one and the same object* is being retained.[56] Such coincidence amounts to the formation of a sense-giving sign; though pre-predicative, this sign has its own signifying power. What is accomplished in this memorial process—accomplished not voluntaristically but by a peculiar passivity-in-activity—is *an object remembered in a mark.* An object is held in memory in such a way that its being explicatively contemplated is equivalent to its constitution as a mark. And conversely: to be a mark is to have been remarked.

The mark in question is a memory-mark. Passing on the mark is passing on the memory generated by an object's having been still-retained-in-grasp. Such a mark does not so much belong *to* mind as it is generated *by* mind. It is generated by a peculiar mindfulness that consists in a remembering located between primary memory and recollection—a remembering that must occur "before the series is terminated." This is mind-as-memory at work beyond the primary way of bare retention: retention has become retention-in-grasp. On the other hand, we can also say with Gethin that in this passive-active operation "memory becomes mindfulness."[57] For in regrasping and explicating what it has just experienced, it becomes mindful of its own object. However subtle the synthesis of such mindfulness, it is, in Kapstein's phrase, "the most natural thing in the world."[58]

This minding-remembering is what preserves the memory-seed first implanted in a given experience. Unretained and unexplicated—cognitive psychologists would say "unrehearsed"—the seed would die stillborn and its object vanish forever. Not the first moment of reception and retention, nor the belated moment of recollection, but the intermediate moment of reapprehensive contemplation constitues the legacy of the mark. This critical but often unacknowledged moment makes possible the passing-on of a mark in still further remembering (whether this occurs as ordinary recollection or as a matter of soteriologically significant "recovery").[59] It is the moment in which the seed becomes a sign. The deposition of the seed becomes the designation of a mark.

As a sign, a memory has a life of its own. It is not strictly dependent on matter or on mind, even though it employs both for its own purposes: matter in sets of traces, mind as series of acts of consciousness. If signs indeed grow, they grow in a semiological soil that is self-nourishing; clusters of signs grow together to compose dense textures of signification. Such clusters, properly totalized, constitute a given language or sign system. But in equipoise with this universalizing tendency, we must remember that one sign—even a dhāraṇī syllable[60]—can stand for many clusters of signs. We bear in mind these clustered blossoms of semiological fruition in a single sign signifying nothing short of "anything and everything."[61]

IV

I have concentrated on the idea of seed-memory for a number of reasons. One of these is that it is not an idea outside the domain of Western phenomenology. This is so even though at first glance it might seem to be an exclusively causal notion: is not a seed the efficient cause of fruit or other organic products? As sheerly causal, seed-memory would be trans- or subphenomenal—not a "phenomenon" in its own right (*phenomenon* derives from *phainesthai*, "to appear"). Causes belong to what Husserl designated as "the natural attitude," which is inimical to phenomenological investigation. But on close inspection the idea of *smṛti-bīja* itself defies the distinction between the causal and the phenomenal, suggesting that the more appropriate distinction is that between the order-of-perdurance and the order-of-reappearance. Essential to reappearance is the quite phenomenological notion of still-retaining-in-grasp. The latter arises from straightforward phenomenological description, and yet it bears on a process that is natural to consider causal. Instead of saying, then, that the store-consciousness entailed by seed-memories calls for "a causal analysis *rather than* a descriptive one,"[62] I prefer to say that the idea of seed-memory and all that it entails (including the notion of store-consciousness) brings the very distinction between the causal and the descriptive into question.

It ensues that the ideas of memorial seeds and their marking and storing do not function as explanatory constructs—constructs that entail causal analysis. They serve instead as boundary concepts that undermine such distinctions as those between the causal and the descriptive, or between the sub- or transphenomenal and the phenomenal—not to mention still more momentous distinctions between ground and recovery, bewilderment and enlightenment, or even between matter and mind, present and past, self and other.[63] For example, what is already true of primary memory (in which past and present are virtually indistinguishable) is also true of the still-retaining-in-grasp of marks: just as the former hovers on the "rearward portion of the present space of time," so the latter clings to the intermediate space between primary and secondary memory—thus deconstructing their very difference. Comparable deconstructions can be performed on the other binary oppositions just listed. With the idea of seed-memory as marked and remarked, we have reached a boundary condition—what Jaspers called a *Grenzsituation*[64]—in which these traditional oppositions dissipate like fading perfume from under our inquiring noses.

Something else that is disseminated by the seed-mark is the notion of *origin*. Just as there is no end of the proliferating growth of signs—which achieve, according to Peirce, a distinctive semiotic immortality for their utterers—so there is no beginning either, no first sign. By the same sign, there is no first memory, not even a first moment of a given memory. A memory arrives *already* "passing on the mark" that identifies it: there is no unmarked memory. By this rather remarkable route, we rejoin an interpretive thesis proffered by Lopez: "the authors of the account of the enlightenment thus construct a model against which all memory is to be measured, a model of *an original memory that reaches back without beginning*."[65] In the experience of enlightenment as in the semiotics of seed-memory, the very idea of a pristine origin, a seedless "first time," is subverted.

V

To say that memory is a marked seed, that is, something semous, is to say that certain experiences—even, at the limit (a limit embraced by Freud and Bergson) *all* experiences—"leave their mark." Such experiences come marked: marked *for* memory and marked *by* memory. They are marked to be remarked; they are made to be remembered. Heidegger speaks of the human condition as that of being "on the way to language" (*unterwegs zur Sprache*).[66] But we are just as much *on the way to memory*. Yet this is so only because to be on the way to memory is already to be on the way to language—on the way to the marking that, as signing, is the basis of language. (A mark, I am assuming, is the design of a word, a sememe, even if it is not yet literally a word as such.)

If we begin to think this way—the way of the memory-seed as memory-sign—we find ourselves in a position to grasp two of the most enigmatic statements in this book:

> "The Buddha needed to remember in order to forget."[67]
> "Remembering is not something buddhas do."[68]

Antinomical as they seem to be in juxtaposition, these bold sentences are clarified by the notion of the (re)marked memory-seed. The Buddha had to remember (certain signs of previous lives)in order to forget (the bewilderment and defilements of any given life). Freud observed that we cannot be said to forget that of which we were not consciously aware to begin with.[69]

Lopez, who wrote the first sentence above, has recourse to Freud for his own interpretation of the Buddha's claim to remember all former lives. According to this interpretation, these lives are recalled as screen memories; that is, as "deferred revisions" of that which is not recollected as such and in detail. Such screened revisions are in effect palimpsests of the past that are incorporated into the Buddha's present life, enriching it immeasurably.[70] If this incorporation counts as remembering, there is no doubt that the Buddha does remember.

Yet Griffiths, the author of the second sentence, claims categorically that the Buddha does *not* remember, not even in a Freudo-Pickwickian manner. In answer to this claim, we need only insist on one proposition which both Lopez and Griffiths affirm: *the Buddha does not recollect.* Not only need he not recollect, to do so in his circumstance would be to misremember: it would bring the past back in a way that mimics defilement itself. (Recollection, in its quasi-sensuous display and personal-mindedness, is remembering in the realm of saṃsāra. In its concern with succession and its obsession with detail, it is an instance of Kapstein's "mnemic engagement *A*"; it thus fails to attain "genuine *dran-pa.*"[71]) But the Buddha *does* remember. He does so by retaining the marks of what has preceded him. Such retaining of marks in mind is reminiscent of what Freud calls "remembering in the old manner—reproduction in the psychical field."[72] Nonrecollective reproduction brings the past back in iconic signs: signs that not only remind by qualitative similarity but that, in Gyatso's way of putting it, are their own signifieds, being equated with them.[73] The old manner, then, is the Buddha's. It is also that of the early Buddhist adepts and virtuosi of memory, for whom remembering occurs as attending to the marks that cluster and grow at the edges of a life—and, at the limit, of all previous lives.

But what is a life, and how is it remembered? Here we enter the treacherous domain of personal identity. Let us take it for granted that there is a decisive difference between the substantial self (e.g., *ātman*) and the person. The former notion is that of a strictly self-identical substance that *continues* to exist over a lifetime and even over many lifetimes without any significant break in its continuity as such. In the Western view, the substantial self is the soul; for example, the *psychē* that is the subject of *anamnēsis* on Plato's account. But in the West, neither this continuant self nor its continual memory is required for personal identity. This was first seen clearly by John Locke, who distinguished rigorously between continuity or sameness of substance and personal identity. The continuity and sameness of personal identity is brought about by consciousness and, in particular, by memory. Pushing the distinction between substance and personal identity to an absurd extreme, he pointed out that twenty different substances or souls in principle could possess the same personal identity; conversely, one substance could possess many personal identities. If Locke is right, all that is required for the identity of the person is that a person be able to connect in consciousness with events earlier in his or her life, or with events in earlier lives. As Locke put it in a classical formulation, "as far as [a person's] consciousness can be extended backwards to any past action or thought, so far reaches the identity of that person; it is the same self [as] it was then; and it is by the same self with this present one that now reflects on it, that that action was done."[74] By "extended backwards" in consciousness, Locke means *remembered*. In his own succinct formulation, "that with which the consciousness of this present thinking thing can join itself makes the same person, and is one self with it, and with nothing else."[75]

And with nothing else. Not continuity of substance but (noncontinual) connection in memory is at once a necessary, sufficient, and exclusive condition of personal identity. The advantages of this view are evident, especially from a Buddhist perspective. First, the Lockean position avoids commitment to enduring substance so far as personal identity is concerned. The sameness of the remembering and the remembered self is a nonsubstantial sameness. The "one self" or "same person" that these two phases of remembering constitute is not a personal, much less a personalized, substance. It is an identical self—a self not so much identical *in time* as constituted *through (discontinuous) memory*. Second, attention is directed to the *present* state of remembering—that is, to the act itself of "owning" the past—rather than to the past content remembered (as occurs perforce in recollection). Third, because personal identity is nothing other than what such an act brings to mind, it deconstructs personal identity as anything existing or lasting independently of consciousness. Indeed, such identity need not be any more constant or continuous than the act of remembrance on which it depends. Fourth, in this paradigm personal identity is not restricted to *this individual life*, but may extend to previous lives. (In fact, Locke expressly allows for the possibility of remembering former lives.[76])Locke might count as genuine remembering any act of reconnecting in consciousness with such diverse and extraindividual things as previous abodes or the principle of emptiness, no matter how disconnected these may be from one's contemporary life. And what counts as remembering counts as the constitution of personal identity.[77] This is so, even though, as Lopez emphasizes, reconnection with previous lives is notably nonpersonal in the sense that it is "topographically flat, without affect . . . disinterested."[78] Locke might well agree that such impersonality of reconnection is a virtue, not a defect, as it voids the cloying personalism of recollective remembering—a remembering that concentrates on the past of a person regarded as a discrete substance.

If we may grant, then, that the author of *An Essay Concerning Human Understanding*, a book first published in 1690 in the heyday of early Western modernism, adroitly eludes the metaphysics of presence and comes into unexpected propinquity with Buddhist thinkers, one nagging question persists. Do we need the idea of "personal identity" at all? Buddhists and Locke alike agree that self-as-substance is dispensable, indeed, detrimental. But Locke clings to the notion of personal identity or, as he sometimes puts it, "the same personal self."[79] A Buddhist such as Vasubhandu appears to reject even this remnant of self-sameness, especially in the passage from the *Abhidharmakośabhāṣya* to which I earlier referred. In that passage, Vasubhandu adopts the minimalist account of self as a radical momentariness, a series (*santāna*) of mental moments (*cittas*) linked only by the cryptic causality of the seed-fruit relation. Remembering is reduced to the scenario that "one mental event of the past, which perceives a certain object and hence can be designated as a 'seeing mental event' (*darśana-citta*) brings about the existence of another, namely, the present mental event, which can be called the 'remembering mental event' (*smṛti-citta*) as it is capable of remembering this object."[80] Not only remembering, then, but the self that is dependent on remembering, collapses into this bare sequence of seeing-event as followed by remembering-event. Both are forms of consciousness, but no conscious self, much less any personal identity of self, is presumed.

Yet it would be a mistake to hold that we have parted company altgether with John Locke at this point. If we ask ourselves what personal identity consists of as discussed in Locke's *Essay,* on close scrutiny we find that such identity is little else besides the conscious acts by which "someone" (even this term becomes problematic in the present context) reconnects with past conscious acts. Consider, for example, this revealing sentence: "For, it being the same consciousness that makes a man be himself to himself, *personal identity depends on that only,* whether it be annexed solely to one individual substance, or can be continued in a succession of several substances."[81] The words I have italicized indicate that, epistemologically considered, personal identity or "self" (as Locke sometimes designates such identity) is constituted by a series of conscious acts—and thus that there is little effective difference between Vasubhandu and the forefather of British empiricism.

It must be admitted that Locke is also concerned with two other senses of the person that are difficult to contain within a *santāna* of mental acts: person as legal entity and person as self-reflective agent.[82] In both of these latter capacities, "person" cannot be entirely dispensed with, even though its epistemological foundation lies exclusively in a discontinuous series of cognitive events. Yet in one crucial respect Locke and Vasubhandu—and, I believe, many other Buddhists as well—might concur that the notion of "person" (or its equivalent) needs to be retained. Let us designate this respect *the (re)owning-of-self in signs.* For Buddhists and Locke, the appeal to self-owning signs is tacit; but it is no less imperative. In Locke's case, he says merely that the personal self "attributes to itself, and owns all [its] ac tions . . . as its own, as far as [its] consciousness reaches, and no further.''[83] But how is such attribution (or ''imputation'' as Locke elsewhere calls it)[84] to be made without the use of signs that pass on—to oneself and others—that which is attributed? Marks are made for holding in mind a person's own self-attributions. The self-attribution itself is a linguistic, or at least a quasi-linguistic, event. Thus Aristotle asserts that ''whenever someone is actively engaged in remembering, he always says *in his soul* . . . that he heard, or perceived, or thought this before.''[85] Such a claim is directly echoed in Griffiths's statement that ''paradigmatically, the judgment in question is of the form *I saw this.*''[86] Several signs are strung together in a self-attributing predicative utterance (or quasi-utterance, such as we experience in ''inner speech''). Wayman quotes Dharmakīrti: ''For in this way the discursive thoughts rightly characterize the sequential occurrence. Thereby, given the perceived entity, one constructs the discursive thought of recognition.''[87]

Aristotle's notion of saying in the soul—*minus* any commitment to soul—is here clarified as a statement of recognition. For signs to serve as vehicles of memories, they must be (1) recognized in themselves as precisely *these* signs, and (2) articulate the recognition of the items remembered (which may themselves be nonlinguistic, as in the recognition of bare perceptual particulars). Recognition is thus doubly inscribed in the process of remembrance; recognition is memory-within-memory; it is another species of *emboîtement.*

To come to the point, if remembering in a minimal state involves an at least tacit judgment of recognition, it also entails a self of sorts: a speaking, or quasi-speaking self, that says to itself ''I have experienced that before.'' This self is the utterer of these signs in a self-ascribed concatenation spelling out recognition. The lingual self is certainly not a substantial self; it is not even a self-reflective or legal self; but it is a self nevertheless. It is a self of signs, a de-signing self. Imputed, and even illusory, as such a self may be, it is nevertheless presupposed by those who deny its existence.

This unselfdeniable self remembers in many ways: in allegory and in myth, in image and in word, in syllable and in letter, in body and in mind, in consciousness and in nonconsciousness. Beyond remembrance by way of primary memory, still-retaining-in-grasp, and recognition—the three main non-recollective memorial modes I have emphasized—there is memory as commemoration. When the Buddha remembers previous lives, or when I more modestly remember my own life, commemorating is going on. Such commemoration is not limited to—though it is lucidly illustrated by—the process of subjective identification discussed by Harrison.[88] As Harrison himself recognizes, ritual and text—bodily action and language—play a central part in commemoration.[89] In both respects, commemoration is indisputably a *practice,* a form of procedural memory. In commemorative practices,

I reconnect with a self (not necessarily my own) in such a way that remembering *is* commemorating. *Smṛti* is *anusmṛti*.[90] Far from merely recollecting this self—that is, recalling a personalized, sensuous presence—I commemorate it as a pre-personal nonpresence. Such a self certainly is not a substance and is not even a person in Locke's attenuated sense. But it is a self of which I am reminded and which I may recognize as well. I recover it despite its ontological emptiness. In commemorating it, I honor it—honor it, among other things, for its having been able to remember itself at all, even once, through the bewilderment of one life and across the vicissitudes of many lives.

Such commemoration of a larger self suggests that something still more momentous is at stake. For Harrison, I ultimately remember (myself as) the Buddha. But if this is so, then I also ultimately remember everything—everything that matters, or, in the language of the Great Perfection, the ground of self-presenting awareness. Or else I remember the emptiness of everything, as in dhāraṇī practice. Just here we rejoin the cognitive-psychological notion of semantic memory in its most extensive outreach; that is, memory in its "generic" or "categorial" capacity.[91] Drawing on this capacity—which belongs to every human being, even those afflicted by severe amnesia—I can be said to possess a veritable "Memory of the World."[92] Such a world-memory is cosmic in scope and has few, if any, effective limits, even though in Buddhism I must act assiduously to cultivate this unlimited memory. I (can) remember myself, the Buddha, and the world-at-large. But that is quite a lot—a lot more in any case than I, or anyone else, can ever recollect.

It appears that in these (p)resumptive pages I have been momentarily standing in for authors and readers of the volume. To this extent, I have been remembering for both—in the double sense discussed at the opening of my essay. By my own memorial practice, then, I have placed myself *between* both parties to the pact of reading, hopefully in and to their common interest. Such in any case has been my assigned task: to be a *mnemon*, a person appointed to remind others of that which they might otherwise forget or overlook in the thick of their ongoing engagements.

But beyond any assignment and remindment there is the pleasure of the text I have here re-viewed. These ten essays commend themselves to the concerted attention of the reader. I am pleased to have commemorated them, however inadequately, in my own commentary.

Notes

1. Rupert Gethin, "The *Mātikās:* Memorization, Mindfulness, and the List," pp. 150–156.

2. P. S. Jaini, "*Smṛti* in the Abhidharma Literature and the Development of Buddhist Accounts of Memory of the Past," p. 47.

3. Paul J. Griffiths, "Memory in Classical Indian Yogācāra," p. 114. My italics.

4. On the use of *mnā,* see Matthew Kapstein, "The Amnesic Monarch and the Five Mnemic Men: Memory in Great Perfection (Rdzogs-chen) Thought," p. 240.

5. Collett Cox, "Mindfulness and Memory: The Scope of *Smṛti* from Early Buddhism to the Sarvāstivādin Abhidharma," p. 78. Other, exactly comparable texts are cited by Cox there.

6. Kapstein, p. 241.

7. Paul Griffiths, p. 122. See also Kapstein, p. 241: "It would be an error to suggest, as some recent writers perhaps have done, that the tradition of thought and practice considered here is to be distinguished as a sort of phenomenology par excellence. This is plainly incorrect." Nevertheless, Kapstein himself points to important phenomenological facets of Great Perfection thought and practice: e.g., on pp. 244, 249, 250, and 258.

8. Griffiths, p. 122.

9. William James, *Principles of Psychology* (New York: Holt, 1890), vol. 1, p. 647. James contrasts the immediate past of primary memory with the "genuine past" of recollection on ibid., p. 646. For James's discussion of attention, see ibid., pp. 402–58. Husserl was deeply influenced by James's account of memory and time in the *Principles;* but he provided a much more complete description of primary memory than James. Hints at such memory are also to be found in Bergson's *Time and Free Will* (first published in 1889 at *Les données immédiates de la conscience*). Indeed, St. Augustine was on the verge of discovering primary memory, for example, in a passage cited by Kapstein from the *De Trinitate:* "as that which is called memory in things past . . . makes it possible to recall and remember them: so in a thing present, as the mind is to itself, that is not unreasonably to be called memory, which *makes the mind at hand to itself*" (my italics).

10. *Principles of Psychology,* vol. 1, pp. 646–47; my italics. The "now-point" (*Jetzt-Punkt*) is Husserl's term for the most focused attention to the stream of events within what he calls "absolute flux." For a discussion of these matters, including primary memory, see his 1905 lectures under the title of *The Phenomenology of Internal Time-Consciousness,* especially sections 11–29, 34–45. "Memory of the present," a notion suggested on several occasions in this volume, is discussed in section 29. (German edition: *Zur Phänomenologie des inneren Zeitbewusstseins,* ed. R. Boehm [Hague: Nijhoff, 1966].

11. Jaini, p. 48.

12. Ibid., p. 54.

13. *Phenomenology of Internal Time-Consciousness*, sections 16–17. Derrida's interpretation of these passages is found in his book. *La voix et le phénomène* (1967) (trans. D. Allison, *Speech and Phenomena* [Evanston, Ill.: Northwestern University Press, 1973], Chapters 2–4).

14. Henri Bergson, *Matter and Memory*, trans. N. M. Paul and W. S. Palmer (1896; English ed.: New York: Doubleday, 1959), p. 18.

15. Nyanaponika Thera, "The Omission of Memory in the Theravādin List of Dhammas: On the Nature of *Saññā*, "p. 62. I shall return to the role of marks in Section III.

16. Nyaponika, p. 64.

17. Cox, p. 83. Note also Cox's claim that "for the Sarvāstivāda-Vaibhāṣikas . . . *smṛti* is a separately existing factor that *operates on present objects*" (p. 84; my italics).

18. Cox, p. 83, my italics. James's formulation, cited earlier, is that the object "never was lost."

19. *Principles of Psychology*, vol. 1, p. 251.

20. As Gethin remarks, "it is hardly surprising to find, at a relatively early date, the Buddhist tradition itself focusing on particular groups of lists and drawing up composite lists; that is, lists of lists" (p. 156). I would suggest that such complex composition of lists may itself serve as a quasi-visual, quasi-verbal metaphor for the multiplicity of memorial modes at stake in Buddhist meditational practices. It is an irony of history that the only serious consideration of lists in Western thought occurs in the two somewhat constricted contexts of mnemotechnics (e.g., in the medieval *ars memoria* tradition) and "serial learning" (i.e., of the sort focused on in recent cognitive-psychological experimentation). Gethin shows convincingly—as did Frances Yates in *The Art of Memory* (London: Routledge Kegan Paul, 1966)—that the memorizing of lists can have a considerable significance beyond any merely instrumental or experimental use.

21. For further comments on remembering-how, see my book *Remembering: A Phenomenological Study* (Blomington: Indiana University Press, 1987), pp. 55–59. The term *procedural memory* was introduced by Terry Winograd in "Frame Representation and the Declarative-Procedure Controversy," in D. G. Bobrow and A. Collins, eds. *Representation and Understanding* (New York: Academic Press, 1975), pp. 185–210. Bergson's idea of "habit memory" is closely related: cf. *Matter and Memory*, pp. 80–84.

22. Cited by Donald S. Lopez, Jr., "Memories of the Buddha," p. 21, from the *Majjhimanikāya*, I. 22. My italics.

23. James, *Principles of Psychology*, vol. 1, p. 646. James adds: "it is brought back, recalled, fished up, so to speak, from a reservoir in which, with countless other objects, it lay buried and lost from view" (ibid.).

24. Ibid., vol. 1, p. 2.

25. Logical problems in the doctrine of remembering former lives are raised by Paul J. Griffiths in his article. "Why Buddhas Can't Remember Their Previous Lives," *Philosophy East and West* 39 (1989): 449–51.

26. See the essay by this title in M. Merleau-Ponty, *The Primacy of Perception,* ed. J. Edie (Evanton, Ill.: Northwestern University Press, 1964), pp. 12–27.

27. On the distinction between adequacy and apodicticity, see E. Husserl, *Cartesian Meditations,* trans, D. Cairns (Hague: Nijhoff, 1960), sections 6–7.

28. On remembering-that, see *Remembering,* pp. 53–55.

29. On semantic memory and its distinction from episodic memory—i.e., "recollection of events vs. recall of facts"—see Endel Tulving's seminal article, "Episodic and Semantic Memory" in E. Tulving and W. Donaldson, eds., *Organization of Memory* (New York: Academic Press, 1972), pp. 590–600, as well as Tulving's later treatment in his *Elements of Episodic Memory* (Oxford: Oxford University Press, 1983), Chapter 2.

30. Paul Harrison. "Commemoration and Identification in *Buddhānusmṛti,*" p. 227.

31. Kapstein, p. 255.

32. See also the discussion of the condensing power of lists in Gethin, pp. 157 and 161.

33. Gyatso, p. 174. In the end, even a single letter can be an entirely effective mnemonic condenser: "from every letter (*yig-'bru*) there is the unobstructed power to remember teachings that were given over many eons" (ibid., p. 186, quoting Rdo Grub-chen). Other condensing expressions include mantras, *mātrikās, parittas,* and single seed-syllable *bījas.* Many such expressions, including the dhāraṇīs, have both a protective and a magical-efficacious function: cf. ibid., pp. 174 and 176.

34. Wayman, p. 138.

35. I take the term *cipher script* from Karl Jaspers, *Philosophy,* trans, E. G. Ashton (Chicago: University of Chicago Press, 1970), vol. 3, pp. 137–43.

36. *Remembering,* pp. 218–21, 259. Cf. also Chapter 5, "Reminding."

37. A. R. Luria, *The Mind of a Mnemonist,* trans. L. Solotaroff (Chicago: Regnery, 1968), especially Chapter 3.

38. Compare the passage from the *Sāgaranāgarājaparipṛchhā* cited by Gyatso: "Letters arise from nowhere, neither body nor mind" (Gyatso, p. 190). In the traditions analyzed by Gyatso, a letter often counts as a seed (*bīja*): cf. ibid., p. 174.

39. Charles S. Peirce, *Collected Papers,* vol. 2, p. 269: "Symbols grow. They come into development out of other signs, particularly from icons, or from mixed

signs partaking of the nature of icons and symbols. . . . A symbol, once in being, spreads among the peoples. In use and in experience, its meaning grows.'' This passage bears importantly on Gyatso's discussion of syllabary dhāraṇī, which can be said to be, on her interpretation, ''mixed signs partaking of the nature of icons and symbols.'' Also closely linked to Peirce's organic sense of signs is Gethin's emphasis on the matrixlike aspect of *mātikās;* Gethin, pp. 156 and 160.

40. Cited in Griffiths, n. 37.

41. The profound link between emotion and memory—''memory mixed with desire''—was first affirmed in Western philosophy in Plato's *Philebus* 33b–36 b.

42. Jaini, p. 53. Cf. especially his n. 33 for further discussion.

43. For a thorough discussion, see Asaṅga's *Mahāyānasaṅgraha* and the *bhāṣya* by Vasubandhu, translated by Étienne Lamotte in ''L'ālayavijñāna dans le *Mahāyānasaṃgraha* (ch. II),'' *Mélanges chinois et boudhhiques* 3 (1934): 239–40. Cf. also Griffiths's lucid discussion cited earlier, pp. 119–120.

44. Lamotte, ibid., p. 241.

45. Aromatic memory may thus be said to offer a limit-case of iconicity as a criterion of remembering. In its very diffuseness, it rejoins the special iconicity which Gyatso ingeniously locates in the dhāraṇī letter as lacking any inherent meaning; cf. Gyatso, p. 190.

46. Griffiths, p. 119, commenting on the *Mahāyānasaṅgraha.* For further remarks on *vāsanā,* see Wayman, p. 134.

47. John Locke, *An Essay Concerning Human Understanding,* ed. A. C. Fraser (New York: Dover, 1959), vol. 1, p. 193: memory ''is as it were the storehouse of our ideas.'' The insertion of ''as it were'' is noteworthy. For Locke, there is a significant analogy between storing up memories and storing up provisions over which one has labored.

48. On this model and offering a critique of it, see Norman Malcolm, *Memory and Mind* (Ithaca, N.Y.: Cornell University Press, 1977), Chapter 8, ''Retention and Storage'' and Chapter 10, ''The Principle of Isomorphism.''

49. S. Freud, ''Project for a Scientific Psychology,'' *Standard Edition of the Complete Psychological Works* (London: Hogarth Press, 1966), vol. 1, sections 1–10. A statement from section 9 is characteristic of Freud's prescient position: ''the sensory path of conduction . . . occurs in a peculiar fashion. It ramifies continually and exhibits thicker and thinner paths, which end in numerous terminal points'' (p. 314). The term *seed neurone* (*Kern-Neurone*) occurs on p. 315.

50. Griffiths, p. 120. Cf. his more complete discussion in his book *On Being Mindless: Buddhist Meditation and the Mind-Body Problem* (LaSalle, Ill.: Open Court, 1986), pp. 94–96.

51. Cox, p. 71, commenting on the *Sūdasutta.*

52. Jaini, p. 54.

53. E. Husserl, *Experience and Judgment*, trans. J. S. Churchill and K. Ameriks (Evanston, Ill.: Northwestern University Press, 1973), p. 108. His italics. For Husserl's most definitive discussion of retaining-in-grasp, see ibid, pp. 106–12.

54. Ibid., p. 113. *Developing contemplation* is in italics. Husserl's example is a perceptual object whose aspects and parts we explicate by retaining them in grasp; but we explicate them only as belonging to this object as a substrate of determinations. Cf. ibid., pp. 113–14. "Substrate" should not be confused with substance. It is a phenomenological given, not a metaphysical posit.

55. The moment in question, when we bring a given object to "explicit intuition," occurs for Husserl" at the *place of origin of the first of the so-called 'logical categories'* " (ibid., pp. 114–15; his italics).

56. On "explicative coincidence," see ibid., pp. 115–19.

57. Gethin, p. 166.

58. Kapstein, p. 259. In italics in his text.

59. On *recovery* as a term appropriate to soteriological remembering in the Great Perfection tradition, see Kapstein, p. 248.

60. *Syllable* traces back to the Greek *syn* + *lambano;* i.e., "seize or take together."

61. I borrow this last phrase from Gyatso's essay in this volume: "The nature of letters is such that they can mean anything, and anything and everything. . . is emptiness" (p. 190).

62. Griffiths, p. 121. My italics. I am not, of course, denying that the language of causality is employed in classical statements of seed-memory or store-consciousness. In a passage cited by Jaini, Vasubandhu says that the "seeing mental event" (*darśana-citta*) and the "remembering mental event" (*smṛti-citta*) "are causally related in the same manner of seed and its fruit, because both belong to the same series (*santati*)" (cited in Jaini, p. 51). But it would be preferable in my view to substitute the idea of a "complex of conditions" for that of causal relation. (The phrase *complex of conditions* is Lamotte's translation of the *Mahāyānasaṅgraha's* term *pratyayasāmagryapekṣa* [Lamotte, "L'ālayavijñāna," p. 239].)

63. I would argue that the intriguing idea of "exchange of self and other" (*parātmaparivartana*) to which Griffiths reverts at the close of his essay is itself made possible by the interpretation of seed-memories as marks. As both Peirce and de Saussure would insist, every sign, including a memory-sign, requires a community of interpreters who are capable of continual semiotic interchange.

64. See Karl Jaspers, *Philosophy*, vol, 2, pp. 177–222.

65. Lopez, p. 37. My italics.

66. See Heidegger's book of this title, translated into English as *On the Way to Language*, trans. P. D. Hertz (New York: Harper, 1971).

67. Lopez, p. 23.

68. Griffiths, p. 123.

69. "Something is 'remembered' which could never have been 'forgotten' because it was never at any time noticed—was never conscious" (Freud, "Remembering, Repeating, and Working-Through," *Standard Edition*, vol. 12, p. 149).

70. "We have in the Buddha's memory of his former abodes a case of deferred revision, in which unassimilated experience from the past is reworked so that it may be incorporated into a meaningful context; namely, that of the four noble truths" (Lopez, p. 38.

71. This last phrase is found in Kapstein, p. 260.

72."[For the psychoanalyst] remembering in the old manner—reproduction in the psychical field—is the aim to which he adheres" ("Remembering, Repeating, and Working-Through," p. 153).

73. Gyatso, p. 192: "the icon can be said already to *be*, in an important sense, its [own] signified" (her italics).

74. *An Essay Concerning Human Understanding*, vol. 2, p. 449 (hereafter referred to as *Essay*). An alternative formulation is this: "whatever past actions [the person] cannot reconcile or *appropriate* to that present self by consciousness [i.e., conscious memory], it can be no more concerned in than if they had never been done" (ibid., p. 467; his italics).

75. Ibid., vol. 1, p. 459. Locke italicizes *can*.

76. See the passage in ibid., vol. 1, p. 458: "it is plain [that] consciousness, as far as ever it can be extended—should it be to ages past—unites existences and actions very remote in time into the same *person*, as well as it does the existences and actions of the immediately preceding moment . . . it matters not whether this present self be made up of the same or other substances—I being as much concerned, and as justly accountable, for any action that was done a thousand years [ago], appropriated to me now by this self-consciousness, as I am for what I did the last moment." It remains, however, that Locke espouses notions of "self" and "sameness" that, despite their antisubstantialist basis in consciousness, would still be troubling to Buddhists, especially as they are represented in the essays by Griffiths and Wayman in this collection. On this and allied questions, see also the excellent treatment by Steven Collins in *Selfless Persons: Imagery and Thought in Theravādin Buddhism* (Cambridge: Cambridge University Press, 1982). For a recent Western discussion of such questions, see Rom Harré, *Personal Being: A Theory for Individual Psychology* (Cambridge, Mass.: Harvard University Press, 1984), especially Chapter 6–8.

77. As A. C. Fraser notes, "all that is essential to the idea of personal identity is, that memory *can* bridge over the apparent interruptions in self-conscious life,

whatever substance may be united with that life'' (*Essay*, vol. 1, p. 451n.; my italics). Locke himself says that I can be ''the same self, as far as the same consciousness can extend to actions past or to come; and would by distance of time, or change of substance, no more [be] two persons, than a man be two men by wearing other clothes to-day than he did yesterday, with a long or a short sleep between: *the same consciousness uniting those distant actions into the same person, whatever substances contributed to their production*'' (ibid., 451–2; my italics). Note that karmic carryover between lives is suggested on this view. Indeed, Locke himself stressed the way in which the remembering self is responsible for what it remembers: ''this personality extends itself beyond present existence to what is past, only by consciousness—*whereby it becomes concerned and accountable; owns and imputes to itself past actions, just upon the same ground and for the same reason as it does the present* (ibid., p. 467; my italics). For Locke's explicit reflections on ''preexistence,'' see ibid., vol. 1, pp. 455–56.

78. Lopez, p. 24.

79. ''For as far as any intelligent being can repeat the idea of any past action with the same consciousness it had of it at first, and with the same consciousness it has of any present action; so far it is the same personal self'' (ibid., vol. 1, p. 451; Locke italicizes *can*).

80. Jaini, p. 51.

81. Locke, *Essay*, vol. 1, p. 451. My italics. Cf. also p. 460: ''This may show us wherein personal identity consists: not in the identity of substance, but, as I have said, in the identity of consciousness . . . ''

82. On person as a legal entity, Locke says: person ''is a forensic term, appropriating actions and their merit; and so belongs only to intelligent agents, capable of a law, and happiness, and misery'' (ibid., p. 467). Regarding self-reflection: a person ''has reason and reflection, and can consider itself as itself, the same thinking thing, in different times and places; which it does only by that consciousness which is inseparable from thinking . . . it being impossible for any one to perceive without *perceiving* that he does perceive'' (ibid., pp. 448–49; his italics). It would be of considerable interest to compare the Buddhist logicians' notion of introspection, as discussed by Wayman in this book, with Locke's notion of self-reflective consciousness.

83. Ibid., p. 459.

84. Ibid., p. 467.

85. Aristotle, *De Memoria et Reminiscentia*, 449 b 21–24, trans. R. Sorabji in his *Aristotle on Memory* (London: Duckworth, 1972), p. 48. My italics.

86. Griffiths, p. 117 (his italics), with reference to Yaśomitra's commentary on the *Abhidharmakośabhāṣya*.

87. Wayman, p. 143, citing Verse 503 of the *pratyakṣa* chapter of the *Pramāṇavārttika*. Wayman comments that ''Thus, even though one does not see an

object or person for a long time, if one can appreciate the feasible changes, it is reasonable to recognize that old house as the one we lived in many years ago and that person as the one we knew long ago'' (ibid.). Note that both examples are perceptual in character.

88. Cf. Harrison, pp. 225–227.

89. I have explored the role of ritual and text in commemorative practices in *Remembering*, Chapter 10, ''Commemoration.''

90. ''The general interchangeability of *smṛti* and *anusmṛti* . . . also suggests that we are dealing with a 'calling to mind' rather than recollection in the strict sense'' (Harrison, p. 228).

91. *Generic memory* is D. L. Hintzman's term in *The Psychology of Learning and Memory* (San Francisco: Freeman, 1978). W. K. Estes discusses *categorial memory* in an article in *Psychological Review* 83 (1976): 37–64.

92. I borrow this last phrase from Merleau-Ponty in *The Visible and the Invisible*, trans. A. Lingis (Evanston, Ill.: Northwestern University Press, 1968), p. 194. Patients with pure anterograde amnesia retain an intact ''knowledge of the world'' and an effective memory of how to navigate in public space. On this point, see the essay by M. Kinsbourne and F. Wood in L. S. Cermak, *Human Memory and Amnesia* (Hillsdale, N.J.: Erlbaum, 1982).

Glossary of Sanskrit/Pāli and Tibetan Terms

Note: Principal terms to whose discussion entire chapters are devoted, such as *smṛti*, *mātikā*, and *dhāraṇī*, are not defined here. Nor are terms such as *saṃsāra*, *nirvāṇa* and *guru*, a working definition of which may be found in English dictionaries.

Abhidharma/Abhidhamma

"Higher" or "further" Dharma/Dhamma; refers to a body of works that systematically elaborate the doctrine expounded in the Buddhist sūtras. A complete set of canonical Abhidharma texts survives only in the "Southern" Theravādin and the "Northern" Sarvāstivādin sects.

Ābhidhārmika

One who is skilled in the doctrine expounded in the Abhidharma.

Āgamas

A later term for Nikāyas (q.v.). In modern scholarly writings this term is used primarily with reference to the Chinese translations of different recensions of texts similar to those found in the Pāli Nikāyas.

anātman/anattā

No-self, selflessness. The doctrine of no-self is renowned as the hallmark of the Buddhist teachings. Ignorance is defined in Buddhism as the belief that there is an autonomous agent, the referent of the term "I," that exists as the owner and controller of mind and body. This ignorance is said to be the root cause of all suffering. To understand through meditative experience that no such self exists effects liberation from suffering and rebirth.

arhat/arahant

A person who is "worthy" of worship; one who has achieved the highest state of enlightenment as described in early Buddhism.

bhakti

Derived from a word meaning "to share," bhakti is the general term in Indian religion for spiritual devotion to gods. A popular mode of practice, especially in Hinduism.

bhāṣya

A primary explanatory work or commentary.

bodhisattva

One who has taken a compassionate vow to liberate all beings from suffering by becoming a buddha through traversing a path that covers millions of lifetimes. Originally applied to real people, the term is also used to refer to a class of semi-mythical figures, the so-called celestial bodhisattvas. Although the bodhisattva doctrine is present in early Buddhism, it is in the Mahāyāna that it is set forth as a universal model of religious practice.

darśana

Lit., "seeing" or "vision," this term refers to a highly charged visual contact between a human being and a divinity who appears in a vision or in the form of a human guru.

Dharma/Dhamma

Most generally, the underlying law of things as they truly are. More specifically Dharma/Dhamma refers to the teachings of a buddha.

dharma/dhamma

Listed in the Abhidharma, the dharmas are the individual, momentary factors that comprise physical or mental states, and which are to be identified by the meditator when analyzing a given state.

dharmakāya

The "body of reality" of a buddha, the term refers also to buddhahood itself. Identified in the Great Perfection tradition with the primordial buddha Samantabhadra, as well as with the realization of naturally present pristine cognition in the meditator's own nature.

dhyāna/jhāna

Generally translated as "concentration," the term refers to a type of practice of meditation involving a sustained one-pointed mental fixation on an object. Such concentration need not possess any insight concerning the nature of the object. Adepts of this type of meditation are said in Buddhism to attain rebirth in certain heavenly realms.

Jaina

An adherent of the teachings of the Jina Mahāvīra, a contemporary of the Buddha, who founded an important religious tradition still widely practiced in India today.

Lokottaravāda

A subsect of the Mahāsāṅghikas (q.v.), deriving its name from its special doctrine concerning the supramundane (*lokottara*) nature of the Buddha.

Mādhyamika

An adherent of the "Middle Position," a Buddhist philosophical school originating in the writings of Nāgārjuna (second century C.E.) which thematize emptiness and dependent origination, and forcefully critique all reifying views.

Mahāsāṅghika

An early school of Buddhism that is said to have represented the views and interests of the majority against the more conservative stand of the Sthaviravādins. Their numerous subsects appear to have been especially active in the development of the Mahāyāna.

mahāsattva

Lit., "a great being," a stock alternative designation for a bodhisattva.

Mahāyāna

Lit., "The Great Vehicle," a movement that spanned several important Indian Buddhist sects that became dominant in Central and East Asia. It called for a reorientation of the religious life towards the goal of buddhahood, to be achieved by following the path of the bodhisattva, and it developed the doctrine of universal emptiness.

Mīmāṃsā

Lit. "reflection" or "investigation," this is the name of a Hindu philosophical school concerned primarily with the interpretation of the Vedas.

Nikāyas

The ancient collections of the Buddha's discourses, compiled c. 3rd century B.C. In modern scholarly writing the term is used especially with reference to the five Pāli Nikāyas handed down by the Theravādin tradition.

Nyāya

A Hindu school of Indian philosophy, traced to the third century B.C. Concerned primarily with logic and episemology. Related to the Vaiśeṣika (q.v.) system of metaphysics.

Piṭaka

"Basket"; refers to the three major divisions of the Buddhist canon which are together known as the Tripiṭaka/Tipiṭaka: Vinaya; Sūtra/Sutta; and Abhidharma/Abhidhamma

Prajñāpāramitā

A group of Mahāyāna sūtras, the earliest examples of which may be dated to the first century B.C. These sūtras are famous for their teachings on emptiness, sometimes stated in paradoxical ways.

Pudgalavāda

The name of a heterodox Buddhist school which believed in the existence of the individual person (*pudgala*), the subject of transmigration.

Rnying-ma

The oldest school of Tibetan Buddhism, tracing its lineage in Tibet to the eighth century. One of its distinctive doctrines is the Great Perfection.

Ṡaivaite

A person or sect devoted to the Hindu god Śiva.

samādhi

A meditative state involving concentration and mental equipoise. The followers of the Mahāyāna identified many samādhis with different names, but in content these are not necessarily distinct from each other.

saṅgha

The Buddhist order or community, usually understood as comprising the renunciant monks and nuns.

Sāṅkhya

A Hindu school of Indian philosophy traced to the sage Kapila, said to have lived in the seventh century B.C. Posits a dualistic metaphysics involving a primordial subject (*puruṣa*) and nature (*prakṛti*).

Saṃyukta/Saṃyutta

One of the principal collections of the sūtras/suttas. Consists of shorter discourses than those found in the Nikāyas.

Sarvāstivāda

Lit., "the position that maintains that everything exists." An Indian Buddhist sect prevalent by the first century C.E. in northern India and Central Asia. The elaboration of Abhidharma became the basis for the later development of this sect, and the focus of controversies with related and rival schools. See also "Vaibhāṣika."

Sautrāntika

Lit., "one who relies upon the sūtras" (rather than the Abhidharma). A Buddhist scholastic sect that flourished in northern and central India from the early years C.E. A major opponent of the Sarvāstivādins, the Sautrāntikas asserted the existence of present factors only, which are strictly momentary.

sūtra/sutta

An authoritative Buddhist text usually taking the form of a discourse delivered by the Buddha to a particular audience at a particular time and place.

sūtrānta/suttanta

In part another term for sūtra/sutta, but one which is often used to characterize the method of teachings embodied in the sūtras as opposed to the method of the Abhidharma. The former is seen as specific to audience, time and place, while the latter is more general and complete.

tantric Buddhism

This form of Buddhism grew out of the matrix of Mahāyāna Buddhism possibly from the 3rd or 4th centuries C.E. onward. In many respects an esoteric tradition, it is distinguished by the wealth of its ritual practices and iconography, its use of all things of the world (including human sexuality) in the quest for enlightenment, and its emphasis on the status of the guru. Shares many features with Hindu tantrism.

tathāgata

A common epithet of the Buddha. Due to an ambiguity in the Sanskrit compound, the term can be read as "one who has thus come," "one who has thus gone," or "one who has thus understood."

Theravāda

The school of the "Elders," i.e. those monks who claim unbroken continuation of the tradition from the Elder Upali, the chief proponent of the Vinaya of the Buddha.

This school is extant in modern times in Sri Lanka, Burma, Thailand, Laos and Cambodia and is distinguished from other Buddhist traditions by its acceptance of the Pāli canon as the only authentic Buddhists scriptures.

Vaibāṣika

Lit., "one who espouses the *Vibhāṣā*." Refers to those Sarvāstivādins who followed the voluminous *Vibhāṣā* commentaries based on the earlier Sarvāstivādin (q.v.) Abhidharma scripture, the *Jñānaprasthāna*. The *Vibhāṣā* commentaries are extant only in Chinese translation.

Vaiśeṣika

A Hindu school of Indian philosophy, traced to the third century B.C., that posited a metaphysics based on a system of irreducible atoms.

Vajrayāna

Sometimes translated as "diamond" or "adamantine," vajra is a mythical stone capable of penetrating and cutting all other substances, and thus stands as a symbol of that perfected insight, or spiritual power, to which nothing can offer any resistance. Vajrayāna, the vajra "vehicle" or "path," is another name for tantric Buddhism.

Vātsīputrīya

Lit., a member of the [faction] of Vātsīputra, the alleged founder of the doctrine of the person (*pudgala*); a synonym for Pudgalavādin (q.v.)

Vedānta

Lit., "culmination of the Veda," this is the name of a Hindu philosophical school which took its origin from the Mīmāṃsā, but which is centrally concerned with systematic metaphysical and epistemological questions.

Vinaya

The discipline and rules governing the life of the community of Buddhist monks and nuns. One of the three major divisions of the ancient canon of Buddhist scriptures.

Yogācāra

Lit., "practitioner of yoga," this term designates a Buddhist scholastic tradition associated primarily with the fourth century works of Asaṅga and Vasubandhu.

Contributors

Edward S. Casey is a professor of Philosophy at State University of New York at Stony Brook, specializing in phenomenology, aesthetics, and philosophical psychology. He is the author of *Imagining: A Phenomenological Study; Remembering: A Phenomenological Study;* and *Spirit and Soul: Essays in Philosophical Psychology.* He has recently completed a phenomenology of place entitled *Getting Back into Place.*

Collett Cox is an associate professor of Asian Languages and Literature at the University of Washington. Her research and publications are in the field of Abhidharma. She is the author of *Disputed Dharmas: Early Buddhist Theories on Existence. An Annotated Translation of the Section on Factors Dissociated from Thought from Sanghabhadra's Nyāyānusāra.*

Rupert Gethin is a lecturer in Religious Studies at the University of Bristol, and a specialist in Theravāda Buddhism and Abhidhamma. He is author of *The Buddhist Path to Awakening,* which elucidates the theory of the Buddhist path as presented in the Pāli Nikāyas and Abhidhamma by way of a detailed study of the 37 "dhammas that contribute to awakening" (*bodhipakkhiyā dhammā*). He is currently working on aspects of Buddhist cosmology and the Abhidhamma theory of rebirth.

Paul J. Griffiths is an associate professor of Theology at the University of Chicago, the Divinity School. His research focuses on the philosophical texts of Indian Buddhism, with special interest in Abhidharma and Yogācāra. His publications include *On Being Mindless: Buddhist Meditation and the Mind-Body Problem, The Realm of Awakening,* a translation and study of the tenth chapter of Asaṅga's *Mahāyānasaṅgraha,* and *An Apology for Apologetics.* He is currently working on a book whose tentative title is *The Doctrine of Buddhahood.*

Janet Gyatso is an assistant professor of Religion at Amherst College. She is the author of several articles on the Treasure (Gter-ma) tradition, Tibetan religious autobiography, and other aspects of Tibetan Buddhism and religious culture. She is currently completing a book that will include a translation of the *The Dancing Water Moon* (*Chu zla gar mkhan*) and *Ḍakki's Grand Secret-Talk* (*Ḍakki'i gsang gtam chen mo*), the "secret autobiographies'' of the 18th century Rnying-ma-pa teacher 'Jigs-med Gling-pa, and a study of visionary autobiography in Tibetan literature.

Paul Harrison has taught Chinese language and literature at Auckland University and (since 1983) Buddhist Studies in the Department of Philosophy and Religious Studies at Canterbury University in his native New Zealand. The primary focus of his research is Mahāyāna sūtra-literature, in particular the first texts to be translated into Chinese. A secondary interest is the history of the Tibetan Kanjur. Publications include various textual studies (an English translation of the *Pratyutpanna-buddha-sammukhāvasthita-samādhi-sūtra*, and critical editions of the Tibetan texts of this and of the *Druma-kinnara-rāja-paripṛcchā-sūtra*) as well as a number of thematic articles on Mahāyāna Buddhism.

Padmanabh S. Jaini is a professor in the Department of South and Southeast Asian Studies at the University of California, Berkeley. He is the author of numerous works dealing with Sanskrit Abhidharma literature, including *Abhidharmadīpa with Vibhāṣāprabhāvṛtti*, and has published extensively on the Pāli apocryphal *Jātakas*, including an edition of the *Paññāsa-Jātaka* (two volumes) which he translated as *Apocryphal Birth-Stories* (also in two volumes). He is also the author of *The Jaina Path of Purification* and his most recent *Gender and Salvation: Jaina Debates on the Spiritual Liberation of Women*.

Matthew Kapstein is an assistant professor in the Religion Department at Columbia University, where he teaches Philosophy of Religion. He was co-translator of the late H. H. Dudjom Rinpoche's *The Nyingma School of Tibetan Buddhism*, and his articles have appeared in *Religious Studies, History of Religion, Idealistic Studies* and other journals and collaborative volumes. He is also editor of the SUNY Series in Buddhist Studies.

Donald S. Lopez, Jr. is a professor of Buddhist and Tibetan Studies in the Department of Asian Languages and Cultures at the University of Michigan. He is the author of *A Study of Svātantrika, The Heart Sutra Explained: Indian and Tibetan Commentaries*, and the editor of *Buddhist Hermeneutics*. He has recently begun a study of a work on Madhyamaka by the controversial twentieth-century Tibetan scholar, dGe-'dun Chos-'phel.

Nyanaponika Thera, a German who became a Theravāda monk in Sri Lanka, studied with Nyanatiloka Mahāthera and worked closely with the Buddhist Publication Society. His numerous studies of Abhidhamma tradition include a German translation of the *Sutta Nipāta; The Heart of Buddhist Meditation;* and *Abhidhamma Studies: Researches in Buddhist Psychology.*

Alex Wayman is professor of Religion at Columbia University. His research studies include *Analysis of the śrāvakabhūmi Manuscript, The Buddhist Tantras, Yoga of the Guhyasamājatantra, Buddhist Insight, Chanting the Names of Mañjuśrī,* and *The Enlightenment of Vairocana.* His principal translations are *Mkhas grub rje's Fundamentals of the Buddhist Tantras, The Lion's Roar of Queen Śrīmālā* (on *tathāgatagarbha theory*); *Calming the Mind and Discerning the Real* and *Ethics of Tibet* (the Bodhisattva section). He is presently translating the 2500 ślokas of the lexicographical work *Viśvalocana,* preparing 24 essays for *Untying the Knots in Buddhism,* and completing *A Millennium of Buddhist Logic.*